China
and the Major Powers
in East Asia

BY A. DOAK BARNETT

Communist Economic Strategy: The Rise of Mainland China
(1959)

Communist China and Asia: Challenge to American Policy
(1960)

Communist China in Perspective
(1962)

*Communist Strategies in Asia: A Comparative Analysis
of Governments and Parties*
(editor, 1963)

China on the Eve of Communist Takeover
(1963)

Communist China: The Early Years, 1949–1955
(1964)

The United States and China in World Affairs
(editor of manuscript by Robert Blum; published posthumously, 1966)

China after Mao
(1967)

Cadres, Bureaucracy, and Political Power in Communist China
(with a contribution by Ezra Vogel, 1967)

Chinese Communist Politics in Action
(editor, 1969)

The United States and China: The Next Decade
(editor, with Edwin O. Reischauer, 1970)

A New U.S. Policy toward China
(Brookings, 1971)

Uncertain Passage: China's Transition to the Post-Mao Era
(Brookings, 1974)

The United States, China, and Arms Control
(with Ralph N. Clough, Morton H. Halperin, and Jerome H. Kahan;
Brookings, 1975)

China Policy: Old Problems and New Challenges
(Brookings, 1977)

China and the Major Powers in East Asia
(Brookings, 1977)

A. Doak Barnett

China
and the Major Powers
in East Asia

THE BROOKINGS INSTITUTION
Washington, D.C.

Library of Congress Cataloging in Publication Data:

Barnett, A   Doak.
  China and the major powers in East Asia.
  Includes bibliographical references and index.
    1. China—Foreign relations—Russia. 2. Russia—
Foreign relations—China. 3. China—Foreign relations—
Japan. 4. Japan—Foreign relations—China.
5. China—Foreign relations—United States. 6. United
States—Foreign relations—China. I. Title.
DS740.5.R8B37   327.51   77-21981
ISBN 0-8157-0824-6
ISBN 0-8157-0823-8 pbk.

1 2 3 4 5 6 7 8 9

In memory of

JOHN M. H. LINDBECK

and

ALEXANDER ECKSTEIN

THE BROOKINGS INSTITUTION is an independent organization devoted to nonpartisan research, education, and publication in economics, government, foreign policy, and the social sciences generally. Its principal purposes are to aid in the development of sound public policies and to promote public understanding of issues of national importance.

The Institution was founded on December 8, 1927, to merge the activities of the Institute for Government Research, founded in 1916, the Institute of Economics, founded in 1922, and the Robert Brookings Graduate School of Economics and Government, founded in 1924.

The Board of Trustees is responsible for the general administration of the Institution, while the immediate direction of the policies, program, and staff is vested in the President, assisted by an advisory committee of the officers and staff. The bylaws of the Institution state: "It is the function of the Trustees to make possible the conduct of scientific research, and publication, under the most favorable conditions, and to safeguard the independence of the research staff in the pursuit of their studies and in the publication of the results of such studies. It is not a part of their function to determine, control, or influence the conduct of particular investigations or the conclusions reached."

The President bears final responsibility for the decision to publish a manuscript as a Brookings book. In reaching his judgment on the competence, accuracy, and objectivity of each study, the President is advised by the director of the appropriate research program and weighs the views of a panel of expert outside readers who report to him in confidence on the quality of the work. Publication of a work signifies that it is deemed a competent treatment worthy of public consideration but does not imply endorsement of conclusions or recommendations.

The Institution maintains its position of neutrality on issues of public policy in order to safeguard the intellectual freedom of the staff. Hence interpretations or conclusions in Brookings publications should be understood to be solely those of the authors and should not be attributed to the Institution, to its trustees, officers, or other staff members, or to the organizations that support its research.

Foreword

ALTHOUGH China is an ancient civilization, it has only recently become a major power. Its influence in the world community has increased greatly since the early 1970s, when it was seated in the United Nations and established new ties with the United States and Japan. One result has been the emergence of an entirely new pattern of four-power relations in East Asia.

There is now widespread recognition of China's growing international importance, but still relatively little understanding of its leaders' motivations and goals and the mainsprings of its foreign policy. In this study, A. Doak Barnett analyzes China's relations with the three other major powers in East Asia—the United States, the Soviet Union, and Japan—and the complex multilateral interactions among the four. He begins by examining in depth China's dealings with each of the other powers during the past quarter-century. His analysis emphasizes the factors that have influenced the evolution of each bilateral relationship and the problems likely to confront it in the future. He then discusses the nature of the new four-power structure in East Asia and China's place in it, and assesses the forces working for and against equilibrium in the region.

The problems dealt with in this book have dominated Peking's foreign policy and the broader regional scene in recent decades and will continue to be important in the future. The prospects for peace and stability in the region will depend both on what policies China's post-Mao leaders pursue and on whether the other major powers adopt policies toward the People's Republic that reflect, among other things, an understanding of Chinese motives, objectives, and strategies. Barnett's purpose is to throw light not only on the past, but also on probable future problems and trends. This book thus complements his *China Policy: Old Problems and*

New Challenges, published by Brookings in April 1977, in which he reexamines U.S. policy toward China and prescribes what he believes to be a realistic and feasible set of policies in the period ahead.

Barnett bases his judgments on his study of China and Asia that began before the Chinese Communists' rise to power and on wide academic, governmental, and journalistic experience dealing with Chinese affairs. While working on this book he made return visits to China, the Soviet Union, and Japan, as well as other parts of Asia.

He acknowledges his indebtedness to those who read and commented on drafts of this study: David Brown, William P. Bundy, Ralph N. Clough, John K. Fairbank, Harry Gelman, Donald C. Hellmann, Hans Heymann, Jr., Harold C. Hinton, Paul F. Langer, Kenneth Lieberthal, James W. Morley, Michel Oksenberg, Lawrence Olson, Henry Owen, Michael Pillsbury, William Sherman, Richard H. Solomon, Rudolf L. Tökés, Ezra F. Vogel, Kei Wakaizumi, and Donald S. Zagoria. They all helped to improve the manuscript, but of course none bears any responsibility for the final product.

He also wishes to thank Thomas G. Rohback, who served as his research assistant in 1973–74 and was particularly helpful in compiling information on Japan and in preparing notes for the study, and to Stacy Delano and David Morse, who typed the manuscript and helped manage his research files. He also expresses appreciation to the East-West Center, where he was a senior fellow when completing the book. And he is grateful to Alice M. Carroll, who edited the manuscript, and to Brian Svikhart, who prepared the index.

The Institution expresses its appreciation to the Rockefeller Foundation, which provided major financial support for this study, and to the Office of External Research of the Department of State, which gave supplementary support.

The views expressed in the book are the author's own and should not be ascribed to the Rockefeller Foundation, the Department of State, or the East-West Center, or to the trustees, officers, or other staff members of the Brookings Institution.

BRUCE K. MACLAURY
President

April 1977
Washington, D.C.

Contents

China
and the Major Powers
in East Asia

Note on Chinese and Japanese Names

Chinese names appear in this study with the surname first in accordance with Chinese usage and common practice in Western writing about China. A modified Wade-Giles system for romanizing Chinese characters is followed except where other spellings are generally accepted in the West. Japanese names appear with the surname last, contrary to Japanese usage but in accordance with the practice most widely followed in Western writing about Japan.

INTRODUCTION

China—A New Major Power

THIS IS A STUDY of the People's Republic of China's relations with the other major powers in East Asia—the Soviet Union, Japan, and the United States. The problem of dealing with these powers has in many respects dominated China's foreign policymaking in recent decades. Despite the expansion of Peking's ties with other nations, how to deal with Moscow, Tokyo, and Washington remains *the* central foreign-policy question for China's leaders. And the ways in which these four powers interact will be critical determinants of the prospects for stability or instability, conflict or cooperation, and war or peace throughout the region in the years immediately ahead.

Many ideological, political, and economic factors have influenced China's policies toward the other powers in the past, but military and strategic considerations have been crucial, and under Mao Tse-tung China pursued very distinctive balance-of-power strategies. A knowledge of these past patterns of behavior is one prerequisite for attempting to look ahead.[1] It is also essential to understand the far-reaching changes that have recently occurred both in China and in the overall pattern of relations among the major powers in East Asia.

As China's political, economic, and military development has progressed, it has pursued increasingly active policies on the world scene. Clearly, it is becoming a major power, capable of exerting a significant influence internationally. Although it is still relatively weak militarily, compared to the powers that it views as its major adversaries, it has nevertheless achieved major-power status in many respects and is gradually assuming international roles commensurate with that status.

Domestically, the People's Republic is undergoing an important political transition. Mao Tse-tung's death in September 1976 marked the end of an era and the start of an entirely new period in China's history, which poses many uncertainties about its future political, economic, military, and foreign policies.

In East Asia as a whole, the basic pattern of big-power relations has undergone fundamental change in recent years. The emerging multipolar structure of power has created new problems and opportunities, for China as well as the other powers, which add to the uncertainties about the future.

The main focus of this study, therefore, is on China's relations with the Soviet Union, Japan, and the United States and on the complex multilateral relationships among these four powers. However, it is necessary, first, to analyze briefly certain broader factors and trends affecting China's international policies: its emergence as a more active participant in world affairs, the basic attitudes and goals influencing its leaders' approach to the outside world, and their changing world views and strategic approaches to the international situation as a whole. These set the general framework within which China determines its policies toward the major powers.

China's International Role

Although China has existed longer as a cultural and political entity than any of the other major powers, it is in some respects a "new nation." Until very recently, it had never played an influential role in the modern interstate system or exerted an international influence commensurate with its size and population.

Before Western imperialist powers forcibly opened China to outside influence in the mid-nineteenth century, the Chinese empire was relatively isolated and deliberately tried to minimize contacts beyond the Sinic area, in which it was dominant. A deep-rooted sense of exclusivity and cultural pride impelled the Chinese to view external influence as threatening to China's identity and integrity.

However, because of its technological backwardness and military weakness in the nineteenth century, it was extremely vulnerable to external encroachment. From the middle of the century until recently, it was subjected to one humiliation after another. Unable to protect itself effectively against foreign threats or to accommodate to the Western-dominated international system, the traditional Chinese empire finally collapsed in 1911.

Ever since then, Chinese leaders have been attempting to come to terms with the modern world and to find China's proper place in it. They have been engaged in a long and complex struggle, on the one hand to revolutionize their own society and create a strong modern state, and on the other to define China's relationship with the international community as a whole. One continuing goal has been to achieve the status of a major power, which virtually all members of the modernized elite in China have believed to be their nation's right.

In a formal sense, China achieved recognition as a major power when it was accepted as one of the so-called Big Four during World War II. But the Chinese Nationalist regime then ruling China was never able to assert its rights, exert a significant influence beyond its borders, or assume an active role as a major power. Throughout the period of Nationalist rule, as in the preceding warlord period, the nation was convulsed by civil war and revolution at home as well as being subjected to unremitting pressure and attacks from abroad.

This situation began to change, fundamentally, once the Communists achieved power in 1949. The new Peking regime rapidly reunified the country and established a strong political apparatus. It built up the country's military strength, initiated an ambitious economic development program, and started to play a more active role abroad. In some respects, therefore, China's emergence as a major power began with Communist rule; no longer did its disunity and weakness compel China simply to submit to external pressure. Yet during the 1950s and 1960s, China's participation in the international community was still limited. The Korean War and subsequent U.S. opposition to acceptance of Peking into the international community, as well as China's subordinate position in the Sino-Soviet alliance and its immense internal problems, delayed its full emergence as a major power. As of the end of the 1960s the People's Republic of China was still barred from membership in the United Nations and most other international organizations. It was still unrecognized by more than half of the world's nations. Perhaps most important, it still lacked official links even with the major powers, other than the Soviet Union, that played crucial roles in East Asia.

In the late 1960s, moreover, Peking turned inward, toward angry isolationism, during the Cultural Revolution. China was at odds with all of the largest nations involved in Asia, including the Soviet Union and

India as well as the United States and Japan. For a brief period it had only one ambassador stationed anywhere abroad, at Cairo. Then, after the Cultural Revolution, Chinese leaders began to look outward again. Since 1971, there have been fairly dramatic changes in China's policies, its international situation, and its role in the world.

These changes have been due less to any far-reaching shift in China's international power position (although its acquisition of a small nuclear arsenal has enhanced its defense capabilities) than to major changes in its policies as well as those of the other powers. For various political, economic, and strategic reasons, Peking's leaders, starting in 1968, reassessed both their domestic needs and the world situation, and redefined China's basic foreign-policy strategy, adopting an increasingly activist approach to the world community. Meanwhile, leaders in Washington, Tokyo, and many other capitals finally abandoned efforts to exclude China from the international community. China's international contacts and involvement expanded rapidly after 1971, and the People's Republic began to assume many of the international roles that a major power is expected to play.

Since 1972, China has had diplomatic relations with all the leading world powers (although its links with the United States are still only quasi-diplomatic). By 1975 it had established formal ties with over a hundred nations—more than double the number in 1968. Its relationships with Third World countries have increased spectacularly. In addition, in 1971 the People's Republic finally replaced the Chinese Nationalists in the United Nations, assuming a seat as one of the five permanent members of the Security Council and acquiring the power of the veto. Since then, as members of most important UN-affiliated bodies (with the notable exception of the World Bank and International Monetary Fund), the Chinese have voiced their opinions on virtually all major international issues.

China's foreign trade and other economic relations have steadily increased during this period. Although its trade is still relatively small, especially in per-capita terms, today it is an important importer of agricultural commodities, capital goods, and advanced technology, and promises to become a significant exporter of petroleum and other commodities. The important compromises that China has had to make in its militantly autarchic stance reflect not only its pressing domestic needs but also a general willingness to involve itself in the international community somewhat more than in the past.

China has also become a more important military power. It remains a regional rather than a global power, however. It is still weak in comparison with the United States and the Soviet Union and therefore continues to maintain an essentially defensive posture. Nevertheless, since its acquisition of a nuclear capability, it has become a new factor in the international nuclear equation that cannot be ignored. The Chinese have also started to take part in international debates on arms control, especially in the United Nations. While still opposing almost all measures sponsored by the United States and the Soviet Union, they have begun to be drawn into international roles in this field too.

China's international position has not been totally transformed, however. Of all the major powers, it is still by far the poorest; its economic strength cannot compare with that of the United States, the Soviet Union, Japan, or the European Community. Militarily, China is clearly still a second-rank power, with no prospect of achieving parity with the two superpowers. Moreover, despite its expanded international activity, it is still the least involved of all the major powers in the increasingly complex patterns of interdependence that characterize the contemporary world.

Nevertheless, China's increasing involvement in world affairs is significant, and its international influence will certainly continue to grow. Its leaders have very ambitious goals, some of which reflect attitudes that shape the policies of other nations, others of which are unique.

Like the leaders in most large nations, Peking's leaders are determined to achieve national power, international prestige, and economic prosperity. Not surprisingly, security—the basic question of survival—takes precedence over all other goals. National pride explains many of their actions. They are extremely sensitive about their international status and "rights," and perhaps because they so recently eliminated foreign privileges that seriously compromised China's national integrity, they are almost obsessively preoccupied with sovereignty and legal equality. They are determined to make their voice heard on all important international issues, to establish a "presence" in critical regions of the world, and to exert a significant influence on the general course of events on the global stage.

Many of China's policies are based on its leaders' practical assessments of how best to pursue limited, concrete national interests. They consistently try to maximize political support for China's current positions on major international issues, to develop economic relationships that will help solve the country's pressing domestic problems as well as expand its influence abroad, and, most important of all, to affect the balance of world forces in ways that will enhance China's security and bolster its position as a power. Especially in devising security policies, Chinese leaders have shown a notable capacity to make hard-headed power calculations, to think in pragmatic realpolitik terms, and while denouncing the power politics of others to pursue balance-of-power goals that they believe are essential for China's survival. When basic security interests have been at stake, ideological predispositions and secondary national interests have generally been subordinated. In these respects, Chinese policies are comparable in many ways to those pursued by other major powers.

Yet, clearly the People's Republic of China is not just like the other major powers. Its policies are strongly influenced by a uniquely Chinese set of factors including deep-rooted traditional attitudes, modern nationalist impulses, and genuine revolutionary aspirations.

Tradition leads Peking's leaders to assume China's greatness, to be convinced that it deserves a leading world role. Like past Chinese rulers, they have faith in China's capacity to achieve its basic goals without becoming dependent on others. They are extremely wary of external influence and involvements that might compromise Chinese values. They also believe that the Chinese example is highly relevant to many other nations.

Modern nationalism motivates them to build a strong nation-state, to strive for total independence, and to oppose any compromise of China's sovereignty. It also impels them to try to minimize Western influence within China and to struggle against all forms of imperialism and colonialism, which they now define so broadly as to include virtually all influences exerted by large powers over smaller ones. China's leaders are determined to redress past wrongs and overcome the trauma of a century of Western dominance.

Ideology and revolutionary aspirations also affect China's foreign policy in very significant ways. For more than a quarter century, China has been ruled by first-generation revolutionary leaders strongly committed to certain universalistic, messianic goals. These leaders have called for revolutionary change not only in China but worldwide. Viewing the world in distinctive Marxist-Leninist-Maoist terms, they have seen international problems through lenses quite different from those of other Communist as well as noncommunist leaders.

Ideology has greatly influenced both the way they have analyzed the interplay of forces in the world and the vocabulary with which they have described the international scene. Their values and their self-image have impelled them to give at least moral support, and at times some material support, to revolutionary parties and movements abroad, especially, though not exclusively, to those that accept Peking's ideological views. Even if the revolutionary component in Chinese foreign policy declines in the future, as seems likely, there is no doubt that ideology will continue to influence China's approach to the world in important ways.

Today, China is unique among the major powers because of the strength of its leaders' commitment to revolutionary values. Chinese leaders have been the most vocal opponents of the international status quo and the strongest proponents of systemic change in the world order. They are the only leaders of a major nation who, in effect, have argued publicly in favor of international instability on the grounds that this will produce needed and desirable political and economic change. They have seen the world in "great disorder"—to use Mao Tse-tung's famous phrase—and welcomed this as the sign of a new world order in the making.

It is not easy to weigh the relative importance of tradition, nationalism, pragmatism, realpolitik considerations, and ideology in shaping specific Chinese foreign-policy decisions. Clearly their relative importance has varied as circumstances have changed. At times, they have been mutually reinforcing. Often, however, they have been in conflict, creating obvious "contradictions" and posing difficult policy choices.

China's World View and Strategy

Although Peking's foreign policies have been influenced by a complex mixture of attitudes, values, interests, and goals, its leaders have always tried to explain and justify their policies in terms of a coherent world view. Neither their world view nor their concrete policies have remained static, however. Chinese leaders have repeatedly altered their schematic analyses of the world situation and their basic foreign-policy strategy as the international environment has changed.

As believers in "scientific socialism," Chinese leaders like to think (or at least give the impression that they think) they are better able than others to understand and influence the broad historical forces shaping the world—the "wheel of history." Periodically they have altered their definition of the current "epoch" or "historical period," specifying each time what broad strategy is needed to deal with changing forces.

During World War II the party leaders, convinced that the nature of the struggle demanded alignments across ideological lines, appealed for a broad united front of Communists and noncommunists against the fascists. After they achieved power in 1949, however, they stressed the basic dichotomy between all Communists and all noncommunists, and called for an intense revolutionary struggle by the "socialist camp," led by the Soviet Union and supported by all "true revolutionaries," against the "imperialist camp," led by the United States and supported by the world's "reactionaries." Then, in the 1950s they again recognized the complexities in the world and moved toward a new united-front strategy. Although they still described the basic world struggle as one between two camps, they now regarded the neutralist nations and diverse noncommunist but antiimperialist groups as potential allies. Their approach during the Bandung period in the mid-1950s was quite flexible, and under the banner of "peaceful coexistence" they actively wooed many neutralist nations. The "Bandung spirit" lasted only a brief period, however. By the late 1950s the Chinese had renewed their calls for revolutionary militancy in the struggle between socialism and imperialism, while continuing to try to attract support from newly independent, noncommunist, developing nations.

As the world situation became steadily more complicated in the 1960s, Chinese leaders declared that "true Marxist-Leninist revolutionaries"—the Chinese and those who agreed with them—must struggle against dangerous "revisionist" trends within the Communist bloc and world movement as well as against the primary enemy, the imperialists. They increasingly stressed the importance of the Third World nations and tried to attract varied independence and liberation movements as well as Marxist revolutionaries to their side in the world struggle. They also perceived a division between the United States, the alleged headquarters of imperialism, and the other developed nations, the "second intermediate zone," which they believed they could exploit to weaken imperialism.

By the end of the 1960s, however, the entire world situation had changed again, in the Chinese view. Peking now divided all nations into three worlds, which cut across the old lines of demarcation between Communist and noncommunist forces. It viewed the underdeveloped nations of the Third World, to which the Chinese said they now belonged, as the crucial revolutionary force. It also argued that they should try to obtain support from the developed nations of the so-called Second World, the industrialized countries other than the two superpowers, the United States and Soviet Union. Peking continued to insist that the basic struggle in the world was between revolutionaries and imperialism, but now its definition of imperialist enemies included the Soviet "social imperialists" as well as the U.S. "imperialists," and its definition of potential allies included most other nations and peoples.

The changes in Peking's articulated world view, reflecting but usually exaggerating changes in the international situation, have had an important influence on Chinese foreign-policy behavior. Often, however, the Chinese world view has revealed more about what Chinese leaders want the rest of the world to believe motivates their policy than about what actually motivates it, and more about their hopes for the future than about their assessment of current realities. The concrete policies they are pursuing provide the best basis for judging their immediate preoccupations and priorities; their world view reveals the general framework into which they try to fit particular policies.

The world view currently propagated by China's leaders is unique. Not only is it unlike that of other nations' leaders, but it differs from earlier Chinese views. In some respects its origins are traceable to China's steadily growing interest in the Third World. More fundamentally, however, it was produced by the Sino-Soviet conflict. By the mid-1960s, in any case, Chinese leaders had adopted a startlingly unorthodox framework for viewing the basic configuration of world forces.

In 1965, Lin Piao, who was then emerging as a possible successor to Mao, issued a major statement on "people's war," which was put forward as a definitive exegesis of Mao's thinking. He proclaimed that the revolutionary experience of the Chinese in their struggle for power provided the best basis for developing a revolutionary strategy globally. This strategy, he asserted, should be one in which forces in rural areas surround and defeat enemy forces in urban areas.[2] "Taking the entire globe," Lin said, "if North America and Western Europe can be called 'the cities of the world,' then Asia, Africa and Latin America constitute 'the rural areas of the world' "; "the contemporary world revolution ... presents a picture of the encirclement of cities by the rural areas." He called for support by "the socialist countries" for "people's revolutionary struggles in Asia, Africa and Latin America" and urged that revolutionaries in these areas employ armed struggle, as the Communists had in

China. Starting in the mid-1960s, Peking's leaders said little about China's participation in the socialist camp. From 1965 through 1968, moreover, they strenuously attacked alleged collusion between the Soviet Union and the United States, claiming that these two nations were pursuing an anti-Chinese conspiracy and developing a nuclear military alliance to dominate the world. In effect, they dissociated China from the Soviet bloc, while holding up China's own experience as the best model for revolutionary struggle against imperialism by the people in all developing nations.

At the Ninth Party Congress in April 1969, Lin—then at the peak of his power, though soon to fall—put forward a somewhat different formulation, but the tendencies evident in his earlier statement were still discernible.[3] He again emphasized Chinese support for revolutionary struggles waged by "the proletariat and oppressed peoples" throughout the world—a vague and very broad grouping—and urged armed struggle in many countries. He also again stressed the importance of revolution by "peoples" in the Third World (later the Chinese emphasis was to shift to a united front of Third World nations). However, although he still labeled the United States as a prime enemy (calling it "the most ferocious enemy of the people of the whole world"), he greatly intensified China's propaganda attack against the Soviet Union (which the Chinese now regarded as the major military threat), accusing it of "social fascism" as well as "revisionist social imperialism." Lin again accused the United States and the Soviet Union of "colluding" in order to dominate the world, but, significantly, he now also accused them of "contending" with each other. He maintained, however, that the United States was "going downhill," while the Soviet Union was encountering increasing difficulties, and that it was possible to prevent world war by expanding world revolution. Analyzing international conflicts in more complicated terms than he had in his earlier countryside-versus-city statement, Lin identified four contradictions as the most important in the world: those between the oppressed nations (mainly Third World nations) and imperialism and social imperialism (the United States and the Soviet Union); those between the proletariat and the bourgeoisie in the capitalist and revisionist countries; those between the imperialists and the social imperialists as well as among the imperialists themselves; and those between socialism (China and other ideologically correct nations and parties) and both imperialism and social imperialism. It was significant that now he put contradictions between the Third World nations and the two superpowers at the top of his list. China's identification of its interests with the Third World was thus taken a step further.

Many of these themes were carried forward, and elaborated upon, at the party's Tenth Congress in August 1973 by Premier Chou En-lai, who now acted as the regime's principal spokesman. While asserting that this is still the era of imperialism and proletarian revolution, Chou stressed the awakening of the Third World and its growing importance in the worldwide struggle gainst imperialism and colonialism, especially against the "hegemonism and power politics" of the two "superpowers."[4] "Countries want independence, nations want liberation, and people want revolution," he declared. The order of goals in this listing was significant; "independence" and "liberation" came before "revolution." Chou also argued that the hegemonism of the superpowers was opposed not only by the Third World but also by Japan and Europe.

The essential feature of imperialism, he asserted, is "rivalry among the great powers, and specifically between the two superpowers" openly struggling for world hegemony. Chou now placed his entire emphasis on the "contention" between these two powers (since the opening of Sino-American relations a short time previously, Peking had had much less to say about U.S.-Soviet collusion). He discussed the need for "necessary compromises between revolutionary countries" (China) "and imperialist nations" (the United States) and he stressed that U.S. influence was on the decline, clearly indicating that the Soviet Union now posed the greater threat. He maintained that the U.S.-Soviet struggle encompassed the entire world, but also argued that its main focus had shifted to Europe, stating that the Soviet Union is "feinting in the East while attacking in the West." Each of the superpowers, he maintained, wishes to divert the other's attention toward China. (Clearly, China's hope was that it could divert the attention of both away from China.)

Overall, Chou argued, the international situation is characterized by "great disorder." The danger of a new world war remains, but revolution is the "main trend," and war can be prevented if the people of all countries unite and struggle together. Slightly over a year later, in a major speech at the Fourth National People's Congress in January 1975, Chou adopted a more pessimistic tone and stated that U.S.-Soviet contention is "bound to lead to world war some day."[5] By using the phrase "some day," however, he indicated that he did not see this as imminent.

Three Worlds

The trends apparent in Lin's and Chou's statements reached their logical conclusion in the formulations, and prescriptions, spelled out by Vice Premier Teng Hsiao-p'ing in April 1974 at the United Nations (Teng, having recovered from his disgrace during the Cultural Revolution, had by that time emerged as a leading contender for top power in China).[6] Teng's speech is the clearest and most explicit statement of the views that Peking's leaders still expound to explain and justify their current approach to the world as a whole. The world view it presents is startlingly different from any articulated in the past by Communist leaders in China or elsewhere.

Teng asserted bluntly that the Communist camp no longer exists; the world now consists of "three worlds"; and China is now a part of the Third World. Although for some time actual Chinese policy had indicated that Peking's leaders were operating on these assumptions, this was the first time a Chinese leader said so, explicitly and openly.

"International relations are changing drastically," Teng declared. "History develops in struggle, and the world advances amidst turbulence." Today, "the whole world is in turbulence and unrest," and there is a "sharpening of all the basic contradictions." Moreover, "all of the political forces in the world have undergone drastic division and realignment." While "the old order based on colonialism, imperialism and hegemony is being undermined," there is an "awakening and growth of newly emerging forces"; the countries of Asia, Africa, and Latin America "are playing an ever greater role in international affairs."

"The socialist [Communist] camp which existed for a time after World War II is no longer in existence," Teng proclaimed, and "the Western imperialist bloc, too, is disintegrating." "The world today actually consists of three parts, or three worlds, that are both interconnected and in contradiction to one another. The United States and the Soviet Union make up the First World. The developing countries in Asia, Africa, and Latin America and other regions make up the Third World. The developed countries between the two make up the Second World." (Labeling the noncommunist industrial nations as the Second World was new, but the idea of identifying them as a distinct group can be traced back many years. In 1946 Mao had talked of an "intermediate zone" between the Communists and imperialists, and this concept had been revived in 1958. Then in 1964 it had been refined to include a first intermediate zone of developing nations and a second intermediate zone of the developed nations other than the United States.[7] This second intermediate zone was now labeled the Second World.)

Teng reiterated the by-now-standard Chinese line that "the two superpowers are the biggest international exploiters and oppressors of today . . . vainly seeking world hegemony." However, although he condemned both, he stressed that "the superpower which flaunts the label of socialism is especially vicious." He also underlined once more that conflict is more important than cooperation between the two: "Since the two superpowers are contending for world hegemony," he said, "the contradiction between them is irreconcileable. . . . Their compromise and collusion can only be partial, temporary, and relative, while their contention is all-embracing, permanent, and absolute." Nevertheless, he argued, while "the danger of a new world war still exists . . . revolution is the main trend in the world today."

The situation of the Second World nations, Teng asserted, is "a complicated one." Some "still retain colonial relations," but "in varying degrees, all of these countries have the desire of shaking off superpower enslavement and control." The implication was clear; in the task of opposing imperialism, the Second and Third World nations have, or should have, common interests.

The emergence of the Third World nations and the importance of their struggle against the superpowers was the most important theme in Teng's speech, however. The developing countries "have won political independence," he said, "yet all of them still face the historic task of clearing out the remnant forces of colonialism, developing the national economy, and consolidating national independence." They are now struggling to consolidate and defend their political and economic independence, which are inseparable. All of them should practice "self-reliance," but this should not be "self-seclusion." They should expand economic cooperation among themselves while working to transform the basic relationships between the Third World nations and the superpowers.

"The struggles of the Asian, African, and Latin American countries and people . . . have exposed the essential weakness of imperialism," Teng declared; "the struggles of these countries against superpower control . . . have a significant impact on the development of international relations." The present international situation "is most favorable to the developing countries and peoples of the world," he asserted. "The old order based on colonialism, imperialism, and hegemonism is being undermined," and there is an "awakening and growth of new emerging forces," as the Third World countries play "an ever greater role in international affairs." These countries "constitute a revolutionary motive force propelling the wheel of world history and are the *main force* combatting colonialism, imperialism, and particularly the superpowers." [Emphasis added.]

After this panegyric stressing the importance of the Third World, Teng asserted that "China is not a superpower, nor will she ever seek to be one." He also declared, dramatically, "China is a socialist country, and a developing country as well. China belongs to the Third World."

Thus, China's public posture is now the reverse, in certain basic respects, of what it was immediately after the Communists came to power. Then Peking's leaders, closely aligned with Moscow, declared that there was no "third road" and called all neutralist developing nations "running dogs" of imperialism. Now they assert that China is not simply aligned with the Third World but is actually a part of it, committed to struggle with Third World nations against the two superpowers and especially against the Soviet Union.

A Dual Approach

Teng's speech reveals a very important facet of Chinese Communist thinking today that clearly has a major influence on Peking's foreign policy. The Chinese, seeking to assert their leadership in the Third World, are making a strong effort to broaden their ties with developing countries.[8] Chinese press reports often give the impression that Peking has become the Mecca for these nations. Heads of state beat a path to China's door, China's trade with the Third World is growing, and well-publicized aid is given to a few, selected countries such as Tanzania and Pakistan. Chinese media give great publicity to meetings of developing nations and generally endorse the positions that leading Third World countries support in international organizations and meetings.

At present Peking's principal emphasis is on strengthening "normalized" state-to-state relations. With relatively little regard for traditional Communist revolutionary criteria, it courts feudal monarchies and military dictatorships as well as "progressive" regimes. Its foreign policy continues, however, to operate on several levels, and in addition to developing official ties, Peking energetically fosters contact with nonofficial groups through "people's diplomacy," and it still endorses revolutionary activity in many areas.

Even though the promotion of revolution is now being given a lower priority in overall Chinese policy than in many periods in the past, the Chinese still enthusiastically endorse armed struggle against selected governments with which China has no formal diplomatic relations, including Israel and the white regimes in South Africa and Rhodesia. Peking's radio and press also continue to give moral support to Communist-led struggles in countries such as Thailand, Malaysia, and Burma, and the Chinese still provide limited material support—for example to the Communists in Burma—while at the same time stressing the need to improve official relations. The conflict between official diplomacy and ideological rhetoric creates inevitable contradictions in China's policy, which seem likely to continue. There is little prospect that Peking will totally end its moral support to revolutionaries abroad; in fact, it could decide at some point to put increased emphasis on revolutionary goals. But, currently, Chinese leaders place a much higher priority on expanding relations with noncommunist states than on exhorting insurrectionaries to overthrow them, and they stress the broad struggle of the developing nations against the leading developed powers much more than the struggle of revolutionary groups to establish new Communist regimes.

Peking has very practical reasons for its current approach to the developing nations. China clearly can enhance its international influence more, at present, by aligning with and supporting Third World governments than by concentrating attention on revolutionary Marxist-Leninist parties and movements, few of which have immediate chances for success. The world may not be experiencing exactly the kind of "great disorder" that the Chinese talk about, but it is undergoing tremendous change, and the pressure to establish more equitable relationships between developing and developed nations, which Peking fully endorses, is strong.

China is, as it claims to be, a developing nation, even though in many respects it is also a major power, and on many transnational economic issues its leaders see a real congruence of interests with other developing countries. By stressing these, it can try to gain political capital among Third World nations. Their reciprocal support for Chinese positions on international issues is obviously very helpful to Peking. Politically and psychologically, moreover, Chinese leaders obtain substantial gratification from the homage paid them by Third World leaders, many of whom view China as unique in part because it is the only major power that, like themselves, is poor and faces huge development problems. Some Third World leaders, despite ideological differences with the Chinese, are intrigued by aspects of the Chinese developmental model, even though Chinese practices are not easily transferable; their praise for Chinese accomplishments bolsters Peking's pride and prestige. Last, but not least, Chinese activities in the Third World are one possible way of diverting and preoccupying the two superpowers—especially the Soviet Union—and though this is not likely to enhance China's security position dramatically, it might do so at least marginally.

China's potential for expanding its influence in the Third World is restricted, however, by its limited ability to project either military or economic influence abroad. Basic ideological and political differences between China and most Third World nations, and Peking's continuing even if low-keyed endorsement of armed revolution, work against close ties in many cases. Nationalism is the dominant force in the Third World nations; the leaders in most of them are wary of excessive influence from any other power and still put China in that category. Moreover, the Third World is not a unitary or cohesive group. It consists of a great diversity of nations, among which there are deep differences and clashes of interest. Although China sees a congruence of many goals with many Third World countries, there is no across-the-board identity of interests, and Peking's ties with particular developing countries vary from extensive to minimal and from friendly to hostile.

Although publicly China places less emphasis on its relations with Second World nations than on its ties with the Third World, for very practical reasons it is now working hard to strengthen its links with both Japan and Europe and is also expanding its relations with other developed nations such as Canada and Australia.[9] As China's need for imported capital goods and advanced technology as well as grain has grown, it has naturally turned to these countries as sources of supply. The developed nations have been responsive, since trade with China, while not essential to them, is clearly of economic benefit.

Far more important than economic factors in Peking's increased interest in the industrialized nations, however, are military and strategic considerations. The Chinese now see these areas as important counterweights to the Soviet Union, and they openly urge them to be militarily strong, to oppose détente with Moscow, and to combat all forms of Soviet influence. Peking hopes that the European nations, in particular, will pursue policies that will prevent Moscow from transferring military forces from Europe to Asia and increasing pressure on China.

In relations with the developed nations as well as the Third World, Peking has had considerable success since the start of the 1970s. Its diplomatic and economic ties have expanded, and sympathetic interest in China has grown. Yet there are limits to what Peking can hope to achieve in relations with these developed countries because of a basic asymmetry in China's relationships with them. Clearly they are potentially much more important to China than China is to them. The crucial immediate interests of the largest noncommunist industrialized nations—the United States, the European Common Market members, and Japan—lie in their relations with each other, despite their growing dependence on resources from the developing nations. Ideologically and politically, moreover, leaders in the industrialized countries are as ambivalent about China as Chinese leaders are about them. Long distances separate most of them from China. The overlap in interests is quite limited. And cultural differences create a deep gulf. It is highly doubtful that Peking will exert a very significant influence on their policies in the period ahead. At times some of China's interests and theirs will be similar, but the parallelism in most cases will be limited. Nevertheless, improved ties with these nations do serve Peking's interests, and it makes good sense from the Chinese point of view to cultivate them.

Peking's three-world schema stressing the importance of the Third World and the potential value of links with the Second World reveals important facets of China's current foreign policy. Yet in many respects it obscures as much as it reveals about Chinese attitudes and policies. Taken at face value, it can be very misleading. In actuality, because Chinese leaders, like most leaders, view security problems as crucially important, and because the industrial powers are much more important in terms of immediate security problems, both as potential adversaries and as potential supporters, than any Third World countries are, many of Peking's most important policies must be explained in terms very different from the assumptions underlying the three-world concept. In practice China clearly places highest priority not on the struggle by the Third and Second Worlds against both superpowers but rather on the need to encourage opposition by the United States, Japan, and Europe as well as China to Soviet expansionism.

In terms of China's security, Peking now appears to view the world as one in which five centers of military or economic power are crucially important, a view similar in many respects to that articulated by President Richard M. Nixon and Henry Kissinger, his main foreign-policy adviser, at the start of the 1970s.[10] The Chinese clearly see the Soviet threat as posing their principal security problem and, despite their denunciation of all "power politics," they are pursuing an energetic, realpolitik-motivated, balance-of-power strategy to counterbalance Soviet influence. Peking's leaders would vehemently deny that this is a valid way to describe their policies, but their behavior makes it evident that this approach is fundamental in their current global strategy. Privately, in discussions with both official and nonofficial leaders from the major industrialized nations, they are unambiguous about the priority they now give to the need to check Soviet power. Even in their public propaganda, this theme coexists with their exhortation to all Third World nations to oppose both superpowers.

In practice, therefore, two different conceptualizations of the world now underlie China's foreign policies—to use a favorite Chinese phrase, China currently "walks on two legs," or pursues dual policies, in its approach to international problems. Sometimes these partially complement each other; for example, both impel China to compete against Soviet influence in the Third World. Often, however, they are in conflict. Both are important; they reflect quite different Chinese goals. But the duality in Peking's policies also creates problems for Chinese policymakers as well as for others who have to cope with the ambiguities and "contradictions" it involves.

In the final analysis the record of China's behavior over the years suggests that when Peking's leaders believe vital Chinese security interests are at stake, these take clear precedence over other interests, and realpolitik considerations and balance-of-power approaches come to the fore. This proposition is a major thesis of this study. Since China's most important security concerns center on its relations with the other major powers in East Asia, its policies toward the Soviet Union, Japan, and the United States are analyzed in detail in the first three parts of this study. In the discussion of its bilateral relations with each of these powers, historical, cultural, ideological, and economic, as well as security, factors are examined. The attitudes and policies of both sides are scrutinized, since neither China's policies nor those of any of the other powers can be fully understood without analysis of the interaction between them. The present state of each bilateral relationship is assessed, and the analysis identifies converging and conflicting interests, China's policy options in the future, and possible trends in relationships in the period immediately ahead.

In the final part, the general policy predispositions, power factors, and multilateral relationships that are likely to shape China's policies toward all the major powers in the immediate future are analyzed. Both the broad patterns of past Chinese policy and the current political, economic, and military trends that will affect its future policy are discussed. Finally, the nature of the new pattern of four-power relations and China's role in the emerging multilateral equilibrium in East Asia are carefully examined, since China's future policies toward the other powers, as well as their policies toward China, will be determined to a large degree by the complex interactions among all of the major powers in the region.

PART ONE

China and the Soviet Union

RELATIONS between China and the Soviet Union are of crucial importance to the prospects for regional peace and stability in East Asia. During the past quarter century two seismic shifts in their relationship have
had worldwide repercussions. First the formation of a Sino-Soviet alliance and then the split between the two countries profoundly altered the
global power structure.

In recent years the hostility between China and the Soviet Union has
been more intense than between any other major powers. Not only in
their dealings with each other, but in the broader world community,
Peking and Moscow have engaged in bitter polemical debate and intense
political competition that have had far-reaching effects on both the atmospherics and the realities of contemporary international relations.

Though other nations may benefit in some respects from the Communist giants' preoccupation with their struggle against each other, major
costs and potential dangers to the entire international community are
inherent in this situation. Examination of China's policy toward all the
major powers can logically start, therefore, with an analysis of Sino-
Soviet relations. The characteristics of the relationship and the underlying causes of the split and continuing conflict between the two countries are the subject of a sizable body of scholarly analysis.[1] In fact, no
other aspect of China's foreign relations since 1949 has been analyzed so
extensively. While neither Peking nor Moscow opens its archives, and
both manipulate the historical record to serve current policy needs, a
great deal is known about the two, especially as a result of Sino-Soviet
debates in the 1960s. Thus it is possible to obtain a reasonably good understanding of what has shaped their relationship in recent years.

Historical Legacy

To understand the situation today, the most relevant historical background concerns the past quarter century, but one cannot ignore memories of earlier relations that China's Communist leaders brought with them when they assumed power. When Mao Tse-tung in mid-1949 proclaimed that China would "lean to one side," toward the Soviet Union, and then in early 1950 signed a military alliance with the Russians, he put overwhelming stress on the unity of outlook, interests, and purpose between the two countries. The rest of the world tended to accept appearances for reality. Probably Mao himself tried hard to put past history behind him. Yet he must have had many more reservations and doubts than he revealed, for numerous frictions and strains had developed between the Chinese and Russian Communist parties during the long revolutionary struggle in China.

The history of the two nations' relations since the first significant contacts between the tsarist and Manchu empires in the seventeenth century had never been intimate or cordial. Up to the early twentieth century, it was, in essence, the story of two great empires colliding.[2] There had been an earlier collision, in the thirteenth and fourteenth centuries, when the Mongols, after conquering China, had expanded westward to what is now Eastern Europe, subjugating Kiev and the other small states in what was later to become western Russia. In the fourteenth and fifteenth centuries, however, important changes occurred in both China and Russia, as the Mongol empire disintegrated. In the mid-fourteenth century the Chinese overthrew the Mongols and established the Ming dynasty, which proceeded to restore control over domains traditionally considered part of the Chinese empire. The rulers of Muscovy won independence from Mongol rule in the fifteenth century and began to create a new Russian empire, which expanded relentlessly eastward during the ensuing centuries.

In the seventeenth century, the Ming dynasty, after a period of decline, was replaced by the Manchus. Although they were foreigners, they proceeded like the Ming rulers before them to reinvigorate the Chinese empire. At about the same time, Russian explorers, traders, and adventurers probing eastward began to have significant direct contact with the Chinese. Friction and tension were inevitable. By the 1680s a number of military clashes had forced the rulers of China and Russia to negotiate a settlement. The Treaty of Nerchinsk in 1689, China's first treaty with a Western state, defined part of the Sino-Russian boundary and opened the way for increased trade and political contact. Although disputes and problems continued, for more than a century the agreements reached at Nerchinsk limited the conflicts.

However, Russian expansion into areas on China's periphery continued, and as it gained momentum, clashes became increasingly frequent. Bit by bit, the Russians occupied portions of territory traditionally regarded by China's rulers as theirs. By the nineteenth century the Manchu dynasty, itself now in a period of decline, confronted mounting imperialist threats and pressures not only from Russia but also from Western maritime powers, and it was forced to sign a series of humiliating "unequal treaties," which compromised its rights in innumerable ways and ceded significant portions of territory to foreign powers.

The areas that the Russians threatened most directly were in the vast borderlands stretching from Manchuria through Mongolia to Sinkiang (Chinese Turkestan). These sparsely populated regions were inhabited largely by tribal peoples who were neither Chinese nor Russian, but the rulers of China had for centuries considered them areas of rightful Chinese control. However, the Manchus were unable to halt the Russians' encroachments, in part because of growing pressure in the east from the European powers and Japan. Russian pressure on China reached a peak at the turn of the twentieth century. It was checked, not by effective Chinese resistance, but by Japan's victory in the Russo-Japanese War of 1904–05 as well as by subsequent revolutionary developments within Russia itself.

Thereafter, the Europeans and then the Japanese posed the greatest immediate threats to China. But Russian pressure and Sino-Russian conflicts continued, despite the Bolshevik leaders' promise after the 1917 revolution to end tsarist Russia's special rights in China. In fact, Russia's new Communist leaders began to intervene in Chinese domestic politics more extensively than the tsars ever had. While conducting relations with the weak Peking government, Moscow also negotiated with local provincial leaders, and, most important, it gave significant support to both the Kuomintang and Communist movements in China.

Russian encroachments in the borderlands also continued. In the years following the 1911 revolution in China, Moscow had supported the breakaway of Outer Mongolia. In the 1930s it established a predominant influence over a separatist provincial regime in Sinkiang. And at the end of World War II, Stalin reasserted Russian rights in Manchuria, acquiring privileges very similar to those the tsarist regime had enjoyed; Moscow also induced the Nationalist regime formally to acknowledge Outer Mongolia's independence.

The leaders of China's struggling Communist party doubtless had a different view of these developments than did the Kuomintang leaders who ruled China from 1927 on. Inspired by the 1917 revolution, they had adopted the Marxist faith in its Leninist form, and they regarded Moscow as the natural headquarters of world revolution. They looked to the Russians for support and probably hoped that once the Chinese revolution succeeded, an entirely new kind of relationship would be possible between China and the Soviet Union. But the memory of past Russian encroachments had certainly not been erased from their minds by 1949 when they assumed power, and they must have been acutely sensitive to any indications that past patterns might persist.

The history of the Chinese Communist party's relations with Moscow also must have created ambivalent feelings and doubts about Russian intentions and behavior on the part of some party leaders, including Mao.[3] In the period before 1949 such doubts were never sufficient to outweigh the importance of the links created by shared values and purposes, but relations were strained on many occasions.

During its first years, the Chinese Communist party, in an organizational sense, was in some respects a creature of Moscow. Though it had its roots in Chinese society, the party was founded in 1921 with the direct encouragement and participation of the Moscow-based Comintern, then only two years old, and continued to be linked to it until the Comintern's demise in 1943. In the 1920s Comintern advisers participated in making many of the Chinese party's most important policy decisions, and through the early 1930s the Russians played a major role in determining who would lead the Chinese party as well as what the party's basic revolutionary strategy should be. Mao was not among those most favored by Moscow.

There is substantial evidence of serious personal friction between the Comintern advisers and Chinese Communist party leaders.[4] More important, the strategies imposed by Moscow on the Chinese were frequently based on serious misjudgments, influenced as much or more by political struggles in the Soviet Union as by the situation in China. Some of these misjudgments led to disasters, such as the debacle of 1927 when the

Chinese Communist party, violently suppressed by the Nationalists, was almost destroyed.[5]

It was only in the 1930s, when the Chinese Communists created new bases for revolutionary power in the countryside, and Mao rose within the party hierarchy without relying on Moscow's backing, that this relationship changed. Thereafter, while continuing to recognize Moscow as the headquarters of world revolution, the Chinese party leaders asserted their autonomy and evolved their own policies. On international issues Mao usually followed Moscow's lead, but within China he tended to go his own way.[6] Moreover, in the party's so-called Rectification Campaign of the early 1940s, the already reduced influence of its most pro-Soviet leaders was further weakened. Soon thereafter Chinese party leaders began stressing the uniqueness of China's revolutionary experience, claiming that Marxism had been "Sinified" by Mao.[7]

Although the Russians maintained a representative in Mao's Yenan headquarters during the wartime years, relationships were not close. Stalin was concerned above all about Russia's defense requirements in the fight against the Axis powers, and in the early war years he gave the Chinese Nationalists important military support.[8] The deprecating remarks he and other Soviet leaders made on several occasions about the Chinese Communists, as well as the policies the Russians pursued, suggested that Moscow had no great faith in the Chinese Communists' immediate chances for success.[9] In many respects, in fact, Stalin seemed ambivalent about them, as they probably were about him, even though both continued to believe their ties were important.

In the critical period from the end of World War II until the Communists' victory in China, the parties' relationships continued to be extremely complicated. When the Russians occupied northeast China—Manchuria—at the end of the war, the Chinese Communists moved major elements of their forces there, and the Russians gave substantial aid, turning over to them large amounts of Japanese military materiel.[10] This timely assistance was of critical importance to the Chinese Communists. It helped them to defeat the Nationalists in Manchuria, which then became a primary base for their nationwide military challenge to the Nanking regime.

But there were many indications that Moscow still lacked complete confidence in the Chinese Communists. Stalin, after obtaining U.S. and British agreement at Yalta, forced the Chinese Nationalists to grant Russia special rights in Manchuria once again, promising in return to respect their regime's sovereignty, and he seized as war booty much of the industrial equipment in the region.[11] He also backed a separatist Turki regime in northwest Sinkiang.[12] Most important, he advised the Chinese Communists to limit their immediate objectives and to join a coalition government with the Nationalists—advice that Mao ignored.[13] Until the Nanking government's final days on the mainland, Moscow continued to maintain relations with it, and, in fact, at the end it was still negotiating with it concerning Soviet interests in Sinkiang. While there is no reason to suppose that Stalin did not hope the Chinese Communists would ultimately win the struggle in China, he hedged his bets until the very end, continuing to give primacy to immediate Russian interests rather than to the goals of revolutionaries outside of Russian territory. It is possible that Stalin feared a rapid increase in Chinese Communist power would provoke increased U.S. intervention. He may even have felt that a China in which the Nationalists and Communists shared power would be preferable in relation to Soviet interests, in the short run at least, to a total Communist victory. Whatever his motives, his support of the Chinese Communists in their revolutionary struggle was clearly limited.

Sino-Soviet Alliance

Despite this background, when the Chinese Communists won their struggle more rapidly than even they had thought possible and established a new national regime in October 1949, both they and the Russians moved rapidly to establish new and unprecedently close ties between the two countries. Whatever mutual doubts Chinese and Soviet leaders may still have had, they both saw obvious advantages in forging an alliance. The cold war was under way in Europe, and the Chinese Communist leaders had already publicly endorsed the Soviet view of a bipolar world dominated by an intense struggle between the socialist and capitalist camps.[14] Both countries feared the power of the United States, and both were committed to foster the spread of Communist influence. Some observers believe that as late as mid-1949 Mao may have considered trying to balance relations with Moscow by developing significant ties with Washington; however, in July he dramatically announced his "lean to one side" policy and rejected any "middle road," committing himself strongly to alignment with Moscow.[15] The Sino-Soviet alliance, concluded soon thereafter, in February 1950, was directed against the United States as well as Japan.[16]

For most of the decade after 1949, the keystone of China's foreign policy was its alliance with the Soviet Union. Not only did the two countries sign a military pact that linked their basic security interests; they also developed far-reaching relations in economic, scientific, educational, and other fields.

Peking's leaders accepted Soviet economic experience as the development model for China and based their programs on Soviet advice and promises of aid.[17] In their dealings with the rest of the world the Chinese and Russians generally followed parallel policies. They cooperated in fighting a war in Korea, in which the Chinese provided most of the manpower and the Russians most of the materiel. And in general they maintained a posture of "monolithic unity." Never had any Chinese leaders gone so far in linking China's interests to, or emulating the model provided by, a foreign nation.

One of the important factors in the decision by Peking's leaders to align China so closely with the Soviet Union and to develop such extensive relations with it was their shared ideology and world outlook. They seemed to have a deep sense of common goals and to face common enemies. Both the Chinese and Russian leaders appeared genuinely to believe, at that time, that common values could unite the two countries and prevent serious clashes of national interests.

Security considerations were of basic importance. The new Chinese leaders knew that their regime was still weak and vulnerable. The United States had filled the postwar vacuum in Asia, occupied Japan, and enjoyed a virtual nuclear monopoly (in 1949 the Russians had only just exploded their first atomic bomb); and it was still linked to the Nationalists. Despite the gradual steps the Americans were taking toward disengagement from China, Peking's leaders doubtless believed that the United States, with Japan as a base, still posed a potential threat of serious proportions, which Moscow's military backing could help to counterbalance. From the Russian point of view, a Sino-Soviet alliance could significantly strengthen the entire socialist camp and bolster Russia's position vis-à-vis the "imperialists" not only in Asia but globally as well.

Economic considerations were also important. Although the Chinese Communists knew how to deal with rural problems, they had had almost no experience in administering large urban areas and developing modern industry. Determined to embark quickly on an ambitious development program, they looked naturally to the Soviet experience for their model and were eager to obtain Russian technical assistance, advice, and aid. In 1949 Mao rejected the idea that China could expect real economic help from the capitalist countries, and Peking began to reorient China's economy away from the West and toward the Communist bloc.[18] As a result, many new economic ties reinforced the military and political alliance.

The alliance was severely tested, less than a year after the Sino-Soviet treaty was signed, by the Korean War, and although it was strained, it survived the test. The war was started by the North Koreans with the endorsement of Stalin, who apparently expected that an attack would trigger revolution in the South and that the United States would not intervene. According to Khrushchev, Mao was informed of the plans and went along with them,[19] but the available evidence suggests that Mao did not expect China to be militarily involved.[20] It was only after U.S.-UN forces had intervened in Korea and the North Korean position was crumbling, and after the United States had reintervened in the Taiwan area, that China, seeing a threat not only to the existence of the North Korean buffer regime but to China itself, sent its own forces into Korea in the guise of volunteers.

Despite the strains it created between Peking and Moscow, the Korean War bolstered China's prestige and strengthened Sino-Soviet ties in certain respects. Moscow sold China large amounts of military equipment, and despite large casualties, Peking's forces were substantially modernized, with Soviet advice and along Soviet lines. Soviet backing was also essential to China in another way; it helped to deter the Americans from escalating the fighting, discouraging Washington from considering direct attacks on China or the use of nuclear weapons. The war accelerated the reorientation of China's economy toward the Communist bloc; the U.S.-initiated, UN-backed embargo against trade with China clearly compelled Peking to become more dependent economically on the bloc than it otherwise would have been.

Far-reaching linkages between the Chinese and Soviet regimes and societies were then forged during Peking's First Five Year Plan, which began in 1953. China's development policies from the start were drafted with Soviet advice, and its First Plan was specifically geared to Soviet promises of technical assistance and capital equipment. From 1952 through 1955, roughly 55 percent of China's annual foreign trade was with the Soviet Union and another 20 percent with other Communist countries.[21] By 1959 Moscow had committed itself to assist China, with equipment, technical data, and so on, on more than 400 industrial projects, of which 250–300 were large ones. In the 1950s, 10,800 Soviet technical specialists and advisers went to China. According to Russian claims the Soviet Union also gave the Chinese about 14,000 sets of scientific and technical "documents," allegedly worth "billions of dollars," and sold them equipment worth 4.7 billion rubles (almost $1.2 billion), including all of the equipment for 166 important industrial projects.

Over 7,000 Chinese were trained in Soviet enterprises during the First Plan period. Under a plan for scientific cooperation, close to 1,000 persons from the Chinese Academy of Sciences reportedly were trained by the Soviet Academy, and 1,500 Chinese technicians and scientists went to the Soviet Union. The Russians also helped to reorganize the Chinese educational system, along Soviet lines. By 1960 they had trained about 1,700 Chinese teachers in the Soviet Union, and by 1962 over 11,000 Chinese students and postgraduates had attended Soviet institutions of higher education (the Russians claim they paid half of the costs). Over 1,300 Soviet educational specialists worked in bodies attached to China's Ministry of Education, and hundreds of Soviet teacher-specialists went to China and helped to train over 17,000 graduates there.

Cultural and educational exchanges of other sorts were also extensive. In eight years, about 230 million copies of over 13,000 titles of Soviet works translated into Chinese were printed in China; by 1955 they included over 20 million copies of over 3,000 technical books. And by 1959 about 750 Soviet films had been shown in China. The flow of Chinese cultural materials to the Soviet Union was much smaller; it was not a balanced two-way exchange.

There were limits, however, to China's willingness to be integrated into the Communist bloc. China did not, for example, join COMECON (the Council for Mutual Economic Assistance), the Communist bloc's answer to the Marshall Plan, or the Warsaw Pact, the Communist equivalent of NATO (the North Atlantic Treaty Organization). Nevertheless, the Chinese did go very far in emulating the Soviet Union and in allowing China to become dependent on it.

It can be argued that in the 1950s China received from the Soviet Union "the most comprehensive technology transfer in modern industrial history."[22] There is no question that in the 1950s it had more extensive economic, scientific, educational, and cultural links with the Soviet Union than it had ever had with a foreign country, which exceeded those it had developed in earlier years, first with Japan and subsequently with the United States and major European countries. Soviet aid was of crucial importance to the Chinese Communists, therefore, as they consolidated their rule and embarked on programs to industrialize and modernize the country. But even in the 1950s the facade of unity was misleading. In spite of the closeness of relations, or perhaps in some respects because of it, there were many frictions and strains, some serious, that were concealed from the rest of the world at the time.

China was clearly the junior partner in the relationship while Stalin lived. The Russians insisted on their primacy, and the Chinese had to accept a subordinate position. As always, the Russians gave priority to their own national interests, sometimes asserting them bluntly, and there was hard bargaining in working out most Sino-Soviet agreements. Khrushchev later asserted that Stalin's high-handedness in dealing with the Chinese had almost wrecked the relationship, and that Sino-Soviet relations might have deteriorated even earlier than they did if Stalin had not died in 1953.[23]

The hard-headed Russian approach must have been apparent to Mao in 1950, when the framework for the Sino-Soviet alliance was hammered out in long negotiations in Moscow.[24] In exchange for military support of the new Peking regime, the Russians asked for a major quid pro quo: the granting of special rights in the Changchun railway and Port Arthur, in Manchuria, and the establishment of joint stock companies in both Manchuria and Sinkiang. Although both the Changchun railway and Port Arthur arrangements were temporary, when the termination date arrived in 1952, the Russians' rights in Port Arthur were extended, ostensibly at Peking's request. Since the Korean War was still in progress, the Chinese may, in fact, have believed that this was necessary for China's defense. But there is little doubt that they also resented these arrangements, which so resembled those imposed on China in earlier years. Some Russian leaders recognized this, for one of Moscow's first moves toward China after Stalin's death was to end all its special rights in China. Khrushchev, in his memoirs, admitted that it had been a major error to establish joint stock companies.[25]

Stalin's propensity to interfere in China's domestic politics must also have created strains. It was symbolically significant that Li Li-san, a Chinese Communist leader who had been in the Soviet Union since the early 1930s, returned to China soon after the Soviet forces entered Manchuria in 1945. The Russians probably viewed him as a lever to exert influence within China, although in fact he never was able to reestablish himself at the top of the Chinese party hierarchy.

Starting at the end of World War II, the Russians did acquire a strong and very special influence in Manchuria, and in mid-1949 they signed a local trade agreement with the Chinese Communist leaders there under Kao Kang. It was later revealed that Stalin had maintained direct communication with Kao, bypassing Mao and the Chinese Polit-buro.[26] There is no hard evidence that Moscow backed Kao's alleged attempt, subsequently, to elevate himself to a position second only to Mao's in China; but it is clear, and is frankly admitted by Soviet officials now, that Moscow viewed Kao as one of the most strongly pro-Soviet of Chinese leaders.[27] It is conceivable that Kao's pro-Soviet views were a factor in his purge in 1953-54.

Economics as well as political relationships between the two countries created friction. The Russians were willing to give major assistance to the Chinese, but they insisted that the Chinese pay for this aid.[28] In early 1950, when Mao was in Moscow, the Russians agreed to give China a $300 million developmental loan, payable over five years, and repayable over the next ten, at a low, one-percent interest rate. In 1954 they granted another loan equivalent to $130 million. But these two were the only Soviet long-term developmental loans to China publicly announced in the entire decade after 1949. Moreover, the Chinese were required to pay for the military supplies they received from the Soviet Union during the Korean War and the Soviet shares in joint stock companies and mili-tary stockpiles at Port Arthur when they were turned over to China.

The total of Soviet credits to China in the 1950s was probably consid-erably larger than the amount of the development loans suggests. One careful estimate places the total credits, for economic development, fi-nancing trade deficits, purchasing Soviet shares in joint stock companies, and providing military aid, between $1.37 billion and $2.24 billion.[29] But on the public record, Moscow gave no free grants of long-term develop-ment aid to Peking.

From their perspective, the Russians probably viewed their financial aid to China as generous. Previously they had not given large-scale eco-nomic assistance to any regime, Communist or noncommunist. In their own descriptions of their aid to China, the Russians emphasize that they charged low interest rates on developmental loans, and they insist that any calculation of Moscow's total financial aid to China should include the value of technical data given free of charge, Chinese savings from the low price for military equipment, and Moscow's contribution to the costs of training Chinese in the Soviet Union.[30]

But from the Chinese perspective, Soviet financial aid probably seemed fairly niggardly. In particular, the fact that China had to pay not only for all industrial and other equipment but also for Russian military aid must have been galling. It is possible that China never requested, or wanted, any large free grants. From the late 1950s on, the Chinese worked to pay off Moscow's past loans as rapidly as possible in order to free China from foreign indebtedness. But as came to light in 1957, during the Hundred Flowers campaign in China, some Chinese deeply resented the Russians' insistence that they pay their own way, bearing even the major costs of the Korean War.[31]

There were doubtless other strains created by the Korean War, which never surfaced.[32] It was not Chinese but Soviet and North Korean misjudgments that led to the American intervention in Korea and reintervention in the Taiwan Strait which impelled Peking to join the costly struggle against U.S. and UN forces. It was the Chinese, not the Russians, who had to bear the major burden of the war and suffer tremendous casualties. In effect, the Chinese, though acting in their own defense, also had to pull the Russians' and North Koreans' chestnuts out of the fire.

The end of the war and Stalin's death in 1953 brought important changes in Sino-Soviet relations. Most obvious were the deliberate efforts of Moscow's new leaders to move toward a more equal relationship and remove past causes of friction. The 1954 visit of Khrushchev and Bulganin to Peking, the first visit of any top Soviet leaders, initiated a period of increased mutual cordiality.[33] The Soviet Union extended a new developmental loan to China, ended the special rights acquired in 1950, and, most important, demonstrated an increased sensitivity to Chinese pride. In 1955 some Soviet leaders, including Molotov, even referred to the Communist bloc as a camp led by *both* the Soviet Union and China.[34]

But in a subtle fashion the death of Stalin altered the relationship in a way that planted the seeds of future discord. While Stalin lived, the Chinese, however much they resented Stalin's insistence on Soviet primacy, seemed prepared to accept, or acquiesce in, a position as junior partner in the alliance. Although Mao and his closest associates undoubtedly did not like much that Stalin did, they respected him as a giant of world communism. When Stalin died, China's leaders doubtless felt that his successors were lesser men. Mao may have begun at that time to view himself as the senior leader in the world Communist movement, even though it was only later that Chinese statements bluntly claimed this position for him. The improvement in Sino-Soviet relations during 1953–56 proved, in any case, to be short lived and superficial.

Sino-Soviet Conflict

Despite strains in Sino-Soviet relations in the early 1950s, the open rift between the two countries did not develop until the second half of the decade, and it did not explode into public ideological debate until 1960. Few observers in the early 1950s, including those who recognized that conflicts of interest existed between China and the Soviet Union that would eventually complicate their relationship, predicted the kind of conflict that ultimately developed. The ties between the two countries seemed so close, the advantages of cooperation so great, and the costs of a rift so obvious that there was every reason to expect leaders in both countries would do everything possible to maintain the alliance. Serious errors of judgment and major policy mistakes on both sides account for their failure to do so.

The rift did not emerge full blown. It developed gradually, and in each major phase the level of conflict escalated and the nature of the conflict changed. Numerous factors aggravated the dispute, but issues relating to military security were the crucial ones at three turning points: in 1957–59, when the strains created doubts about the alliance on both sides; in 1962–63, when the alliance became a dead letter for all practical purposes; and in 1968–69, when the political confrontation between the two countries was transformed into a military confrontation.

The Chinese date the start of the conflict to Khrushchev's de-Stalinization speech in 1956. Peking's leaders were surprised and shocked by the speech. Khrushchev had not consulted them, or even informed them of his intentions, beforehand. The Russian leaders apparently viewed de-Stalinization as a policy they alone could decide. But from the Chinese point of view it had far-reaching implications for China and the entire Communist bloc and world movement. The attack on Stalin raised ideological and political questions of tremendous import. China's leaders feared that it might threaten the legitimacy of Communist regimes and parties everywhere, weaken the unity of the Communist bloc, and affect the worldwide struggle against the capitalist world adversely. Moreover, the sweeping attack against Stalin's "cult of personality" inevitably raised questions that Mao must have felt might threaten his primacy within China. In ideological terms, the Chinese were disturbed by Khrushchev's stress on the noninevitability of war, the possibility of a nonviolent transition to socialism, and the idea of "peaceful coexistence" as basic principles underlying Soviet policy. These positions conflicted with many aspects of the model for revolution espoused by Mao (even though the Chinese themselves had strongly endorsed the "coexistence" theme in 1955). They also implied a willingness to compromise with the capitalist nations, and in particular the United States, in ways that Peking felt could weaken its position in its confrontation with the Americans, for example over Taiwan. From Peking's viewpoint, the speech called into question both the judgment of Moscow's new leaders and their willingness to take Chinese views and interests fully into account in making their policy decisions.

The upheavals that occurred later in 1956, first in Poland and then in Hungary, seemed to confirm some of Peking's worst fears. The Chinese responded by involving themselves directly, for the first time, in East European affairs and articulating, also for the first time, their own views on the major ideological and political issues facing the Communist world.[35] These actions indicated that Peking no longer automatically accepted Moscow's authority to define the correct line on critical issues affecting other Communist regimes and parties. Moscow clearly had mixed feelings about China's actions, even though its leaders appreciated China's efforts to limit the trend toward "polycentrism" that Khrushchev's speech had unleashed.

Once the seeds of Sino-Soviet conflict were sown, in 1956, a clear divergence in the basic strategic outlook of China and the Soviet Union developed during 1957–59, when the interests of the two countries clashed. Differences in strategic outlook first became evident at the Moscow conference of Communist parties in November 1957. Even though Mao, who attended the conference, argued for the need to acknowledge Soviet leadership of the Communist bloc, and the Chinese and Russians avoided public confrontation over their views, the divergence between their assessments of the global situation and prescriptions for world strategy became clear. While the Russians argued for a relatively cautious strategy toward the noncommunist world, Mao, proclaiming that the "east wind prevails over the west wind," urged a more militant worldwide struggle.[36]

One explanation of their divergence lay in the different assessments

Moscow and Peking made of the significance of the Russian successes in launching their first intercontinental missile and earth satellite just before the conference. Mao argued that the world balance had shifted in favor of the Communist bloc, and that, led by Moscow, all Communists should actively exploit the new situation. Khrushchev was much less sanguine. Increasingly concerned about the risks of nuclear conflict, he was trying to evolve a policy of "coexistence" with the United States.

As these broad ideological and political differences surfaced, divergent political trends within the two countries also created new strains in their relations. Development issues had been a matter of debate in China for some time, and Mao, who had become increasingly concerned about domestic trends and increasingly disenchanted with Soviet influence, began in the fall of 1957 to push for more radical domestic policies. By 1958, when the Great Leap Forward and commune program took shape, he had clearly abandoned the Soviet model. Thus, increased radicalism in internal policy paralleled growing militancy in foreign policy. In contrast, the trends within the Soviet Union were toward less revolutionary domestic policies, which reinforced the pressure pushing Khrushchev to pursue a coexistence policy toward the West.

Critical Issues

Chinese and Russian differences on many specific foreign policy issues became painfully apparent in 1958 and 1959. Khrushchev, determined to achieve a more nearly equal strategic balance with the United States and minimize the risks of nuclear war, moved ahead in his attempt to devise a new policy toward the United States. His efforts to promote coexistence, which later would be called "détente," culminated in his visit to Washington in 1959. The Chinese, convinced that Soviet-American détente would compromise important Chinese interests in the Taiwan area and elsewhere, clearly opposed this trend. As a major nuclear power, the Soviet Union feared the possibility of local military conflicts escalating into confrontations between the major powers. In contrast, Chinese leaders, who were acutely dissatisfied with the status quo, argued that armed struggles were necessary for successful revolutions, and they apparently believed that in order for China to achieve its national objectives, including the recovery of Taiwan, the Soviet Union as well as China would have to apply increased pressure on the United States.

This broad divergence of strategic perspective led to serious differences over many specific issues during 1958–59, several of which had a crucial effect on overall Sino-Soviet relations. In particular, the offshore islands crisis of 1958 was a key event in this period. As much as any other development, it highlighted, to leaders in both Peking and Moscow, the conflicts of Chinese and Soviet national interests.

Chinese leaders had regarded the recovery of Taiwan as one of China's highest priority goals ever since 1949. In 1954–55 they had tried to work toward their goal by exerting military pressure on the Nationalist-held offshore islands, near the China coast. When this failed, they briefly adopted a policy of political attraction. Then in 1958 they decided to try pressure once again.

For some time the Chinese Communists had observed the steady strengthening of ties between the United States and Taiwan; they now were fearful that Moscow's coexistence policy would reduce the prospect of recovery of the island. In fact, they suspected that Khrushchev was trying to signal both Washington and Peking that in his view Taiwan was not an issue of high priority and should be laid aside, at least for the present.[37] In deciding to renew military pressure on the offshore islands, the Chinese probably hoped to compel the Russians to give them greater support. In a sense, they were testing the basic value of their alliance with the Soviet Union.

They began by subjecting the offshore islands to massive artillery barrages, but this soon created an international crisis involving the major powers. At the height of the crisis, Khrushchev did conclude that Moscow's alliance with Peking compelled him to threaten retaliation against the United States if it attacked the China mainland. However, in reality Moscow wished to avoid direct involvement in any conflict there, and, as subsequent Chinese statements stressed, Khrushchev's strongest pledges of support came only after the crisis had passed its peak.[38] In addition, Khrushchev made clear that he would not aid any offensive Chinese Communist action to take either the offshore islands or Taiwan.

From the Chinese point of view, the crisis demonstrated that the Soviet Union was not prepared to give China the support it desired, even on an issue that Peking regarded as fundamental to its national interests. From the Soviet point of view, the crisis highlighted the danger that the Chinese might draw the Soviet Union into conflicts, involving possible confrontation with the United States, that it wished to avoid.

The 1958 crisis almost certainly helped precipitate a rift over another crucial issue—Soviet aid to the Chinese for the development of nuclear weapons. Limited collaboration between the two countries in the nuclear field had begun in the mid-1950s, when the Russians aided the Chinese in building their first nuclear reactor. Then in the fall of 1957, in what was obviously a major policy decision, the Soviet Union agreed to help China build its own nuclear weapons. The Chinese claim that the Russians promised to give China a "sample" bomb as well as the technical data required to build nuclear weapons.[39] Thereafter, Moscow did give substantial assistance to the Chinese in constructing major nuclear facilities, including their first gaseous diffusion plant, but it never delivered a sample bomb.

It is surprising that Moscow was ever willing to promise such support, since, as the Russians have subsequently stated, they were disturbed during the November 1957 Moscow conference by statements Mao made that seemed to them to reveal a cavalier, even reckless, attitude about the risk of nuclear war. Perhaps they believed they had to offer help with nuclear development in order to win Chinese support in the task of re-uniting the Communist bloc. By 1958, however, Moscow began to have serious doubts about the wisdom of this policy, and the 1958 offshore islands crisis heightened these doubts.* Finally, in mid-1959, according to the Chinese, the Russians "tore up" the 1957 nuclear agreement.

This rift over nuclear weapons, unpublicized at the time, was unquestionably one of the most important causes for the eventual open split between Peking and Moscow.[40] From Peking's perspective, it indicated that the Russians were not willing to use their power to back China even in the pursuit of its highest priority national interests and that they wished to perpetuate a relationship in which the Chinese would continue to be militarily dependent on the Soviet nuclear umbrella, and subordinate. This reinforced Peking's determination to go it alone, and thereafter China's efforts to develop its own nuclear capability were accelerated.

The Russians argue that in this period Khrushchev decided that priority must be given to arms control, including efforts to prevent prolifer-

---

* M. S. Kapitsa, a leading Soviet government specialist on Asian affairs, asserted in an interview with me in April 1974 that the Chinese had not informed the Soviet Union of their intentions regarding the off-shore islands, even though Khrushchev had visited Peking just before the crisis began. When the crisis developed, Foreign Minister Gromyko, accompanied by Kapitsa, made a secret visit to Peking. At a meeting they held with the Chinese Politburo, Kapitsa asserts, Mao made statements similar to those he had made in Moscow deprecating the dangers of nuclear conflict. Shortly after this visit, according to Kapitsa, Moscow reassessed its policy of nuclear assistance to China.

ation, and that it was therefore logical to end nuclear assistance to China.[41] Actually, it appears that Moscow concluded that a nuclear-armed China, especially under Mao's leadership, might be more of a liability than an asset, and that it was not in Russia's interest to hasten the emergence of such a China. Moscow probably underestimated the political costs of reneging on its promise of nuclear assistance. The consequence was a profound change in its military and security relations with China.

Other military issues that arose in 1958–59 also exacerbated Sino-Soviet tensions. According to a Soviet official, Peking requested large-scale Soviet assistance to help expand the Chinese navy, which Moscow was not willing to give.[42] The Russians apparently proposed the formation of a joint Sino-Soviet fleet and requested permission to use Chinese territory for Soviet ships and naval facilities, which Peking refused. For the Chinese, who later charged that Moscow's aim had been to achieve "control" over China,[43] the Russian proposals probably evoked bitter memories of the humiliations China suffered from imperialist gunboat diplomacy.

In 1959 another territorial dispute developed in which the Russians failed, as they had in the 1958 Taiwan crisis, to give Peking the backing it desired. The Sino-Indian border dispute had earlier origins, but in 1959 it was brought into the open and the clash of Chinese and Indian claims became clear. At the same time, general relations between Peking and New Delhi deteriorated and became increasingly hostile. As the border dispute developed, instead of exerting pressure on New Delhi, Moscow adopted a neutral stance and continued its economic aid to India. From the Chinese viewpoint this constituted a clear tilt toward India, and later the Chinese angrily charged that this was the first time one socialist state had failed to support another in a major dispute with a noncommunist regime.[44]

Whatever the Russians may have felt about the border claims, they apparently disapproved of China's general shift from friendly relations to hostility in its policy toward India. Several years earlier, the Russians had begun economic aid to India, and they now showed a growing political interest in it as an instrument of their policy toward the Third World. Moscow was now stressing the need to deal with existing anticolonialist, neutralist, bourgeois regimes. In this context, relations with India were increasingly important in Soviet policy, as they had been in Chinese policy during the short Bandung period before 1959. Moscow therefore felt not only that China's dispute with India was unwise but that it conflicted with the general thrust of Russian policy toward the Third World.[45] The Chinese felt, however, that in failing to back Peking in its dispute with New Delhi, Moscow was again betraying important Chinese national interests. In Peking's eyes it was unthinkable that the Russians would give higher priority to their relations with a bourgeois nationalist regime than to their obligations to a socialist ally.

Economic factors also contributed to the parting of the ways between China and the Soviet Union during this period. Moscow's development loans dried up, and China decided to go its own way in its internal economic programs. The final installment of the Soviet Union's long-term credits to China was drawn by the Chinese in 1957, and no further loans of this sort followed, even though the Russians were at the time providing substantial aid to noncommunist countries such as India and Indonesia. Whether this was the result primarily of a decision by Moscow not to grant further long-term loans to China or a decision by Peking that it did not desire more, it reinforced other factors impelling Chinese leaders to adopt a much more independent, or "self-reliant," approach to China's problems.

The Chinese leaders' decisions in 1957–58 to abandon the Soviet model and to initiate the Great Leap Forward and communes program posed a direct ideological and political challenge to Moscow, since some Chinese statements implied, at least for a brief period in 1958, that China had now leapt ahead of the Soviet Union in moving from socialism toward the ultimate goal of communism. Khrushchev did not conceal his disapproval of—and, in fact, contempt for—Mao's innovations,[46] and he felt compelled to refute Chinese ideological pretensions. Some Russians now privately admit that the Chinese claims had a significant impact for a brief period on many people in Eastern Europe and some in the Soviet Union itself.[47] Within China the shifts in policy created serious friction between Soviet experts and the Chinese with whom they were working, as the Russians increasingly argued against the wisdom of actions taken during the Great Leap and the Chinese increasingly ignored or rejected Soviet advice.[48]

Throughout the period following the 1957 Moscow conference, growing problems in bilateral relations were accompanied by intensified Sino-Soviet ideological debate. Competition for influence between Peking and Moscow both in the Communist bloc and world movement and in the Third World steadily increased. And the split had inevitable repercussions in the domestic politics of both countries. Mao accused his domestic opponents, and in particular P'eng Teh-huai, of subversive links to Moscow.

By the end of 1959 the Sino-Soviet relationship was severely strained —far more so than was apparent either to the people of China and the Soviet Union or to the outside world. Peking and Moscow concealed many of their differences, and it was difficult to know how much weight to assign to the frictions that were evident or what consequences they might have. The economic and other linkages between the two societies had yet to be significantly weakened; in fact, Sino-Soviet trade reached its peak in 1959 when it totaled over $2 billion, the highest figure it has ever reached.[49] However, in light of what is now known, it is clear that under the surface the rift was already extremely serious. Early in the following year it became a matter of open debate.

Open Rift

The Chinese took the initiative in early 1960 in bringing the dispute into the open by launching a frontal ideological attack on the Soviet Union. They still did not explicitly name the Soviet Union as their target, but Moscow and the world knew it was. Mao doubtless played the crucial role in deciding to launch this attack, and there is evidence of differences at the time on policy toward Moscow. The essential issue, probably, was whether to exert new pressure on Moscow to alter its policies even at the risk of exacerbating tensions, or to search for compromises in order to try to repair relations. Minister of National Defense P'eng Teh-huai was charged, in effect, when he was purged in late 1959, with favoring a compromising approach.[50] Mao obviously favored a direct ideological attack, and his view prevailed.

The Chinese assault, contained in a bitter polemical article in the party's main theoretical journal, Red Flag,[51] was a sweeping ideological condemnation of the Soviet Union for abandoning Leninist principles and basic Communist values. Although the article, entitled "Long Live Leninism," referred to Soviet leaders simply as "modern revisionists," there was little attempt to disguise the target and no ambiguity in the charges. The Chinese focused primary attention on questions of basic ideology and revolutionary strategy, arguing the necessity for continuing class struggle, the need for violence and "armed revolution" rather than reliance on "peaceful transformation," the dangers inherent in the Soviet brand of "peaceful coexistence," and so on. These were real and important issues in the minds of China's leaders, and especially Mao. However, ideological differences were obviously not the only reasons for the Chinese attack. More important were the clashes of national interest that had occurred during the previous three years.

One can only speculate about what Mao hoped to achieve by launching this attack. He probably had not yet decided that Chinese and Soviet views and policies were irreconcilable; that came later. The most plausible explanation is that in April 1960 he hoped that strong ideological pressure would force Moscow to modify its attitudes and behavior. Although in one sense he was retaliating against what he felt were Soviet betrayals of Chinese interests and the world revolutionary cause, he probably aimed at inducing Moscow's leaders to see the error of their ways and return to the correct path. If this was Mao's hope, however, he made a serious misjudgment of the likely Soviet response.

Moscow's reaction became clear within a few months. It consisted of strong counterpressures against the Chinese. Not content to respond with ideological counterattacks alone, the Soviet Union took concrete punitive action. In the summer of 1960 almost all Soviet advisers and technical experts in China were recalled, a move that had an extremely damaging economic impact on China.

The ex post facto Russian explanations for this move stress that, from 1958 on, the Chinese increasingly ignored the advice of Soviet experts in China and made their conditions of work "unbearable."[52] After trying repeatedly, without success, to improve the situation, the Russians concluded, they say, that they had no recourse but to call their personnel home. The decision was not sudden, they argued, but was the culmination of two years of harassment. And they maintain that it was not their intention to remove the Soviet experts permanently, and that, in fact, as early as November 1960 they expressed their willingness to return the specialists.[53] If so, the Chinese probably had little faith in the sincerity of such offers.

While there is some truth in Moscow's charges that the Chinese created increasing difficulties for Soviet personnel from 1958 on, the decision to recall them suddenly and rapidly in mid-1960 was a drastic act of economic retaliation for Peking's ideological pressure on Moscow. Soviet leaders probably hoped to induce Chinese leaders to change their attitudes and be more compromising. They may have believed that Peking would have no alternative to knuckling under on Russian terms. Their later statements that they meant to send the Russian experts back to China suggest that they badly misjudged the likely Chinese response. Peking chose to be more uncompromising than ever. Even though the withdrawal of the Russian experts did have severely damaging economic effects on China, at a time when the Chinese economy was already in serious trouble as a result of the failures of the Great Leap Forward and of bad weather, the Chinese did not knuckle under. They were extremely bitter, and despite their relatively weak position, they decided to go it alone, whatever the problems and costs, determined to end their economic dependency and vulnerability.[54]

Just as the disputes over nuclear and naval issues profoundly affected the basic nature of their military-security relationships, the clashes over development strategy, the end of aid, and the withdrawal of experts had far-reaching effects on the basic economic and social relationships between China and the Soviet Union. China began, deliberately and systematically, to reduce its links to the Soviet Union, gradually extricating itself from the web of ties the two economies and societies had created in the mid-1950s.

The Soviet experts were never invited back. China proceeded systematically to repay all Soviet loans, to free Peking of indebtedness to Moscow.[55] And it began to shift its trade to the noncommunist world. The process of disengagement was inevitably gradual in some respects, and it was not clear at the start how far Peking would go. Moscow made some efforts to restore the economic relationship and as late as 1961 offered sizable short-term trading credits, which Peking accepted because of the severe economic depression in China. And reportedly the Russians periodically reiterated, in late 1960, 1961, and 1963, their offers to return their technical experts to China.[56] But once started, the process of economic disengagement soon became inexorable and irreversible. It gained momentum over time, accelerating as political relationships continued to deteriorate.

One important measure of this change was the decline of China's trade with the Soviet Union. From the $2.06 billion peak in 1959, it declined steadily until by 1970 it reached the almost negligible figure of $45 million, before beginning to rise somewhat again.[57] The drop in trade was accompanied by a gradual weakening of all other ties—scientific, educational, cultural—that had linked the two countries. As a result, whereas in the mid-1950s China had seemed well on its way toward full incorporation into a Moscow-dominated "Communist world system," by the end of the 1960s it had nothing more than minimal diplomatic contact with Russia. China's ties with Russia were now far less extensive than its links with many noncommunist countries, including some such as Japan with which China had not yet even established formal diplomatic relations.

From 1960 on, also, tension increased between China and the Soviet Union along their forty-five-hundred-mile common border. Since 1949 the border had remained calm, although some issues had been raised, and a few incidents had occurred. However, the long history of tensions in the borderlands made problems inevitable.[58] So too did the fact that major minority groups tended to regard national borders dividing their people as artificial barriers.

After achieving power, the Chinese Communists took steps in strategically important areas to consolidate control of minority populations such as the Uighurs, Kazakhs, and others in Sinkiang (especially in the Ili region which had been ruled by a Soviet-sponsored semiautonomous regime immediately before 1949) and the Mongols in Inner Mongolia. In doing so, they cut back those ethnic groups' contacts with similar groups across the border. The Soviet Union and Mongolian People's Republic took comparable actions. Peking, Moscow, and Ulan Bator all understood the dangers inherent in the situation. As early as 1954, when Khrushchev first visited Peking, Mao posed the issue of the status of Outer Mongolia. Khrushchev refused even to discuss the question, however, and Mao did not try then to force the issue.[59] Before 1960, therefore, no major border tensions, disputes, or crises had yet emerged.

After 1960, however, the situation basically changed. As political relations between Peking and Moscow deteriorated, frictions in the border regions became increasingly serious. In 1962 they reached a point of high tension when thousands of Kazakhs and Uighurs left China for the Soviet Union. The Chinese claimed that this exodus was the direct result of Soviet subversion and incitement. The Russians asserted that it was the result of excessive Chinese control over, and oppression of, these minority groups.[60] The incident poisoned the atmosphere all along the border, and thereafter the number of incidents greatly increased; the Russians claim there were over five thousand Chinese border violations in 1962 alone.[61] Both sides took measures to tighten border controls and strengthen local defenses, and both began to reinforce their regular military forces near the border.

Then in 1963–64 the border problem was transformed into a dispute over conflicting territorial claims. Khrushchev may have inadvertently provoked the Chinese into raising broad territorial issues. In December 1962, responding to Chinese criticism of Soviet behavior during the Cuban missile crisis, he taunted the Chinese about their toleration of continued colonial control of Hong Kong and Macao.[62] In March 1963 the Chinese replied by raising basic questions about all past "unequal treaties," including those between China and Russia, indicating that the settlements agreed to in all of them required reexamination.[63] The Soviet response was that no territorial issues existed. But Moscow was clearly worried, and it proposed discussions on the subject with the Chinese. At the end of 1963 Khrushchev, in a letter to all heads of state and government, called for a global treaty renouncing the use of force in solving any territorial disputes or border problems.[64]

In February 1964 the two sides finally met in Peking to discuss border and territorial problems, as Moscow had proposed the previous May.[65] These "consultations," as the Russians insisted on calling them, proved to be fruitless, however, and they were broken off before the end of the year. The Chinese stated that they were prepared to accept the existing border as a basis for negotiation, but insisted that Moscow admit that all the old treaties were "unequal" and invalid. This the Russians refused to do, insisting that past border treaties were still valid and that only minor adjustments should be discussed. While the discussions were in progress, Mao told a group of Japanese Socialists that the Soviet Union had occupied huge areas of other nations' territory, both in Asia and in Europe.[66] He hinted that China might ask for the return of an enormous area east of Lake Baikal. The Russian press responded with ominous warnings that if China asked for major territorial revisions, it could suffer the fate of the Japanese empire. Some time later, in May 1966, Chinese Foreign Minister Ch'en Yi asserted, in another interview with a Japanese visitor, that tsarist Russia had seized more than one and a half million square kilometers of Chinese territory through "unequal treaties," which China considered wholly unjustified; he indicated that Peking was not demanding the return of all the territories ceded under these treaties, but he pointed out that the Soviet Union had occupied certain areas "in violation of the treaties"—that is, beyond the areas ceded.[67]

The border and territorial issues that came to the fore in the early 1960s clearly were not the main causes of increasing Sino-Soviet conflict. They were symptoms of deeper, more serious problems. But they did exacerbate fears and raise the level of tension. The once placid boundary became a long line of hostile confrontation, and each side feared the other would exploit the situation. Then, from 1965 on, the Russians began to build up their military forces near the border, and the Chinese responded in kind; this raised tension to a still higher level. All of these developments aroused intense Chinese fear of Soviet expansionism, as well as Soviet fear of irrational Chinese action to recover "lost territories."

In fact the Chinese never advanced specific claims to large portions of Soviet territory; their official statements indicated that they recognized that no more than adjustments of the border would in fact be possible. The hints about huge territorial claims, and the demand that Moscow admit—as the Chinese probably recognized it would not—that past border treaties were "unequal," were weapons of political and psychological warfare. From their position of relative weakness, the Chinese did not have many instruments with which to exert leverage on Moscow. Consequently, they again attacked with words, as they had in April 1960. However, if Mao thought that this would induce Moscow to be more compromising, he made another misjudgment. Instead, the Russians stepped up their military buildup around China.

The deterioration in Sino-Soviet relations affected their policies throughout the world. On issue after issue they attacked each other's positions or actions and actively competed for influence and leadership of the Communist bloc and world movement.[68] Whereas before 1960 their debates had seemed esoteric to much of the world, from 1960 on the schism had an increasing impact on others, especially other Communist nations and parties, reinforcing the trend toward factional struggle and disunity.

The November 1960 conference of Communist parties in Moscow, the first such meeting since 1957, was designed to restore unity in the Communist world movement. Instead, Sino-Soviet differences accelerated the trend toward polycentrism.[69] China asserted the right of those holding "minority" opinions to propagate them openly, and it energetically proselytized its own views while denigrating Moscow's. Directly challenging Soviet authority, the Chinese tried to convince the Communist leaders that they should repudiate Moscow's leadership and align with Peking, or at least take a neutral stance in regard to the Sino-Soviet dispute. Their influence was a major factor in the factionalism that swept the Communist world movement.

Albania became a symbol of this competition and a kind of proxy for Sino-Soviet conflict during 1960–61.[70] A de facto alliance took shape between Peking and Tirana, and when Soviet leaders mounted a major political attack on Albania at the Twenty-second Congress of the Soviet party in 1961, Chou En-lai ostentatiously walked out. The program finally adopted at the congress was deliberately designed to counter the Chinese ideological and political positions. Peking, not surprisingly, denounced it as "out-and-out revisionist."[71]

Thereafter, the worldwide competition between China and Russia became increasingly bitter, and this further poisoned their bilateral relations. Everywhere it could, China encouraged radical pro-Peking Communist groups to break away from more orthodox pro-Moscow parties, and many did so. Altogether more than thirty pro-Peking groups looked to the Chinese for encouragement and aid. This trend peaked in the mid-1960s, however, and thereafter Moscow demonstrated that it still had greater leverage over most well-established parties, although many, including some important ones, increasingly tried to avoid clear alignment with either Moscow or Peking and asserted more independent positions.

Competition for influence over Communist states proved to be more important in the long run than the struggle for the allegiance of minor Communist parties. In Eastern Europe, proximity gave the Soviet Union an overwhelming advantage, but in time China was able to develop important new relationships with Rumania and Yugoslavia. Peking's aim, clearly, was not only to increase its own influence in Eastern Europe but also to complicate Moscow's problems there, and it had some limited success. The countries that expanded their ties with Peking hoped thereby to check excessive Soviet pressure and to improve their chances of pursuing independent policies, which to a certain extent they probably did.

Intense competition also developed in the two nations' relations with Third World governments and organizations. By the mid-1960s this competition helped to wreck the Afro-Asian Solidarity Movement and to torpedo plans for a second Bandung conference, to be held in 1965.[72] Eventually both Peking and Moscow gave high priority to competition against each other in virtually every area of the Third World, including South and Southeast Asia, the Middle East, Africa, and Latin America.

Several crises in the early 1960s also contributed greatly to the intensity of the global conflict. The Cuban missile crisis of 1962 was one. Following the crisis, the Chinese accused the Russians both of reckless "adventurism" in precipitating the crisis and of craven cowardice and "capitulationism" in backing down under U.S. pressure.[73] Such accusations at a time when Russia's relations with the United States were at their most dangerous clearly outraged Moscow. The Russians were equally critical of Chinese "adventurism" during the Sino-Indian border war which also occurred in 1962.[74] Moscow gave obvious support to the Indians in this period, through continued delivery of war materiel to New Delhi despite the Chinese-Indian clashes. This Soviet action, at a time when Sino-Soviet border relations were deteriorating in northwest China and Peking also feared renewed pressures on China in the Taiwan Strait region, outraged the Chinese, who denounced the Russians for openly betraying "proletarian internationalism."[75]

Political Battles

During 1962–63 the Sino-Soviet conflict escalated to a new level. In fact, it reached a "point of no return." The major cause was a dispute between Peking and Moscow over a limited ban on the testing of nuclear devices.

In the fall of 1962 the Soviet Union, responding to American proposals, indicated to Washington that it was seriously interested in several possible agreements on control of nuclear arms, and it so informed Peking. Peking quickly dispatched a series of memorandums to Moscow warning that China "would not tolerate" steps aimed at limiting its nuclear options.[76] When the Soviet Union, despite this clear opposition, proceeded to sign a Limited Test Ban Treaty with the United States and Britain in July 1963, China vehemently denounced it as a "fraud" and accused Washington and Moscow of trying to "consolidate their nuclear monopoly."[77]

The Russians obviously faced a difficult choice in 1963: to continue pursuing a coexistence policy toward the United States, which would require at least minimal moves toward strategic arms limitations and would further damage their relations with China, or to give priority to good relations with China, and heed Peking's objections to an arms control agreement, which would result in a setback in their relations with Washington.[78] They chose the former course. Peking regarded the treaty as an act of U.S.-Soviet collusion aimed directly against China, and it reacted accordingly.

The dispute over the test ban treaty widened the chasm between Peking and Moscow. Just before the signing of the treaty, during late 1962 and early 1963, debate between the leaders in the two countries began to escalate. Thereafter, increasingly acrimonious charges were traded, in several exchanges of letters between the Chinese and Soviet Communist parties as well as in a series of major polemical editorials published in both Peking and Moscow, in which the wide differences between the two sides were clearly spelled out.[79] After the signing of the test ban treaty, plans for new interparty discussions collapsed, and the Sino-Soviet polemics became more overt, explicit, and bitter than ever before.

In July 1963 the Central Committee of the Communist Party of the Soviet Union (CPSU) published an "open letter" to the party's organizations and members, summarizing its version of the origins of the conflict and its views on the key issues.[80] In response, the Chinese published a series of nine major editorials, in late 1963 and early 1964, starting with their account of "The Origin and Development of the Differences Between the Leadership of the CPSU and Ourselves" and culminating in "On Khrushchev's Phoney Communism and Its Historical Lessons for the World."[81] The Chinese gave a very different version of the story. Both sides were more explicit than ever before in revealing conflicts of national interest as well as the ideological issues dividing them.

The link between domestic problems—especially in China—and these developments in Sino-Soviet relations was important. Such a link had been apparent since the late 1950s when Mao had decided to reject the Soviet developmental model and the Russian leaders had heaped scorn on his policies. In 1964 the connection became even clearer. Peking's blast against "Khrushchev's phoney communism" revealed Mao's deep apprehension about the main direction of political, economic, and social trends in China, his fear that Chinese society might be subverted by Soviet influences, and his determination to prevent China from following the "negative example" of Moscow's "revisionism."[82] The long struggle in China over power and policy that culminated in the Cultural Revolution was approaching a climax in this period. Mao seemed obsessed with the dangers of revolutionary backsliding, caused by both foreign and domestic "revisionist" influences, and he escalated his attacks on everything the Soviet Union, and specifically Khrushchev, stood for. During this same period, political opposition to Khrushchev was growing in the Soviet Union.

There was a brief lull in the conflict in the fall of 1964, when Khrushchev was ousted from the Soviet leadership and China simultaneously (doubtlessly by happenstance) exploded its first nuclear device.[83] Polemical debate was temporarily muted, and each side explored whether, in the new situation, the other would moderate its stand. But it soon became clear that both remained inflexible and uncompromising, and before long the Chinese resumed their ideological attacks. The Russians soon renewed their counterattacks.

During 1964–65 a new issue exacerbated Sino-Soviet relations.[84] As the United States intervened more deeply in the Vietnam war, both Moscow and Peking became increasingly concerned about the outcome. Moscow's response was to press Peking for "united action"—closer Sino-Soviet cooperation in aiding North Vietnam—and other Communist parties also urged this course on the Chinese. But Peking remained adamant and rejected (apparently after considerable debate) all efforts to induce it to cooperate with Moscow. Instead it deliberately obstructed Russian efforts to assist North Vietnam, while carrying out its own aid programs independently. The fact that China pursued an independent course, even though its leaders feared the possibility of military clashes with the United States in 1964–65, indicated how deep the Sino-Soviet division had become.

Then, during 1966, China was engulfed by the political struggles that erupted during the Cultural Revolution. Although broad foreign policy questions were among the issues that divided China's leaders, the Cultural Revolution was caused above all by differences over domestic problems. But the struggle had an immediate and great impact on foreign policy as the dominant leaders in Peking, on the one hand, adopted a revolutionary posture of extreme militancy and, on the other, turned inward toward extreme isolation, greatly reducing China's actual ties abroad. Because of the spillover effects of the struggles within China, Peking's relationships with most nations, including the Soviet Union, reached a low point during 1967–68.[85] In Peking, Red Guards besieged the Soviet embassy—and many others—and in Moscow militant Chinese students became involved in open brawls. Chinese propaganda against the Soviet Union was now savage, and the Russians reciprocated by condemning virtually everything Mao was attempting to do in China. Moscow also renewed its efforts to isolate China internationally.

Confrontation and Stalemate

The most important development in Sino-Soviet relations in the 1960s was not, however, the two nations' noisy, public confrontation. It was the emergence of a tense, dangerous military confrontation. Both sides had begun strengthening their border defenses in 1960. Then, starting in 1965, the Russians initiated an ominous military buildup around China.[86] The scale of the effort inevitably raised questions about whether Moscow was considering offensive military action against China.

As a result, another basic qualitative change occurred in Sino-Soviet relations in the late 1960s. Previously the clash between the two countries had been essentially ideological and political; now it developed into a direct military confrontation. Each side saw a growing threat to its security, and both prepared for possible military conflict. The climax came in 1968–69 when there was real danger of war.

Several factors probably help to explain the Russian buildup. Soviet leaders were disturbed by China's entry into the "nuclear club," by possible Chinese claims on Soviet territory, and by the seeming unpredictability of Peking's leaders during the Cultural Revolution.[87] In addition, they may well have decided to use military pressure to force Peking to compromise. And once the buildup began, bureaucratic momentum probably helped carry it forward.

Chinese fears understandably mounted as the Soviet buildup proceeded. Clearly Moscow's military superiority gave it the option of initiating major action, and the potential threat to China's security was obvious. Finally, in 1968 the Soviet occupation of Czechoslovakia and Brezhnev's so-called doctrine of limited sovereignty greatly alarmed Peking,[88] since it established a precedent for possible Soviet intervention in China. Peking's leaders began revising their entire foreign policy strategy soon thereafter.

The danger of Sino-Soviet war reached a peak in 1969 when two serious military clashes took place, on March 2 and 15, at Chenpao (Damansky) Island, in the Ussuri River.[89] The Chinese seem to have initiated the first of the major Chenpao incidents. They doubtless acted, in part, to retaliate against the Russians for earlier incidents they had instigated. But Peking may also have had several important political motives. The clash, which occurred on the eve of China's Ninth Party Congress, dramatized the Soviet threat and helped to mobilize domestic support for Peking's policies. And a major Chinese aim may have been to demonstrate clearly to the Russians that China would stand up to Soviet pressure, in the hope that this would deter Moscow from considering large-scale military action. The Russians apparently initiated the second clash, in retaliation for the first, but they did not escalate the scale of the conflict significantly.

These incidents could have precipitated war; however, both sides chose to draw back from the brink, even though Chinese leaders at the height of the crisis refused to accept a telephone call from Premier Kosygin.[90] Nevertheless, tension continued at a high level thereafter, and the shrillness of Peking's and Moscow's mutual denunciations reached a new peak in 1969. Further border clashes occurred; the most serious, in August, was at the Dzungarian Gate in Sinkiang.[91] The Russians did escalate their threats and pressure on Peking in 1969. Most important, they deliberately hinted at the possibility of a nuclear strike.[92] They also convened another international Communist conference, in July, which they probably hoped would make a collective condemnation of the Chinese, but no such action was taken because several important parties opposed it.[93]

Perhaps because the tension was so great, China and the Soviet Union then moved to defuse the situation. In June 1969 their joint commission on border rivers met, in the first important Sino-Soviet talks in several years. Then in September Kosygin, en route home from Ho Chi-minh's funeral, met with Chou at the Peking airport and discussed the resumption of border talks.[94] New talks, between deputy foreign ministers, finally began in Peking in October.

In the ensuing period there were minor improvements in state relations. Diplomatic representation at the ambassadorial level was restored in 1970, and two-way trade rose from $45 million in 1970 to $310 million in 1975.[95] But nothing occurred to fundamentally alter the hostile relationship.

Since 1969 the situation has remained virtually frozen. The border talks have dragged on without significant results, and minor clashes or disputes have occurred from time to time—for example, over navigation rights on boundary rivers. Other sorts of incidents have also highlighted the continuing hostility. In 1974 Peking, for instance, expelled several Soviet diplomats for alleged spying. In the same year, it jailed the crew members of a Soviet helicopter that had made a forced landing on the Chinese side of the Sinkiang border, accusing them of spying.[96]

From 1974 on, both governments periodically made gestures that stimulated speculation that their policies might be changing. In November 1974 Peking aroused worldwide interest when it sent a message to Moscow proposing a nonaggression pact (something the Russians had proposed on several occasions previously), but there was no follow-up.[97] In December 1975 there was even greater international speculation when the Chinese released the Soviet helicopter crew seized in 1974 and admitted that they had been in error in accusing them of being spies.[98] Many observers saw this as a deliberate signal, perhaps initiated by Teng Hsiao-p'ing, whose influence was then rising, to probe the possibility of reducing Sino-Soviet tensions. But again there was no significant follow-up.

On their part, the Russians for many years have alternated conciliatory statements with new pressure in a rather transparent carrot-and-stick approach[99] without significantly altering their basic policies. In April 1976 *Pravda* published an authoritative article that seemed to suggest Moscow would be conciliatory and compromising once Mao died, yet after Mao's death, in October, it issued a new veiled threat against China. The April article, signed by I. Alexandrov (a pseudonymn for high foreign ministry officials), stated that there was "no objective reason" for Sino-Soviet hostility; it deemphasized the scope of the border problem and repeated previous "constructive" Soviet proposals.[100] The October threat, contained in an article by Victor Louis, a well-known journalist, warned that unless the new Chinese leaders "find a common language" with Moscow "within the coming month," it will not be possible to prevent "an irreversible decision" by Soviet leaders—a vague but ominous threat that provoked Henry Kissinger to state publicly that the United States "would consider it a grave matter" if China was to be "threatened by an outside power."[101] On balance, the Soviet Union's pressure and threats tended to cancel out its conciliatory gestures.

Political relations between Peking and Moscow since 1969 can best be described as a continuing hostile stalemate; and the military confrontation between the two countries has yet to be defused. It is probably true that China's fears of imminent military conflict have declined somewhat. In fact by 1973, after it had emplaced a number of nuclear missiles and had opened relations with the United States, Peking began to play down the direct Soviet military threat to China and emphasized the dangers posed for Europe, a change of line that was probably tactical in part but may have reflected some real easing in China's fears. However, the Russians continued their military buildup, and the Chinese continued to construct underground shelters and warn their people of possible war.

Moscow's basic policy appears to have been based on the premise that it should maintain a clear position of strength and, while making conciliatory gestures from time to time, continue to exert unrelenting pressure on China through military deployments. The Chinese, on the defensive in military terms, have maintained an intransigent posture on border problems and other concrete issues, rejecting all of Moscow's conciliatory proposals as fraudulent. Their aim, apparently, has been to hold the Russians at bay while doing everything possible to improve China's political and military position—and therefore its bargaining power. In short, while the confrontation between Peking and Moscow has been limited and controlled, as of the end of 1976 it remained fundamentally unchanged.

With their bilateral relations stalemated, China and Russia have pursued their struggle through competition primarily on the global stage. The most dramatic changes have been in Peking's policies. Even though it has repeatedly denounced power politics, since 1968–69 Peking has energetically pursued a balance-of-power strategy designed to strengthen China's position vis-à-vis the Soviet Union. Even in its policies toward the developing world it has focused its main efforts on countering the influence of the Soviet Union rather than the United States. In fact, the keystone of Peking's global strategy since the late 1960s has been its struggle against the Soviet Union.

Moscow's global policies have also been profoundly influenced in recent years by its determination to compete against and exert pressure on China wherever and whenever possible. Brezhnev's proposal of an Asian collective security pact, advanced in 1969, was clearly directed against China; even though the Russians later said that China would be welcome to join, they knew that Peking strongly opposed the idea.[102] Moscow's treaty with India in 1971 and its backing of India in the India-Pakistan war that year, its efforts to improve its relations with Japan, its expanded naval activity in both East Asian waters and the Indian Ocean, all have been motivated to a significant degree by its desire to compete against Chinese influence.[103] Its major moves toward the United States and Europe—Strategic Arms Limitation Talks, the Nixon visits of 1972 and 1974, and the pursuit of all-Europe agreements on security— obviously have had complex and multiple motives and aims, but the desire to isolate and exert pressure on China has been a constant theme or subtheme in these as in all aspects of Moscow's global strategy.[104]

Ideological and National Differences

Analysis of Sino-Soviet relations over the past twenty-seven years does not provide automatic answers to questions about how the relationship may evolve in the future. But it does provide some basis for identifying the factors that have influenced the relationship in recent years and for weighing the variables that could affect the direction of change in the future.

Ideology has obviously been one of the important factors shaping Sino-Soviet relations in recent years.[105] Paradoxically, while it operated at first as a strong unifying force, for some years it has been an extremely divisive factor. Ideology has been such a salient element that some observers have tended to explain both the alliance and the subsequent split between China and the Soviet Union primarily in ideological terms.

It is no simple matter, however, to separate ideology as an independent factor, determining Chinese and Soviet views on other issues, from its role as a manipulable element used by both sides to support positions determined by other factors. A key question is whether the clashes of Chinese and Soviet views on concrete security and territorial issues have been due to ideological differences, or whether those differences have been rationalizations and justifications of conflicts having little to do with ideology. The evidence suggests that ideology has been both an independent and a dependent variable, but it is difficult to define and weigh its role as an actual determinant of policy at different periods.

It has often been noted that Marxist-Leninist doctrine can operate as a quasi-religious secular faith, creating bonds that transcend and outweigh more concrete factors and interests. This was true to a certain extent in Sino-Soviet relations during the early years after 1949. But like the adherents of many religions, Communists have had great difficulty in coping with heterodoxy. As communism spread, its numerous adaptations created many versions of "national communism," mixing Marxist-Leninist "universal" principles with local nationalist aspirations. In the 1960s the trend toward ideological polycentrism was so rapid and extensive that some observers called the process "the disintegration of a secular faith."[106]

It has not been easy for Communists anywhere to accept this trend. And it has been particularly difficult for the ruling elites in Peking and Moscow, who have tended to stress the universal validity of their own particular doctrines, to think globally, and to act as the ultimate arbiters of orthodoxy and heterodoxy for all of "world communism."

For at least a decade and a half, ideology has clearly been a divisive factor in the Sino-Soviet relationship and a cause of intense mutual hostility, in part because leaders in each country have reacted emotionally to the presumed heresy of the other. Like true believers generally, leaders in Moscow and Peking tend to be more hostile toward apostates than toward heathens or agnostics. Each group's conviction that the other has betrayed the faith has helped to intensify the ideological competition. Millions of words have poured forth from Peking and Moscow in the ideological debates, and numerous volumes have been written analyzing the debates. However, the issues in dispute have changed in character and importance over time. Some have focused on fairly abstract, basic doctrinal issues. Most, however, have concerned the application of doctrinal principles to analysis of current social realities and practical questions of strategy and policy.[107]

Many Chinese and Russian divergences have been based on differing assessments of the overall world situation—in Marxist terminology, the "nature of the epoch"—and its implications for international strategy. Moscow and Peking have differed in their views on the world balance of forces, their identification of primary enemies, their assumptions about the inevitability of war, and their views on "peaceful coexistence." They have quarreled about what kind of relations to establish with national liberation movements and bourgeois nationalist regimes, and whom to include in any Communist-led united front. They have differed too on the desirability of pursuing a "peace strategy" or a militant revolutionary strategy, worldwide, and on the feasibility and desirability of seeking arms control agreements with capitalist states.

Other differences have concerned strategies for revolutionary parties struggling to achieve power. These have been based on divergent assessments of revolutionary opportunities in particular societies, different views on the worldwide relevance of alternative models of revolution, and arguments about definition of potential friends and enemies and desirable domestic united-front strategies. They have also involved differing concepts of the proper role of various classes and groups in revolutionary struggles, the revolutionary stages and goals applicable to particular revolutionary movements, and the question of whether revolutionaries must use "armed struggle" and violence or should try to pursue nonviolent methods of "peaceful transition."

Other disputes have focused on differing "roads to socialism" pursued by Communist regimes already in power. Moscow and Peking have had divergent views on the desirable forms of political organization and state power in particular countries, on the basic nature of class struggle and the dictatorship of the proletariat, on class relationships in the period after a Communist takeover, and on the proper stages for socialization and socialist construction. They have differed fundamentally on the validity of various models, and acceptable priorities, for economic development and social change.

Underlying all these issues have been basic differences concerning the locus of authority and desirable forms of organization within the Communist bloc and world movement. These have involved questions about how to determine who belongs to the Communist "camp," how much autonomy should be tolerated within the world movement, what the "universals" of Marxism-Leninism are, and what the limits of local adaptation in particular situations should be. The Chinese and Russians have differed on whether decisions in the Communist bloc and world movement should be centralized, whether they should be by unanimity or majority vote, and whether minority views and factions should be tolerated. All of these have reflected divergent views on what the basic pattern of interparty and interstate relations among socialist nations should be, and most important, where ideological authority for the entire Communist world should ultimately rest.

Although Chinese and Russian debates on such issues have involved widely differing interpretations of basic doctrine, they cannot be explained simply in terms of divergent scholastic analyses or exegetical interpretations by the leading ideologists on both sides. Ideological views have been shaped by extremely complicated factors reflecting the differing national situations, interests, and outlooks of the two countries. Each side has harnessed ideology to support its own nationalism and cultural predispositions.

The question of where authority—the ultimate power of decision on ideological and political questions—resides has been fundamental. From the early years of the world Communist movement, and especially since the Comintern was established as the headquarters of world communism in 1919, Soviet leaders have generally insisted that there must be one center of ultimate authority—one Communist Rome—namely Moscow. Chinese Communist leaders for many years accepted this only with reservations, and from the 1930s on they were increasingly inclined to make their own interpretations as well as political decisions. And when the Chinese party assumed the reins of power in a country almost as large as, and more populous than, the Soviet Union, Peking became a potential competing source of authority. Even though by the mid-1950s Moscow hinted that it was willing to take some steps toward accepting

Peking as an equal, in reality it was never willing to accept another center of ideological authority.

It was probably inevitable that the Chinese Communists would reject the idea that any outside authority was superior to Peking's. Peking began to make competing claims in the 1940s and 1950s. Then in the 1960s the Chinese openly questioned Moscow's authority and began asserting Peking's own. Subsequently, the Chinese demanded, in effect, a coequal position of ideological authority on a worldwide basis. Finally they tried to establish the primacy of Maoist thought, and Peking's ideological authority, over that of Moscow.[108]

In practice, for more than a decade, both Moscow and Peking have had to confront the reality that at least two major (and several minor) centers of Communist authority exist in the world. Neither has any realistic basis for successfully establishing its authority over the other, yet each has attempted to assert its own primacy and to increase its influence over other Communist parties, states, and revolutionary movements. Though Peking maintains that the "Communist camp" no longer exists, it continues to try to proselytize other Communist groups, albeit with limited success.

Ideology clearly must be viewed, therefore, as a real cause of Sino-Soviet conflict, not simply a symptom or a tool to rationalize positions on nonideological issues. From the late 1950s on, many Chinese leaders, and above all Mao, strongly felt that Moscow was betraying basic Marxist-Leninist values, threatening to subvert Chinese society, and undermining the entire world Communist revolution. To many intensely egalitarian Chinese leaders, the Soviet Union has appeared to be an increasingly elitist, bureaucratic, bourgeois society, led by men dedicated to promoting Russian interests, not world revolution.

Ideology has probably been less important in shaping Soviet policies, yet it has nevertheless been a significant factor influencing the attitudes of many Russian leaders, especially those responsible for international Communist affairs. Probably most Soviet leaders in recent years have viewed China as a deviant society pursuing domestic policies that are populist, utopian, un-Marxist, and destined to fail, and implementing policies abroad that are either motivated solely by Chinese nationalism or that express an unrealistic revolutionary messianism divorced from social reality.[109] They have regarded Mao's "deviations" and his frontal challenge to Moscow's authority as both dangerous and subversive. From their perspective the Chinese ideological challenge has posed immediate dangers to the unity of the world Communist movement and long-run threats to Moscow's world role and even to the legitimacy of Russia's leadership.

In basic respects, however, ideology must be regarded as a dependent variable in shaping Sino-Soviet relations. Many of the doctrinal disputes have been reflections of fundamental differences rooted in differing cultures and societies, revolutionary experiences, and stages of economic development, all producing real conflicts of interest. Chinese views have been those of first-generation leaders who achieved power on their own following independently evolved strategies and who have ruled a huge, poor, underdeveloped nation. The Chinese historical legacy and the problems faced by China's new rulers both at home and abroad have differed in basic respects from those confronting the Soviet Union. The present "postrevolutionary" leaders of the Soviet Union rule a nation that is far more developed than China and a society that has been gradually adopting bourgeois values. These leaders appear to be motivated less by revolutionary goals than by the desire to strengthen the USSR and establish it firmly as one of the world's two superpowers.

In sum, many of the divergences in Chinese and Russian perspectives are attributable to differences in the societies. The leaders in each country have deliberately manipulated ideology to defend their particular outlooks, interests, and policies, and to attack those of the other. More than a decade of debate has infused their differences with considerable passion, and ideological conflicts have come to reflect emotions as much as rational beliefs and calculations. And over time, ideological differences have increasingly reflected deep conflicts of national interests.

Many of the issues considered crucial by both sides in the Sino-Soviet ideological debate have changed over time. Some that appeared vitally important only a few years ago have become relatively unimportant, while others have come to the fore. Both sides have altered their positions on a number of issues, and at times have actually reversed them. Moreover, neither Moscow nor Peking has been consistent, by any means, in following the logic of its own ideological beliefs in formulating concrete policies. While it is true that ideological conflicts have highlighted the chasm between the values and outlooks of the dominant leaders in Peking and Moscow, neither the issues nor the intensity of the debates have been immutable.

In some respects the ideological conflict has acquired a life of its own, with positions changing as a result of the action-reaction cycle of the debates themselves. In other respects the changing issues have reflected changing national interests, constantly redefined as each side has reassessed its goals and the ways ideology could be used to serve them.

There are strong reasons to believe that ideology will continue to be a divisive factor in Sino-Soviet relations for a long time to come.[110] The hypothesis that somehow, sometime, ideology will suddenly again be a unifying force, as it appeared to be in the 1950s, is not plausible. Each side will doubtless continue to insist on making its own interpretations of doctrine, and neither can be expected to defer to the ideological authority of the other. Both will probably continue to proselytize their views and to promote their revolutionary models globally. Their competition will probably continue to reinforce trends toward polycentrism and pluralism within the Communist world and prevent the reestablishment of ideological unity. The more intense their ideological conflict is, the more this could limit the worldwide ideological influence of both. Continuing ideological differences mean that there is little prospect of reestablishing close party relationships between Moscow and Peking.

It would be a mistake, however, to assume that ideological positions are unalterable, or that ideology poses an insuperable barrier to improved intergovernmental ties.[111] If leaders in Peking and Moscow decide that urgent national interests—the avoidance of war, for example—demand some improvement of state relations, they are quite capable of moderating their ideological debate, whether or not their differences are resolved. They could do this for limited periods, for purely tactical reasons. Or at some point they could tacitly or explicitly agree on a longer ideological truce.

In time, moreover, the intensity of the ideological conflict may decline. If radical ideologues had been able to achieve a dominant influence in China's leadership, this would have become less likely. However, the trend in China's post-Mao leadership points toward an increase in the power of relatively pragmatic men, who are likely in time to give considerably less priority to ideological issues than Mao did. In Moscow, the ascendancy of technocratic and realpolitik values over traditional Marxist-Leninist values has been evident for some years. It is quite possible that future leaders in both Peking and Moscow could decide to deemphasize ideological conflicts. At some point they might make a conscious effort to compromise ideological differences and stress areas of agreement. If so, the result might eventually be a kind of ecumenism in ideological relations among the major Communist parties, and some convergence of political views. What seems more likely, however, is that both might simply adopt a more tolerant live-and-let-live attitude, a form of ideological coexistence. On balance, however, far-reaching changes in the basic ideological relationship between Peking and Moscow do not seem likely to occur suddenly or soon. Basic changes will at best require time—and further changes in the nature of the leadership and social conditions in both countries.

In the period ahead, therefore, ideological differences will continue to impose severe limits on how far any improvements of Sino-Soviet relations might go. There is virtually no foreseeable possibility of restoring intimate party relations. And competition for influence over other parties, movements, and countries will doubtless continue, even if its intensity declines. Its termination would be possible only if Peking and Moscow were to agree, in effect, to accept different spheres of ideological influence, which seems improbable.

But limited détente in governmental relations between Peking and Moscow is a real possibility. In recent years, leaders in both Peking and Moscow, even while stressing the irreconcilability of their ideological positions, have at times called for steps to improve state relations. Their lack of success has been due more to their uncompromising positions on nonideological issues than to their ideological conflict. It is quite conceivable that military, political, or economic imperatives could impel Peking and Moscow to consider limited compromise, whether or not their ideological conflicts can be resolved, or even substantially moderated.

The Cultural Gulf

One result of the conflict between Peking and Moscow has been to arouse among both Chinese and Russians deep-rooted historical apprehensions, increasing the awareness on both sides of the wide cultural gap separating the two countries. Immediately after 1949, leaders in the two countries appeared genuinely to believe that an intimate relationship between their societies was both desirable and possible. Their assumption was that the common political values of Marxism-Leninism would bridge the historical cultural gulf between the two societies. Peking's 1952 slogan, "The Soviet Union of today is the China of tomorrow," symbolized the Chinese leaders' commitment to this goal.[112] The relationship was always one-sided, however; there were never any Russian slogans calling for Soviet borrowing of Chinese values.

This sense of shared values lasted only briefly and was probably relatively superficial. When conflicts of national interest emerged, it became clear that the cultural gap had not been significantly narrowed, and as political relations deteriorated, intense animosity and distrust, rooted in history, came rapidly to the surface.

Today it is clear, not simply from public polemics but also from the emotions revealed in private conversation, that both Chinese and Russians are acutely aware of their profound cultural differences and have a deep sense of distrust based on revived historical memories.[113] Members of the Chinese elite again stress the uniqueness of their nation and the need to preserve its distinctive values. Since their first contacts with the West in the nineteenth century, a central problem for the Chinese has been how to preserve essential Chinese values in the face of what many have considered to be dangerous subversive influences from abroad, while at the same time borrowing the scientific and technical knowledge necessary for China's self-strengthening and modernization. In light of this, China's dependence on the Russians in the 1950s was in many respects an aberration. Now the Chinese tendency is again to view the Soviet Union as a white, Western, imperialist power which is the carrier of values that are both alien to China and potentially subversive. The memories that appear to have the greatest influence on Chinese attitudes now are not those of the brief period of close interaction between the two societies, but the centuries-long history of friction, conflict, and animosity.

Before 1949, despite geographical propinquity, China clearly had less cultural contact with Russia (except in Manchuria and Sinkiang) than with the maritime colonial powers. In most of China there were few Russian educators, doctors, missionaries, or businessmen, and the Russians appeared to be even more culturally remote to most members of China's modernized elite than other foreigners. The prevailing Chinese stereotype of the Russians was often particularly derogatory.

There is little reason to believe that the extensive contacts between the two countries in the 1950s basically or permanently changed earlier attitudes. Recently, traditional attitudes appear to have revived, perhaps even in more extreme forms than before. The virulence of Chinese expressions of suspicion, hostility, and fear of the Russians today is striking even in the light of past Chinese tendencies toward xenophobia.

Perhaps more favorable attitudes toward the Russians persist among some Chinese who were trained in the Soviet Union or worked with

Russian colleagues in China in the 1950s. If there should be any tendency toward Sino-Soviet détente, those who are unable now to express favorable views of the Soviet Union may feel freer to do so. But it is highly doubtful that even such persons would call for the kind of close identification with the Soviet Union that Peking favored in the 1950s.

Traditional suspicions and apprehensions have also been revived in the Soviet Union, where they are even more striking in some respects. Despite the Soviet Union's overwhelming military superiority over China, Russians' fears of their neighbor appear, to judge from private as well as public expressions of opinion, to be real, and, like current Chinese attitudes, they are deeply rooted in an acute awareness of the cultural chasm between the two countries.

A great many Russians now tend to view China as extremely alien: a yellow, Asiatic, chauvinistic country that is not only the carrier of subversive values but is directly threatening to the Soviet Union, even militarily. Many, including some who have had substantial contact with China, say that they simply cannot understand the Chinese. Not a few allege, and may actually believe, that China's recent actions reveal disturbing irrationality. There is clearly an element of racism in the attitudes of some Russians, however much they deny it and blame the Chinese for attempting to exploit antiwhite feelings. (Feelings of racial superiority have been equally characteristic of the Chinese.)

Vague and crude geopolitical concepts also shape the attitudes of many Russians. Viewing the huge spaces of Siberia and the Soviet Far East, underpopulated and relatively undeveloped, and the huge population of China, disciplined and in the prevailing Russian view chauvinistic, they believe the situation is inherently dangerous.

One of the most striking facts about the Russians' attitudes today is the degree to which memories of the Golden Horde's invasion, centuries ago, have been revived. A sizable number of Russians seem to compare the potential Chinese Communist threat with the Mongol onslaught. They tend to exaggerate the "China threat" tremendously, much as Americans did in the 1950s, and appear genuinely to worry about a new Yellow Peril. Not only are these attitudes revealed in official propaganda and in remarks made by members of the Soviet establishment; they also are reflected in the comments of ordinary Russians. And they have appeared repeatedly in the writings of Russian intellectuals, including leading antiestablishment figures. Men as diverse as Sakharov, Yevtushenko, Almarik, and Solzhenitsyn have revealed deep apprehensions about the

Chinese and the dangers of Sino-Soviet war in the future.[114] (Even though such attitudes are not now prevalent among Americans and Europeans, there were many, not so long ago, who evoked images of a Yellow Peril.)

It is difficult to assess how much such culturally rooted attitudes may influence policy. Clearly they do influence it in subtle ways since leaders are often captives of their cultural stereotypes, but they do not determine it. The intensity and salience of such attitudes can vary tremendously. In periods of acute tension in foreign relations, their intensity is heightened, but in periods of relaxation and "normal" relations it tends to decline. Leaders can either deliberately arouse primordial feelings and try to exploit them, or they can consciously dampen and de-emphasize them.

The predominant cultural attitudes in both China and the Soviet Union at present clearly exacerbate Sino-Soviet tensions, but there is no reason to conclude that they will be the major determinants of how the two countries' relations develop in the future. Cultural attitudes—like the existing ideological conflicts—will tend to limit how far any moves toward improved relations might go in the years immediately ahead, but they will not prevent steps toward limited détente if the leaders in both capitals decide that there are compelling practical reasons to reduce tension and repair state-to-state links. If relations were to deteriorate further, however, cultural animosities would tend to heighten tension and increase the danger inherent in the hostile confrontation between the two countries.

The Political Context

Sino-Soviet relations have not been determined solely by impersonal factors and objective interests; they have also been influenced by the personalities, idiosyncratic styles, and individual beliefs of particular leaders. Clearly, there have been important differences and debates among the leaders of each country on policy toward the other. Domestic political trends within one have often had a direct impact on the other's internal politics, as well as on relations between the two countries. During the period of closest relations there were probably few major decisions made in either country that did not have important reverberations within the other. In addition, each—and especially the Soviet Union—has attempted to exert a direct influence on the domestic affairs of the other.

Mao's influence on the development of Sino-Soviet relations was extraordinarily important—as it was on most policy issues China faced.

He personally contributed greatly to the growth of hostility between the two countries. By the early 1960s he appeared in many respects to be obsessed, for a combination of ideological, political, and personal reasons, with the dangers posed to China and the world by the Russians. The nine anti-Soviet editorials reflecting Mao's views, published during 1963–64, attacked virtually every aspect of Soviet society.[115] The Moscow regime and its policies were held up as the prime "negative example" for China; they became the model for what China should *not* be and should *not* do.

There is considerable evidence—for example in Khrushchev's memoirs—that Mao's personal relationships with key Soviet leaders were generally unsatisfactory, to him and to them.[116] It is difficult to know whether he or they were more to blame. Prejudices and insensitivities on both sides clearly affected relations adversely. There is no evidence that intimate or understanding personal relationships were ever established. Khrushchev described his dealings with Mao, in retrospect, almost entirely in terms of a series of irritations and misunderstandings.

Mao had reason to be annoyed and angered by many Soviet policy decisions which had adverse effects on Chinese interests. But the passion that infused his attitude toward Moscow by the 1960s appeared to be a good deal more intense than that of some of his colleagues. Soviet leaders eventually concluded that Mao was implacably and unalterably hostile to the Soviet Union. By the late 1960s they seemed inclined to place the blame for the sad state of Sino-Soviet relations primarily, and at times almost wholly, on Mao personally.[117] At some point they concluded, probably correctly, that as long as Mao lived, essentially hostile relations would continue; they hoped, however, that once Mao was gone, improvement in relations would become possible.

Several factors probably help to explain Mao's intense hostility toward the Soviet leaders. Unlike some Chinese Communist leaders, he had had little personal contact with the Russians, or any foreigners, before his first trip to Moscow in 1949–50. Basically a "nativist," with deep roots in China but little in his background to mold a cosmopolitan outlook, Mao was always a "revolutionary nationalist" who looked at problems from a distinctive Chinese perspective.[118] From the start he was strongly inclined to "Sinify" communism, to domesticate it to the China scene. This probably predisposed him to be suspicious, and in many respects resentful, of Russian attitudes and behavior toward China. His intense personal ideological commitments, embodied in his particular brand of

Maoist revolutionary values, seemed to impel him to regard many points at issue with the Russians as ones involving uncompromisable principles, which explains in part why he made such strongly negative judgments about post-Stalin trends in Soviet society. Mao was probably personally offended, moreover, by actions such as Khrushchev's de-Stalinization speech that reflected on his own position as party leader in China. Though these factors might not have impelled Mao to adopt a bitterly anti-Soviet stance if there had been no open clash in Chinese and Soviet national interests, they probably would have made him view Moscow with considerable suspicion under any circumstances.

Obviously, Mao was not alone in his resentment of Moscow's policies. But clearly not all Chinese leaders fully concurred with him.[119] It is significant that some of the most prominent of Mao's purged opponents, including P'eng Teh-huai, Liu Shao-ch'i, and Lin Piao, were accused explicitly or implicitly of subversive links to the Soviet Union; P'eng, Liu, and perhaps others such as Kao Kang and Lo Jui-ch'ing, may have argued in favor of efforts to reduce Sino-Soviet tension and to avoid uncompromising positions.[120] Right up until Mao's death, new evidence periodically appeared of high-level differences on policy toward the Soviet Union.[121]

It is not plausible to believe that any of Mao's purged opponents favored actions that were genuinely subversive of Chinese interests. Some may not even have favored policies toward Moscow drastically different from his. But the men Mao accused of pro-Soviet subversion were probably critical of his inflexibility and insistence on policies that would heighten rather than reduce tension.

Military men have been prominent among those who seem to have failed to give Mao full support in his anti-Soviet policies. Some of the top leaders of the People's Liberation Army appear to have argued in the 1950s that it was necessary to maintain military cooperation. In the 1960s and 1970s, most doubtless shared Mao's growing concern about a Soviet threat, but some apparently argued that compromise was desirable to avoid the risks and costs of hostile confrontation. It is likely that some of China's leading civilian bureaucrats also had doubts—on practical economic and political grounds—about the wisdom of Mao's confrontation approach. In recent years the most vocal support for Mao's anti-Soviet stance came from China's radical ideologues.[122]

As long as he lived, Mao, as an individual, unquestionably had an enormous impact on Sino-Soviet relations and probably did, as the Russians asserted, make compromise and détente virtually impossible. Since his death, the possibility of change has clearly increased. This does not mean that a more flexible Chinese policy, a moderate Soviet response, and compromise are inevitable. It does mean, however, that one fundamental obstacle to Sino-Soviet détente has been removed and that there is a real possibility that China's new leaders may reassess policy toward Moscow.

The Soviet side of the equation has been somewhat different. While most top Soviet leaders, including Joseph V. Stalin and Nikita S. Khrushchev, appear to have had remarkably little understanding of the Chinese and an ingrained suspicion of them, probably none was so passionately committed to hostile confrontation as Mao.

The personalities and styles of individual Soviet leaders did influence Sino-Soviet relations, however. Stalin's toughness, arrogance, and aloofness set the tone for the Moscow-Peking relationship until he died. And Khrushchev's insensitivity, erratic style, unpredictability, and bluntness probably alienated Mao and many other leaders in Peking, as they eventually did his own colleagues in Moscow. However, the individual characteristics and styles of Soviet leaders have been less important since Khrushchev's political demise. Since then, the top Soviet leaders, including L. I. Brezhnev, A. N. Kosygin, and N. V. Podgorny, seem to have shared a strong antipathy toward all that Mao stood for, but have never appeared to be so implacably committed to hostile confrontation as Mao. They may have genuinely desired to improve relations with the Chinese, even though they saw little chance of doing so while Mao lived. They have not, however, seemed willing to acknowledge that the Chinese have legitimate grievances and reasons for fear of Moscow, and so far they have not been prepared to make the kind of compromises that will almost certainly be necessary to open the door to real détente with China.

There is evidence of some differences among Soviet leaders in their views on how to deal with China.[123] Leaders such as M. A. Suslov and B. N. Ponomarev, who are primarily concerned with ideological matters and the international Communist movement, appear to have given high priority to the "China problem," to have been particularly opposed to compromise with the Chinese, and to have argued for a comparatively hard line in Soviet policy toward Peking. Some military leaders also seem to have supported a comparatively hard line, emphasizing military rather than ideological and political considerations. In contrast, others in the Soviet elite, probably including government leaders such as Kosygin and some foreign affairs specialists, appear to have been more concerned about the need to repair state relations than about ideological conflict.

Differences on how to deal with China have doubtless influenced debates in Moscow on certain Soviet policies elsewhere. For example, there is reason to believe that leading ideologists such as Suslov had doubts about Soviet policy toward Czechoslovakia in 1968 because they felt attention should be focused on the task of convening a new world Communist conference and mobilizing support against Peking.

Although there have certainly been differences on what tactics to pursue toward China, especially on how tough or conciliatory to be, and on what mixture of carrot and stick to employ, there does not appear to have been any top Soviet leader comparable to Mao who has been unalterably opposed to Sino-Soviet détente. Consequently, there is no reason to believe that a change of leadership in the Soviet Union will be a prerequisite for Moscow-Peking détente, although some shifts in Soviet policy clearly will be necessary, and changes in the Russian leadership might make it easier for both Moscow and Peking to consider détente.

In a deeper sense, the Sino-Soviet relationship has been greatly affected, and complicated, by political interactions between the two societies. In earlier years, most major policy decisions in either country, even those based principally on domestic considerations, tended to have repercussions in the other.[124] Khrushchev's de-Stalinization moves in 1956, for example, raised serious questions affecting the stability of the leadership in China. Peking's response, in its statement "On the Historical Experience of the Dictatorship of the Proletariat," had important repercussions within the Soviet Union and significantly affected its relations with Eastern Europe. Mao's "contradictions" speech and Hundred Flowers campaign in 1957 were viewed with great unease by Moscow's leaders because of their possible effects elsewhere. And Mao's Great Leap and commune programs in 1958 compelled Soviet leaders to make a direct political response, particularly at the Soviet Union's Twenty-first Party Congress, designed to demonstrate that Moscow still maintained its ideological and political leadership.

In both China and Russia a complicated interplay of competing forces has affected decisions on such critical issues as the emphasis to be given to ideological concerns or to pragmatic problem-solving, the need to tighten discipline or to relax political controls, and the impulse to centralize or to decentralize authority. The interactions between the two societies on these issues have been subtle and intricate, but there is no doubt that the dynamics of political and economic change within each country has significantly affected developments within the other, and major internal shifts in either power or policy within one have often had a significant impact on the other. As a result, each has been sensitively attuned to the course of internal developments in the other.

This kind of interaction has obviously declined in recent years, however, as a result of the severance of past links between China and Russia. Each now attempts, in fact, to immunize its own society against contamination and subversion from the other. But each nevertheless continues to be very sensitive to the potential impact on its own society of trends within the other.

Sino-Soviet relations have also been significantly affected by deliberate attempts on the part of the leadership in each country to influence the political situation within the other. Soviet leaders in particular have on many occasions tried to support certain Chinese leaders against others. Before 1949, their interference was blatant. In the early 1950s Moscow was probably still trying to move China in a pro-Soviet direction, and looked to men such as Li Li-san and Kao Kang for help. And there may be at least an element of truth in some of the charges Mao made against his later enemies that implicate the Soviet Union. Over time, however, Moscow's ability to intervene in China's internal politics has obviously declined. Nevertheless, as late as the 1960s the Russians were giving open political support to the exiled Wang Ming, general secretary of the Chinese party during 1931–32, who was still violently attacking Mao and urging opposition forces in China to overthrow him.[125]

The Chinese have never had comparable opportunities to exert political influence within the Soviet Union. In the 1950s, however, Mao probably tried to indicate his preferences between possible successors to Stalin, and may in fact have had a marginal influence on the leadership struggles in Moscow. Some observers believe, for example, that Mao's favorable predisposition toward Khrushchev at one point may have helped him—though necessarily not decisively—to achieve his political victory over Malenkov.[126] And Mao's later hostility toward Khrushchev was probably damaging to him.

Since the late 1960s neither Moscow nor Peking has been able to intervene effectively in the domestic politics of the other. Both have been determined to prevent any external interference or subversion. Nevertheless, each has attempted in its propaganda efforts—mainly by radio—to exploit disaffection and incite domestic opposition against the other country's leaders, in effect calling on the people to overthrow their leaders.[127] The main effect of the propaganda appears to have been to further poison the atmosphere of the relationship.

In the future, either country—and in particular the Soviet Union—could decide to increase its efforts to meddle politically in the other. The principal danger is that the Soviet Union might be tempted to intervene more actively in Chinese affairs. For example, if there were a severe power struggle in China, Soviet leaders might choose to support certain Chinese leaders against others; if so, the possibility of conflict could rise dangerously. One prerequisite for any long-term improvement in Sino-Soviet relations will be a willingness by each side to demonstrate convincingly that it is not actively attempting to subvert the other, even with incendiary propaganda, and that it is genuinely prepared to adopt a live-and-let-live approach.

The Role of Economics

One striking feature of the interaction between China and the Soviet Union since 1949 is the fact that economics has clearly been the handmaiden of politics in relations between these two nations. Economic factors have been important, first in a positive way and then in a negative sense, but politics has dominated economics in the policies pursued by each side toward the other.[128]

The original decision by China to turn its economy away from the West, and toward the Soviet Union, was made for political and military as well as economic reasons, as was the Soviet decision to give China economic aid. Both sides believed that economic cooperation was required to cement the political link between the two countries.

Peking and Moscow had differing perspectives on their economic ties, however. The Chinese, though grateful for Soviet assistance in the early years when it was so important to China's development, eventually came to resent intensely the Russians' tough bargaining and their propensity to interfere and impose their own ideas on China. The Russians, on their part, resented Peking's lack of gratitude and regarded the Chinese as unreasonable in ignoring Soviet advice. Nevertheless, the economic relationship was extremely important to both through the late 1950s. Soviet assistance was crucial to China's development program, as initially conceived, and Moscow considered its economic ties essential to a strong political relationship with China.

The first signs of economic dissension, which appeared in 1957–58 at the end of China's First Plan period, were in part a reflection of diverging political interests and priorities; they were also the consequence of decisions by the Chinese leaders to halt the trend toward increasing Russian involvement in China and increasing Chinese dependence on the Soviet Union. Mao's decision in effect to abandon the Soviet model made it certain that Peking would reduce its economic ties with Moscow whatever the state of its political relations. Even if no open political break had occurred, therefore, the two countries would have made major adjustments in their economic relations, but perhaps less far-reaching and more gradual than they were.

What radically and suddenly changed the picture was the rapid deterioration of political relations between the two countries, followed by Moscow's decision in 1960 to exert strong economic pressure on China by withdrawing all Soviet technicians, and Peking's subsequent decision to reorient China's external economic relations away from the Communist bloc and toward the noncommunist world, in a fashion almost as dramatic as the earlier reorientation away from the West toward Moscow.

The Soviet Union's drastic economic moves against China in 1960 not only had extremely harmful economic effects, which lasted several years; they had political consequences that have persisted to the present. Whoever China's leaders are, and whatever changes occur in Sino-Soviet relations, for the foreseeable future the Chinese will almost certainly avoid any significant economic dependency on the Soviet Union, or any other country.

It would be a mistake, however, to assume that Sino-Soviet economic relations cannot improve, and possibly have some effect on political relations. A gradual expansion of trade could, for example, be a prelude to improved political relations. And if real political détente occurs, trade will probably increase to a significant level, even if not to that of earlier years.

On purely economic grounds, a good case can be made that both countries would benefit from expanded trade and other forms of economic cooperation. In a less tense political atmosphere the advantages might seem compelling to economic planners and bureaucrats in Peking as well as Moscow. China could usefully draw on Soviet technology and import more capital goods as well as raw materials from Russia. It would be less expensive for the Chinese to buy replacement parts from the Soviet Union for machinery and equipment purchased there in the 1950s than to manufacture them themselves. There is reason to believe China's leaders have recently considered increasing their purchases of such replacement parts. The Soviet Union could benefit from increased imports of Chinese agricultural commodities, certain raw materials, and light manufactures, for use especially in Siberia and the Soviet Far East. Proximity and low transportation costs would be an advantage to both countries. The fact that both have planned economies, manage foreign commerce through state trading agencies, and see advantages in two-way barter arrangements would be regarded as a plus by some planners in both Peking and Moscow.

For all of these reasons Soviet experts in Sino-Soviet economic relations have long argued that there is a natural complementarity between the two economies that will operate in favor of expanded economic relations once the major political obstacles are removed.[129] Yet in purely economic terms, the situation has changed greatly since the heyday of the Sino-Soviet alliance. China in the 1970s, in contrast to the 1950s, has many options in choosing its trading partners. For numerous reasons, including concern about quality, Peking will probably wish to obtain most technologically sophisticated items in the years ahead from Japan and the West, as the Russians themselves are now forced to do. The Chinese cannot satisfy their need for grain imports from the Soviet Union; large supplies can only be obtained from the world's major food-surplus nations in North America and Australia. Moreover, today, probably many Chinese see advantages in competing in world markets rather than having to bargain bilaterally with the Russians. If China decides that it is necessary to finance imports with credit, it seems likely to seek commercial credit from varied noncommunist sources to avoid the political implications and dangers of receiving state credit from Moscow.

Soviet economic policies will of course influence the calculations of Chinese planners in the future. If Moscow were prepared to sell at low prices, offer credit on attractive terms, and accept the necessity of establishing a new economic relationship on a very different basis from that of the 1950s, the economic attractions to Peking might, in time, be substantial. Possibly Soviet leaders might at some point try to make attractive offers; they have not been noted, however, for flexibility or generosity in their foreign economic policies. Nevertheless, they obviously have a strong desire to expand trade and other economic relations with China, and they might very well make a major effort to offer liberal trade terms if they thought this could have a favorable impact on Chinese political attitudes. Peking would probably be wary of such a move; Chinese leaders, whoever they are, will continue to be suspicious and fear that flexible Soviet economic policies might simply represent an effort to buy a change in China's policy. But they could be cautiously responsive.

In sum, although the political legacy of the past decade and a half will continue to impose severe limits on the degree to which Sino-Soviet economic relations can be expanded in the years ahead, eventually the potential benefits to both countries of increased trade should work in favor of improved economic ties. But this will depend on overall relations, and the economic factor will certainly not be a governing influence. Economics will not compel the two countries to improve relations. However, if a serious effort is undertaken to improve political relations, some increase in trade will doubtless occur and tend to reinforce the process.

In a minor way the responsiveness of trade to political developments has been demonstrated even in recent years. When the tensions that reached a peak in 1969 began to cool, Peking and Moscow signed a new trade agreement, and Sino-Soviet trade immediately increased from its nadir of $45 million in 1970 to $272 million in 1973.[130] During 1974 and 1975 it rose only slightly to $285 million and $310 million; this new plateau represented only about one-sixth of Sino-Soviet trade at its peak, reflecting the fact that no real détente between Peking and Moscow was yet in sight.

If détente does occur, however, there will doubtless be a more significant increase in Sino-Soviet trade, although Peking will probably restrict it to a relatively small percentage of its total foreign trade. Economic relations between China and the Soviet Union will doubtless continue, in short, to be subordinated to politics. Instead of being a key factor determining the state of overall relations, trade will reflect overall trends determined by other factors.

Territorial and Security Issues

Ideological, cultural, political, and economic factors will continue to influence the evolution of Sino-Soviet relations. But clearly another variable is far more critical, namely, conflicts focusing on major national interests, especially border and territorial issues and basic military-security relationships. The direction in which Sino-Soviet relations move in the period ahead will depend above all on this range of problems.

After the ideological schism began in the late 1950s, serious divergences of national interest increasingly strained relations between Peking and Moscow. Major problems were created by the Taiwan Strait crisis of 1958, differences over military and particularly nuclear cooperation, and the Sino-Indian crisis of 1959. As the range of contentious issues rapidly broadened, Peking and Moscow came to see their interests as conflicting in virtually every major geographical area of the world and on a majority of the most salient international issues.

By far the most volatile and dangerous conflicts of interest concern bilateral military-security relations and disputes over the regions where China and Russia are in direct physical contact. The transformation of the military relationship from a close alliance to a hostile confrontation was the most profound change that occurred in the long course of the Sino-Soviet conflict, and today each views the other as posing a direct threat to its security. Observers who believe that the Sino-Soviet border conflict was predestined point, rightly, to the long history of clashes in the borderlands as well as to the built-in possibilities for conflict when two huge nations face each other across a forty-five-hundred-mile border. But any thesis of inevitability is highly questionable. Actually, in the 1950s, when China and Russia were on friendly terms, the borderlands were calm. Tension arose only when their political relationship deteriorated. In a fundamental sense, therefore, their border problems should be viewed more as a symptom than as a basic cause of conflict between the two countries, although, as they have assumed a life of their own, they have added fuel to the conflict.

Blame for the numerous border incidents that occurred in the early 1960s probably must be assigned to both sides. Each felt that the other was exerting pressure and creating provocations, and both countered with pressure and provocations of their own. The process of action and counteraction fed upon itself, irritation turned into fear, and tension steadily increased until it reached a peak at the time of the 1969 clashes when war appeared to be a possibility.

Whoever was to blame for specific incidents in the early 1960s, by 1964 the Chinese had begun to use border and territorial issues as a political weapon, an instrument of verbal attack and psychological warfare against the Russians. The hints that Mao and others made that China might push claims to large portions of Soviet territory were clearly provocative. Conceivably, Peking's leaders felt that, because of China's relative weakness, they could do little else to counter Soviet pressure. Possibly their main aim was simply to discredit the Soviet leaders and mobilize opposition to them. Whatever the Chinese motives, the Russians' angry reaction was not surprising. The Russians could not be sure of Chinese intentions and apparently decided that they must prepare for the worst. Their large-scale military buildup around China, which began in 1965, was doubtless due, in part, to Peking's provocative territorial pronouncements.

But the Russians went far beyond what was required for strengthening local border defenses. They were clearly responding to broader problems: China's explosion of its first nuclear device in 1964, the uncertainties resulting from the confused political struggles in China during 1966–68, and the bellicosity that Chinese leaders exhibited at that time. At some point Soviet leaders seem to have concluded that the best way to deal with Peking was to exert strong pressure, at times subtle, and sometimes not so subtle, and to build up a position of overwhelming military strength in the areas immediately around China—in the Soviet Far East, Siberia, Outer Mongolia, and Central Asia. But this buildup served simply as a catalyst for fear and hostility in Peking, which created a new and much more dangerous situation. Today, therefore, the Sino-Soviet confrontation involves not only specific territorial but broad military-security issues. Negotiations between the Chinese and Russians on the enormously complicated border and territorial questions have remained secret.* However, both sides revealed their basic positions in 1969, and they have changed little since then. The Chinese, while not pressing claims to huge territories, as the Russians have often claimed they do, still do insist that certain territories now in Soviet hands should be transferred to Peking's control. They have also put forward certain other conditions for a settlement, including some that are wholly understandable (for example, a mutual withdrawal of forces) and some that they doubtless know the Russians will not accept (such as the demand that Moscow admit that previous treaties were "unequal"). In contrast, the Russians,

---

* Specific border and territorial questions and their historical background are described at length in other studies.[131] It is impossible to know precisely the positions the Chinese and Russians have taken, but the broad outlines are revealed by their actions and private statements as well as their major public statements. The essentials of their official positions are contained in Chinese government statements of May 24 and Oct. 7, 1969, and Soviet statements of Mar. 29 and June 13, 1969.[132]

while indicating a willingness to make minor concessions and adjustments, have basically been defenders of the status quo.

The Chinese, in insisting that all past treaties defining the borders
were "unequal," have sought their annulment and replacement by a
new "equal" treaty. They have said, however, that China is prepared to
take the old treaties "as a basis for an overall settlement." Peking emphasizes that it "never demanded" the "return of the territory tsarist Russia
has annexed." But it charges that the Soviet Union has taken additional
territory that should be Chinese even under the old treaties and that
these "disputed areas" must be returned to China. "Pending a settlement," the Chinese say, the status quo should be maintained and all armed
conflicts avoided; and both sides must withdraw their forces from the
"disputed areas."

The Russians have officially rejected virtually all Chinese claims and
demands. In reality, they say, any "unequal" treaties between China and
Russia were annulled years ago; they assert that the border treaties do
not fit into this category. They insist, therefore, that there is no "territorial problem" now, since the entire length of the border has a "definite
and clear legal formulation" in existing treaties. The territorial "problem," they maintain, is an artificial creation of the Chinese; it is not the
Russians who have encroached on the Chinese territory, they argue, but
the Chinese who have initiated provocations and advanced unjustifiable
territorial claims against the Soviet Union. However, they assert, current
differences can be settled through "consultations" for the "clarification
of the border line's location," and they acknowledge that minor "mutual
concessions" may be necessary and desirable.

The territories that are the focus of real contention are fairly limited.
The most important are several hundred small islands in the rivers that
form the border between northeast China (Manchuria) and the Soviet
Union, and an area of several thousand square kilometers in the Pamir
Mountain area overlapping China's Sinkiang Province and the Soviet
Union.[133]

The disputed islands, with one exception, are not intrinsically important to either country, although understandably both sides are extremely
sensitive to any violations of their assumed rights concerning them. The
Chinese have maintained from the start that the river border should follow the main or deepest channel of the river, according to the "thalweg"
principle, and that the Russians are illegally occupying many islands that
are on China's side of the channel. The Russians first maintained that the

border line delineated on the original treaty maps, which the Chinese say were vague and invalid, followed the Chinese bank of the river in many places and that the Soviet Union has not violated that line. However, in the course of the negotiations, the Russians have apparently indicated their willingness to accept the main channel as the dividing line for much of the border; privately they say they have told Peking that they are willing to turn over to China a sizable number of islands on the Chinese side of the main channel. There is one island complex, however, the Russians make clear they will not consider giving up, whatever legal or political case the Chinese may put forward. This is Hei-hsia-tzu (in Russian, Chimnaya and Tarabarovsky), which is adjacent to a major Soviet city, Khabarovsk, at the confluence of the Amur and Ussuri rivers, and is strategically important in relation to it.[134]

The Pamir area in dispute is larger and perhaps of greater significance than most of the disputed islands, but even this area is not of crucial strategic, economic, or other importance to China or the Soviet Union. Historically, there may be some validity to the claims of the Chinese regarding their earlier authority over the area. There is little reason, however, to believe that the Russians, who have controlled and administered the territory for many years, will consider major concessions there, or that the Chinese really expect them to, although Moscow might make minor concessions if this is the price for a definite settlement.

One basic problem that has made agreement impossible is the Chinese demand that Moscow admit that the old treaties were unequal and negotiate a comprehensive new treaty. The Russians are virtually certain to refuse to accede to this demand, at least in any broad sense. They believe that such an admission might not only open the door to future Chinese territorial claims but also encourage other nations to consider reopening claims of lost territory against Russia. The Chinese may already have backtracked on this issue; they have in any case not emphasized it since late 1974.

Another major obstacle is the failure of both sides—which each blames on the other—to carry out a "withdrawal of forces." The Chinese assert that in 1969 the Russians agreed to a mutual withdrawal from all "disputed areas" but that they have refused to carry out the agreement. The Russians maintain that no agreement was ever reached, at least in the form the Chinese allege. How could they have agreed to this, they ask, since they do not even acknowledge the existence of "disputed areas"? All they have been willing to say is that if a settlement is reached, an adjustment of force deployments would follow naturally.

Despite these differences, it is still possible to conceive of a border settlement. In reality, the border problems do not greatly threaten the national interests of either country and are not insoluble. But a settlement will only become possible when both sides decide that a lessening of tension is desirable and show a willingness to make significant concessions. Any settlement will require difficult decisions by leaders in both Peking and Moscow that they are not likely to make until both sides make a commitment to improve overall relations. Until then, the border question will probably continue to be stalemated, and will remain a symbol of hostility, a cause of friction, and a potential focus of serious conflict.

If both Peking and Moscow do seriously try to improve overall relations, however, the border situation could probably be defused fairly rapidly. Steps in this direction could be taken, in fact, without a formal border agreement. To a very limited extent, border tensions have already moderated, since the peak of tension in 1969, as both sides have scaled down their border patrolling, thereby decreasing the chances for local military clashes. However, a serious search for a far-reaching détente will require a formal border agreement of some sort.

The atmosphere on the border and in the negotiations concerning it will therefore serve as a barometer of the intentions on both sides in the period ahead. If general relations were to deteriorate further, border tension would inevitably rise, creating a danger of expanded clashes. But if the two countries were to try to move toward détente, progress toward a border settlement would be an important sign of their serious intentions.

In a genuine settlement, each side will probably have to make certain compromises. The Russians will have to be willing to make at least the limited concessions they have indicated are possible, such as accepting the thalweg principle for defining most of the river boundary, turning over a sizable number of islands to the Chinese, and possibly making symbolic concessions in the Pamir area. Clearly, however, the Chinese will have to make equal or greater concessions. They will doubtless have to abandon their effort to get Moscow to admit that the old treaties are unequal. They will probably also have to accept the Hei-hsia-tzu Islands as Russian and give up their claim to most of the disputed Pamir area.

But any significant agreement will in all likelihood depend on Moscow's making a much more important concession. Beyond merely accepting adjustments of the border, it will probably have to alter its military posture toward China, which will not be easy for it to do.

The Chinese insistence on a mutual withdrawal of forces from disputed areas may in a narrow, legalistic sense have to be modified, since Moscow may continue to resist acknowledging that any significant "areas" are "disputed." In a broad sense, however, Peking is likely to insist on evidence that Moscow is willing to redeploy its forces in such a way as to reassure the Chinese about its basic military intentions toward China.[135]

Since the late 1960s Chinese concern has clearly focused less on the border itself than on the large Soviet military buildup around China and the Soviet Union's threatening military posture. They seem to have felt, with justification, that Moscow has been trying to exact compromises from them by its buildup of military strength on China's border. Just as they did in response to the U.S. pressure they perceived in the 1950s and 1960s, Chinese leaders have responded to Soviet pressure by adopting a tough, inflexible, and at times bellicose stance. They seem to have believed that with a superior power "breathing down China's neck" militarily, any Chinese compromise would be interpreted as a sign of weakness. One prerequisite for significantly improved overall Sino-Soviet relations will probably, therefore, be increased Chinese confidence in their own defensive strength and military capabilities; another will be a Russian willingness to alter their military posture to reassure the Chinese.

The Soviet Union's military capabilities today are overwhelmingly superior to China's in terms of both strategic nuclear missiles and sophisticated conventional materiel. The overall balance between the two countries has not changed fundamentally in recent years, even though the Chinese now have a minimal nuclear deterrent. What has changed greatly in the military equation in the past decade has been the deployment of forces in the borderlands.

Peking charges that the Russians have concentrated a million troops around China, while Moscow asserts that China maintains two million men on its side of the border.[136] Although these are inflated figures, each has significantly strengthened its border forces in recent years.

According to Western estimates, the Soviet Union since the fall of 1974 has maintained about thirty-nine divisions close to the Chinese border.[137] In the same region, there were about fourteen divisions a decade ago. A large number of the recent deployments were made in 1969–

71, after border talks had started. A decade ago the fourteen divisions probably had about 150,000 men. At full strength, the divisions now in the region would total close to half a million men; they probably now total between 350,000 and 400,000, but they could be brought up to full strength rapidly. These forces have advanced, sophisticated equipment, far superior to what the Chinese possess. Not only do they have large numbers of aircraft, tanks, artillery, and other conventional weapons; they also have short-range nuclear missiles. Moreover, a sizable number of long-range Soviet nuclear missiles are also directed at Chinese targets.

On the Chinese side of the border, about 1.2 million men are stationed in the Shenyang, Peking, Lanchow, and Sinkiang Military Regions, adjacent to areas where the Soviet forces are located. A few highly strategic defense positions close to the border are manned, but the bulk of the Chinese troops are stationed farther back (perhaps to avoid provocation and perhaps in part because Chinese strategic concepts have called for a defense in depth). Although the number of troops in the border regions has been increased in recent years, the scale of Chinese redeployment has not been comparable to that of the Russians. And although the materiel supplied to these Chinese forces has improved, it is still clearly inferior to that of the Russians. However, the Chinese do have in operation a limited number of nuclear missiles directed at Soviet targets east of the Urals.

The Russian forces are considerably larger than what would be needed to cope with limited border clashes. Yet they are not really large enough to support a large conventional war. The Soviet buildups can probably best be explained as an overreaction by Soviet leaders in the late 1960s and early 1970s to what they saw as a growing potential Chinese threat. Military planners in Moscow, like their counterparts elsewhere, doubtless plan on the basis of "worst case" possibilities, and they may have argued the need to prepare for contingencies such as attempts to disrupt the trans-Siberian railway, Russia's lifeline to the Far East, or to threaten Soviet territory in that region. Once the buildup began in a crisis atmosphere, bureaucratic momentum may have kept it going. In addition, Soviet leaders probably felt that China's growing military capabilities, including its nuclear capabilities, argued for strengthening the Soviet position sufficiently to ensure that at every point the Russians would have clear superiority, to deter Peking from considering any "adventurist" moves.

Russian planners probably also have had in mind various Soviet military actions other than pressure against China. Some observers believe that in 1969 they may have considered a preemptive strike against Chinese nuclear installations, as propaganda from Moscow hinted. It seems unlikely, however, that Soviet political leaders ever came close to deciding on such a move, although individual military leaders in Moscow may very well have considered the possibility (as some individual military men in Washington did in the 1950s). But the Chinese could not exclude this possibility, and they not only warned the Chinese people of the danger of "surprise attack" by the Soviet Union but also carried out a massive campaign to construct underground shelters.[138]

Although a nuclear strike is highly unlikely, there are more plausible contingencies the Russians may have built up their forces to deal with. If serious border clashes were to occur again, they could consider launching the kind of large-scale punishing attacks they made against Japanese forces in China's border areas before World War II.[139] Or, if there were to be violent power struggles in China, the Russians might be tempted to support one group of leaders against others by providing military aid, exerting military pressure in the border regions, or directly intervening as they did in Sinkiang in the 1930s.[140] The Russians conceivably may also have considered other situations in which they might wish to move militarily into such key areas as Manchuria or Sinkiang. Although contingencies such as these may not have rated high as probabilities, Russian planners doubtless considered them, and they may have influenced the size and nature of the buildup. Leaders in Peking, as they watched the Soviet buildup, could not exclude such possibilities.

In addition, the Russians seem to have decided that, in view of the existing tension and hostility, the best way to deal with China would be to create a "position of strength" and exert constant pressure on China's periphery, sometimes overtly, sometimes subtly. The fact that such an approach was likely to be counterproductive does not make it any less possible that this premise shaped Soviet policy. And it is almost certain that Chinese leaders viewed the Soviet buildup in this light.

China's actions—and its military posture in the borderlands—have, of necessity, been essentially defensive, even though its border initiatives in 1969 were accompanied by renewed claims to contested territory. At some point, Peking's leaders apparently concluded that an effective defense against Moscow's buildup required forward patrolling in the border regions, even though they doubtless recognized that this would appear provocative. One primary motive, probably, was to exhibit China's defensive capabilities in order to deter the Russians from initiating—or even considering—large-scale military action. The Chinese clearly lacked the capability of initiating large-scale offensive military action against the Soviet Union. However, if Moscow were to launch a major attack, they could attempt retaliatory attacks.

There is no question that since the late 1960s Chinese leaders have felt the Soviet military threat to be real. Since 1973, they have deliberately played it down—they now say the Russians have "only" a million men around China[141] but this line cannot be accepted as an accurate reflection of Chinese attitudes. Peking's fear of Moscow may be less acute now than in 1969, but Chinese leaders' actions as well as statements indicate that they still believe the Russians are determined to exert continuing pressure not only on China's northern and western borders but everywhere possible on its periphery, and preoccupation with the Soviet Union's "encirclement" policies continues to be a basic determinant of Peking's policies.

The danger inherent in the Sino-Soviet military confrontation persists, therefore, and as long as the situation continues unchanged, the risk of serious clashes and of escalation to war will remain. For the situation to improve, both sides have to avoid provocations and make concessions, and the Soviet Union will doubtless have to make convincing moves to relieve the pressure the Chinese perceive. In the long run, improved relations will require a more stable military balance, based on mutual deterrence and mutual restraint. This may become somewhat less difficult to achieve as China's military capabilities improve, but it will not be easy; the huge discrepancies between Soviet and Chinese military power will continue to pose obstacles to stability in their military relationship for a long time to come.

The Period Ahead

Among several theoretically possible developments in future Sino-Soviet relations is a continuing "no war–no peace" state of controlled but intense hostility. The persistence of hostility for so many years reinforces a natural tendency to expect present trends to continue into the indefinite future. Yet the dramatic shifts that have occurred during the past quarter-century make it clear that important changes could occur in the future. In recent years, different observers have predicted such widely different trends as escalation of the conflict and possibly war, or a far-reaching Sino-Soviet rapprochement, and possibly reestablishment of a close alliance. None of these possibilities can be totally excluded, but obviously they cannot be regarded as equally probable.

Escalating tension and even open conflict will remain a danger as long as the deep hostility between China and Russia continues and huge forces confront each other across their long border. If serious border clashes recur, both sides might feel compelled to demonstrate that they cannot be forced to capitulate, and either might miscalculate the consequences of the actions it might take.

The level of conflict could escalate if either country—most likely the Soviet Union—were to try to exploit political struggles within the other to achieve its own goals. If, for example, the first round of the post-Mao succession struggle fails to create a stable new leadership, and new struggles break out between competing groups backed by different military leaders, the temptation in Moscow to exploit the confusion by supporting leaders who might be pro-Soviet, or by exerting new pressure to try to improve the Soviet position in border regions, might be irresistible. Either tactic could provoke the Chinese to retaliate, in which case the danger of war could be substantial.

War would clearly have disastrous effects on China particularly, but in certain respects on the Soviet Union as well, and it would have costly and potentially dangerous repercussions regionally and globally. It would doubtless end the worldwide movement toward détente between major-power adversaries and turn them again toward political polarization, militarization, and confrontation—even if other powers were not drawn into a Sino-Soviet military conflict.

However, open Sino-Soviet military conflict, while still a theoretical possibility, today can be viewed as an improbability. The peak period of danger was 1969, and even then both sides, recognizing the dangers, pulled back from the brink. Even the Soviet Union, despite its military superiority, appeared to recognize that it could not impose its will by open force. Both governments were aware that the entire international community would oppose such a war and, in all likelihood, react strongly against it—especially against the country that appeared to be the principal aggressor.

The reduced danger of war can be attributed to several developments. China's acquisition of a limited nuclear deterrent has substantially increased the risks of conflict, and therefore altered the power equation. The major shifts that have occurred in the configuration of power among the big powers since 1969—in particular China's opening of relations with the United States, normalization of relations with Japan, and expansion of ties with Europe—have imposed new restraints on the Soviet Union. So too, to a lesser extent, has China's growing stature in the Third World. And the rapidity and relative smoothness with which the first stage of the post-Mao succession has taken place has reduced the possibility that violent power struggles might weaken China and encourage intervention or manipulation from outside. Today, even if border tension were to increase or new clashes were to occur, both Peking and Moscow would probably act to contain them. As of early 1977, therefore, the probability of Sino-Soviet war must be rated as very low.

At present, speculation about possible changes in Sino-Soviet relations centers less on the danger of war, therefore, than on the possibility of a sudden swing of the pendulum, under post-Mao leaders in China, toward rapprochement or even restoration of a military alliance. Much of this speculation ignores the profound effects of the Sino-Soviet conflict over the years since 1956—and especially since the late 1960s—on the leaders and people in both countries. The many unresolved conflicts of interest, the obvious differences in ideological and cultural attitudes, and the deep emotions on both sides make it almost impossible to conceive of any far-reaching rapprochement in the foreseeable future. Even if both sides attempt to improve relations, deep-rooted resentment and hostility will severely limit how far the improvement can go. No Chinese leaders in this generation—or the next—are likely to consider restoring the kind of linkages the two countries had in the 1950s, or to risk new forms of dependency. Even if compromise becomes possible on some important issues, the two countries will basically remain competitors. And even if their military confrontation can be gradually relaxed, each will continue to view the other as a potential—if not actual—security threat for many years to come.

Fear and suspicion, however deep-rooted, are not immutable, of course. But attitudes can change only gradually, and only under very favorable conditions will fear and suspicion moderate. For the foreseeable future, therefore, even though some form of "peaceful coexistence" between China and the Soviet Union conceivably could evolve, there is little possibility that a genuine, far-reaching rapprochement can occur.

The prospect that a significant military alliance can somehow be restored between the two countries is close to nil. Even if overtly pro-Soviet leaders achieved power in Peking—which is highly unlikely in the period immediately ahead—they would probably not favor the kind of close military alignment that characterized relations in the 1950s, since this would place China in a subordinate, dependent position once again.

The possibility of restoration of the alliance is not *absolutely* nil, however. Both Peking and Moscow have demonstrated in the past that, if their security needs demand it, they can suddenly reverse course and cooperate with former adversaries for purely practical, realpolitik reasons. The Russians demonstrated this when Stalin signed a pact with Hitler in 1939; so too did Mao when he altered his basic approach toward Washington in the late 1960s and early 1970s. It is difficult, however, to foresee circumstances that could impel leaders in Peking to consider restoring a close military alliance with Moscow. This would become a plausible possibility only if China's leaders were to conclude that the United States, or a rearmed Japan, again posed the greatest and most immediate military threat to China's security—and that the Soviet threat had been greatly reduced. Even under such circumstances, future Chinese leaders would not necessarily follow the precedent set by Mao, who was almost always inclined to concentrate attention on one major enemy. They might opt instead for a more flexible approach. Yet they could, under such conditions, consider reestablishing a close alignment with Moscow, which at best would doubtless be an uneasy alliance in which mutual suspicions were subordinated but not eliminated. Restoration of an effective Sino-Soviet alliance seems highly unlikely, however, in the foreseeable future unless basic reversals in American or Japanese policies cause Peking to view them as extremely threatening. At present this seems highly improbable. The probability is that the Sino-Soviet alliance, already dead in fact, will formally expire in 1980, at the end of its thirty-year term, and that it will not be revived.

If neither open military conflict nor a far-reaching rapprochement between China and the Soviet Union seems likely, the most reasonable prognostication, in the view of many observers, is for continuation of the present pattern of Sino-Soviet relations for an indefinite period. This is a real possibility, which would mean continued bilateral confrontation and unrelenting worldwide competition. Tension would probably continue at a fairly high level, although with some ups and downs, but it would probably be contained in such a way as to prevent war. Most of the problems between the two countries would remain unresolved, however. And the unrelieved fear and suspicion on both sides would impel each to continue devoting major resources to the task of countering the perceived military threat from the other. Much of the rest of the world would continue to see benefits in the constraint that the conflict imposes on both Peking and Moscow. But the international community would also have to continue living with the danger of war inherent in such a situation and with the international tension and potentially destabilizing effect that Sino-Soviet competition creates in many parts of the globe.

Limited Détente

Although the continuation of hostility at its present level is a plausible and widely accepted projection of the likely trend in the period ahead, it is not what is probable. There are reasons to believe that, with Mao dead, China's new leadership may cautiously explore the possibilities of gradual, limited détente with the Soviet Union.

In the months immediately following Mao's death, there was no overt sign of any decline in Peking's hostility toward Moscow. On the contrary, China's anti-Soviet propaganda was particularly strident, and when Moscow made gestures that might have been viewed as conciliatory, Peking rudely rejected them. But this should have been expected, in light of the legacy of Mao, the power struggle against China's top Maoist radicals, and the inevitable uncertainty about what Moscow might do in reaction to the purges in China. To establish their legitimacy, post-Mao leaders, whatever their views, had to assert their nationalism and avoid any taint of "capitulationism" (the term used by the Maoists to attack all those favoring increased flexibility or compromise in dealing with the Soviet Union). Their initial obeisance to Maoist values does not, therefore, provide a reliable basis for predicting their future policies. The new leadership that has so far emerged under Hua Kuo-feng, moreover, appears to be dominated by pragmatists and moderates—in the Chinese context, men moved more by practical concerns than by dogmatic ideological assumptions. In domestic policy, they began very soon to move away from Maoist policies while still proclaiming Maoist slogans. They may in time decide to do the same in foreign policy.

Both the character of China's new leadership and the broader problems of multilateral relationships that China faces today make it plausible to expect a reassessment of China's policy toward the Soviet Union—possibly quite soon. There is convincing evidence that for some years a number of Chinese leaders, including important military men, have questioned Mao's uncompromising, confrontational approach to the problem of dealing with the Soviet Union. The death of Mao has automatically

removed what was an insuperable barrier to serious consideration of such
views.

The international situation that they face is extremely complex, and it
seems highly likely that some Chinese leaders will see disadvantages in
past approaches to dealing with both the Soviet Union and perhaps the
United States as well. They are doubtless as concerned with the Soviet
threat as Mao was, but conceivably they could decide that it would be
better to deal with Moscow by compromise than by hostility, in order to
reduce the risk of open confrontation. They will almost certainly wish,
if possible, to maintain a reasonable relationship with the United States,
to encourage Washington to continue serving as a counterweight to
Moscow. Some Chinese leaders, however, may question the desirability
of relying heavily on U.S. deterrence of the Soviet Union. Others clearly
are impatient with the pace of normalization of U.S.-China relations and
would like to see Washington compromise further on the Taiwan issue.
Many would doubtless like to see Peking evolve policies that might give
China maximum maneuverability in dealing with both Moscow and
Washington—and, in fact, with all the major powers.

It is very possible, therefore, that Peking's new leaders could decide
that cautious probing of the possibilities of reducing Sino-Soviet tension
might help to defuse the Soviet threat, and at the same time increase the
pressure on Washington to make additional compromises regarding Taiwan and further moves toward normalization of relations with China,
without fundamentally endangering or upsetting the U.S. role as regional
counterbalance to Moscow and a check against Soviet pressure on China.

If the new Chinese leaders were to start such probing, Moscow would
probably be responsive. Its hope would be to encourage a major shift in
Chinese policy that might alter the entire international balance. The process could involve a sequence of steps—a decline in ideological polemics,
increased civility in diplomatic contacts, a gradual expansion of trade,
restoration of some cultural contacts, and at some point serious negotiations on territorial and military issues. Conceivably all of this might
happen rapidly, but the likelihood is that the process would be gradual.

Even if Peking's leaders consider this course, however, there is no
guarantee that even a limited détente will automatically occur. At some
point the Russians would almost certainly have to be willing to alter their
deployment of military forces around China, and many leaders in Moscow may be reluctant to do this. The Chinese would have to be willing to
moderate—although not necessarily abandon—their worldwide attacks

on Soviet "social-imperialism," which many leaders in Peking may op-
pose, since there have been political advantages, domestically as well as
internationally, in having a clearly defined enemy against which to direct
China's hostility. Nevertheless, the potential benefits of reducing Sino-
Soviet tension could be a compelling argument for both Peking and
Moscow.

Any move toward Sino-Soviet détente would have significant international repercussions. A far-reaching rapprochement could fundamentally alter the configuration of global power; though a radical change
seems highly unlikely, any sign of improved Peking-Moscow relations is
likely to arouse unrealistic fear of a major shift in the world balance of
power.

The international consequences of a very limited Sino-Soviet détente,
of the kind that is realistically possible, would be more limited, but they
nevertheless could be important. They would depend, in large part, on
the state of U.S.-China relations at the time. If a reduction in tension
between Peking and Moscow occurred when U.S.-China relations were
still frozen, or deteriorating, Peking's posture toward the United States
—especially on the Taiwan issue—could harden, although probably not
to the extent of creating confrontations comparable to those of the
1950s. Any such trend, however, would have destabilizing effects regionally, the seriousness of which would be difficult to predict.

If limited détente between Peking and Moscow were to occur after
U.S.-China relations had been normalized, or were improving, the effects
would be much more limited, and mixed. Globally, some effects would
be adverse, since Europe would worry that Moscow might be able to
transfer some of its forces and increase its pressure on the West. This
danger should not be exaggerated, however, since a limited détente
would not eliminate Moscow's concerns to the east, and even if Russia
were to reduce its forces on China's borders, it would not be able to
ignore what it regards as a potential "China threat."

In the East Asian region, a limited Sino-Soviet détente would have
some favorable as well as unfavorable effects. It would doubtless arouse
some fear of a basic shift in the balance of power, which could revive,
unjustifiedly, the specter of a return to a bipolar world. But if, as is very
possible, it reduced the intensity of Sino-Soviet competition in the key
areas of conflict in the region, especially in Korea and Southeast Asia, it
might increase possibilities for cooperation among the major powers to

reduce tension, prevent conflicts, and work toward increased regional stability.

From Peking's viewpoint, limited détente with Moscow, if successful, could make it reasonable for China to adopt a posture of "equidistance" in dealing with all the major powers, which might increase its general maneuverability. From the point of view of the international community, there would definitely be some short-term costs, but they might well be outweighed by long-term benefits if a reduction in Sino-Soviet tension were to reduce the danger of war, reinforce broader trends toward détente, and open the door to increased cooperation among the powers.

PART TWO

China and Japan

JAPAN occupies a very special role in Chinese foreign policy.[1] It is clearly the most important nation, apart from the two superpowers, with which China must deal. Geography, history, security considerations, and economics all make this so.

In their current schematic division of world forces, the Chinese do not place Japan in the same category as the United States and the Soviet Union. Unlike these two nations, Japan today, despite its great economic strength, lacks the military power to pose any security threat to China; at present it has no global or even regional military role of significance. But China's leaders have not forgotten Japan's aggression in the decades before 1945, and they are acutely aware of its military potential. Because Japan could rapidly become a military power again, Peking's leaders cannot ignore its weight in the balance affecting China's security.

Proximity and cultural ties have created unique historical links between China and Japan. Moreover, Japan's economic strength creates opportunities as well as problems for the Chinese. Since the Sino-Soviet split, China has developed more extensive economic links with Japan than any other nation.

Even though Peking's leaders now categorize Japan simply as one of many countries in the Second World, they actually view it as a very special case: a nation whose past policies were of critical importance to China and whose present economic strength makes it a major power whose future policies will greatly affect China's interests.

Chinese policies toward Japan have been far from static; over the past quarter-century, they have been repeatedly modified or adjusted. Some of the changes have paralleled broad shifts in Peking's world view and global strategy. Many, however, have reflected Chinese leaders' changing perceptions of Japan's domestic situation and foreign policy. At different times, in defining their immediate goals and current tactics in relation to Japan, the Chinese have given quite different weight to ideological, economic, and other considerations.

Historical and Cultural Links

Historical ties between China and Japan make their relationship significantly different from any other relationship between major powers in East Asia. Japan, like Korea and Vietnam, belongs to the Sinic civilization area, which was profoundly affected by China's culture.[2] Even though Japan was never subjected to Chinese political control, as Korea and Vietnam were, its cultural borrowing from China was extensive.

More than a thousand years ago, during the seventh and eighth centuries, Japan's leaders deliberately embarked on one of the most massive programs of cultural borrowing in history. The result was far-reaching social change, based on the model of T'ang dynasty China. Through numerous missions sent to China, and more informal contacts—many of them through Korea—the Japanese imported the T'ang dynasty's dominant religion, Buddhism, and its Confucian values, as well as its basic political principles, forms of government organization, patterns of bureaucratic administration, and codes of law. They borrowed much of China's technology and many of its economic institutions. They also looked to China as Japan's model for art and music, and for architecture and city planning. Perhaps most important, they borrowed the Chinese writing system, adapting it for their own use; with it they acquired a great deal of Chinese history and scholarship. But the result was not simply the creation of a miniature Japanese version of Chinese society.

Chinese cultural influence probably reached its peak in Japan in the ninth century. The political and social system that subsequently developed in Japan was not a Chinese type of bureaucratic empire run by scholar-officials, but a distinctive Japanese feudal system dominated by hereditary aristocratic groups and infused with a unique military ethos.

Perhaps in part because they were separated by a large expanse of water, China and Japan remained very different; each went its own way. In certain periods, significant trade and other contacts were maintained, and some Japanese rulers sent tribute missions to China, but there were long periods, during which both countries pursued essentially isolationist policies, when actual physical contact was limited.[3] Awareness among Japanese of their society's enormous cultural debt to China continued, however. So too did the Chinese tendency to view Japan as a subordinate member of the cultural area that China dominated.

Even today, despite the tremendous changes in both China and Japan since the influx of Western ideas in the mid-nineteenth century, the historical cultural links between the two countries remain important. In a sense China has been the Athens and Rome of the Sinic area, from the Chinese as well as the Japanese point of view. Though the political significance of this fact is debatable, these cultural links are a unique element, absent from China's relations with the Soviet Union or the United States.

During the past century, however, both the internal and the foreign policies of China and Japan diverged, creating a new, and more immediately relevant, context for their relations. Beginning about the middle of the nineteenth century, although China and Japan faced similar challenges from Western colonialism, their responses were very different.[4] By the end of the century a rapidly modernizing and increasingly strong Japan came into open military conflict with a weak and disintegrating China.

Japan in the nineteenth century abandoned its isolationism and deliberately embarked, as it had during the seventh and eighth centuries, on a program of massive cultural borrowing, this time from the industrial nations of the West. The Meiji Restoration in the 1860s resulted in a peaceful revolution with far-reaching consequences. Japan's new leaders set about to modernize, on the Western model, as rapidly as possible, and they had remarkable success. Although a primary Japanese aim was to acquire the technology necessary to develop modern military power in order to stand up to the West, the Japanese deliberately tried, as they had a millenium earlier, to change their society in fundamental ways, borrowing foreign political, legal, and economic institutions as well as many of the intellectual and social underpinnings for them. And again they showed a remarkable capacity to be eclectic, and to assimilate influences from abroad without fundamentally compromising the integrity of their cultural and social system. While carrying out one of the most successful programs of modernization in history, Japan remained distinctively Japanese.

The Chinese, perhaps because their society had maintained its strength and integrity for so long, and had normally exported rather than imported cultural influences, were much more resistant to change than the Japanese were. In the latter half of the nineteenth century, some Chinese leaders attempted to import Western technology while rejecting basic Western values, but with only very limited success. Instead of undergoing a peaceful transformation, the Chinese empire went through a painful process of disintegration, which ultimately resulted in the collapse of the old empire in 1911. There followed several decades of civil conflict, foreign invasion, and violent revolution, leading first to the Nationalists' rise to power in 1927–28 and ultimately to the Communist party's victory in 1949.

Despite Japan's increasing political pressure on China, many Chinese reformers and revolutionaries viewed it during the early part of the twentieth century as the principal mediator between modern Western ideas and values and Asian traditions. Following Japan's military defeat first of China in 1895 and then of Russia in 1905, thousands of young Chinese, impressed by the Japanese success in modernization, went to Japan to obtain their education. During the early 1900s, especially after 1905, ten thousand or more went every year.[5] They became a key group in China that pushed for reform, or revolution, and modernization. Later the flow of Chinese students shifted to the United States and Europe, and after 1949 to the Soviet Union, but Japanese-trained leaders continued to play important roles in both the Kuomintang and Communist movements.

The early attraction of Japan to modern-minded Chinese leaders declined, however, as conflict steadily grew between the two countries, and ultimately Japan became a prime target of Chinese nationalistic fervor and hatred. As it developed economically and built up its military strength, Japan began to extend its influence abroad in competition with the major Western colonial powers. Ultimately it embarked on an ambitious program of expansionism aimed at regional supremacy, and China was obviously a major target.[6] The most important milestones in this process included the establishment of Japanese control over the Ryukyus in the 1870s, pressure on Taiwan and Korea from the 1870s on, and the military defeat of China in 1895, which resulted in Japanese annexation of Taiwan as well as the detachment of Korea from China. Then followed the first attempt of the Japanese to annex parts of Manchuria, their takeover of Russian special rights in Manchuria in 1905 after the Russo-Japanese War, their annexation of Korea in 1910, their presentation of the notorious Twenty-One Demands to China in 1915 (which if fully accepted would have given Tokyo a high degree of control over China as a whole), and their takeover, albeit temporary, of German rights in Shantung Province as a result of the Versailles Treaty in 1919.

Increasingly, the Japanese not only seized pieces of Chinese territory but also became deeply involved in the chaotic internal politics of the country, extending their influence through manipulative financial and political policies. They also tried, with limited success, to induce the other major powers to give them a free hand in China and accept Japan's hegemony in the region.

Finally, in the 1930s, soon after the Kuomintang established a new national government in Nanking, Japan embarked on major aggression against China. It first seized Manchuria, creating the puppet state of Manchukuo there in 1931–32, then extended Japanese control over north China, and finally in 1937 launched a full-scale military effort to conquer China. Japan is the only nation that has attempted, in the modern period, to achieve overall control of China.

Not surprisingly, as Japanese pressure mounted, Japan came to be viewed as China's main enemy. As early as World War I it became clear to many Chinese that Japan was trying to outcompete the Western imperialist powers in their encroachments on China, and the Versailles Treaty provoked an unprecedented outburst of Chinese nationalism directed against both Japan and the Western powers. When the Chinese Communist party was founded in 1921, this nationalistic outpouring was in full flood, and the party was profoundly influenced by the mood of the times.[7] A decade later, following the Japanese invasion of Manchuria, the Chinese Communist party, though still a relatively small revolutionary group fighting for survival in rural areas, "declared war" on Japan,[8] and in 1936 it switched to a united-front policy to try to mobilize political support within China as well as to resist Japanese aggression. From 1937 through 1945 both the ruling Nationalist regime and the Communists were engaged in a bitter war of survival against the Japanese, though both continued, especially from 1941 on, to struggle against each other for supremacy within China.

The war against Japan was a primary factor making possible the Chinese Communists' ultimate rise to power.[9] They succeeded during the war in achieving control of most of the north China countryside. The Japanese invasion created a vacuum in rural areas, which the Communists filled, winning the support of millions of peasants—as well as many intellectuals—with their patriotic and reformist appeals. While the Communists' strength was gradually increasing, the Nationalist regime underwent a steady process of disintegration. By the end of the war, the Communists were prepared to challenge the Nationalists for control of all China, and by 1949 they were victorious.

By then, the entire situation in East Asia had been radically altered. Japan was defeated and prostrate, and the United States was the predominant power in the region. China's Communist leaders faced a very new kind of world, therefore, and perceived new threats and new opportunities. Relations with the Soviet Union and the United States had priority. However, Chinese leaders who had spent most of their adult lives fighting China's "war of national resistance" could not forget a half century of Sino-Japanese conflict.

Early Communist Policy

When China's new leaders began to formulate their regime's foreign policy in 1949–50, they faced a Japan that was prostrate but still a potential danger because it was the main base for U.S. power in Asia.[10] Peking now viewed the world in bipolar terms, as a bitter struggle between two camps. Japan, with a key strategic position and a skilled population, under the allied (in reality American) occupation, clearly belonged to the "enemy camp." Moreover, U.S. efforts had begun to improve Japan's capacity to resist communism. One of Peking's first aims, therefore, was to strengthen its defenses against any threat from U.S. power based in Japan, and the Sino-Soviet treaty of 1950 was specifically designed to do that.[11]

The instability and revolutionary change that characterized much of Asia in 1948–49 apparently led both Moscow and Peking to hope that the Japanese Communist party might be able to seize power by violence (or at least seriously weaken the Japanese government), and in early 1950 Moscow directed the Japanese Communists to attempt such a seizure. The Chinese Communists, who had long maintained close contact with key Japanese Communist leaders, some of whom had spent part of the wartime period at Yenan, strongly backed this approach.[12] Moscow's action could have been the result of an overestimate of the potential for violent revolution in Japan (the Communists had won roughly 10 percent of the votes in Japan's 1949 election), or simply a belief that militant action, even if unsuccessful, would indirectly support other Communist efforts in East Asia.

The Korean War, initiated by North Korea[13] in June 1950, basically changed the situation. Both Stalin who backed the war and Mao who reportedly endorsed it must have believed that, if successful, it would have significantly altered the balance in East Asia in favor of the Communist camp. Instead, the war provoked a strong U.S. response; and in a sense some of the Communists' worst fears about the United States and Japan became a reality.

Japan, as the principal base for the American war effort in Korea, became extremely important in the calculations of U.S. strategic planners. The Japanese government took harsh countermeasures against the Communist party, which rapidly lost political support (the party was driven underground; some of its leaders sought refuge in China). With the stimulus of American wartime procurement, the Japanese economy started on the road to recovery. The United States, moreover, accelerated its efforts to convert Japan from a defeated enemy into a strengthened ally; John Foster Dulles, for example, began encouraging Japan to start rebuilding its defense capability.[14] And Washington also prepared to sign a peace treaty with the Japanese.

Japan's emerging conservative leaders, who achieved a political predominance in this period that has yet to be destroyed, followed closely in the footsteps of the United States, and moved toward an overtly anticommunist policy. Whereas in 1950 Premier Shigeru Yoshida had said that he was prepared to send trade delegates to China as soon as the Americans would permit it, and even as late as 1951 expressed the view that geography and economics would eventually prevail over ideological differences in Sino-Japanese relations, such views disappeared as the Korean War continued. Yoshida, and Tokyo's conservative leadership as a whole, aligned Japan strongly with the United States against China and the Soviet Union.[15] Japanese leaders really had no alternative, since Washington exerted strong pressure on them to make such an alignment.

In the fall of 1951, within a year after China's intervention in Korea, the United States and its major Western allies signed a peace treaty with Japan, ending the state of war that had legally continued up to that time. Both the Chinese Communist and Chinese Nationalists regimes were excluded from the peace conference. The Soviet Union took part, but in the end refused to sign the treaty. Peking asserted that the peace treaty was invalid without its participation, but neither Chinese protests nor Moscow's obstructionism significantly affected the outcome.

One article of the treaty obligated Japan to conclude peace separately with China, without specifying which Chinese regime it should deal with, within three years. The question of Taiwan's future was left in abeyance; Japan renounced title to it, but the treaty did not specify to whom title now belonged.[16]

In theory, Japan, an independent nation once again, could decide whether to deal with Peking or Taipei. Actually, it had no choice, for at the time the peace treaty was signed, the United States and Japan concluded a security treaty tying Tokyo closely to Washington. And in December 1951, Secretary of State Dulles obtained from Premier Yoshida a letter pledging that Japan would sign a peace treaty with Nationalist China, as soon as possible, and would refrain from establishing relations with Peking.[17] This treaty was concluded soon thereafter, in April 1952. Tokyo hedged its bets somewhat by insisting that it be made clear that the treaty applied only to territory actually under Nationalist control.[18] But the treaty nevertheless locked Japan into the anticommunist, pro-Nationalist posture adopted by the United States.

Political Manipulation

By 1952 Peking may have felt that it now confronted the worst of all possible worlds in relation to Japan. In the intense, cold-war hostility developing between East and West, Japan was closely allied with, and subordinate to, the United States, and it now maintained diplomatic relations with Taipei rather than Peking. Within Japan, the conservatives were so clearly dominant that Peking must have realized that violent Communist-led revolution in Japan was not possible. Japan's economic recovery had progressed further, and Japanese rearmament was now a possibility.

Yet Peking was not totally lacking in means to try to influence Japanese politics and policies. Important individuals and political groups in Japan were very critical of government policy and favored the establishment of friendly relations with the Chinese Communist regime. These included not merely the Japan Communist party but a large percentage of the membership of the Socialist party and other opposition groups, and even some leaders in the conservative parties.

Moreover, important currents of opinion in Japanese society were susceptible to Chinese Communist influence and manipulation.[19] Many businessmen were attracted by the lure of China trade, especially after the truce in Korea resulted in a decline in U.S. procurement in Japan. A large number of Japanese intellectuals, influenced by Marxism, tended to be ideologically sympathetic toward Peking. Few Japanese felt any sense of threat from China. Many favored establishing relations with China's new regime because of a sense of cultural affinity to China, guilt about past Japanese aggression, a pacifistic outlook resulting from Japan's World War II defeat, or growing resentment about the excessive American influence in Japan and Tokyo's apparent subservience to Washington.

Starting about 1952, with the Korean war stalemated, Peking began to evolve a new policy toward Japan.[20] It went through many complicated changes in the ensuing years, but through much of the 1950s some Chinese goals remained fairly constant. Lacking official ties with Tokyo, Peking attempted to develop trade and cultural and political links with a wide range of Japanese. It tried to influence and manipulate political opinion in Japan so as to encourage the strengthening and coalescence of pro-Peking forces, and then to stimulate these forces to exert pressure on the Japanese government to change its policies. Eventually, the Chinese tried to establish semi- or quasi-official links with the Japanese government itself, in order to exert direct influence on it. Broadly, its aims were to strengthen the Japanese left and to weaken and eventually end Japan's alliance with the United States and involvement with Taiwan. It hoped to lay a basis for opening official relations with Tokyo on Chinese terms, and in the longer run to encourage Japan to be either pro-Peking or neutralist and perhaps even to align with China.

The wide variety of groups in Japan that Peking believed would push for changes consistent with its aims included the Japan Communist party and other leftist parties (notably the Japan Socialist party), leftist intellectuals and students, such "people's organizations" as the Dietmen's League for the Promotion of Japan-China Trade (founded in 1950), and businessmen desiring to trade with China (especially, at the start, those associated with small and medium-sized businesses). Later, the Chinese focused their attention increasingly on the ruling Liberal Democratic party itself and on big business. Although some of Peking's propaganda was directed at the "masses," much of it was targeted at specific groups or factions.

In pursuit of its policies Peking used, and manipulated, extremely varied issues: trade, fishing problems, Japanese prisoners of war and war criminals in China, and a wide range of problems related to "peace" and Japan's American ties such as U.S. bases in Japan, nuclear arms, the return of Okinawa to Japan, and the U.S.-Japan security treaty.

Chinese policy often reflected political shifts within China, but it was also fine-tuned to fit the changes Peking perceived in Japanese domestic politics. Chinese leaders had to make difficult tactical choices about which groups and factions to cultivate, the mixture of attraction and pressure to use, and the problems and issues to stress at any particular time. In setting immediate goals they had to decide whether to try mainly to increase nonofficial contacts, establish de facto official ties, or work for full diplomatic relations. More broadly, they had to decide whether to give priority to strengthening the political left within Japan, weakening Japan-U.S. relations, or improving Sino-Japanese relations. The choices were not clearcut; they required delicate calculations and difficult decisions on questions of priorities.

The Chinese in the 1950s became deeply involved in Japanese politics. In this respect Peking's Japan policy was, and remains, unique; in no other foreign policy area (even in relations with other Communist nations) have the Chinese seen comparable opportunities to pursue their aims by attempting to influence domestic politics in the country involved. Within Japan, problems relating to China policy had become one of the most controversial foreign policy issues by the mid-1950s, and they were to remain so for more than a decade and a half thereafter. China policy confronted every Japanese premier with extremely difficult dilemmas, and most conservative administrations felt themselves to be politically vulnerable on these issues. In a sense they were caught in the middle, between conflicting, irreconcilable pressures, on the one hand from Peking, pro-Peking political forces in Japan, and broad public opinion, which shifted steadily in favor of improved relations with China, and on the other from Washington, Taipei, and pro-Nationalist or pro-Taiwan forces in Japan.

Trade was Peking's most important policy instrument in dealing with Japan in the 1950s, and the Chinese sometimes used it with sophistication and skill. Yet Sino-Japanese trade remained small, in part because the U.S.-sponsored system of controls limited trade in strategic items; and trade policy proved to be a less effective political weapon than Peking hoped.

Eventually, it became clear that although Peking could influence Japanese opinion in many respects, it was unable to make significant progress toward its basic goals through political manipulation, no matter how fine-tuned its policy was. Chinese leaders simply did not have sufficient leverage to induce the Japanese government either to alter its relations with the United States, which remained the keystone of Japan's foreign policy, or to make basic changes in its China policy.

People's Diplomacy

Within the general framework of Chinese policy throughout the 1950s and much of the 1960s, different aspects were dominant during different periods. The initial Chinese moves toward defining a new policy toward Japan in 1952 were part of a broad policy shift, made in concert with the Soviet Union, toward a "peace" and "coexistence" strategy. Peking's first step was to develop a campaign of "people's diplomacy" directed primarily at leftists and secondarily at businessmen. In June 1952 the Chinese signed a nonofficial trade agreement with a group of Japanese businessmen, and in the fall they invited a group of leading leftists to attend a so-called Asian and Pacific Peace Conference in Peking.[21]

Not surprisingly, Peking was extremely hostile to the incumbent, pro-American, Yoshida administration in Tokyo, and it appealed to the Japanese people as a whole to oppose Yoshida and end the U.S. occupation. Its main efforts, however, were aimed at the Japan Communist party which it regarded as the most important group to cultivate, despite the party's declining popular support (it did not win a single Diet seat in the 1952 elections). In 1952 Peking established Radio Free Japan to support the revolutionary cause. The Chinese probably were no longer sanguine about immediate revolutionary prospects in Japan, however, and they began to widen their contacts with noncommunist leftists who advocated the establishment of relations with Peking and those conservatives who viewed the Peking regime as more nationalist than Communist.

The nonofficial trade agreement signed in 1952 was obviously designed to induce the Japanese government to remove or reduce the restrictions imposed on China trade. It divided the commodities to be exchanged into three categories and specified that the Japanese could only purchase the goods they wanted most if Japan would sell to China goods still on the restricted list.[22]

In December 1952 Peking announced that it was willing to return Japanese prisoners of war still in China. It did this in a way deliberately designed to embarrass the Japanese government, insisting that the arrangements be made through private, pro-Peking Japanese organizations —the Japan-China Friendship Association, Japan Peace Liaison Committee, and the Japanese Red Cross.[23] The first repatriated groups that

arrived in Japan were well indoctrinated and their pro-Chinese statements had a significant impact on Japanese public opinion. Within a
year, however, Peking declared that the repatriation program was ended,
which dismayed many Japanese since some prisoners were still detained
in China.

The Chinese worked assiduously to broaden their contacts with Japanese trade, fishing, and labor groups during 1952–53. In effect, they
began encouraging the formation of a pro-Peking, leftist-oriented united
front to increase political pressure on the government. Despite Yoshida's
reelection in early 1953, leftist forces, in particular the Socialists, were
growing stronger and they increasingly accused Yoshida of subservience
to the United States and hostility toward China. The left wing of the
Socialist party called openly for recognition of Peking and abrogation of
Japan's treaty with the Chinese Nationalists.[24] The party's right wing
did not go that far, but it did call for greater trade. So too did many
leading conservatives such as Ichiro Hatoyama. In mid-1953, in fact, the
lower house of the Diet voted unanimously to recommend reduced restrictions on China trade.[25] At about the same time, China extended the
first nonofficial trade agreement for six months, at the request of the
Sino-Japanese Trade Promotion Association and the Japan-China Trade
Promotion Council.

Starting in late 1953 the major Communist nations began showing an
active interest in establishing official diplomatic ties with Japan, and
Russian and Chinese leaders in a joint declaration in Peking in late 1954
called for the normalization of relations with Japan.[26] In reality, however, Moscow's and Peking's positions differed; the Russians were fully
prepared to establish official diplomatic relations, which they did shortly
thereafter, but the Chinese were not, because Japan continued to maintain ties with the Nationalists on Taiwan. Nevertheless, Peking's explicit
expression of interest in establishing official relations, and its talk of a
possible Sino-Japanese nonaggression pact, represented a significant
change on its part. Chinese leaders made it clear, however, that it would
be necessary first to remove the "obstacles" created by Tokyo's ties with
the Nationalists and "subservience" to the United States.[27] Chou En-lai
told some visiting Japanese that the signing of a peace treaty, establishment of official relations, and conclusion of a nonaggression pact were
desirable but would be possible only when Japan became truly independent, democratic, and free, implying that its relations with the United
States would first have to change. At other times, however, the Chinese

implied that they were prepared to deal with any Japanese government willing to sever its ties with Taiwan. In sum, they pushed for normalization of relations but set a price they knew Japan's conservative leaders could not consider paying, at least immediately. However, they continued to make conciliatory gestures, offering to settle the war criminals issue, and issuing an invitation to a private Japanese fishery mission which had indicated a desire to go to China.

China's immediate practical aims in this period were simply to expand "people's diplomacy," stimulate the growth of pro-Peking groups in Japan, and encourage political pressure from the left on the Japanese government. People's diplomacy did develop further.[28] In 1953 the Dietmen's League for the Promotion of Sino-Japanese Trade sent a delegation to Peking; it was the first Japanese group representing all parties to go. The Chinese also signed a second private trade agreement with the Japanese. In October 1954 a Red Cross mission went to Tokyo, the first major Chinese Communist group to visit Japan. Later that year private Japanese groups established a National Council for the Restoration of Diplomatic Relations with the Soviet Union and China, a Japan-China Fishery Problems Council, and an International Trade Promotion Association.

Increased Contacts

In December 1954, Ichiro Hatoyama replaced Yoshida as premier, first as head of a caretaker government, then in early 1955 on a longer term basis. Peking thereupon reassessed its Japan policy, as it was to do whenever Japan's leadership changed. The Chinese at first seemed uncertain about how to deal with Hatoyama. They obviously approved his statements favoring increased trade with China but strongly opposed the kind of two-Chinas policy he proposed.[29]

By early 1955, seeing no immediate basis for establishing full diplomatic relations, and not content to rely entirely on unofficial contacts, the Chinese began to work toward de facto relations with the Japanese government. Chou En-lai met with Tokyo's official representatives at the Bandung conference in Indonesia in early 1955.[30] When a private fishing agreement was signed in China in April, the Chinese emphasized that an intergovernmental agreement would be preferable.[31] And in May the first Chinese Communist trade delegation visited Japan and signed a third private trade agreement, stressing the desirability of exchanging permanent trade missions.[32]

Japan's Liberal Democratic party (LDP) was now clearly interested in other contacts with China, but not prepared to make any moves that would strain relations with the United States. It did, however, take limited initiatives, and it raised the issue of Japanese still held in China. Peking initially stated that Japanese war criminals would be dealt with according to law, but then its position softened. Emphasizing that they desired to take further steps to normalize relations, the Chinese indicated clearly for the first time that the San Francisco peace treaty would not pose any obstacle to the signing of a peace treaty between Japan and the People's Republic of China. Chou also indicated he was now prepared to meet with a representative of Hatoyama.[33]

The Chinese seemed to vacillate in this period. Briefly in late 1955 and early 1956 Peking again called for full relations, indicating that until this could be achieved, concrete problems relating to repatriation, trade, and fisheries would have to be postponed.[34] Mao proposed that Japan send a representative of ambassadorial rank to Peking to discuss normalization of relations.

Later in 1956, however, the Chinese reverted to a more flexible approach. After Tanzan Ishibashi became premier, Peking resumed efforts to establish de facto governmental relations. Ishibashi favored steps toward a rapprochement, but his foreign minister, Nobusuke Kishi, wanted to restrict new moves to the field of trade.[35] Peking, as a conciliatory gesture, repatriated most of the Japanese war criminals held in China (working through "people's organizations" rather than government channels, however). It agreed to continue the private fishery agreement, and in a joint communiqué called for an intergovernmental agreement in this field as in others.[36] Then, when the third private trade agreement was extended, the Japanese negotiators and the Chinese agreed that permanent, nonofficial trade missions would be exchanged in the future. However, various problems blocked implementation until considerably later.[37] In 1956 Chinese leaders also suggested once again that conservative Japanese leaders such as former Premiers Hatoyama and Yoshida visit Peking.

The trends in Chinese policy that had been developing since 1952 reached a peak during 1956–57. "People's diplomacy" appeared to have paid off substantially. Public opinion in Japan had swung strongly in favor of recognition of Peking, although many ordinary Japanese still favored some kind of two-Chinas policy. Peking's contact with many and varied "people's organizations" in Japan was close. The number of Japanese visiting China had steadily risen, from somewhat over eight hundred in 1955 to more than sixteen hundred in 1957.[38] And by the end of 1957 the Chinese had signed more than forty nonofficial agreements with various Japanese groups.[39]

Most important, Peking had established a kind of quasi-diplomatic relationship with Japan's leading opposition group, the Socialist party, and by 1956 obviously regarded the Socialists rather than the Communists as their most important potential allies in Japan. Numerous Socialist leaders visited Peking in 1956–57, and the most important visits produced joint communiqués calling for basic changes in Tokyo's China policy.[40]

Sino-Japanese trade had risen from $34 million in 1953 to $150 million in 1956 (its peak year until 1964) and many businessmen in Japan pressed for more.[41] Yet it was still relatively unimportant. It constituted a tiny percentage of Japan's overall trade, and it was still only a small proportion even of China's trade. China was starting to increase commercial relations with noncommunist countries, but gradually and cautiously; its economy was still closely tied to the Soviet Union. Political factors in both China and Japan still prevented the development of large-scale trade. Thus, it was the lure of future trade, consciously manipulated by Peking, more than the actual level of current trade that was important in the 1950s.[42] Nevertheless, trade policy was a major political weapon of the Chinese throughout this period, employed to increase pressure on the Japanese government.

In 1957, another change of administration occurred in Tokyo, and Nobusuke Kishi formed a new government after Ishibashi resigned for health reasons. Peking's immediate reaction was again one of uncertainty, but not for long. Kishi was in favor of increased China trade, but he strongly opposed recognition of Peking. In July his government, together with the major European trading countries, reduced existing trade restrictions, eliminating most of the so-called China differential (which had imposed greater restrictions on trade with China than on trade with the Soviet Union ever since the Korean War).[43] However, this was Kishi's one departure from the U.S. approach to China policy. He moved vigorously to strengthen Japan's ties with the United States, visiting Washington, where he obtained agreements putting the two governments' relations on a more equal and solid basis. And he committed an unpardonable sin, from Peking's viewpoint, by visiting Taiwan, and reemphasizing the importance of Japanese ties with Chiang Kai-shek.

Strong Pressures

Peking reacted to Kishi's moves in an extremely hostile fashion and stepped up its political pressure on him. The Chinese encouraged the Socialists to oppose him more strongly and manipulated trade policy to weaken his position. In late 1957 they canceled plans to hold trade fairs in Japan and stalled negotiations for a new private trade agreement, objecting to Japanese regulations that would require fingerprinting of members of any Chinese trade mission sent to Japan. Peking demanded that trade mission members be given certain diplomatic or quasi-diplomatic privileges.[44] Things seemed to improve briefly in early 1958 when a fourth private trade agreement was finally signed and a five-year contract for an exchange of Japanese steel for Chinese iron and coal was concluded. But in the trade agreement Peking insisted on the right of any future Chinese trade mission in Tokyo to fly the Chinese Communist flag, knowing that the Japanese government opposed this. When the Chinese Nationalists protested, the Japanese government assured them that it had not changed its China policy and would not grant diplomatic privileges to any Chinese Communist trade representatives or grant them to the right to fly their flag.[45]

The Chinese further stepped up their pressure between March and May 1958, on the eve of new national elections in Japan. They vehemently denounced the Japanese government's policies. Then they seized upon an incident in which a Chinese Communist flag was desecrated in Nagasaki as the pretext for an abrupt and almost complete severance of economic relations with Japan. They canceled existing contracts and virtually halted trade. They also harassed Japanese fishing vessels and encouraged a boycott of Japanese goods in Southeast Asia. The fourth trade agreement became a dead letter.

These drastic actions were the most blatant pressure Peking has ever used for political purposes.[46] They were supplemented by increased political pressure on various Japanese groups. All of this came at a time when China's overall policy had just shifted toward a more militantly radical position, both at home and abroad, and it was doubtless in part a product of that shift. However, it also seemed to be based on Peking's misjudgment of the political situation in Japan—and China's ability to exploit it. The Chinese probably hoped, by discrediting Kishi, to help the Socialists improve their position in the coming election. They also seemed to believe that by creating economic problems for Japan, thereby shocking the Japanese government and people, they might induce even Kishi to change his foreign policy.[47] If these were their aims, their actions clearly boomeranged. The Socialists in Japan were hurt rather than helped by Chinese actions. Many Japanese expressed strong criticism of Peking's moves, and public attitudes hardened. And Kishi refused to alter his policies. Some pro-Peking groups in Japan, such as the Dietmen's League, soon fell into decline, and the left in Japan became increasingly fractionalized.[48]

Until the end of Kishi's premiership in 1960, Peking kept up its pressure on Japan, and relations reached a low point. In late 1958 China's foreign minister openly called on the Japanese to repudiate Kishi and abrogate the U.S.-Japan security treaty, and in 1959 Peking's propaganda focused almost exclusively on this issue.[49] Although small-scale trade with certain "people's trade" companies continued, the overall level dropped precipitously, to the almost negligible figures of $22 million in 1959 and $23 million in 1960.[50] Chinese purchases from Japan in these years were about one-tenth of one percent of Japan's total exports.

Despite the overall decline in contacts, Peking continued its efforts to cement relations with the Japanese Socialists, with some success. When a second Socialist party mission went to Peking in 1959, its leaders joined the Chinese in asserting that "American imperialism" is the "common enemy of both the Chinese and Japanese people."[51] However, this rather dramatic statement probably harmed the Socialists more than it helped Peking's cause. It played a part in causing one group in the Socialist party to break off in late 1959 and form the new Democratic Socialist party. Peking also began paying greater attention to the Japanese Communist party once again, and in 1959 issued two joint statements with its leaders, Kenji Miyamoto and Sanzo Nosaka. It also cultivated certain Liberal Democratic party members such as Ishibashi and Kenzo Matsumura.

Chinese policy in this period played a role in exacerbating the conflict in Japan over the U.S.-Japan security treaty. Mass rallies were organized in Peking against it, and various Japanese groups were urged to oppose it. However, the agitation in Japan, which escalated up to the time of the treaty's renewal, was caused by deeper political currents which impelled many Japanese to press for greater independence and a more equal relationship with the United States. The issue became ensnarled in domestic Japanese politics and was a major point of argument between competing groups. Finally in mid-1960 the treaty was revised and renewed for ten years. However, Kishi, who had never been popular, was ousted as premier and was replaced by Hayato Ikeda. Once again Peking was impelled to reassess its Japan policy.

A New Context

Soon after Kishi's resignation, Peking took steps to improve communication with varied Japanese groups, but its room for maneuver was now limited. Its focus was primarily on the extreme left in Japanese politics and on those businessmen, large and small, who pushed most strongly for China trade. Slowly, Peking moved to reopen trade.

In some respects Sino-Japanese relations during the ensuing decade did not appear very different from the 1950s. Peking continued to try to influence Japanese politics through its unofficial relationships, but with limited results; the Japanese government continued its close alignment with the United States and its nonrecognition policy toward China. Nevertheless, important changes did occur, gradually. In fact, the basic context for Sino-Japanese relations was altered as a result of important developments both within the two countries and in the overall pattern of relations among the big powers in Asia.

The most important development in the period was the Sino-Soviet split. The Soviet cutoff of aid in 1960, and the economic depression in China in the early 1960s, compelled Peking to view trade with Japan increasingly in economic terms, rather than as a political tool.[52] Eventually, the Chinese were impelled to reassess security relations with Japan as well. Within China, a shift in the political balance in the leadership during 1960–61 brought to the fore relatively pragmatic men, who took steps toward more flexible and moderate policies, both at home and abroad, and after Kishi's fall they adjusted their policies toward Japan.

Before 1960 the Chinese had put forward three political principles that they insisted the Japanese government or private groups would have to observe if they wished to establish friendly relations with Peking: abandonment of hostility toward China, renunciation of all "two-Chinas schemes," and the end of obstructionist moves delaying the restoration of political relations.[53] They also had indicated that the establishment of political relations would be a prerequisite for significant economic relations. Peking had persistently tried to link economics and politics as a means of pressing for changes in Japanese policy, but the Japanese government had insisted that economics and politics should be separated, and had favored the development of trade before political issues were resolved.

In late 1960 a shift in China's policy became evident when Chou En-lai defined a set of principles applying specifically to trade. He indicated that China was prepared to reopen trading on a new basis: it would supply certain specified types of commodities to Japan and deal with selected Japanese traders, on a private basis, deferring attempts to arrange intergovernmental trade agreements until after the normalization of political relations.[54]

On the basis of these two sets of principles, the Chinese gradually expanded what was labeled "friendly trade." But they dealt only with designated Japanese firms—mostly small and medium-sized ones, although some were dummy fronts for big businesses—which fulfilled China's political preconditions and were vouched for by the Japanese Communists or pro-Peking organizations such as the Japan-China Trade Promotion Association.

By the end of 1962 more than two hundred firms had been designated "friendly," and most trade was conducted through these channels.[55] But trade had increased only modestly, to $47 million in 1961 and $84 million in 1962[56] and the "friendly trade" mechanism was clearly not satisfactory from the Japanese point of view. The Chinese, who now wanted to expand trade more rapidly, also concluded that it was not adequate.

A major step toward increased trade was the signing of an important agreement in 1962 between Tatsunosuke Takasaki, former head of Japan's Ministry of International Trade and Industry, and Liao Ch'eng-chih, head of the China-Japan Friendship Association. Their "private" memorandum, which created the basis for what came to be known as "L-T trade," covered a five-year exchange of goods and called for an average annual two-way trade of 36 million pounds[57] (roughly 100 million dollars). It included provisions for some deferred payments or installment purchasing. The Chinese indicated a special interest in commodities that could help their agriculture recover from its post-Leap slump. Under the new arrangements, trade was partially exempted from Peking's previous political conditions.

From 1962 on, Sino-Japanese trade developed fairly rapidly through both "friendly trade" and "L-T trade" channels. In 1964 the mechanisms to promote increased exchanges were further strengthened when "private" trade missions, which had been discussed for many years, were finally exchanged. But Peking was unwilling to give up the leverage that dealing through designated firms gave it. Gradually, L-T trade declined from an almost equal share of total trade in 1962 to little more than a third of friendly trade by 1967.[58] (In 1968 the arrangements were re-negotiated and L-T trade became, simply, memorandum trade.)

In the mid-1960s Peking began to show an increased interest in buying prototype plants from Japan. Once again, however, politics intruded, but this time the pressure on Tokyo was exerted primarily by Taipei, not Peking. When the Japanese discussed the sale of a vinylon plant to Peking, with possible Japanese Export-Import Bank backing, the Chinese Nationalists strongly protested and took economic and political action to back up their protest. As a result, in 1964, the Japanese government backtracked. Premier Ikeda had former Premier Yoshida deliver a letter to the Nationalist government pledging that the Japanese government would not authorize Export-Import Bank financing for such deals.[59]

Despite such complications, Sino-Japanese trade grew fairly rapidly—from $137 million in 1963 to $310 million in 1964, $470 million in 1965, and $621 million in 1966, before dropping during China's Cultural Revolution and then recovering to about the 1966 level in 1969.[60] Trade with China could no longer be viewed by Peking mainly in symbolic terms, or as a lever to obtain political concessions; it was now very important to China in economic terms. Although it remained small in proportion to Japan's overall trade, it began to be important to certain Japanese industries.

Politically, from 1962 on the Chinese gradually seemed to lose hope that an effective, left wing, united front could emerge in Japan. The left appeared to fractionalize and weaken even further, and Chinese actions probably contributed to this trend. For example, in 1962 the Chinese pressured members of a Socialist party mission to take political positions that unquestionably hurt them at home and helped to divide the leftists from the moderates in the party.[61] By late 1963 the Chinese had become much less active in cultivating the Socialists, although they did continue to deal extensively with the most extreme leftists in the party.

Their main interest in left-wing groups shifted back to the Japan Communist party. A new factor that impelled them to shift emphasis was the Sino-Soviet split which convinced the Chinese that they should actively compete against the Soviet Union for influence over all other

Communist parties.[62] But they had only limited success. For a while the Japanese Communists leaned toward Peking, and later toward Moscow. The main long-run effect of the Sino-Soviet dispute, however, was to push them toward greater independence from both China and the Soviet Union.

Despite its renewed interest in the Japanese Communists, Peking continued to invite a fairly wide range of leftists to China and in its propaganda attempted to appeal to Japanese opinion more broadly. Ikeda, however, continued Kishi's China policy for the most part, actively supporting, for example, the U.S. position on Chinese representation in the United Nations. It was not surprising, therefore, that Peking strongly attacked him.[63]

The China issue, though still important, was now somewhat less salient in Japanese politics. Chinese propaganda began to stress new issues, such as Tokyo's efforts from 1962 on to improve relations with South Korea, and problems arising from the U.S. bases and other issues relating to U.S. relations with Japan. While Peking strongly criticized Japanese policy on these issues, it took some positive steps to expand trade and people-to-people contacts, agreeing, for example, to an exchange of news correspondents as well as trade agencies in 1964.[64] In general, public opinion in Japan continued strongly to favor improved relations with Peking; however, Peking's explosion of a nuclear device in 1964 provoked widespread criticism.

The most important new element in Peking's people's diplomacy was its increasing interest in expanding contacts with conservative politicians and big businessmen belonging to the ruling establishment in Japan. The 1959 visits of Kenzo Matsumura and Ichiro Kono to Peking were tentative steps in this direction. From the time of Takasaki's visit in 1962, the Chinese gradually broadened their links with Japanese conservatives, recognizing that China's economic and political interests required direct dealings with those who exercised real power in Japan.

Retrogression Again

When Eisaku Sato succeeded Ikeda as premier in 1964, Sino-Japanese relations entered another period of decline, and by the end of the 1960s they had reached another low point. Although in general Sato (who was a brother of Kishi) simply continued Ikeda's China policy, in Peking's eyes he appeared even more hostile. He favored increased trade, but he continued to insist that economics and politics be separated, and he endorsed the "Yoshida letter" which pledged that Japan's Export-Import Bank would not finance China trade.[65] Most important, he took major steps to strengthen Japanese-American ties and formed closer links with both the Nationalist regime on Taiwan and the government of South Korea. Not all in his party agreed with him, and two factions in the Liberal Democratic party emerged with different views on China policy, the pro-Taiwan Asian Study Group and pro-Peking Afro-Asian Study Group.

Soon after Sato came to power, Peking briefly suspended trade negotiations and canceled some trade contracts, probably because of its increasing concern about Japan's tendency to support "two Chinas." Nevertheless, overall Chinese-Japanese trade continued to grow, and in 1966 Japan's trade with China surpassed its trade with the Soviet Union and other Communist countries. However, politics continued to intrude. The semiofficial L-T trade declined, and Peking again put pressure on the firms on its "friendly trade" list to endorse Chinese political views.

From 1966 on, during the Cultural Revolution, China's relations with Japan, as with most of the world, deteriorated. Peking's preoccupation with its domestic struggles, and its indiscriminate militance toward most of the outside world, contributed to a major decline in Japanese visits to China. A number of Japanese businessmen and newsmen in Peking were expelled, arrested, or mistreated. And lurid Japanese press reports of political excesses in China affected broad public opinion in Japan adversely.

The Chinese and Japanese Communist parties openly split in 1966–67 on issues relating to the Sino-Soviet conflict, Vietnam, and revolutionary strategy, with Mao himself playing a key role in the split.[66] In the resulting polemics, Peking strongly denounced "Miyamoto revisionism," while backing a radical splinter Communist party in Japan. The Japanese left during this period was further fractionalized, and a number of groups, including the Japan-China Friendship Association, split apart.

Even though the Vietnam War strained Japanese relations with the United States, public attitudes toward China were also affected adversely, because of the confusion that prevailed during the Cultural Revolution and China's nuclear testing from 1964 on. Sino-Japanese trade dropped from $621 million in 1966 to $557 million in 1967, to $549 million in 1968.[67]

Peking's hostility toward Sato increased, especially after his 1967 visit to the United States, Southeast Asia, and Taiwan, when Peking accused him of "treading Tojo's old road."[68] Although Peking seemed to lower the priority given to Japan in its overall foreign policy—perhaps because of its increasing preoccupation with the Soviet Union and Vietnam—it continued to try to influence Japan's politics and policies. As Japanese policy became more active under Sato, the Chinese became increasingly apprehensive. During 1968 and 1969 it became clear that major changes were occurring in the entire pattern of big-power relations in East Asia and that Japan was emerging as a more important factor in the equation as a result of its growing economic power and political activities. The Chinese showed intensified anxiety about Japan's involvement in South Korea, Southeast Asia, and above all Taiwan.

Peking's apprehensions came to a head during 1969 when President Nixon and Premier Sato reached agreement on the return of Okinawa to Japan (the transfer occurred in 1972). Included in the reversion, the Japanese insisted, were the Tiao-yu-t'ai or Senkaku Islands, which Peking also claimed. Nixon and Sato also signed a joint communiqué that Peking found extremely disturbing.[69] Apparently at U.S. urging, the communiqué indicated that in Tokyo's view Korea was "essential" and Taiwan "important" to Japan's security.

The Okinawa agreement and the joint communiqué constituted a milestone in Japanese-American relations, highlighting Japan's increasing independence, yet strengthening the ties between the two countries. From Peking's viewpoint, the communiqué hinted that Japan might be moving to assert a new regional role in Asia, possibly even a military role, in collaboration with the United States and with American backing. Peking's leaders probably asked themselves whether Tokyo intended to fill any vacuum left by the Americans, especially in Northeast Asia and, above all, in Taiwan and Korea. Washington had already taken steps toward military withdrawal from Vietnam, and Nixon had announced his "Guam doctrine."

The Chinese reacted strongly against what they labeled a U.S.-Japan "criminal plot," and they launched an intense campaign to denounce Japanese "remilitarization." Chou En-lai stressed this danger in a communiqué he signed with Kim Il-sung in North Korea in early 1970.[70] Peking also intensified its cultivation of a broad range of Japanese opposition groups. As trade with Japan rose once more—from $625 million in 1969, to $822 million in 1970, to about $900 million in 1971—Peking again attempted to manipulate it for political purposes,[71] although in a more restrained way than in 1958.

China's activities directed at political groups once more broadened.[72] Peking relied heavily on organizations such as the revived Dietmen's League, but it paid special attention to the most radical leftists—Communists and others—in Japan. It also showed renewed interest in the Socialists who sent another party mission—their fifth—to China, and it established much wider contact than before with other opposition parties and groups such as the Democratic Socialist party and Komeito and even LDP leaders belonging to factions other than Sato's. By 1971 Peking had significant contacts with most important Japanese groups except for the "mainstream" Japanese Communist party and Sato's faction in the Liberal Democratic party. In sum, China's pre-Cultural Revolution modus operandi was revived, but on an even broader basis than previously. The Chinese adopted a fairly tough posture in dealing with most groups, demanding that they endorse Peking's basic principles for the normalization of Sino-Japanese relations. Because pressure within Japan to establish official relations was rising again, Chinese tactics achieved some success.

In early 1970, not long after the Nixon-Sato communiqué, Chou Enlai defined a new and tougher set of four principles to govern the development of Sino-Japanese trade.[73] He warned that China would not trade with Japanese firms that helped (that is, traded with) or invested in Taiwan and South Korea, sent arms to the Indochina states, or were linked with American enterprises in Japan. Peking canceled contracts with some companies in these categories, and many Japanese firms, including some large ones, fell into line. In 1970, memorandum trade dropped to 8.5 percent of total Sino-Japanese trade, and an increasing number of large Japanese firms became involved in the highly politicized "friendly trade,"[74] many of them through "dummy companies."

Although Peking's new tough line had discernible political effects, it is questionable whether it significantly affected either the level of trade or its composition. Sino-Japanese trade by now had developed an economic rationale and dynamics of its own that shaped its course more than political factors did.

Throughout 1970 and much of 1971, Peking kept up its hostile propaganda campaign against Japanese remilitarization, attacking Tokyo's Fourth Defense Plan and warning that Japan was on the way to becoming a regional threat. There is no doubt that the Chinese knew that Japan still lacked the capability to pose any real military danger; they deliberately exaggerated the threat for political effect. Nevertheless, they probably were genuinely disturbed by the implications of the Nixon-Sato communiqué, by Japan's increasing economic influence in Northeast and Southeast Asia and its growing involvement in Korea and Taiwan, as well as by Moscow's stepped-up efforts to improve its Japanese ties.[75]

Peking's campaign was obviously designed to reactivate debate in Japan over China policy as well as to check military trends. Pressure in Japan to establish formal relations with Peking did, in fact, mount, and even Sato modified his stand; he was not willing to meet all of Peking's preconditions, however.

By 1971 it was clear that there were three basic Chinese prerequisites for normalized Sino-Japanese relations: recognition by Tokyo that there is only one China and that the People's Republic of China is its sole legitimate government; recognition that Taiwan is a province of China; and abolition of Japan's treaty with the Nationalists.[76] Sato now began using the term *People's Republic* in referring to China, and he indicated a willingness to hold official talks, but he was not prepared to accept the Chinese Communist position on Taiwan. He also continued to support the American position on Chinese representation in the United Nations. By now, however, virtually all major opposition parties and groups in Japan had indicated their willingness to accede to Peking's major conditions. It was also evident that Sato would probably soon be replaced as premier.

Agreement to Normalize Relations

Then, in mid-1971, Henry Kissinger made his dramatic secret visit to Peking, to prepare for a trip by President Nixon. In the fall Peking was seated in the United Nations. The sudden prospect of Sino-American détente in a single stroke changed the fundamental context for Sino-Japanese relations.

The Chinese immediately adopted a more flexible and moderate posture toward Japan. They dropped both their campaign against remilitarization and the political conditions they had set for trade. They also began to signal strongly that they wished to move rapidly toward full normalization of relations as soon as Sato was replaced as premier, which appeared imminent.[77] China's flexibility in early 1972 in agreeing to a basis for a limited relationship with the United States raised still higher Tokyo's hopes for solving the problems obstructing its relations with Peking, even though it was clear that Japan would probably have to go further than the United States in compromising past positions.

Political pressure in Japan to change China policy intensified. Kissinger's trip, undertaken without Tokyo's knowledge, had a traumatic impact. For two decades Japanese leaders had shaped their China policy to conform to Washington's; they had avoided moving ahead of Washington, but they had always believed that it would be disastrous to fall behind. They felt a sense of betrayal in not being consulted before the U.S.-China opening. (This "Nixon shock" proved to be only the first of several shocks in 1971–73 that severely strained Japanese-American ties.) Most leaders in Tokyo concluded that Japan should now move rapidly to establish full diplomatic relations with Peking. The position of those who had favored some kind of two-Chinas policy was undercut.

Although Sato modified his China policy in early 1972, by authorizing Export-Import Bank financing of China trade and disavowing the Yoshida letter,[78] Peking waited to deal with his successor. Kakuei Tanaka, a major contender for Sato's job, indicated his desire to initiate talks on normalization of Sino-Japanese relations as soon as possible, and Chinese leaders indicated that they would be prepared to deal with him. They seemed to regard him, a new postwar figure, as more acceptable than previous leaders such as Kishi and Sato.

In the elections the Japanese public made clear its strong desire for rapid change in China policy. Opinion was overwhelmingly in favor of ending the pattern of nonofficial relations and starting a new period of official ties. When Tanaka was elected in July 1972 he moved so quickly on the China question that some knowledgeable Japanese feared he had not made adequate preparations. By September he was in Peking, and he and Chou En-lai signed a joint statement that finally opened up formal diplomatic relations between China and Japan.

The Tanaka-Chou agreement, like the Nixon-Chou communiqué preceding it, was a skillfully and subtly drafted document.[79] Just as the signing of the Shanghai communiqué had stimulated debate as to whether the Chinese or Americans had made the greatest concessions, the Tanaka-Chou statement provoked debate on the degree of compromise by both sides. Actually, both sides made important compromises in order to overcome, or finesse, past obstacles to formal relations.

Freed from many past restraints by the U.S.-China opening, the Japanese were prepared to sever diplomatic relations with the Nationalists, but a variety of political and legal problems made it impossible for them to accept in full the three principles specified for formal relations with Peking. While the Chinese reaffirmed their principles, they were quite flexible in applying—or not applying—them, and in the end did not insist on full compliance. It was clear that by 1972 they also placed a high priority on establishment of full diplomatic relations.

The Tanaka-Chou statement spoke of a "long history of traditional friendship" between the two countries and declared the recent "abnormal state of affairs" in Sino-Japanese relations to be "terminated." The five principles of coexistence would now be the basis for "peaceful and friendly" relations. Both sides stated that the agreement was not directed against anyone else, that neither sought hegemony in the Asian and Pacific area, and that both would oppose others who might. The statement called for the immediate establishment of formal diplomatic ties, to be followed by further negotiations to conclude specific intergovernmental agreements on "trade, navigation, aviation, fishery, etc." as well as a broad "treaty of peace and friendship." (At certain times in the past Peking had implied that a peace treaty would have to be concluded before diplomatic relations could be established.)

The Japanese government stated that it "proceeds from the stand of fully understanding the three principles for the restoration of diplomatic relations," but it specifically endorsed only one of them: recognition of the People's Republic of China as the "sole legal government of China." Although Peking reaffirmed its claim to Taiwan, the Japanese did not explicitly recognize that claim. Instead they simply said that the Japanese government "fully understands and respects" it, and "adheres to its stand of complying with Article 8 of the Potsdam Proclamation." Later the Japanese Foreign Ministry pointed out that the Potsdam agreement merely endorsed the Cairo agreement, which stated that Taiwan "should be returned" to China.[80] Foreign Minister Masayoshi Ohira explained: "Japan actually has not said that Taiwan is a territory of the People's Republic of China. We are only saying that it is a territory that ought to belong to China. There is no difference at all from the past."[81] The Japanese government's stand—that it was not in a position to make any pronouncement on the legal status of Taiwan—contained inevitable ambiguities. Significantly, Peking made no protest when this interpretation was publicized, although it continued to insist that, in its view, the issue had been resolved. Since then, Tokyo's policy has continued to be one of "avoiding commitment as to Japan's legal position on the status of Taiwan."[82]

The Tanaka-Chou statement made no mention of the Japanese treaty with the Nationalists, which Peking's three principles had maintained was illegal and must be abrogated. Immediately after the issuance of the statement, however, Ohira explained that the treaty "has lost the basis for existence and is considered to have ceased to be effective."[83] Japan, in short, fulfilled this condition, but unilaterally, and without acknowledging that its treaty with the Nationalists ending the Sino-Japanese war had been illegal.

The Chinese renounced any claim to reparations from Japan for World War II damages. The Japanese, who had never been prepared to pay China reparations, apologized for the war by stating that they were "keenly aware of Japan's responsibility for causing enormous damages," for which they "deeply reproached" themselves.

The agreement made no mention of two other issues which at times had appeared to be serious obstacles to normalizing relations: the U.S.-Japan security treaty and Japan's economic ties with Taiwan. Peking was remarkably relaxed about Japanese trade with Taiwan. Even though Tokyo immediately cut formal diplomatic ties with the Nationalists, and made clear that it would not back any Taiwan independence moves, the Japanese, with Peking's obvious acquiescence, proceeded to expand trade with, and investment in, Taiwan. They also established a new structure of ostensibly unofficial but actually quasi-official relations with the Nationalist regime. The Nationalist embassy in Japan was converted into a new East Asian Relations Association and the Japanese embassy in Taiwan was transformed into a so-called Interchange Association. Foreign service officers on leave from their official positions staffed these associations, and consulates were made branches of these organizations.[84]

The Tanaka-Chou statement made no mention of the U.S.-Japanese security treaty. Moreover, not only did Peking refrain from denouncing it, soon thereafter it began to make statements indicating that China actually favored it under existing circumstances, as a counterbalance to the power of the Soviet Union. Instead of attacking Japanese militarism, Peking now stated that Japan obviously needed a competent military force for its own defense.

From 1972 on, Chinese approval of Japan's defense policies and security treaty with the United States became increasingly explicit. In early 1973 Chou En-lai told Takeo Kimura that "Inasmuch as Japan constitutes a nation, weapons of self-defense are essential to it."[85] Not long thereafter, Liao Ch'eng-chih stated: "I cannot support the U.S.-Japan Security Treaty structure but its functions directed toward China have already lost substance, and we will not take particular issue with it at this late date. As a practical question, Japan will probably have to rely on America's nuclear umbrella for some time to come."[86] In late 1973, Foreign Minister Chi P'eng-fei reportedly told a Japanese parliamentary mission that "it is quite natural for Japan to maintain the security treaty with the United States while it lacks sufficient self-defense capacity."[87]

Teng Hsiao-p'ing subsequently told Takeo Kimura in January 1974 that "China does not affirm the Japan-U.S. security treaty, in principle, but since a threat exists, we think it unavoidable for Japan to defend its own country by maintaining ties with the United States."[88] Later that year, in an interview with Aiichiro Fujiyama, Teng was explicit about the threat: "The U.S. is not so dangerous as the U.S.S.R., up to a certain stage. The reason is that the U.S. is at present devoting its power to the point of maintaining its own rights and interests at various places in the world and is standing on the defensive. The U.S.S.R. is standing on the offensive."[89]

Finally, in 1975, Chou En-lai went even further when he stated to Foreign Minister Kiichi Miyazawa that he "could understand the specially deep relations that had grown up between Japan and the United States because of the process following the Second World War," adding that he thought that they "should develop even more intimate ties" and that it is "only natural" for Japan to maintain self-defense forces.[90] Statements such as these reflect the profound change in China's basic strategic outlook since the late 1960s, when its perception of the Soviet threat to China had begun to shape its new approach to Japan and to the United States.

China also increased the priority given to economic interests in its foreign policy. The process of expanding Sino-Japanese trade had gained momentum since the end of the Cultural Revolution; it now speeded up even more. From levels around $900 million in 1971 and $1.1 billion in 1972, Sino-Japanese trade soared to just over $2 billion in 1973,[91] almost $3.3 billion in 1974, and $3.8 billion in 1975.[92] And in 1973 the Chinese began exporting oil to Japan—roughly 1 million tons in the first year, about 4 million in 1974, and about 8 million in 1975—and the Chinese indicated they wished to raise the amount in the future.[93] (At the same time, Japan's trade with Taiwan also soared; in fact, in 1973 it amounted to $2.25 billion; only in 1974 did it fall below trade with the mainland.[94])

People-to-people contacts between China and Japan also rose to a new peak. In 1973 more than ten thousand Japanese visited China, including over two hundred groups representing business, technical, medical, cultural, and sports interests, as well as a broad spectrum of politicians and a growing number of representatives of local areas. About five thousand businessmen attended the Canton trade fairs.[95] Chinese visits to Japan grew significantly too. In 1973 Liao Ch'eng-chih led a highly publicized "friendship mission" to Japan, and during the year more than fifty economic missions, most with highly specialized technical or economic interests, made visits to explore the possibilities of technical cooperation and trade.[96] China's intercourse with Japan was now many times larger than that with any other country. (For Japan, however, its ten thousand visitors to China in 1973 compared to over four hundred thousand visitors to Taiwan.[97])

The Path to Full Normalization

The task of converting the promises in the Tanaka-Chou statement into reality proved to be more gradual and difficult than many had expected. There was hard bargaining on a number of agreements, reflecting inevitable differences of national interests; various unresolved political issues complicated the process.

The agreement on trade proved to be the easiest to achieve, although even it took time. An interim memorandum trade agreement was concluded in late 1972, in record time.[98] From then until the official agreement was signed in January 1974, there were almost uninterrupted negotiations. Finally, the two sides agreed on reciprocal most-favored-nation treatment, procedures for settling accounts (in yen, jenminpi, or other mutually acceptable currencies), the promotion of technical interchanges, and the holding of trade exhibits.[99] They also agreed to try to settle disputes through "friendly consultation" but, if that were to fail, to submit to arbitration; an official "joint committee" was to be established to help implement the agreement. The agreement was to be valid for three years and would continue thereafter unless either side gave three months' notice of its intention to terminate it. Problems concerning registration of trademarks, protection of industrial property, procedures affecting visiting businessmen, and arbitration procedures were left for future negotiation. But on balance the agreement placed Sino-Japanese trade on a more solid basis.

Negotiations on an aviation agreement proved to be far more difficult, with Taiwan the crux of the problem.[100] Peking's initial demand that the Japanese end their flights to Taiwan before starting flights to the China mainland aroused the pro-Taiwan forces in Tokyo and reactivated debate on the Taiwan issue. The Japanese government spent months in complex negotiations with both the Chinese and its domestic opposition. Finally, however, Peking softened its position, and its ultimate demands amounted, in some respects, to no more than symbolic measures designed to underline the fact that in principle Peking would not accept any two-Chinas policy. But China's more flexible position did not end the political debate in Japan.

In January 1974 Ohira returned from a visit to Peking with a proposed deal under which Japan-Taiwan flights would be considered "private" and would be undertaken by some airline other than Japan Airlines (which would handle the Peking flights). Japan would require that "Taiwan" be added to the name of the Nationalists' "China Airlines" flying to Japan, it would refuse to recognize the Nationalists' flag as a national flag, and it would require that the Nationalists' airline work through local agents in Japan rather than through an office of its own.[101] Reaction against these proposals was strong. The Nationalists actively lobbied against such a deal and threatened strong reprisals. Pro-Taiwan groups in the Liberal Democratic party asserted that the steps demanded were tantamount to granting recognition of Taiwan as part of China, which Japan had avoided doing in the Tanaka-Chou agreement. Competing Japanese business interests lined up on different sides of the issues. And right-wing groups, such as the Seirankai within the LDP, seized upon the dispute to attack Tanaka.[102]

Finally, in April 1974, Tokyo and Peking signed an agreement.[103] At the time, Ohira issued a statement in which he said Japan would now consider Taiwan's flights to Japan to be "private," would not recognize China Airlines as representing a "state," and, most important, would no longer recognize the Nationalist flag as a "so-called national flag."[104] The latter statement in particular angered the Nationalists. They canceled all flights between Tokyo and Taipei, both by Japanese planes and their own, and threatened action against any Japanese plane that entered Taiwan's "flight identification zone."[105] This action had a real impact, both economic and psychological, on Japan. (Japan Airlines, for example, had been carrying about thirty thousand persons a month to Taiwan, whereas the projected Peking flights would carry only a very small number.[106]) But the ban hurt Taiwan itself in a potentially serious way; more than a year later, Taipei quietly agreed to the resumption of flights.[107]

The airline episode not only strained Japan's relations with Taiwan but also dampened the fairly euphoric atmosphere in which "normalized" Sino-Japanese relations had begun, highlighting the fact that many dormant problems could easily surface. It also made it apparent that when concrete issues arose, particularly ones involving Japan's relations with Taiwan, negotiations might be difficult. And it demonstrated that important political divisions within Japan persisted which Peking clearly still had a capacity to exploit.

Once the airline agreement was concluded, the Chinese were willing to begin formal negotiations in 1974 on navigation and fisheries issues. The navigation agreement was the simpler of the two to conclude as it could be patterned on existing private agreements between the Japan International Trade Promotion Association and China Council for the Promotion of International Trade. Initially the Japanese were concerned that the Nationalist flag issue would again be raised or that the ports that ships from Taiwan might use would be questioned. Peking did initially raise the Taiwan issue, which led to temporary suspension of talks. When negotiations resumed, however, agreement was reached fairly rapidly, and no reference was made to Taiwan.[108]

The fisheries negotiations encountered major difficulties right from the start over substantive issues.[109] For years China had enforced restrictions on shipping and fishing in certain unilaterally defined military and conservation zones along its coast. Private Japanese fishing interests had accepted these restrictions, but now the government had to decide whether or not to do so. Moreover, Peking now proposed extending some of the zones, arguing that more stringent measures were required for conservation. Tokyo opposed this and also voiced strong opposition to Chinese "military warning lines."[110] In mid-1974, negotiations were suspended and existing private arrangements extended for one year. The negotiations were resumed later in the year, and finally in 1975 an agreement was signed.[111] The Japanese had to make many compromises, however, by accepting numerous restricted zones.

Over time it became clear that other problems would also complicate the process of stabilizing Sino-Japanese relations. Some of the most ticklish related to ocean areas and natural resources. Although Peking's exact stand on many law-of-the-sea issues remained undefined, the Chinese objected to any steps taken by others that conceivably could infringe on China's claims. For example, when Japan and South Korea signed an agreement in 1973 calling for joint exploitation of oil resources in certain undersea areas where their jurisdictional claims overlapped, Peking in early 1974 declared their moves invalid, arguing that such issues had to be "decided by China and the other countries concerned through consultation."[112] The Japanese government, thus placed in an awkward position, equivocated and postponed putting the agreement up for ratification by the Diet.

China also continued to assert its own claim and contest Japan's to the Tiao-yu-t'ai/Senkaku Islands.[113] (Tiao-yu-t'ai is the Chinese name, Senkaku the Japanese.) When Tanaka was in Peking in 1972, Chou chose not to inject this issue into negotiations, but Tokyo remained uneasy about Peking's intentions. The Japanese were relieved when Vice Premier Teng Hsiao-P'ing told a group of visitors in October 1974 that Peking was prepared to discuss a general friendship treaty once agreements on navigation and fisheries were completed, and that it was willing to lay aside the Tiao-yu-t'ai/Senkaku dispute in order to do so.[114] However, as long as the territorial dispute remained unresolved, Tokyo was inhibited from taking any action in the area (including oil exploration) that could complicate its relations with China. The dispute remained a potentially troublesome issue, therefore.

The Chinese also did all they could from 1972 on, using both the stick and the carrot, to discourage the Japanese from negotiating agreements with the Russians for joint development of resources, especially oil and gas, in Siberia. They gave several verbal warnings. For example, in 1973 Liao Ch'eng-chih told Japanese visitors that China would harbor "bitter feelings" if Japan assisted the Soviet Union in building a pipeline to carry oil from Tyumen, since this would help to supply fuel to Soviet military forces on China's borders.[115] And Peking hinted at greatly increased Chinese oil production and exports to Japan, suggesting that by the end of the decade China should be able to sell more oil to Japan than the Soviet Union could even if the Japanese agreed to support Russian development projects. (Interestingly, the Chinese indicated that if the Japanese did go ahead on certain joint economic projects with the Russians, it would be better if they did so with U.S. participation and cooperation rather than on their own.[116]) At the same time they strongly supported Japan in its dispute over four northern islands the Russians had held since World War II. The Japanese nevertheless continued discussions with the Russians and were able to reach a few agreements on developmental projects, though not on the largest projects that had been proposed. Peking's pressure on Tokyo was one of several factors that complicated Soviet-Japanese negotiations.

Despite the many problems, overall Chinese policy toward Japan from 1972 on clearly accented the positive and aimed at cementing relations between the two countries. There was no doubt that both the Chinese and Japanese were strongly committed to the task of broadening ties, and concrete progress was made toward this end. In 1974 both indicated that they hoped to complete negotiations on a "treaty of peace and friendship" before the end of 1975.[117] (The Japanese use the term "treaty of peace and friendship" instead of "peace treaty" because of the peace treaty with China that they concluded with the Nationalists in 1952.) Both felt that conclusion of a treaty would be a symbolically important capstone to the entire process of normalizing relations.

However, when discussion of the contents of a treaty began in 1975, serious trouble arose.[118] Peking insisted that one clause spell out the opposition of both nations to hegemony over the area by any power. This was obviously aimed at the Russians, and the Japanese, committed to a policy of equidistance toward Peking and Moscow, were disturbed. The Russians were too, and indicated that they would regard Tokyo's agreement to such a clause as an unfriendly act.[119] Within Japan, the issue became a subject of major controversy, used by many different groups for political purposes. As a consequence, latent differences over foreign policy were reactivated, and debate over policy toward both China and the Soviet Union was renewed. The Japanese government decided that it could not simply acquiesce to Peking's proposal. Even though statements opposing hegemony had been included in both the U.S.-China Shanghai communiqué and the Tanaka-Chou statement, the Foreign Ministry felt that such a clause should not be included in a formal treaty.

Eventually the Japanese indicated a willingness to include a statement on hegemony in the preamble of the treaty to resolve the impasse. Peking, however, stood firm in insisting on a separate clause. The result was a prolonged deadlock. However, in early 1977 the Japanese hinted that they might reconsider the inclusion of the clause if the Chinese would indicate their understanding and acceptance of Japan's interpretation of its meaning.

The hard line Peking took on this issue was consistent with its worldwide effort to counter Soviet influence. In 1975–76 its major goal seemed to be to complicate the relations of all other nations with Moscow. Chinese leaders may have felt that if they could induce Japan to take a step that Moscow clearly regarded as unfriendly, this would suggest a tilt toward China and thereby weaken the Japanese-Soviet relationship, which in Peking's eyes would be a gain significant enough to risk creating strains in China's relations with Japan.

In practical terms, however, the deadlock over the treaty did not seem to have far-reaching immediate effects; Sino-Japanese trade and exchanges continued to develop satisfactorily. It did, however, highlight the fact that interactions between the two countries will continue to be complex, and at times difficult, and that questions of China policy could still create very troublesome political issues within Japan and in its relations with third countries.

Basic Attitudes

The basic attitudes and domestic political factors that play a very special role in the Sino-Japanese relationship make it different from any China has with other major powers.[120] There are important differences between China and Japan in this respect, however. Broad public opinion is obviously not a primary determinant at present of China's policy, as it is of Japan's. However, the attitudes of the country's leaders and elite are critically important. There is little sentimentality in Chinese views of Japan today. Realistic, practical calculations outweigh other factors in shaping China's policies. Nevertheless, China's present leaders are obviously moved by many emotions that are rooted in past history. Though the Chinese have traditionally regarded Japan as a subordinate member of the Sinic world, they have also viewed the Japanese, justifiably, as island people whose culture is different in basic respects from that of the Chinese. Their most vivid memories are not of the two countries' centuries-old cultural links but rather of the threat posed by Japanese imperialists to China from the late nineteenth century on. Moreover, their ideology predisposed China's leaders to view Japan as a member of the enemy "camp," a bourgeois capitalist nation closely linked to imperialism.

Overall, the Chinese have looked on Japan with a complicated mixture of apprehension, hostility, envy, and admiration. Watching its rapid economic recovery and growth, with American assistance, from the early 1950s on, Chinese leaders almost certainly resented the fact that the wartime aggressors were surging ahead of their victims. And they obviously looked with some apprehension at Japan's growing economic strength.[121] However, in recent years they have become increasingly interested in obtaining Japan's advanced technology. Nevertheless, Peking's leaders make clear that in economic as well as ideological-political terms they continue to regard Japan as "one of them," rather than "one of us." They see it as a leading member of the industrialized Second World, closely linked to one of the superpowers, rather than as a member of the Third World, as China now claims to be.

While these perspectives have significantly influenced Peking's leaders' views on Japan, Chinese policy has been based above all on concrete security concerns, pragmatically defined economic interests, and hard-headed political calculations. Nevertheless, basic Chinese attitudes bar any really intimate relationship with the Japanese in the foreseeable future. (It is in no sense intimate today; Japanese, like all foreign visitors to China, are isolated, physically and politically, and denied opportunities for close interaction with the Chinese people.) If political relations between China and Japan were to go sour, Chinese suspicions and hostilities, rooted in recent history, would almost certainly come to the fore very rapidly.

Public attitudes have been more important in shaping Japan's approach to China. A large number of Japanese, probably including the great majority of intellectual and other elite groups, seem to believe that Japan's historical-cultural links to China are extremely important. The sense of cultural affinity appears definitely stronger on the Japanese than on the Chinese side. Many Japanese exaggerate the affinity, underplaying basic differences and often projecting images of what they think ought to be rather than what is. Aside from academic specialists on Chinese affairs, or persons who spent many years in China during the Sino-Japanese war, few can speak or read Chinese, despite the fact that the Japanese language uses Chinese ideographs. In a Chinese environment many would probably feel as alien as a Western European visiting Athens, or an American visiting Paris, viewing a culture that is obviously important to his heritage yet indisputably foreign.

The sense of cultural affinity to China has been politically important in Japan, nevertheless, and it has reinforced widespread feelings favoring close relations with China. It has not, however, answered the question "which China" Tokyo should deal with, and not a few Japanese—a minority but an articulate one including some key political leaders—have been pro-Taiwan rather than pro-Peking.

Japanese generally indicate in opinion polls a strong desire for good relations with China, but they also reveal mixed attitudes toward the present Chinese regime[122] (although they are far more favorable than toward the Soviet Union). There is no widespread sense of threat from the Chinese.[123] However, as new generations that have matured in a modern industrial society, and have had little contact with China, have come to the fore, the traditional Japanese sense of cultural affinity with China has begun to decline.

Another factor whose influence has probably already declined is the guilt many older Japanese have felt because of Japan's past aggression against China.[124] Some younger Japanese have a patronizing attitude toward China. Japan's far greater success in economic development has made them feel that their highly developed nation is obviously superior to "backward" China.[125]

Ideology has also shaped the attitudes of many Japanese toward China. Marxism has strongly influenced a large proportion of Japan's intellectuals and students, its labor movement, and key opposition parties. Members of these groups have tended to be pro-Chinese and to admire Peking's revolutionary ethos, even though their versions of Marxism have differed markedly from the Maoist brand. Ironically, most Japanese Communists in recent years have been far more skeptical of Maoist policies than most other leftists, although the splinter party that broke away from the mainstream Communists is, together with certain student groups, the most pro-Maoist.

Even though many Marxist-oriented opposition groups have worked to improve Sino-Japanese relations, this has not created close ideological and political bonds with the Chinese. The "academic Marxism" that has predominated among the Japanese Socialists and intellectuals and the distinctive version of "national communism" that has recently guided the Japanese Communists are both so different from Chinese Maoism that they provide little basis for genuine ideological agreement; in the long run, ideology could just as well lead to political conflict as to political cooperation.

More than counterbalancing all of the pro-Peking factors in Japan today is the fact that Japan is now a highly developed, capitalist, pluralistic, and relatively open society, and a parliamentary democracy. While unique in many respects, it is far more similar to the industrialized Western nations than to the socialist, underdeveloped, authoritarian, and relatively closed society of China. In their recent modernization efforts and economic development the Japanese have looked primarily to the United States for inspiration. Even culturally they now borrow from the West, not China. Japan's younger generation in particular knows the West much better than China. The majority of Japanese recognize these facts, as well as their close economic and security links with the Western nations. Japanese today do not feel toward the Americans the kind of historically rooted cultural affinity that they felt toward the Chinese in the past, but they nevertheless recognize the strength of present links with the West and believe many should be lasting.[126] In the period ahead there could be new strains in relations with the United States as the Japanese assert their independent views, and these could be serious if intense Japanese nationalism is revived, but such trends do not seem likely to create a closer sense of affinity with the Chinese.

In a sense, Japan today is a part of, and yet stands apart from and between, two worlds: the Asian world, in which it is the only highly developed industrial nation, and the developed industrial world encompassing North America and Europe, in which it is the only Asian member. Being part of both, yet not fully belonging to either, creates psychological problems for the Japanese. Subjected to pulls from opposite directions, most Japanese hope they can maintain close, friendly relations with both China and the West. This is what they are now trying to do. Yet if forced to choose, Japanese leaders—at least of the post-World War II kind—would probably opt to maintain close ties with the United States, even if this meant a deterioration of links with China; pragmatic calculations of Japan's concrete interests rather than intangible factors would govern their choice. Conceivably, however, they might adopt a more nationalistic and independent posture, designed to preserve equidistance from both.

In sum, there seems little possibility that general cultural, ideological, or political attitudes will impel Japan to consider close political alignment with China at the expense of its ties with the West. Most Japanese —even the opposition parties—recognize the practical imperatives of maintaining close ties to the West, and Peking's leaders seem to understand this fact.

Domestic Political Factors

Domestic politics have had an important influence on relations between China and Japan, but in different ways and degrees within each country. While the Chinese in recent years have involved themselves deeply in Japanese domestic politics, the Japanese since 1949 have had no direct impact on politics within China's closed society. (In contrast, the Russians intervened in Chinese politics in the 1950s much more than the Chinese did in theirs, and in the prewar period it was the Japanese who intervened politically in China, not the opposite.)

Even though Chinese Communist policy toward Japan has not been significantly influenced by Japanese pressure in recent years, it has been affected in important ways by major domestic political trends in China. Continuing policy disputes in Peking have caused major policy shifts that have directly affected Peking's policy toward Japan. Probably the most striking example of this was China's decision to apply strong economic pressure on Japan in 1958. Peking's definition of its goals and tactics in dealing with Japan has generally fluctuated in accord with China's periods of militance (immediately after 1949, in the late 1950s, and during the Cultural Revolution) and periods of relative pragmatism (the mid-1950s, early 1960s, and early 1970s).

If China should shift to extreme militancy in its overall policies in the period immediately ahead it could conceivably adopt the kind of hard-line policy toward Japan that it pursued in the late 1950s. Many security and economic factors, however, would impose limits on how far even a leftist Communist leadership in China would go in pushing a radical policy toward Japan. And the clear trend toward increased pragmatism shown by Peking's leaders in the months following Mao's death appeared to reduce the possibility of any shift toward increased radicalism.

A speculative but plausible case can be made that Chinese policy toward Japan may have been significantly influenced in recent years by a group of Japanese-trained leaders who played important roles, not in determining the basic direction of policy—a function reserved to the top leaders in the Politburo—but in analyzing specific problems and opportunities, in fine-tuning Peking's tactical line, and in conducting direct dealings with the Japanese. Liao Ch'eng-chih has been the most conspicuous of these "Japan experts" in Peking, but others such as Kuo Mo-jo have probably been important too.[127] Such men have probably tried to use their influence to promote "realistic" approaches, tailored to fit political, economic, and social realities in Japan (they clearly have also played key roles in Chinese attempts to manipulate Japanese politics). As this generation of experts disappears, it is possible that it will be superseded by a new group of Japan specialists composed largely of technocrats, trade specialists, and others whose concerns focus primarily on practical technical and economic matters.

Whatever the influence of internal political factors may be on Chinese policy toward Japan, domestic politics has clearly been a key factor in recent Japanese policy toward China.[128] Since the normalization of Sino-Japanese relations, the "China question" in Japanese politics seems to have been defused to some extent, and China's ability to exert leverage within Japan through antigovernment forces has probably declined. Today, differences within the Liberal Democratic party over China policy may be more important politically than those between the LDP and opposition parties, and Chinese leaders must now pursue their most important goals by dealing with the Japanese government and the conservative establishment. This imposes some real limits on the extent to which they can use Japanese opposition groups manipulatively.

However, issues relating to policy toward China have not been removed from the arena of Japanese politics, as controversy stimulated by the aviation negotiations in 1973–74 and the dispute over the hegemony clause in the proposed friendship treaty have made evident. Many pro-Peking and pro-Taiwan pressures are still exerted on Japanese leaders. And if Peking were to decide to step up pressure on the Japanese government to make concessions on particular issues, it could probably mobilize some support for its positions and activate new debates on China policy within Japan. In sum, there is still no equivalent of bipartisanship in Japan on China policy, and while the China question appears to be less divisive today than it once was, it is certainly not dead.

Yet it does not seem likely that Peking can soon regain the kind of political leverage that it appeared to have in the 1950s and 1960s. Renewed attempts to manipulate Japanese politics to the degree China did then might well arouse Japanese nationalism and provoke a strong counteraction. Few Japanese now see China simply as an aggrieved supplicant for recognition. An increasing number will now view Chinese manipulations in terms of conflicting national interests, and increased Chinese pressure might unite rather than fragment Japanese opinion and increase opposition to China. In the future, both Chinese and Japanese policies will be shaped above all by how the two countries' top leaders perceive their national interests and the most feasible (and least costly) ways to achieve them.

These judgments seem reasonable if the nature of Japan's political leadership remains essentially unchanged. However, some political change in Japan is likely. A variety of economic, social, and demographic, as well as political, trends in recent years have resulted in a steady weakening of the Liberal Democratic party which has ruled Japan since the 1950s. The party is clearly losing the Diet majority it has enjoyed.

The LDP is the only party that has unequivocally supported the existing alliance with the United States as well as the policy of equidistance in dealing with China and the Soviet Union. Even its leaders have favored greater Japanese independence of action, although they have continued to maintain Japan's basically pragmatic, and reactive, "low-posture" approach to foreign policy. Important opposition leaders have argued that Japan should move toward a neutralist posture and should abrogate the U.S.-Japan security treaty. This would obviously have important implications for Japan's relationships with all the other major powers, including China. Logically, a loosening of Japanese-American relations might argue for a strengthening of Japanese-Chinese relations.

Yet, even if erosion of the Liberal Democratic party's position results in loss of its Diet majority, no drastic sudden changes in Japanese policy seem probable. None of the opposition parties seem likely to replace the LDP in this decade, or even to supersede it as the strongest single party, nor is a left-wing coalition likely to displace it soon. The Japanese left remains too fragmented.

As the Liberal Democratic party loses strength, new alignments will probably take shape both within and without that party, but the present ruling establishment, consisting of key elements of the party, bureaucracy, and big business, is likely to retain a predominant position. Possibly there will emerge a Liberal Democratic–led coalition, incorporating middle-of-the-road elements from the Democratic Socialist party or even the right-wing Socialists and the Komeito.

Among many factors that are likely to work against sudden, drastic policy shifts is the relatively strong and stable Japanese bureaucracy which will be a force for continuity, whatever political changes occur. Another is the noticeable, though gradual, change in the attitudes of the opposition party leaders on major policy issues during the past three years. Not only do the Social Democrats, for example, now favor the security treaty, even some Socialists have become notably less hostile toward it, indicating that if they controlled Japan's foreign policy, they would reexamine the treaty but not abrogate it immediately. All the parties, in short, appear to be reassessing their positions in the light of domestic political trends and new international circumstances.

No radical change in Japanese foreign policy seems in prospect, therefore, but adjustments are likely. Within the Liberal Democratic party
itself there has been pressure to modify U.S.-Japan security relationships
without abandoning them, and Japanese desires for greater independence
of action are strong. Conceivably, the trend to accommodate many view-
points could weaken the leadership and make all decision making more
difficult than at present. At worst this could lead to inertia or immobilism.
If this resulted in ineffective government and national frustration it could
eventually create crises resulting in drastic political changes—such as a
revival of nationalism or remilitarization. However, this does not appear
likely in the period immediately ahead.

Even if there is some loosening of Japan's links with the United States,
and a broadening of contact with China, Japan seems likely to continue
through the 1970s both its special security relationship with the United
States and its policy of equidistance toward China and the Soviet Union
(although it might tilt slightly toward China).

From Peking's perspective, all of this will probably argue for continuing its present basic approach toward Japan. As long as its leaders
are essentially pragmatic, and the quadrilateral power balance in Asia
does not change radically, China's policy will probably be based on the
premise that it should pursue its interests by gradually improving its relations with Japan, dealing mainly with established leaders, and that it
should view the security relationship between the United States and
Japan not only as tolerable but as actually desirable as a counterweight
to Moscow. However, Sino-Japanese relations will be complex. Although
in some areas, common or intersecting interests will foster cooperation,
in others there will be friction and strain, and there could be new conflicts, possibly serious ones.

Economic Relations

One of the most important trends fostering closer Sino-Japanese relationships in recent years has been the rapid growth of trade.[129] Although
in the 1960s two-way trade never came close to $1 billion, it approached
that figure in 1971 and it soared to $3.83 billion in 1975.[130] This rapid
rise is traceable to decisions made in Peking. For years Japanese businessmen had pushed for more trade with China but with only limited
success. Then in the early 1970s Peking decided to expand its participa-

tion in the international economy generally and to give economic considerations high priority in its policy toward Japan.

The trade now is of real benefit to both countries. China obtains needed steel and metals, machine tools, vital chemicals including fertilizers, and important machinery including transportation and mining equipment, as well as complete plants, from Japan. The principal Japanese imports from China are textiles, foodstuffs, and raw materials. Clearly, however, the trade is of far greater importance to China than to Japan. The commodities China imports are of fundamental importance to both its industrialization efforts and its agricultural development program; Japan's imports from China are much less critical to its economy. In 1974 the $3.33 billion total of Sino-Japanese trade amounted to only 2.83 percent of Japan's overall trade of $117.6 billion but it was 23.76 percent of China's overall trade of $14 billion.[131]

Japan is now China's largest trading partner by a large margin and it is Peking's most important external source for advanced technology and capital goods. The prototype, "turn key" plants Peking is purchasing are of special importance for China's development. In some fields, such as petrochemicals, Peking is developing entirely new industries with plants imported from Japan, Europe, and the United States. About one-half of China's $2.5 billion contracts in 1973–74 for foreign plants, machinery, and equipment was for complete plants, and Japan was the largest single supplier.[132] Imports of Japanese chemical fertilizers are also extremely important to China's agricultural programs. Moreover, Japan has become a major source of credits since China began accepting medium-term foreign credits—generally five years at 6 percent and in the form of "extended payment agreements"—to finance a portion of its imports.

Geographical proximity, low prices, and long and close historical contact and familiarity with Japanese trading practices are important factors that encourage China to expand its trade with Japan. So too does Japan's flexibility in responding to China's needs. And Japan's military weakness probably makes the Chinese less concerned about the danger of political influence than in their dealings with some other countries. Clearly, also, China believes that increased trade is important to strengthen its political ties with Japan. The Japanese government likewise sees trade as politically beneficial. And even though China trade is a tiny fraction of Japan's total trade and is not critical to the Japanese economy, Tokyo views it as important. *All* trade is important for the

Japanese, and many businessmen still hope for a great increase in Sino-Japanese trade. For certain industries, including some of Japan's largest, it is already quite important. Recently, China has been Japan's second largest foreign market for iron and steel, and in some years has purchased about 60 percent of Japan's chemical fertilizer exports.[133] A growing number of Japanese enterprises have a strong vested interest in trade with China, therefore. Theoretically, this might give Peking a new lever to exert political influence in Japan. However, since the trade is now more important to China than to Japan, manipulating it for political purposes would probably be counterproductive from Peking's viewpoint.

Sino-Japanese trade will almost certainly continue to grow, but the rate of growth is likely to be lower than in the recent past. In 1973 and 1974, while China's total foreign trade rose by 67 percent and 43 percent, its trade with Japan increased by 83 percent and 64.3 percent.[134] In the period ahead, the rate of growth in overall trade will probably be less dramatic, and the rise in Sino-Japanese trade is not likely to exceed the overall rate significantly. Nevertheless, some Japanese analysts estimate that by 1980 China's foreign trade could reach $23 billion and that the Japanese share could be 20–25 percent or between $4.6 billion and $5.8 billion (not counting possible price rises).[135]

China's petroleum could become an extremely important factor in its trade with Japan. For more than a decade, up to 1976, China's oil output increased at a rate averaging over 20 percent a year, and its oil exports to Japan rose from 1 million tons in 1973 to about 8 million tons in 1975. Chinese officials have indicated to the Japanese that they hope to be able to produce about 400 million tons of petroleum a year by 1980 and to export as much as 40 million to 50 million to Japan.[136] Such a rise would give Sino-Japanese trade a big boost. In the past, China's limited export capacity has been a fundamental factor limiting its trade. If China's oil exports increase rapidly, not only would China's overall trade prospects change significantly, but the importance of China trade to Japan would substantially increase. (According to some estimates, 50 million tons might meet one-tenth to one-sixth of Japan's need for oil imports in 1980.) However, the most optimistic forecasts may be unrealistic. In 1976 the rate of increase both in China's petroleum output and in its oil exports dropped significantly.[137]

China's exports to Japan of labor-intensive, low-technology, light manufactured goods will probably continue to rise gradually. In some respects the Chinese and Japanese economies are complementary and should remain so for many years. Both can benefit greatly from the exchange of Chinese light manufactures and raw materials for Japanese advanced technology and heavy manufactures.

There are clearly limits, however, to how far the development of closer Sino-Japanese economic ties can go. China will almost certainly bar direct investments and may continue to reject Japanese proposals for joint projects. China's limited export capabilities will continue to restrict trade even if oil exports rise significantly. And even if the Chinese finance some imports with credits, they will probably set limits to their indebtedness; in a few years the need to repay past credits will impose new constraints on imports.

Peking will probably not conduct a much larger share of its trade than at present with Japan, to avoid developing a new relationship of dependency. If Japan's share were to become "too large" (say, above one-third of total trade) the Chinese would probably begin to pull back and redirect some of the trade elsewhere. On its side, the Japanese government will also be wary of becoming dependent on China for particular commodities (for example, purchasing 15 or so percent of Japan's oil imports from China might be acceptable, but a significantly larger figure might not be). The Japanese may also wish to avoid excessive dependence on the China market for sales of commodities such as steel.

Japan, China, and Southeast Asia

While bilateral trade should in general strengthen ties between China and Japan in the period ahead, their economic activity as well as political interests elsewhere in Asia could strain them. There is an obvious potential for competition and conflict between the two countries in Southeast Asia, as well as in such traditional areas of Sino-Japanese conflict as Korea and Taiwan.[138]

The Chinese have given conflicting hints about their views concerning Japan's economic role in Southeast Asia. In January 1973 Chou Enlai stated to Takeo Kimura that "if Japan is to pursue profits too intensively, this will lead to 'exploitation' and cause repulsion among peoples in these areas.... (while laughing) If this is to happen, this will be what China is waiting for."[139] However, Yasuhiro Nakasone reported at about the same time that Chou had told him that in its aid to underdeveloped countries China would stress agriculture and light industries while Japan would concentrate on heavy industrial materials, implying a tacit understanding involving a division of function. Nakasone's conclusion was that "China and Japan will probably not come into conflict."[140]

An American specialist on Asian affairs who has studied Japan's economic role in Asia argues that a Sino-Japanese economic partnership in Asia is quite possible. He quotes influential Japanese who support his views. For example, Shingo Moriyama, director of the Bangkok office of the Japan External Trade Organization, is quoted as saying: "We in Japan used to think of China as a threat to our interests overseas. . . . But we have a better understanding of China now. . . . It is necessary and possible for China and Japan to adopt coordinated policies and create a bloc of our own in Asia."[141] An influential Japanese businessman is reported to have said: "There is room enough for both of us. . . . China will have to expand its trade with its Asian neighbors eventually, but we can avoid damaging competition. We are not competing for natural resources. There is no reason why we should have serious conflict politically if we are able to harmonize our economic interests. We will phase out our light industrial exports to make room for them and concentrate on high-technology heavy industry."[142]

Other knowledgeable Japanese, however, are concerned about the possibility of growing competition in the future. And Russian observers alternately warn against economic collusion between the Chinese and Japanese in the short run and predict intense competition and conflict in the long run.

At present there is not much of a contest, economically. Japan's economic dominance in Southeast Asia is growing, while China's role in the region is still very limited in economic terms.

In the past decade, as Japan's total economic growth and foreign trade have skyrocketed, its trade with Southeast Asia, which consists essentially of an exchange of manufactured goods, both heavy and light, for Southeast Asian raw materials, has steadily increased. Whereas in 1964 the two-way trade totaled about $1.6 billion, in 1970 it reached $3.97 billion, by 1972 it had jumped to around $5.3 billion,[143] and it has continued to rise. In most recent years, Japan has had an export surplus in this trade.

By 1972 Japan was the largest trading partner of all Southeast Asian countries except those in the Indochina area. In many instances, its domination of other nations' import markets was overwhelming—over 40 percent of the Philippines', about 35 percent of Thailand's, and over 25 percent of Indonesia's.[144] Southeast Asian leaders have become increasingly concerned about their trade dependency on Japan.

Japan's trade dominance has been paralleled by increased investment and aid. Its global foreign investment rose from under $1 billion in 1965 to almost $7 billion in 1972 and about $10 billion in 1974.[145] Southeast Asia, only one of many regions of Japanese interest, by early 1973 had received a total of at least $1 billion in Japanese investment; some observers put the figure, including disguised or indirect investments, at as much as three times the official figure.[146]

Foreign aid has also contributed to Japan's increasing influence. By 1973 the flow of all Japanese capital to underdeveloped nations reached an annual level of close to 1 percent of gross national product—over $4 billion, about $1 billion of which was government development aid and the remainder private capital.[147] A significant portion of the aid has gone to Southeast Asian nations, and Japan, even more than most nations, has tended to link its aid and investments to trade, thereby strengthening its overall economic position in the region.

Southeast Asia has not become more important, relative to other areas, to Japan, in recent years, however. On the contrary, in Japan's total trade Southeast Asia's importance has declined and is expected to keep declining.[148] But for Southeast Asian nations, Japan's relative importance has steadily risen.

The contrast presented by China's ties with Southeast Asia is striking.[149] Its total two-way trade with the region in 1972 was only $420 million, about 8 percent of Japan's trade with Southeast Asia. Although by 1974 the figure had risen, it was still only $1 billion. Moreover, China had no investments in the area, and its aid—outside of Indochina—has been minimal, consisting of a small amount of assistance to Burma and, in earlier years, Indonesia.

The volume of trade—primarily in Chinese foodstuffs and light manufactures (with the latter growing in importance) and Southeast Asian raw materials (of which rubber is particularly important)—increased in the decade from 1959 through 1969 by about one-half, and then from 1970 through 1973 it roughly tripled from $270 million to $825 million, partly due to price increases. Yet in relation to China's total trade, it has not grown significantly; it was 8–9 percent in 1967–69, 6 percent in 1971, 7 percent in 1972, and 8 percent in 1973. There is a heavy imbalance, moreover; the Chinese buy remarkably little from Southeast Asia. In 1972, while China's exports to the area totaled $330 million, its imports were only $90 million. Actually, this discrepancy has given the trade its principal economic significance from Peking's point of view; China earns a sizable amount of hard currency from trade with Southeast Asia (as it does to an even greater extent from trade with Hong Kong and Macao) which it uses to finance imports from the industrialized countries.

Economic competition between China and Japan in Southeast Asia would obviously increase if China decides to make a major effort to step up its trade with the area, in order to earn more foreign exchange and obtain greater quantities of needed raw materials, or to use it for political reasons. The Chinese could probably expand their exports of labor-intensive light manufactures and certain types of machinery and machine tools. If they do, Sino-Japanese trade competition would increase, but not necessarily by very much. Conceivably, there might be a tacit division of functions, with Japan stressing exports of capital-intensive and high-technology commodities and China exporting mainly low-cost, labor-intensive manufactures. The Japanese are already shifting their exports in this direction. In addition, their investments are spurring the development in Southeast Asia of local light industries which are closely linked to Japan because they rely on semi-processed Japanese products. This creates a strong foundation for the continuing growth of Japan's trade. The main competitors of the Japanese for markets in the area are likely to be the United States and European nations. If China's exports of light manufactures to Southeast Asia increase, they will, to an increasing degree, be competing not primarily with Japan's but with the output of the local light industries that are now being developed within the Southeast Asian nations themselves as well as with the export industries of Korea, Taiwan, and Hong Kong, many of which also have varied Japanese involvements.

The trade competition between China and Japan is not likely soon to develop into an equal economic contest, but it could stimulate a competition for political influence. Japan so far has maintained a low posture, politically, in Southeast Asia and has avoided deliberately trying to translate its economic power into political influence. Yet its political influence has unquestionably increased, and its trade, investment, and aid have had a large political impact in the region—causing a strong political reaction in some countries. Southeast Asian leaders have complained bitterly that many Japanese businessmen are parochial in their outlook and unresponsive to local needs. Moreover, in their dealings with local business-men and officials, the Japanese have inevitably influenced local politics.[150] They are sometimes charged with reinforcing corruption and antidemo-cratic trends and contributing to the polarization of local political forces.

Many Southeast Asians are apprehensive that in time Japan will overwhelm the region economically. As a result, some political backlash —like the demonstrations during 1973–74 when Tanaka visited Thailand and Indonesia—is already apparent. If anti-Japanese nationalism grows, local politicians of various kinds could try to exploit it for their own purposes. Many Japanese leaders are fully aware of these problems, and the dangers they pose, and they have urged self-restraint and tried to promote corrective measures on the part of both the Japanese govern-ment and Japanese business, but the problems persist.

To date, Peking appears to have taken a remarkably relaxed view of Japan's growing economic influence in the region and has made no obvi-ous effort to exacerbate or exploit Southeast Asian anxieties. This for-bearance could continue as long as the Chinese put high priority on maintaining their friendly relations with Japan as part of a broad policy aimed at counterbalancing Soviet influence. However, if the basic situa-tion in Asia were to change, the Chinese could easily switch to a more competitive posture in Southeast Asia and intensify their competition with the Japanese.[151] Their main instruments for influence would be political. They could certainly attempt to exploit existing economic tension, however. One obvious strategy would be to try to foment anti-Japanese nationalism in the region, to tar Japan with the brush of neo-colonialism, and to encourage Southeast Asian political groups and gov-ernments to resist its growing economic influence. Peking could also encourage local opposition groups to attack the existing Southeast Asian regimes for their "subservience to Japan." And it might exert increased pressure on leading businessmen, many of whom are Overseas Chinese, to reduce their links with Japan. This could involve political costs for Peking, and it might or might not succeed, but it would certainly com-plicate Japan's problems.

Intense Sino-Japanese competition does not seem likely soon in South-east Asia, however, unless relations between China and Japan begin to deteriorate over other issues, or unless Japan moves overtly to translate its economic dominance in Southeast Asia into increased political, or even military, influence. Chinese leaders will probably watch Japanese activi-ties in the region with some unease, remembering Japan's pre-World

War II slogans calling for a Greater East Asian Co-Prosperity Sphere, but they, like the Japanese, will try to avoid overt, hostile competition, since both countries today give less priority to the problems they face in Southeast Asia than to their big-power relationships elsewhere.

Japan, China, and Northeast Asia

If serious tension does arise between China and Japan in the period immediately ahead, problems in Northeast Asia are more likely to be the cause than competition in Southeast Asia. Conflicts of interest in this region have created many unresolved problems relating to the Tiao-yu-t'ai/Senkaku Islands, ocean resources, Korea, and Taiwan. Since 1972 both sides have deemphasized these problems in order to foster improved overall relations, but it is uncertain how long solutions to some of the problems can be deferred. The future approach of both sides to the problems will depend on their basic flexibility and willingness to compromise, which will be greatly influenced both by the general state of their bilateral relations and by the overall regional situation.

The Tiao-yu-t'ai Islands

One unresolved territorial dispute complicates relations between China and Japan. It concerns the Tiao-yu-t'ai or Senkaku Islands,[152] a small cluster of five uninhabited islands north of Taiwan and west of Okinawa, which were largely ignored until geological surveys in the 1960s indicated that the area might have large undersea oil deposits. The islands then became a focus of intense interest in Tokyo and Peking (as well as in Taipei). (An American citizen also got into the act, asserting that an imperial edict in 1893 had granted title to three of the islands to her Chinese ancestor.)

The Chinese claim that these islands have been theirs since at least the sixteenth century, that they are geographically and legally a part of the island complex belonging to Taiwan Province, and that, although Japan took possession of the islands at the end of the Sino-Japanese war in 1895, legal rights to them were returned to China after World War II, along with Taiwan, as a result of the Potsdam agreement and subsequent Allied acts.[153] The Japanese government bases its claim to sovereignty on contacts made by an 1884 Japanese expedition, and on the fact that in 1895 Tokyo approved their annexation by Okinawa Prefecture, which thereafter administered them.[154] Although the United States assumed control of the islands after World War II, the Japanese assert that they retained residual sovereignty over them, as over all of the Ryukyus, and recovered full sovereignty when the Ryukyus were returned to Japan. The United States, adopting a noncommittal position, stated that it was returning "administrative rights" to Japan, but that it had no definite position regarding sovereignty over the islands, and that the parties directly concerned would have to resolve the problem. The fact that the United States had administered the Senkakus along with Okinawa tended to bolster Japan's claims, however.

Both the Chinese and the Japanese have put forward serious arguments, including legal ones, to bolster their claims.[155] But the issue is not likely to be settled on the basis of these arguments. The problem now is essentially political and economic. Theoretically, the two countries could submit the case to international arbitration, but there is little basis for believing that either—but especially Peking—would consider doing so. Conceivably, one side could simply accept the claims of the other, if it concluded that crucial security interests demanded quick resolution of the dispute. But this too seems unlikely in the near future. Territorial issues tend to assume an exaggerated political importance because they involve national prestige and face. In this case the abandonment of territory is made doubly difficult by the possibility that rich oil deposits may be located in the area. The Nationalists' claim to the islands adds a serious complication, although ultimately Peking and Tokyo are likely to be the most important actors in the dispute.

Recently, both sides appear to have concluded that the problem should be temporarily laid aside. But the Japanese may have difficulty maintaining a posture of patient waiting, especially if the reports of large oil deposits are confirmed. The Japanese now have administrative control of the islands, and over time they may feel impelled to exercise their control more actively. Clearly, Japan's need for oil argues for energetic exploitation of any resources accessible to it. In contrast, the Chinese, with large oil reserves inside China and near its coast, can more easily afford to sit and wait.

The Japanese are forgoing important economic opportunities at present to avoid precipitating a crisis. In time, however, Tokyo may feel under pressure domestically to pursue a more active policy aimed at a solution that would permit development of oil resources in the area. It could try to negotiate with China and offer some quid pro quo for Chinese concessions. Tokyo might, for example, offer to assist the Chinese in other oil development, or propose joint development of this and other areas, on a basis similar to that agreed upon with the Koreans. At some point, however, if there is no prospect of a solution, the Japanese could simply decide to go ahead with active exploration on their own; if so, Peking would certainly protest, and it might try to block Japanese efforts. Overall Sino-Japanese relations would inevitably be affected adversely. It is also conceivable that Peking could eventually precipitate a crisis by sending vessels into the area to try to assert Chinese claims.

None of these possibilities seems imminent. However, the dispute remains a source of irritation and potential conflict. Clearly, a compromise of some sort is desirable. Joint development of the oil reserves, even without resolution of the legal conflict, would help to stabilize the region and improve Sino-Japanese relations. Conversely, if either side were to try to force the issue, or if Sino-Japanese relations were to deteriorate for other reasons, the Tiao-yu-t'ai Islands could become a focus of active dispute.

The Oceans in East Asia

China and Japan also differ, for understandable reasons, in their basic approach to a wide range of issues concerning the law of the sea that directly affect their economic, political, and security interests. The difficulty of resolving these differences is compounded by the lack of success in recent international efforts to agree on comprehensive new laws of the sea.

Though China has not yet clarified its position on many critical issues, in general it has supported proposals made by Third World nations designed to maximize coastal nations' areas of control and to restrict the freedom of action of the major fishing and maritime nations.[156] It has, for example, not only endorsed the idea of a two-hundred-mile economic zone, but also supported the arguments of those favoring full sovereignty and control by coastal states over this zone. Japan initially opposed and resisted all such proposals, which would greatly restrict its freedom of action. When it became clear that international acceptance of two-hundred-mile economic zones was likely, the Japanese accepted the idea, but they still oppose granting unlimited rights in these zones to coastal states. The continuing uncertainty about the outcome of efforts to codify the law of the sea leaves a wide range of questions unanswered, which for the moment affects Japan's interests more adversely than

China's. The Japanese do not like the restricted fishing and security zones that China has defined along its coast, extending as far as fifty miles. They are also very seriously concerned about what their rights will be to exploit the resources of the continental shelf and seabed in the East China Sea.[157] China's position on this remains unclear, probably deliberately so. While it supports the concept of two-hundred-mile economic zones, it has hinted that it could base its own claims on the theory of the "natural prolongation" of the continental shelf. If it were to do the latter, it theoretically might insist on China's exclusive right to exploit oil and other resources up to the so-called Okinawa trough which lies close to Japan's coast. If, however, the UN Law of the Sea Conference finally approves of two-hundred-mile zones, this would seem to imply, logically, that the jurisdictional line between China and its neighbors should be drawn along a median line in the ocean between them.

Two-hundred-mile zones will work against Japan's fishing interests, but a median-line settlement of shelf and seabed claims will work in its favor, giving Japan the right to exploit oil resources in the East China Sea. In the long run this could conceivably be more important to Japan than access to fishing areas, although obviously both will affect its economic interests significantly.

These issues pose problems that will not be easy to resolve. China and Japan will both find themselves under pressure to respond to competing domestic interests as well as to compromise with neighboring nations. The problems are greatly complicated by the fact that North and South Korea and Taiwan are also involved and should participate or acquiesce in the solutions to many of the problems. China's protests, including one asserting that Japan's 1973 agreement with South Korea on joint oil development is "illegal" and "null and void" and that "division of jurisdiction" must be "decided by countries concerned through consultations on an equal footing,"[158] have demonstrated how the Chinese can create problems for Japan even in its relations with other nations in the area over ocean issues.

As with the Tiao-yu-t'ai/Senkaku problem, Japan may feel a greater sense of economic urgency than China about finding solutions for these issues. In theory, multilateral agreements involving all the claimants would be desirable, but the multiplicity of claimants, and the open hostility between some of them, make such agreements difficult to conceive at present. Parallel bilateral agreements would be an alternative. But

China's attitude makes even this solution seem unpromising. The intrinsic complexity of the issues will make them difficult to resolve even if international agreement is reached on a new law-of-the-sea code.

The Chinese and Japanese may be compelled eventually to devise a series of piecemeal compromises, or working arrangements, agreed to either formally or tacitly. In some respects, it will be in the interests of both to work toward this end. Yet basic differences between the interests and approaches of the two countries will continue. They will inevitably create friction, and at worst they could lead to open clashes that would affect their overall relations very adversely.

The salience of these ocean problems probably will be determined by broader political and security considerations, however. As long as Peking and Tokyo give priority to the need for a friendly relationship, both will doubtless try to avoid exacerbating the conflict inherent in the situation. But if overall relations were to deteriorate, conflict over these issues could become increasingly serious and have far-reaching effects.

Taiwan and Korea

For much of the past century, Taiwan and Korea have been critical focuses for conflict between China and Japan.[159] A key question for the future is whether stability can be achieved and maintained in both areas on a basis tolerable to both Peking and Tokyo.

There are basic differences in Chinese and Japanese views on the importance of both Taiwan and Korea. Peking regards Taiwan as an unliberated province, albeit a unique one because of its history and geography. It still feels that liberation of the island is an important national goal. It regards Korea as an independent, though still divided, nation with special historical and strategic ties to China, which are very important even though they are qualitatively different and less important than Taiwan's links to China. Japan views both of these former colonies as areas of special strategic and economic significance for Japan. It regards Korea, especially, as vitally important to Japan's security. And it has a large economic stake in both Korea and Taiwan.

As Peking's leaders look back on China's interaction with the outside world from the nineteenth century on, they see Taiwan and Korea as focal points of virtually continuous competition and conflict with foreign powers. Japan annexed Taiwan in 1895 and Korea in 1910, and it used both as springboards for further aggression. The persistence of historical images was well illustrated by Peking's bitter accusation in 1950 that Washington was following the path of past Japanese aggressors in its intervention in both Korea and Taiwan.

Today Peking's leaders still view Korea as an arena where big-power competition could ignite conflicts threatening to China. It was, after all, from Korea that Japan launched invasions against Manchuria, and from which, as Peking sees it, U.S. forces posed a threat to China as well as to North Korea in the 1950s. This past history appears to have convinced China's leaders that it is essential to maintain North Korea as a buffer state and to prevent control of it by any regime hostile to China. They would obviously like also to see political regimes on the peninsula friendly to China.

Peking views Taiwan primarily in irredentist terms. In the prewar period, when the island was still under Japanese rule, Mao Tse-tung apparently was willing to accept Taiwan's independence, but during the war, recovery of the island became an important Chinese national goal, and since 1949 the liberation of Taiwan has been high on Peking's list of unfulfilled national aims. The issue became critical from the Chinese Communist point of view both because the Nationalist regime which they overthrew on the mainland survived there and because American support of the Nationalists symbolized continuing foreign intervention in Chinese affairs. Since 1949 they have not deviated, in principle, from their stated goal of recovering control of Taiwan. Until recently, moreover, they persistently tried to end all of the Nationalists' ties with Japan and the United States, the foreign nations most involved in the area.

Japan, too, regards both Korea and Taiwan in a very special light. For half a century these were core areas of Japan's empire, where thousands of Japanese lived and worked, and Japan profited greatly from them. The Japanese also had a large cultural and political impact on both. Strong historical and sentimental ties as well as economic and security interests led to Japan's gradual but steady reinvolvement in both areas after World War II as Japan rebuilt its economy and increased its activities abroad.

Throughout the 1950s and most of the 1960s, when Peking regarded Japan primarily as a tool of, and military base for, a hostile United States, it viewed Japan's relationship with Korea and Taiwan as an extension of American policy. The Chinese tried to check the growth of Japan's influence and to encourage divisions between the Japanese and Americans on issues relating to both areas.

Their attitudes began to change in the late 1960s as they became increasingly worried about a Soviet threat, a possible reduction in the U.S. military presence in Asia, and Japan's reemergence as an independent political and economic factor in the region. The Chinese became particularly concerned, after the signing of the Nixon-Sato communiqué in 1969, that Japan might again become a major independent military force in the area and try to fill any vacuum created by the lessening of the U.S. role. In the communiqué the Japanese government stated that it regarded "the security of Korea" to be "essential to Japan's own security," and "the maintenance of peace and security in the Taiwan area" as a "most important factor for the security of Japan." This obviously disturbed Peking, as did Japan's rapidly growing economic involvement in Taiwan and Korea.

It is highly likely that one motive for Peking's decision to move so rapidly toward normalization of relations with Japan in 1971–72 was its desire to prevent Tokyo from developing a predominant influence over Taiwan and Korea. To induce Tokyo to cut formal diplomatic ties with Taipei, however, the Chinese had to adopt a tolerant position on Japan's economic relations with Taiwan.

The present modus vivendi between China and Japan concerning Taiwan is based on a conscious decision by both sides to set aside some difficult political issues and to tolerate deliberate ambiguity: Tokyo now acknowledges that Taiwan *should* be a part of China, but not that it *is*. It deals diplomatically with the People's Republic of China as the sole legal government of China, but has maintained quasi-diplomatic, "nonofficial" ties with Taiwan. In effect, Japan, like the United States, has promised not to encourage moves toward independence on the part of Taiwan (this is important, since Tokyo was formerly a major base for Taiwanese independence movement leaders), but it is apparent that the dominant leaders in Tokyo believe that de facto separation is likely to continue for a long time, and most of them hope this will be the case.

Present security relationships in the area are based on the willingness of both Peking and Tokyo to accept continuing ambiguity. The Japanese have not explicitly renounced the statement in the Nixon-Sato communiqué about the importance of Taiwan to Japan's security. In fact, Foreign Minister Ohira reportedly said in late 1972 that they had no intention of doing so.[160] Moreover, the U.S.-Japan security treaty grants the United States the use of bases in Japan for the purpose of "maintenance of international peace and security in the Far East."[161] In theory this gives the Americans the right to use such bases to fulfill their defense commitment to Taiwan. Actually, because of public opposition the Japanese government might find it very difficult to grant this right. It obviously hopes that it will never be asked to do so. In late 1972, Tanaka stated that since the United States operates "on the premise that China will not resort to armed force against Taiwan" there is "no possibility of such a situation arising."[162] Subsequently, the Japanese government asserted that "the possibility of armed conflict arising has disappeared."[163] Yet in debate in the Diet, Tanaka said that "the Taiwan area" was still considered part of the "Far East," to which the security treaty applies. The potential for misunderstandings and problems in this situation is obvious.

Because of these ambiguities, continuation of the present situation will depend fundamentally on Peking's willingness to forgo the use of force or even major military threats against Taiwan. While it seems likely to exercise restraint, one cannot exclude the possibility of a switch in Chinese policy resulting in renewed pressure. Even if it did not contemplate the actual use of force, Peking conceivably might exert new pressure for political reasons, to force difficult decisions on both Japan and the United States on the key unresolved issues. If it did, this would pose serious new dilemmas for Tokyo in its relations not only with Peking and Taipei but also with Washington.

The expanding economic relationship between Japan and Taiwan must also trouble Peking's leaders. Japanese trade with and investment in the island have soared to the point where economically the island is becoming increasingly dependent on Japan. Until recently, Japan's trade with Taiwan (whose population is roughly 2 percent that of the People's Republic's) consistently surpassed trade with all of mainland China. In 1973 Japan's Taiwan trade exceeded $2.2 billion (about $1.4 billion in exports to Taiwan and about $800 million in imports),[164] and in 1974 it was close to $3 billion.[165]

Japan's investment in Taiwan has also grown rapidly. By the end of 1972, overt direct investment there totaled over $100 million, and some estimates of the real total, including disguised or indirect investment, are as high as $650 million.[166] Through technical and licensing links, Japan's role both in Taiwan's internal industrial development and in its trade with third countries has also become enormous (by late 1972 there were more than five hundred link-ups between Japanese and Taiwanese enterprises).[167] Since 1972, because of the importance it has placed on Sino-Japanese relations, Peking has not tried to reverse these trends, even though Tokyo's trade and investments clearly have strengthened Taiwan's economic viability and ability to remain separate from China. Taiwan has become so closely linked to the Japanese economy that it would be difficult for Taiwan and Japan to disentangle their interests.

For the Japanese, as little change as possible in Taiwan's situation would be desirable. A few rightists would favor an independent Taiwan, but the government and the majority of the public probably favor continuation of the existing de facto separation. Japan might accept without too much difficulty a peaceful and gradual reunification of Taiwan with the mainland, if this eventually occurs. However, it would find it very difficult to accept any violent or sudden change that sacrificed Japan's economic stake in the island's economy, or turned Taiwan into a strongly armed military base for Chinese Communist forces which could pose new dangers to Japan's security.

Whether the Taiwan issue will seriously complicate Sino-Japanese relations in the period ahead will depend above all on the Chinese Communists' tactics in working toward their goal of reunification. If Peking continues its recent approach, stressing gradualism and reliance on nonviolent methods, this may prevent Taiwan from becoming a serious issue in Sino-Japanese relations again. However, if this approach fails to draw Taiwan toward reunification, the long-term trend could be toward permanent separation and increasingly close economic links between Taiwan and Japan. A shift by Peking to a more militant approach involving open threats, or even intimidating political and economic pressure, would almost immediately create serious problems in Sino-Japanese relations. Peking will continue to confront hard choices in its policy toward Taiwan, therefore, and will have to consider carefully how Japan might react to various Chinese policies. As long as Peking gives high priority to good relations with Tokyo, this will tend to inhibit it from making overt threats to Taiwan. However, excessive Japanese political involvement in and influence on Taiwan might provoke the leaders in Peking eventually to consider more militant policies. Besides the adverse effects on Sino-Japanese relations, this would create new U.S.-Japanese strains and it could affect the entire equilibrium in East Asia adversely.

As in the case of Taiwan, the Chinese and the Japanese have differing attitudes toward and conflicting interest in Korea, but recent trends have made the issues somewhat less salient and disturbing to Peking and Tokyo than they once were. Nevertheless Korea, like Taiwan, remains an area of potential Sino-Japanese conflict.

Because it regards Korea as an area of great importance to its security interests, China strongly supports its North Korean ally. However, because its priority goal today is to strengthen counterweights against the Soviet Union, Peking now places greater stress on preserving the present situation than on pressing for change. It supports most of North Korea's political proposals, but it emphasizes the need to achieve them peacefully. Privately, during 1972–73, Peking indicated that it was not as eager as its public statements indicated for a total American military disengagement from the peninsula.[168] Chinese leaders probably are still tolerant of the U.S. military presence, though they no longer say so.

Because of its preoccupation with the Soviet Union, Peking is now remarkably tolerant of Japan's growing role in Korea, but it probably disapproves, in a fundamental sense, of the huge Japanese economic involvement in the South, and may see in it new dangers of neocolonialist control. However, for the present China is not allowing this to complicate its relations with Japan.

Japanese interests in Korea are even more substantial than in Taiwan. Though not all Japanese today view Korea as "the dagger" pointed at Japan, many still do, and key political and governmental figures believe that Japanese security requires that the peninsula not come under the control of a hostile regime. The Nixon-Sato communiqué was consistent with this view. And during 1975–76 Japanese leaders publicly emphasized that stability in Korea was still regarded as basic to Japan's security.[169]

Economically, Japan's involvement has grown rapidly, especially since 1965 when relations with South Korea were normalized. By 1972 Japan's exports to South Korea totaled close to $1 billion; outstanding Japanese government loans amounted to over $200 million and commercial loans probably to more than $500 million. Publicly known direct investment in Korea by Japanese exceeded $128 million and direct and indirect investment may have totaled as much as $775 million.[170] Hundreds of South Korean enterprises have been linked directly to Japan through varied and complicated arrangements, and thousands of Japanese businessmen are involved in projects in Korea. Although mutually beneficial, these ties also create major problems. The combination of a huge Japanese economic stake, Korean fear of being economically overwhelmed by Japan, Japanese businessmen's insensitivity in dealing with Koreans, and the Koreans' pride and nationalistic resentment of the Japanese has created serious tensions. In 1973–74 they exploded and created severe strains between Tokyo and Seoul. Despite the decline of tension since then, its causes have not been removed.

The Korean peninsula is a dangerous conflict zone not only because of the intense hostility between the two Korean governments but also because of the deep involvement of the major powers. Military conflict, or even increased instability, would have far-reaching effects on relations among all the powers involved. New crises in Korea would inevitably have extremely adverse effects on Sino-Japanese relations, reversing recent trends. A new Korean war could destroy the existing regional equilibrium. It might well impel Japan to undertake major rearmament, which would fundamentally change the entire situation in Northeast Asia. Sino-Japanese relations would doubtless then move toward increasing conflict rather than compromise and détente.

Security Issues

The crucial determinant of the basic policies of China and Japan toward each other in the period ahead will be security. Their relationship will be shaped not only by the perceptions each has of the possibility of military threats from the other but also by the calculations each makes of the effects of the general big-power balance on their security.[171]

The importance of security considerations in determining Sino-Japanese relations during the past quarter century may not be as self-evident as in the case of Sino-Soviet or Sino-American relationships. During this period, neither has feared any immediate, direct threat from the other. The Chinese have known that since Japan's defeat in World War II it has lacked offensive military capabilities. The Japanese, though wary of China's military progress, have generally not shared the view, held first by the Americans and then by the Russians, that China has posed immediate and serious threats to its neighbors. Tokyo has recognized that a large expanse of water separates China from Japan, that the Chinese have lacked strong naval or amphibious forces, and that Peking has been preoccupied with the threats it has perceived from the Americans or the Russians. Nevertheless, both Peking and Tokyo have been uneasy about the other's close links to another power that has appeared threatening, and each has recognized that the other could itself pose serious military threats in the future.

Chinese policy was shaped throughout the 1950s and 1960s by Peking's perception of Japan as a base for American power which the Chinese at that time saw as the principal immediate threat to them, and one of Peking's basic aims was to weaken Japanese-American ties. In contrast, since Chinese leaders have given priority to the Soviet threat they have viewed their relations with Japan—linked to the United States—as necessary to create a counterweight to Soviet power. However, there is little doubt that China's present view of Japan is relatively benign in large part because Japan itself is still militarily weak. It could change rapidly if the Japanese embarked on major remilitarization.

The Japanese, throughout the 1950s and 1960s, regarded the Soviet Union rather than China as the main potential threat to their security, and, while gradually rebuilding a conventional defense capability of their own, they relied primarily on U.S. nuclear and naval power for protection. Although they could not ignore the possibility of future threats from China, and showed concern over China's development of nuclear weapons and missiles, when both Sino-Japanese and Sino-American relations rapidly improved during 1971–72, the possibility of a Chinese threat seemed increasingly remote. Today, Japan's primary security concerns focus even more clearly than before on the Soviet Union, in part because of increasing Russian naval activity in Asian waters.

Tokyo can be relatively relaxed at present about China because of the security provided to Japan by its treaty with the United States and the restraints imposed on China by the Sino-Soviet split. Japanese attitudes and policies could change if either of these factors changed.

Peking can look favorably on Japanese policies today not only because Tokyo is linked to the United States rather than to the Soviet Union but also because its military establishment is limited in size and wholly non-nuclear and defensive, and lacks the capability either to threaten China or to project Japanese power to other Asian areas such as Korea, Taiwan, or Southeast Asia. If there were any dramatic increase in Japanese military capabilities, or if Tokyo began to assume any regional military roles, Peking's attitudes and policies would undoubtedly change. In theory a Japan with no U.S. security guarantees might remain militarily weak and either adopt a neutralist stance or develop closer ties with China. But Peking probably fears that it would be more likely to remilitarize or accommodate to the Soviet Union. It is clearly in China's interest to pursue policies that minimize the danger of these possibilities.

Even though China now endorses the U.S.-Japan security relationship, it would probably be disturbed if the ties were greatly strengthened, especially if Japan were to assume regional military responsibilities with U.S. encouragement. From 1969 to 1971 the Chinese appeared genuinely disturbed about such a possibility, and they will undoutedly remain alert to any sign that it might occur in the future. In sum, while Peking seems relatively well satisfied with Japan's present security policies, it probably continues to be uneasy about the future and is more ambivalent than it appears to be about the development of Japan's defense establishment.

Today, Japan is unique among the major powers. Its postwar constitution renounces war and contains provisions prohibiting the maintenance of land, sea, and air forces.[172] Strong pacifist feelings, which are a legacy of its defeat in 1945, reinforce these constitutional barriers to major remilitarization, and Japan's experience as the victim of atomic weapons has resulted in a deep-rooted public "nuclear allergy" which creates strong opposition both to Japan's acquisition of nuclear weapons and to the introduction of such weapons into Japan by the United States.

Yet, despite all these limiting factors, Japan has gradually built a small, highly modernized defense establishment which includes sophisticated land, sea, and air forces. The first step toward rebuilding defensive forces was taken in 1950 when Tokyo established a national police reserve. Then, in 1952 the Japanese began organizing a regular defense establishment, which in 1954 became the Japan Defense Agency. Tokyo's basic security policy, which was defined in 1957, is focused wholly on defense of Japan's home territory and the waters immediately surrounding it.

Under Japan's four defense plans, covering the years 1957 through 1976, its military expenditures, calculated as a percentage of gross national product, have remained the lowest of any major nation. During the 1950s they amounted to 1–2 percent of GNP, and during most of the 1960s they were less than 1 percent.[173] As late as 1972, the Defense Agency estimated its fiscal-year expenditures at 0.87 percent of GNP and 6.78 percent of the government's budget.[174] However, Japan's actual expenditures by the late 1960s exceeded $1 billion a year, and the Fourth Defense Plan, for 1972–76, called for military expenditures of about $15 billion over five years.[175] The Japanese forces have remained relatively small, with about 180,000 men authorized for ground forces, 38,000 for the navy, and 42,000 for the air force since 1972.[176] Actually, the Defense Agency has had difficulty filling its quotas; there is no conscription in Japan.

While the defense forces are modest in size, they are well armed with technologically sophisticated weapons.* One analyst in the Japan Defense Agency estimates that by the early 1970s Japan had "the most well-balanced force in Asia" and the "seventh in the world in terms of total strength."[178] This may exaggerate Japan's existing military strength. However, it has clearly improved its defense capability in recent years, and in fields such as electronics, antisubmarine warfare, and the like, its forces are quite advanced. They are designed to cope with any conventional attack long enough to allow the United States to come to Japan's assistance.

There is no evidence that Japanese leaders are planning to increase the size of their forces significantly. Yet there is no doubt that Japan already has the core of a military establishment that could be expanded fairly rapidly. The Japanese possess both the industrial and technological prerequisites for rapid conventional remilitarization, and they are acquiring the knowledge of both missile and nuclear technology that would enable Japan to "go nuclear" fairly rapidly if Tokyo decided to do so.

Some people, both in Asia and in the West, believe that it is inevitable that Japan will ultimately become a major military power again. Chou En-lai implied this in his 1971 interview with James Reston. "When they [the Japanese] have developed to the present stage," Chou said, "they are bound to develop militarism. . . . Economic expansionism is bound to bring about military expansion."[179] But informed Japanese deny the inevitability of such a trend. In fact, some of the country's most knowledgeable strategic thinkers argue that because of Japan's special vulnerabilities, the strength of its possible adversaries, and the fears of other nations of revived Japanese militarism, major remilitarization would result in less rather than more security for Japan. Most of them maintain that continued reliance on American defense guarantees, especially the nuclear umbrella, and emphasis on the building of peaceful foreign relations primarily through economic means, represent Japan's best hope for protecting its security and other interests.

* In 1972 the navy had 48 destroyers (totaling 97,000 tons), 15 submarines (totaling 21,000 tons), and 170 tactical aircraft; the air force had 880 aircraft and 4 nonnuclear NIKE missile groups; and the ground forces had 660 tanks, 650 armored personnel carriers, 310 tactical aircraft, and 5 HAWK missile groups. The Fourth Plan set the following targets: 54 destroyers (totaling 121,000 tons), 15 submarines (totaling 27,000 tons), and 200 tactical aircraft in the navy; 770 aircraft and 6 NIKE groups in the air force; and 820 tanks, 650 armored personnel carriers, 350 tactical aircraft, and 8 HAWK groups in the ground forces.[177]

The thesis that Japan will move inexorably toward major remilitarization is certainly challengeable, therefore. It is quite conceivable that it will choose to continue maintaining its military forces at relatively low levels, even though this would be unprecedented for a nation of its size and potential, if the Japanese continue to feel secure. However, there is no certainty that Japan's present approach to its security problems will continue unchanged. Several possible developments could alter the outlook. A steady incremental improvement of Japan's military forces, accompanied by subtle changes in public attitudes, could lay the groundwork for a major change of defense policy. There could well be much greater questioning of present policies if Soviet naval pressures appeared to increase, or if China were to expand its naval power rapidly (even if the Chinese were motivated more by a desire to counter Soviet naval power than a desire to increase pressure on Japan). Or, if Japanese-American economic and political relations were to deteriorate, Japan's confidence in U.S. defense commitments would probably erode, in which case a change in Japanese policies would almost certainly occur.

The most plausible cause of a sudden and basic change in Japanese defense policy would be some major international shock, or series of shocks, that greatly altered Japanese perceptions of the regional security environment in East Asia and the threats facing Japan. If the U.S.-Japan security treaty were to come to an abrupt end, or if Moscow or Peking were to make overt military threats against Japan, or if there were either a far-reaching rapprochement or a war between China and Russia, the shock to Japan would doubtless impel its leaders to reassess their policies. Any major conflict in Korea or the Taiwan Strait area, or possibly even large-scale fighting in Southeast Asia, could have similar effects. One or more of these developments could lead to revived nationalism in Japan and accelerated militarization, including even the development of nuclear weapons.

Japanese militarization, and especially the acquisition of nuclear weapons, would obviously create a totally new context for Sino-Japanese relations. It would doubtless result in a much more competitive relationship and significantly increased tensions. It would greatly increase the danger of serious Sino-Japanese conflict. At present, Peking seems to take these possibilities fully into account in designing its policy toward Japan. Its interest in encouraging Tokyo to resist any blandishments or pressure from Moscow and in deterring the Japanese from choosing the path of major remilitarization should continue to inhibit Peking from taking actions that would threaten to destabilize the present situation.

Although some changes in the quadrilateral big-power relationship in East Asia are very possible, they are not likely to be so far-reaching in the years immediately ahead as to alter Peking's desire to encourage counterweights to the Soviet Union. Hence, Peking will probably continue to see a modestly armed Japan, maintaining its treaty with the United States, as desirable. Japan will probably continue to maintain its special security relationship with the United States and to pursue a policy of equidistance toward China and the Soviet Union.

Unless unexpected destabilizing developments occur, the most likely prospect in bilateral Sino-Japanese relations in the next five to ten years is for a complex mixture of cooperation and competition. Neither close alignment nor open conflict is probable. Economic and other ties will continue to expand, but the relationship will not be intimate. Certain issues will create difficult problems, and there will be hard bargaining over conflicting national interests, but both Peking and Tokyo will probably try to contain their differences and minimize frictions. The key to policy on both sides will continue to be security, and both will probably continue to feel that their security interests demand maintenance of a viable, nonhostile relationship.

PART THREE

China and the United States

ALTHOUGH today the primary foreign policy goal of Peking's leaders is to counter the threat that they perceive Moscow posing to China, for most of the past quarter century Mao and his colleagues were preoccupied by their conflict with the United States. From the outbreak of the Korean War in 1950 until 1971, Sino-American confrontation was, in fact, the dominant factor shaping international relationships in the Far East. The Shanghai communiqué of 1972 marked the end of that confrontation and symbolized a major shift in the world balance. Like the signing of the Sino-Soviet alliance in 1950 and the development of the Peking-Moscow split in the 1960s it had far-reaching international repercussions. Both Peking and Washington now stress their commitment to move, step by step, toward full normalization of relations. The two countries have forged new links that are significant but still fairly fragile. Difficult problems continue to block the establishment of full diplomatic ties. Moreover, Peking and Washington are still divided by deep ideological, cultural, and political differences, very different world perspectives, and basic disagreement on a large number of global issues.

The Sino-Soviet split was clearly the primary factor leading to U.S.-China détente in the early 1970s. More than anything else, China's fear of Soviet intentions and its desire to create counterweights to restrain Moscow induced Peking's leaders to alter their policy toward the United States. And recognition that Sino-Soviet conflict had ended the bipolarity of forces in East Asia was a basic factor impelling leaders in Washington to reassess their policy toward China.

Historical Legacy

Sino-American relations have been shaped by a complex mixture of ideological, cultural, political, and economic, as well as geopolitical and military-security, influences.[1] To understand how they have evolved, it is essential to analyze the factors affecting the attitudes and policies of *both* countries, and the *interaction* between them. Special attention must be given to two periods: the early period of contact between Americans and Chinese Communists that led to conflict at the start of the 1950s, and the period of détente starting in the late 1960s when leaders in both countries decided to end two decades of hostile confrontation. Understanding the motives and objectives of both Chinese and Americans is a prerequisite for any attempt to project how the relationship will develop in the period just ahead.*

American Views

The "historic policy of the United States" toward China has been one of "friendship and aid toward the people of China," Secretary of State Dean Acheson stated in transmitting the U.S. white paper on China to the President in 1949.[2] This official view, broadly shared by ordinary citizens (but increasingly questioned or qualified by historians), has emphasized the mutuality of American and Chinese interests, and the historical importance of religious, philanthropic, and cultural ties. It has also highlighted American backing for the administrative and territorial integrity of China against threats of foreign domination, and the U.S. desire to support "stable government and progress along democratic lines" in China.[3]

According to this view, China in the century preceding the Communist takeover in 1949 in many respects had friendlier relations with the United States than with any other major power. It had no major military clashes with the United States—as it had with Great Britain, Russia, Japan, and others. Unlike the major European colonial nations and Japan, the United States did not seize significant portions of Chinese

---

* Surprisingly few analyses are available of the relationship from the perspective of the Chinese, particularly for the period since 1949. That is due in part to a lack of knowledge about China's policymaking process and in part to Americans' difficulty in overcoming their own parochialism. Much closer examination of how China's U.S. policy has been shaped, and the factors that have influenced it, is needed.

territory, or demand direct control of major territorial concessions, or try to stake out exclusive spheres of interest.

From the start of clipper ship trade in the 1780s, American businessmen competed actively to open the China market. At the same time American missionaries and educators played a major role in developing modern universities, schools, and medical institutions in China and in training a key group of China's emerging elite, roughly thirty-five thousand of whom studied in the United States.[4]

From the turn of the century, the United States, pursuing its Open Door policy, was the most vocal defender of China's territorial and administrative integrity and repeatedly protested the attempts of other powers—especially Russia and Japan, which were trying to catch up with the British economically in China—to compromise it. In 1899, the year after U.S. annexation of Hawaii, Puerto Rico, Guam, and the Philippines, Secretary of State John Hay, inspired by a British suggestion, attempted to persuade the other powers to agree that there should be equality of commercial opportunity in China. Then in 1900, when Russia was trying hard to extend its influence in China and occupied Manchuria, he expanded his proposal to include support for China's "territorial and administrative entity" (or "integrity," as it was later called).[5]

These principles of equal commercial opportunity and support of China's territorial and administrative integrity became the foundations of Washington's China policy and its broad Asia policy. Washington protested almost all foreign encroachments against China.[6] It opposed Russian expansionist policies in Manchuria in 1902–03, appealed for respect for China's neutrality and integrity at the time of the Russo-Japanese War in 1904–05, proposed neutralization of the railways in Manchuria in 1908 to try to prevent foreign domination of the area, and during World War I opposed both Japan's attempt to control China through its notorious Twenty-One Demands and its desire to take over all German territory and rights in China. In 1922 the United States attempted to codify the Open Door principles in the Nine-Power Treaty formulated at the Washington Conference. In 1927 it opposed foreign punitive action in response to Kuomintang atrocities in Nanking; in 1928 it recognized the new Nationalist government; and it was the first signator of a treaty that restored China's tariff autonomy.

After Japan invaded Manchuria in 1931, Secretary of State Henry L. Stimson in his famous nonrecognition doctrine informed Japan that the

United States would not recognize agreements or acts impairing U.S. treaty rights in China, including those relating to China's territorial and administrative integrity. Repeatedly, thereafter, Washington protested Japanese actions in China. When Japan embarked on a full-scale China war in 1937, President Franklin D. Roosevelt in his October "quarantine speech" warned against the spreading "epidemic of world lawlessness," and this was followed by many U.S. protests against aggressive Japanese actions.[7] In 1939 Washington began using economic measures to exert some pressure on Japan. Finally in 1941 it proposed that all Japanese forces be withdrawn from China, and it froze Japanese assets in the United States, steps that helped to provoke Tokyo to attack Pearl Harbor.

American sympathies clearly were with China in its conflict with Japan, and the United States began cautiously to give China aid even before Pearl Harbor. For example, it authorized American airmen to fly as volunteers on the Chinese side. After the United States and China became de facto allies, American military and economic support was substantially increased.[8] Americans trained and equipped a sizable number of Chinese divisions and built up the Chinese air force, and American air units fought in China. Sino-American "stabilization" agreements helped to combat inflation in China, and in 1942 Washington authorized a $500 million credit to the Nationalist regime. Although the United States was never as heavily involved in China as in Europe or the Pacific, thousands of American soldiers served in training, advisory, intelligence, and some combat positions there; and U.S. support was extremely important in preventing the defeat of the Nationalist regime.

The United States also became the principal sponsor of the Chinese in the international community. President Roosevelt overcame the resistance of Britain's Prime Minister Winston Churchill and the Russians to obtain acceptance of China as one of the Big Four. Washington helped to obtain promises that territories lost to Japan would be returned to China at war's end. And in 1943 the United States relinquished its extraterritorial rights in China and repealed exclusion acts that restricted Chinese immigration into the United States.

During and immediately after the war the United States was deeply involved in domestic Chinese politics.[9] Although the United States did not take part in the fighting that erupted inside China in 1946, it continued aid to the Nationalists while attempting to mediate their conflict with the Communists. Hundreds of millions of dollars' worth of economic aid was sent, mostly through the United Nations Relief and Rehabilitation Administration. American forces helped transport Nationalist forces to take over key areas from the Japanese. And General George C. Marshall was sent by President Harry S. Truman to China to try to work out a Nationalist-Communist compromise that could bring internal peace to the country. However, when it became clear that U.S. mediation efforts could not succeed, that full-scale war could not be stopped, and that the Communists were winning the struggle, Washington began a process of gradual disengagement, waiting to "let the dust settle."

Before the Communist takeover in 1949 the predominant American view of relations with China tended to be self-congratulatory. In general terms, the U.S. policy toward China was friendly, and U.S. support of the Nationalist government was substantial. Americans had formed close links with China, and many felt a strong attraction to and identification with the Chinese. In the early years of World War II many Americans tended to idealize China in its struggle against Japan, which helps to explain the deep sense of American disillusionment and "betrayal" about the "loss of China" when the Communists overthrew the Nationalist regime. As has been frequently noted, unrequited love often leads to unrestrained hostility, and American attitudes underwent a profound change when China was transformed from an ally to an adversary in 1949.

Chinese Views

Not surprisingly, Chinese views of relations with the United States have been different from those of most Americans.[10] Even among the strongly pro-American group of Chinese who were highly influential before 1949, few could view U.S. policy in terms of unalloyed altruism. And a large number of Chinese have always been anti-Western.

Many Chinese saw U.S. influence on China in the nineteenth century as part and parcel of the Western colonialist and imperialist expansion that broke down the Ch'ing dynasty's self-imposed isolation, compromised China's sovereignty, and helped to undermine the values and institutions of the traditional Chinese political and social system. The United States did not take the lead in this process, in part because its position in Asia was relatively weak and in part because it was less moved by colonial ambitions than countries such as England, Russia, and Japan. But in 1844 it obtained, through a most-favored-nation clause in the Sino-American Treaty of Wanghia, a guarantee that it would gain whatever treaty rights and privileges the Chinese gave to others with respect to trade, tariffs, residence rights, religious activity, and so on.[11] Thus when Great Britain and the other powers broadened their extraterritorial privileges in China, the United States was a beneficiary. Its citizens, like all Westerners, belonged to the special foreign community which was protected by Western laws and military forces (including American units). In a sense, the Americans clung to the coattails of the British in the nineteenth century and benefited from what they did in, and to, China.

For a time in the late 1890s and early 1900s, American official policy was sympathetic to Japanese aspirations in the region. This changed fundamentally only after the Sino-Japanese War of 1904–05, when it appeared that Japanese ambitions might threaten the interests of the Western powers. The Open Door policy was initially aimed less at protecting China's interests than at deterring Japan and Russia from taking action that could erode American commercial interests and other rights in China.

When Chinese actions threatened the safety or special rights of foreigners in China, the United States usually joined the other powers in efforts to protect their privileges. American troops, for example, participated in the international expeditionary force sent to Peking in 1900 when foreigners there were under attack from members of the Boxer secret society. The American decision to use indemnity funds extracted from China after the Boxer episode to finance the education of Chinese was a generous act; this did not obscure the fact, however, that American leaders had been as ready to intervene militarily to protect their citizens as were the leaders of other interested powers.

Washington's Open Door policy, and its many protests against threats to China's territorial and administrative integrity, were helpful to China, and the United States did at times exert influence within the concert of powers involved in Chinese affairs to restrain Russian and Japanese ambitions and help to prevent a total partition of China by the colonial powers. But there was a large gap between rhetoric and action in American policy. Clearly Washington often lacked either the intention or the power to back up its protestations, and it frequently compromised with unpleasant reality at China's expense. In 1915, when Japan sent its Twenty-One Demands to China, the United States reiterated its support for China's territorial integrity, but it also recognized that "territorial contiguity" "created special relations" between countries, and in 1917 Washington concluded in the Lansing-Ishii Agreement that "territorial propinquity" justified Japan's claim that it had "special interests in China."[12]

At the Versailles conference in 1919 when the United States acquiesced to Japanese takeover of German rights in Shantung, the Chinese clearly felt betrayed. The Versailles Treaty provoked the first great outpouring of popular, nationalist feeling in China—the May Fourth Movement.[13] Anti-Japanese feelings predominated at the time, but the major Western nations including the United States were also targets of growing nationalism and antiimperialism.

As Japanese aggression against China steadily escalated in the 1930s, although the Chinese appreciated Washington's verbal support, they were repeatedly disappointed by its failure to back up its words with action to restrain the Japanese.[14] American indignation alone could not protect China. The United States continued to trade with Japan, thereby contributing to Tokyo's ability to pursue its expansionist policies. The strong economic measures that Washington finally took against Japan in 1941 were provoked less by a sense of obligation to China than by Japanese threats to Western interests in Southeast Asia.[15] Until the United States itself was attacked by Japan, American material support to China remained small; in fact, from 1937 to 1941 the Russians gave Chiang Kai-shek's regime its most significent aid, through loans and military supplies.[16]

Even after Pearl Harbor, American assistance was far less than the Chinese hoped for. This was due in part to the difficulty of supplying China, by road through Burma or by air over "the Hump," but fundamentally it was due to the priority the United States placed on the war effort in Europe and the Pacific. The Chinese hoped, toward the end of the war, for American landings on the Chinese coast which Washington seriously considered but never undertook.

The extensive involvement of Americans in Chinese domestic affairs during the war led inevitably to friction.[17] Americans were dismayed by the corruption and inefficiency of the Chinese government and frustrated by the inability of the Nationalists and Communists to collaborate in the war effort. From 1944 on, the United States increasingly pressed the Chungking government to reform and broaden its base. Chiang Kai-shek deeply resented what he regarded as unjustified American intervention in China, and he rejected Roosevelt's proposal that General Joseph Stilwell be appointed commander of Chinese forces. Chiang's opponents—including many Western-oriented leaders as well as the Communists—felt that U.S. pressure was not sufficient to force changes in the Nationalist regime and its policies; from their perspective U.S. policy simply bolstered a reactionary regime.

Chinese national pride was deeply offended by the failure of the United States, despite its words, to accord the same major-power status to China that it gave the other powers. The prime symbol of China's lack of genuine major-power status was the Yalta Conference, where the United States, Britain, and the Soviet Union made far-reaching decisions affecting China's interests without consulting the Chinese. (Though the Nationalists' first reaction to the Yalta Agreements was positive, they later denounced them as a sell-out of Chinese interests.)

The behavior of some American soldiers in China also created frictions. Though many formed friendships that promoted good relations, others behaved, as foreign troops frequently do abroad, with insensitivity and arrogance, offending Chinese cultural pride.

The ambiguities and dilemmas in Sino-American relations steadily increased after the war. In its attempt to mediate the Nationalist-Communist conflict, the United States found itself in the vortex of a struggle between irreconcilable forces. Its attempt simultaneously to support the Nationalist government and to induce it to reach a compromise with the Communists was probably destined from the start to fail. In the end virtually all major Chinese groups were bitter and disillusioned with the United States—the Nationalists felt the Americans had failed to give them full-scale aid and in attempting to push for reforms and compromises had meddled excessively in Chinese internal affairs; the Communists felt the Americans had failed to maintain a really neutral posture but instead had bolstered the Nationalist regime throughout the period of mediation.

Many of the Nationalist leaders did not genuinely share American values and views. Though they had staked their future on American support, they resented American pressure for reform. However, a significant number of Chinese were greatly influenced by Western values and the American model. Among them were noncommunist opponents of the Kuomintang, Western-educated intellectuals and professionals, and liberal politicians and technical bureaucrats within the Nationalist regime, key members of China's modern elite, who had an intellectual influence out of proportion to their numbers. They pinned their hopes on U.S. influence to force both the Nationalists and the Communists to reform, compromise, and make peace.[18] But in a civil war, they proved to be politically impotent, and ultimately they were disillusioned by the destruction of the values they believed in, as a result of both the Nationalists' and the Communists' policies.

After World War II a large number of Chinese, especially educated youth, came to view the United States in extremely nationalist terms. Americans, inheriting the imperialist onus formerly borne by the Japanese, British, and Russians, became for many of them the symbol and embodiment of Western colonialist intervention in China. Antiimperialism and the determination to end a century of "national humiliation" were almost universal; in fact, Chiang Kai-shek's book *China's Destiny* stressed this almost as much as Communist writings did. In the end, many nationalistic Chinese simply wanted the "Yankee" to "go home" and let China solve its problems in its own way.

The Chinese Communists, not surprisingly, held antiimperialist views in their most extreme form. Although some evidence suggests that in the 1940s the leadership of the Communist party was comparatively flexible in defining its policies toward the United States, in a fundamental ideological and political sense the Communists viewed the United States as the leader of world imperialism, the principal supporter of reactionary forces in China, and the most influential advocate of bourgeois values that the party hoped to eradicate.[19]

To the mass of Chinese, especially in the rural hinterland, the United States, like all foreign nations, always seemed extremely remote. Before 1949, ordinary Chinese, to the extent that they had discriminating views about foreigners, tended to view Americans comparatively favorably.[20] There is some basis, therefore, for the view that during the first half of the twentieth century the United States created small, scattered reservoirs of goodwill in China.

But the extent and significance of this goodwill should not be exaggerated. Whenever the leaders of Chinese political movements attempted to arouse either traditional xenophobic emotions or modern nationalistic fervor, the target usually included Americans.[21] And although before 1949 the cultural influence of the United States had been extended more widely in China through religious and educational efforts than that of most foreign countries, it had not penetrated very deeply.

The Western impact did have revolutionary effects, many unintended, on elite groups in China. In a sense, the entire history of China from the mid-nineteenth century on can be viewed as a complicated struggle in which these elite groups attempted to protect China from external threats and at the same time tried to accommodate to and borrow from the West. However, the bulk of the Chinese continued to live in a world of their own, to have only a superficial knowledge of foreign nations, and to hold attitudes toward all foreigners that were highly manipulable by political leaders.

Early Communist Attitudes

The Chinese Communists' ideological and political assumptions impelled them, from the start, to be hostile toward the United States. Accepting Marxist-Leninist tenets that portrayed international conflict in fairly dichotomous terms, they saw the worldwide struggle as one between Communist revolutionaries, led by the Soviet Union, and capitalist, imperialist forces, supported by their "running dogs" in colonial and "semi-colonial" areas.[22] They viewed the United States above all, therefore, as a leader of the enemy camp.

As long as the party was a small revolutionary group, however, there was no pressing need for its leaders to formulate very specific policies toward the United States. In the 1920s the Americans seemed less important in China than the British, French, and other imperialists, whose policemen harassed the Chinese Communists in treaty ports such as Shanghai. Even though the Communist leaders attempted to apply united-front concepts to their struggle within China, they looked to the Soviet Union and Comintern-led world Communist movement as their one important source of external support and aid. After their move to the Kiangsi countryside in the late 1920s, the Chinese Communists, without extensive contact even with the Soviet Union, evolved their own strategy, tactics, and policies. Most international actors, except for Japan which clearly posed a growing military threat, appeared to be of limited relevance to the party's immediate situation, problems, and goals.

By the mid-1930s, however—especially after the Communists' move to northwest China in 1935, the outbreak of major Sino-Japanese conflict in 1937, and the mounting evidence of possible war in Europe—Mao and his colleagues saw, more clearly than before, direct linkages between their own domestic struggle for power and the changing international situation as it affected China.[23] They started, therefore, to work more seriously at defining their policy toward particular nations, including the major noncommunist nations. Even though they did not begin to have significant dealings with representatives of noncommunist nations until the latter years of World War II, or develop conventional state-to-state relations until after their victory in 1949, the origins of the Chinese Communists' foreign policy can be traced to the late 1930s.

During 1935–36, as the fascists in Europe and the Japanese in Asia became increasingly threatening, the Communist leaders in China, as well as the Russian leaders and men heading the Communist International in Moscow, moved to adopt an international united-front strategy. The concepts and principles that Mao gradually refined at that time were to guide the Chinese Communists' foreign policy as well as their domestic strategy in the decades ahead.* Many of these have strongly influenced party leaders' thinking right up to the present.

Because Mao, like most Communist leaders, saw the fundamental worldwide conflict as a struggle between all revolutionaries and all non-revolutionaries, and especially between the Communists and the capitalists and imperialists, he assumed that the Soviet Union was the only fully dependable ally of Communists anywhere.[25] Hence, he believed at that time that the Chinese Communists had to lean to one side, toward Moscow. However, Mao also viewed the world in terms of complex and changing "contradictions," among capitalists and imperialists as well as between Communists and their enemies, and he argued that Communists should fully use such contradictions to their own advantage. He stressed self-reliance as one crucial requirement for revolutionary success. But he also argued that it is necessary to identify the party's primary enemy at any particular time and then to search for "limited allies," even among capitalists and imperialists, in order to build a broad united front against the main enemy. While it is essential, he asserted, not to compromise fundamental revolutionary principles, it is also necessary to employ flexible tactics.[26] In Mao's view, limited allies are temporary allies who may eventually become enemies again, but for limited periods they can be of critical importance in the balance of forces affecting the struggle for power.

In line with such views, the Chinese Communists began to make important distinctions between various imperialist nations, identifying the fascist states (Japan, Germany, Italy) as the main enemies and the capi-

* There is still debate among scholars about whether the Chinese evolved their new policies autonomously or in parallel with the Russians, simply followed the Soviet lead, or acted on directions from Moscow.[24] I believe they developed many of their policies on their own.

talist democracies (in particular, the United States, Britain, and France) as potential limited allies. When Edgar Snow visited Yenan in 1936—the first American correspondent invited to the Communists' wartime capital—Mao stressed to him the common interest of the Americans, British, and French, as well as the Chinese and Russians, in opposing Japanese imperialism. The Communists, he said, "expect at least that friendly nations will not help Japanese imperialism, and will adopt a neutral position. We hope that they will actively help China to resist invasion and conquest." All nonfascist countries, including imperialist nations that oppose Japan, Mao asserted, should be "organized into antiwar, anti-aggression, anti-Fascist world alliances."[27]

During the war years, the Chinese Communists frequently reassessed the impact of the changing international situation on their interests, and although they supported Moscow's views on crucial issues, they often made their own independent judgments. Periodically they modified their posture toward the United States and other capitalist democracies, sometimes stressing the importance of general opposition to imperialism, but at other times emphasizing the need for a broad united front including the imperialists. For example, whereas after the Molotov-Ribbentrop pact in 1939 and the outbreak of war between Germany and the West European nations, the Chinese Communists reverted to their dichotomous world view, condemning both sides of the conflict as imperialists, by late 1940 they were once more stressing the differences between the fascists and antifascists. Following Germany's attack on the Soviet Union in mid-1941, they argued strongly in favor of a very broad, antifascist, international united front.

Mao's innerparty directive "On Policy," issued in December 1940 even before Germany's attack on the Soviet Union, was a classic statement of his views on united-front tactics (it was reemphasized years later, in 1971, when the party leadership was trying to explain and justify its new policy of limited détente with the United States). "The Communist Party opposes all imperialism," Mao stated, but "we make a distinction" between Japanese imperialism and those imperialists who now oppose Japan. "We build our policy on these distinctions," he declared. "Our tactics are guided by one and the same principle: to make use of contradictions, win over the many, oppose the few and crush our enemies one by one."[28]

These tactics became increasingly important after both the Soviet Union and the United States had been drawn into the war. In fact, how to deal with the United States, which was now the Western power most deeply involved in China, became a priority problem for the Communists as well as the Nationalists. Thereafter, although the Communists' attitudes toward the United States changed periodically in line with Yenan's approval or disapproval of specific American wartime policies, the party continued to push for an antifascist coalition. Mao hoped not only for American assistance to the broad Chinese war effort but also for direct aid to his own forces and for support that would help to shift the balance within China in the Communists' favor. Formerly, the Communists had no way to apply political leverage on the United States, but now they could hold out the possibility of military cooperation against the Japanese to try to induce the Americans to take their views more seriously. During the last two years of the war, in particular, they worked assiduously to induce the United States to increase its military assistance to China, to give direct military aid to Communist forces, and to put pressure on the Nationalists to change their policies. The leaders in Yenan now looked to the United States rather than to the Soviet Union for possible assistance in the form of diplomatic leverage as well as military aid. They could expect little help from the Russians, who were preoccupied in Europe and had given no significant military aid to China since they had signed a neutrality pact with Japan in 1941.

In 1944 the Communists opened Yenan to visits by a number of American correspondents, who gave wide publicity in the West to the Communists' views.[29] More important, they engaged in extensive negotiations with Patrick Hurley, President Roosevelt's special emissary to China who was attempting to promote a Nationalist-Communist compromise. And they agreed to the stationing in Yenan of a U.S. military group (the Dixie mission) that included diplomats,[30] thereby establishing the first quasi-diplomatic contacts with the Americans. (Over the ensuing years, despite the lack of formal relations, there were to be many more such contacts, at Nanking and Peking during the Marshall mission period, at Panmunjom after the Korean War, at Geneva and Warsaw from the mid-1950s on.)

During 1944-45 the Communists clearly hoped for a U.S. military landing on the China coast, as well as for military aid to their forces. Mao offered military cooperation, and he stated that the Chinese Communists' forces would be willing to serve under an American commander. "We will accept your help with gratitude any time," he said, "now or in the future. We would serve with all our hearts under an American

General, with no strings or conditions attached. . . . If you land on the shores of China, we will be there to meet you, and to place ourselves under your command."[31]

Mao also pressed for a coalition government in China, for foreign-policy as well as domestic reasons, and attempted to get the Americans to persuade the Nationalists to accept this. To convince them that coopera-tion, even in the long run, was both possible and desirable, he disin-genuously assured the Americans: "Even the most conservative Ameri-can businessman can find nothing in our program to take exception to."[32]

Mao also argued in favor of long-term American economic assistance for China's modernization. "China's greatest postwar need," he said, "is economic development. She lacks the capitalistic foundation necessary to carry this out alone. . . . America and China complement each other economically. . . . America needs an export market [and] an outlet for capital investment. . . . America is not only the most suitable country to assist this economic development of China; she is also the only country fully able to participate."[33] In January 1945, Mao and Chou proposed that they visit President Roosevelt in Washington, as unofficial repre-sentatives of "a primary Chinese political party," for an "exploratory conference," presumably to discuss, among other things, military co-operation.[34] This never materialized, but the Chinese Communists were able to send a party representative to the San Francisco conference at which the United Nations was founded.[35]

Some American representatives in China strongly urged that the United States give direct military aid to the Communists—for practical military reasons and also because they suspected that the Communists would ultimately win the struggle for power in China.[36] However, be-cause of Chiang Kai-shek's adamant opposition to the idea and Patrick Hurley's backing of Chiang's position, and perhaps also because of the decision not to land on the Chinese coast, Washington decided against such aid.

Washington's failure to develop closer relationships with the Com-munists in 1944 and early 1945 is viewed by some scholars as the first of several lost opportunities to influence Chinese Communist policies.[37] If Washington had been more flexible, it is argued, it might have prevented the Communists, once they achieved power, from adopting a clearly pro-Soviet and anti-American "lean to one side" posture. Even assuming the Communists remained committed to Leninist views and long-term revo-lutionary goals, perhaps their wartime cooperation with the United

States might have "mortgaged" their "future options" and made it "difficult if not impossible [for them] to abandon the policy of cooperation" with the Americans after the war.[38]

But the fact that the Nationalist regime was at that time an internationally accepted government, recognized by the Soviet Union as well as the Western powers, and an ally of the United States, whereas the Communists were a revolutionary movement committed to the Nationalists' overthrow, certainly limited if it did not absolutely predetermine American choices. Moreover, even if it had been possible to establish satisfactory working relations during the war, Mao's deep commitment to revolution and antiimperialism as well as the basic American opposition to communism would probably have come to the fore again eventually. If, as seems plausible, Mao viewed the United States at that time only as a potentially useful "temporary ally," it seems likely that his opposition to imperialism would have put him in open opposition to the United States again after the war.

In the event, as Chinese Communist hopes for American aid dissipated, there was renewed debate within the party in 1945 over foreign-policy issues,[39] and eventually the party's ideological position hardened. This became clear at the Seventh Party Congress, when renewed stress was placed on fundamental revolutionary aims. After Yalta, seeing the possibility once more of increased Soviet involvement in China, the party began to look again to Moscow for assistance, even though at times party leaders were clearly disturbed about aspects of Soviet policy, especially Moscow's increased dealings with the Chinese Nationalists in 1945.

As the end of the war approached, both the Communists and the Nationalists prepared for open civil war, and in August 1945, with the U.S. atomic attack on Japan, Moscow's entry into the war, and Japan's surrender, both sides moved to strengthen their military and political positions by seizing territory and arms from the defeated Japanese. This competition was already well under way when President Truman sent General Marshall to mediate the conflict in China.

The American attempt to prevent civil war in China was a remarkable episode.[40] There are probably few close parallels. The United States assumed responsibility for trying to mediate between the leaders of a friendly government and the leaders of a revolutionary movement committed to that government's overthrow. General Marshall faced the task of reconciling virtually irreconcilable interests and overcoming animosities and suspicions that were the legacy of more than two decades of bitter struggle. His mandate was to try to achieve a cease-fire, a broadening of the Chinese government, and a nationalization of military forces that could lead to peace.

Initially it appeared that Marshall was making progress. In January 1946 both a cease-fire and political agreement on establishment of a coalition government were concluded. A complex tripartite mechanism to implement these agreements and to compromise remaining differences was then established, with a top-level Committee of Three in Chungking (later moved to Nanking), an executive headquarters in Peking (then Peiping), and many truce teams to supervise the cease-fire in the field—in all of which there were American as well as Nationalist and Communist representatives. But the initial optimism rapidly dissipated, as it became clear that many issues—including the nationalization or integration of military forces—were not resolvable. Fighting between the two sides resumed, particularly in northeast China (Manchuria), and gradually escalated. By mid-1946 major civil war was under way, and by the end of the year Marshall concluded that it was impossible to persuade the two sides to exercise restraint and reach a viable compromise. In January 1947 he returned home, blaming both sides for their intransigence.[41]

The contacts between General Marshall, America's top wartime military leader and subsequently its secretary of state, and Chou En-lai, the Communists' foremost specialist on foreign affairs and later premier and foreign minister, as well as between many Americans and Communists of lesser rank, created the most significant relationships between Americans and Chinese Communist leaders up to that time. (Many of those on the Chinese side became foreign policy professionals, with whom the United States still must deal.) If domestic peace in China had, in fact, been achieved in 1946–47, these relationships might have had considerable significance. Instead, the ultimate failure of the mediation effort helped to create intense Chinese Communist bitterness against the Americans, which unquestionably was a major factor shaping their hostile attitudes and policies when they achieved power not long thereafter.

Some of the Communist leaders during the mediation period may have been prepared to make compromises, both domestically and in their international orientation, if these had been matched on the Nationalist side and by the Americans. Chou En-lai is reported to have said to Marshall: "Of course we will lean to one side. But how far depends on you."[42] The party was probably never prepared, though, to give up control of its autonomous territories and armed forces. It remained committed to a long-term revolutionary struggle to achieve total national power, and it still regarded the United States basically as an imperialist adversary. In any case, the strategy the Chinese finally decided to pursue was one of "fight and talk," in which they attempted to expand their areas of military control while at the same time negotiating with the Americans and Nationalists.

As soon as Japan surrendered, in August 1945, the Chinese Communists sent a large portion of their best forces into northeast China and Inner Mongolia, where they linked up with the newly arrived Soviet forces. In the northeast, Soviet forces turned over large quantities of captured Japanese arms to the Communists[43] and timed their withdrawals from many key areas to facilitate Communist takeovers. The Russians were inhibited from giving the Communists full-scale, overt support, however, by their new treaty with the Nationalist regime, signed in August, as well as their desire to avoid provoking large-scale American military intervention. (Stalin actually advised Mao after the war to join a coalition with the Nationalists.[44])

The Americans' large-scale involvement in China impelled the Communists to participate in the negotiations held under Marshall's aegis, in order to achieve certain important objectives; they hoped to minimize American support for the Nationalists and with American help to extract concessions from Chiang that they could not hope to obtain by their own efforts alone. But they strongly opposed, from the start, the help the United States gave to the Nationalists right after the war in moving their forces by air and sea to take over key areas of east, north, and northeast China from the Japanese.

From the official American perspective, Marshall made a genuine attempt to be objective and neutral in dealing with both the Nationalists and Communists. The United States put considerable pressure on the Nationalists to introduce reforms and make compromises—even cutting off the flow of military supplies for a time to demonstrate American evenhandedness as well as to try to influence Chiang. But from the Communists' perspective, the Americans never seemed truly neutral. The fact that the Americans were the principal supporters of the Nationalists when full-scale civil war got under way clearly intensified the hostility that the Communists felt toward the United States.[45] In all probability, the passage of a major new China Aid Act in 1948 in Washington and the resumption of American economic and military aid simply confirmed the Communists in their belief that they should view the United States as an imperialist enemy committed to supporting the Nationalists' anti-communist efforts.

The Communists' attitude and policy toward the United States after full-scale civil war was resumed in China were summarized by the party's propaganda chief, Lu Ting-yi, in January 1947, about the time that Marshall's recall was announced: "After the [sic] World War II," he asserted, "the American imperialists took [the] place of the Fascist Germany, Italy and Japan becoming a fortress of the world reactionary forces."[46] The Chinese Communists again called for a worldwide united front but this time against the world's "reactionary" forces consisting of the "American imperialists," the "reactionaries in various countries," and "other fascist remnants." Within China they embarked on an all-out military struggle to achieve power.

The Takeover Period

The Chinese Communists' antagonism toward the Americans was doubtless heightened by their disappointments and disillusionments during 1944–46. From 1947 on, in any case, they adopted a clearly hostile attitude toward the United States and took various actions that strengthened American hostility toward them. The policies they pushed during 1948–50 created new barriers to the establishment of any friendly links with the Americans, or for that matter formal relations of any sort, even after they won power.

The 1948–49 period was one of steady, albeit gradual, U.S. disengagement from China.[47] By 1948, after the Communists had won a series of major military victories and demonstrated their ability to seize major cities, it was clear to the U.S. government that it was only a matter of time before the Communists would win the civil war and establish a new national government. By then, Secretary of State Marshall had for all practical purposes decided that there was no alternative but to write off China (including Taiwan). The Truman administration was firm about not intervening directly with U.S. forces. However, the process of disengaging from the Chinese civil war was extremely difficult.[48] As the Nationalists' situation deteriorated, Republican opponents of U.S. policy pressed for more, not less, U.S. aid and involvement. Washington's moves toward disengagement were thus gradual and cautious and, in the face of severe domestic criticism, defensive. The combination of limited aid and limited withdrawal inevitably created considerable ambiguity.

Nevertheless, from late 1948 through early 1950 the United States took a series of steps that the Communists could have interpreted to be evidence of Washington's probable willingness to accept the realities of the situation in China and possibly to consider establishing relations with a new Communist regime, despite the Communists' anti-American stance. In late 1948 Washington instructed its diplomatic personnel in consular posts in key cities such as Peking to remain where they were when the Communists took over and to try to establish local contact with the new authorities. More important, Ambassador Leighton Stuart, who was accredited to the Nationalist regime, stayed in Nanking in April 1949 when much of the diplomatic community moved with the Nationalists to Canton. Soon after the Communist takeover, Stuart entered into discussions with a senior Communist official in Nanking, Huang Hua (who in 1976 became China's foreign minister), and over the next two months they discussed varied issues, including the question of recognition.[49] Huang indicated that the United States should make the first move toward recognition of the new regime by cutting its ties with the Nationalists. Stuart indicated that the preconditions for American recognition were evidence of acceptance of the new government by the Chinese people and a demonstration by that government that it was willing and able to "perform its international obligations."[50]

In the United States, the Truman administration opposed Republican efforts in Congress to vote additional aid to the Nationalists, and in August 1949 it took the extraordinary step of issuing a white paper (*United States Relations with China*) which contained a devastating critique of the Nationalist regime. In his letter of transmittal, Dean Acheson, who had succeeded Marshall as secretary of state, asserted: "The unfortunate but inescapable fact is that the ominous result of the civil war in China was beyond the control of the government of the United States. Nothing that this country did or could have done within the reasonable limits of its capabilities could have changed the result."[51] The white paper made clear that the United States accepted the inevitability of a Communist takeover, and not long thereafter, in January 1950, both Truman and Acheson made it clear that the United States did not intend to intervene to prevent a Communist takeover even of the island of Taiwan to which the Nationalist government had retreated.[52] In this period Washington urged its allies not to recognize a new Communist regime precipitously, but apparently it only sought delay, not long-term ostracism of Peking. In the United Nations, although the United States opposed immediate seating of the new Communist regime, it indicated that since this was a procedural matter, it would accept the majority view.[53]

However, the Chinese Communists throughout this period maintained an extremely hostile posture toward the United States, in their press, their radio broadcasts, and their public statements. More important, they openly proclaimed their close alignment with the Soviet Union in the Soviet-American cold war. As early as November 1948, Liu Shao-ch'i, second-ranking leader in the party, asserted, in a major article on "Internationalism and Nationalism": "The world today has been divided into two mutually antagonistic camps: on the one hand, the world imperialist camp, composed of the American imperialists and their accomplices—the reactionaries of all countries of the world; on the other hand, the world antiimperialist camp, composed of the Soviet Union and the New Democracies of Eastern Europe, and the national liberation movements in China, Southeast Asia and Greece, plus the people's democratic forces of all countries of the world . . . people line up with one side or the other. . . . To remain neutral or sitting on the fence is impossible. . . . neutrality . . . is nothing but deception."[54]

In March 1949, Mao in his report to the Party Central Committee's Second Plenum, looked forward to the party's takeover of power and defined a tough antiimperialist line, both domestically and internationally. He called for a "policy of systematically and completely destroying imperialist domination in China . . . in the political, economic and cultural fields." "We are willing to establish diplomatic relations with all countries on the principle of equality," he said, "but the imperialists, who have always been hostile to the Chinese people, will definitely not be in a hurry to treat us as equals. As long as the imperialist countries do not change their hostile attitude, we shall not grant them legal status in China." He declared that the Chinese Communists would refuse to recognize foreign diplomats and the "treasonable treaties" of the Kuomintang period. However, "wherever there is business to do, we shall do it."[55]

The most important declaration of policy in this period was Mao's June 30, 1949, statement, "On the People's Democratic Dictatorship."[56] In this statement, Mao asserted in unambiguous terms that China "must lean to one side," toward the Soviet Union, emphasizing that there is no "third road." "Internationally, we belong to the side of the anti-imperialist front headed by the Soviet Union," Mao declared, and he reiterated his strong support for an "international united front" against the imperialists. He ridiculed as "naive" the idea that the United States or Britain might be willing to give China help on a basis of mutual benefit.

In August, Mao reacted scornfully to the issuance of the U.S. white paper on China, labeling it a "counter-revolutionary document which openly demonstrates U.S. imperialist intervention in China."[57] In November, Liu pledged strong moral support to antiimperialist revolutions throughout the colonial and semicolonial world. Holding up the Chinese "road" as a model, he bitterly attacked the imperialists as "robbers armed to the teeth."[58] Finally, China's antiimperialist, "lean to one side" policy was signed and sealed by Mao in Moscow, in February 1950, when the Sino-Soviet treaty was concluded, creating a defense alliance against Japan and "any other state that may collaborate with Japan directly or indirectly"[59]—clearly meaning the United States.

The Chinese Communists' hard line toward the United States during this period was highlighted by several cases of mistreatment of American diplomats: in Mukden, in late 1948, they placed Angus Ward, a consul, under house arrest, not releasing him until almost a year later; in mid-1949 a vice consul in Shanghai was physically harassed and mistreated; and other consuls were isolated and ignored. Even though the majority of American citizens in China were not mistreated at the time of the Communists' takeover, the U.S. government interpreted the Ward case in particular as a sign of a deliberately hostile policy, and that case inflamed American public opinion and hardened government attitudes.

Finally, in January 1950, the Chinese Communists seized American government property in Peking, despite Washington's "announced intention to withdraw all American official personnel from Communist China if the Communist Chinese attempted to seize our offices and properties."[60] Soon thereafter, all American officials left the country. Peking doubtless knew that this would delay recognition of the new regime by the United States, but it now seemed in no great hurry to establish relations with Washington. If there had been no Korean War, the delay might have been relatively brief. But, in the event, it proved to be crucial. By the end of 1950 the United States and the People's Republic of China were locked in direct military conflict in Korea, and a two-decade-long period of bitterly hostile confrontation had begun.

The Communists doubtless wished to establish relations with the United States in due time. However, in the flush of revolutionary victory, they were determined to prove that China had "stood up"—to use Mao's phrase—against the imperialists and that they would be prepared to establish relations with countries such as the United States only after they had met all of the Chinese Communists' terms and preconditions. This approach clearly proved to have costly long-run consequences for the Chinese—just as Washington's propensity to delay proved to be costly to the United States.

The bulk of evidence points to the conclusion that it was in 1948, when the U.S.-Soviet cold war as well as full-scale civil war in China were under way, that the Chinese Communists made a basic decision to align with the Soviet-led Communist camp and adopt a tough line toward Washington and a militant revolutionary posture in the worldwide struggle against the "imperialist camp." Recently, some analysts have disputed this, arguing that there was continuing debate among Chinese Communist leaders during 1948–49 and that some, possibly including even Mao and Chou, may have remained open to the idea of adopting a more balanced approach to the Soviet Union and the United States until publication of Mao's article "On People's Democratic Dictatorship" in mid-1949.[61] These analysts believe there were unresolved differences within Chinese Communist party councils over policy toward both the Soviet Union and the United States, and they stress the importance of the fact—which was not publicly revealed until 1972—that in June 1949 the party's leaders invited Ambassador Stuart to visit Peking.[62] According to information now available, the question of such a visit had come up early that month in the Huang-Stuart conversations, and then on June 28 Huang told Stuart that he had received a message from Mao and Chou stating that they would welcome him in Peking, as a private citizen. Stuart cabled this information to Washington on June 30, indicating he wished to accept the invitation. On July 1, however, the State Department instructed him to refuse it.

This episode raises intriguing questions about whether this was another lost opportunity to establish significant contacts with the Communists' top leaders, contacts that might have led the Chinese to decide not to align so closely with the Soviet Union. It is highly doubtful, however, that as late as June 1949 the United States could have induced the Chinese Communist leaders to opt for a foreign-policy posture basically different from the one they actually chose. The invitation was not extended to Stuart until June,[63] and Mao's "lean to one side" statement must have been based on decisions made well before it was released on June 30 (it was clearly prefigured, moreover, by Liu's November 1948 article). As of June 30, Mao and Chou did not know whether Stuart might accept their invitation, and they clearly were not waiting for his response before defining their basic foreign-policy stance. If Stuart had gone to see Mao and Chou, therefore, it would have been after the party had publicly defined in a fairly dramatic fashion its pro-Soviet, antiimperialist, "lean to one side" position.

Some Soviet scholars also now argue that in early 1949 Mao was still considering the possibility of pursuing more balanced policies toward both the Soviet Union and the United States. They assert that certain Russian representatives in China at that time believed that Mao felt it would be best if Soviet recognition of a new Communist regime would come at roughly the same time as American recognition, even if this required some delay in action by Moscow.[64] This is very questionable, however; if it were so, Chinese Communist statements and actions in dealing with the Americans throughout this period probably would have been substantially different than they were. Even though there may have been continuing debate in late 1948 and early 1949 within the Chinese Communist party's councils on some aspects of future policy toward both the Soviet Union and the United States, therefore, it seems clear that China's "lean to one side" decision, first articulated by Liu in late 1948 and strongly reaffirmed by Mao in mid-1949, set the basic framework for their overall policy in the period that followed.

The Korean War

Peking's leaders in the months immediately following their establishment of a new national regime on October 1, 1949, were primarily concerned with domestic rather than foreign-policy problems. Though the Communists were still uneasy about U.S. intentions, their apprehensions about U.S. military involvement in China probably had declined. The Truman-Acheson statements of January 1950 must have contributed to this, but the insurance provided to China by the Sino-Soviet treaty was doubtless the crucial factor. Peking actually moved in early 1950 to cut back its military forces for economic reasons.[65]

Within China, however, the Communists began the effort that Mao had proposed in March 1949 to "systematically and completely destroy imperialist domination in China . . . in the political, economic, and cultural fields." The expulsion or takeover of American and other Western institutions and interests, accomplished in large part by subtle pressure instead of expropriation, was highly effective and soon resulted in a major exodus of Westerners. At about the same time a major influx of Russians began. In its propaganda, Peking kept up a stridently antiimperialist, anti-American line, in part to mobilize support within China but also to sustain the pressure on the United States to disengage totally from China. Simultaneously it carried out a massive propaganda campaign to promote Sino-Soviet friendship.

United States policymakers in this period viewed the new Chinese regime as part of a monolithic, Soviet-controlled Communist bloc, stressing, in their public statements, the likelihood that Chinese nationalism and the Soviet desire for domination would eventually come into conflict. Accusing Peking of being a servile satellite of Moscow, they made clear their hope that in time the Chinese Communist leaders would become "Titoists" and break with the Russians—a line that probably angered many leaders in Peking.[66] In fact, the evidence never supported the idea that Peking was a supine Soviet satellite, and it is difficult to know whether the Washington line reflected real misconceptions or was simply a tactic to try deliberately to exacerbate Sino-Soviet frictions.

In early 1950 the prospects certainly were not favorable for an immediate establishment of relations between Washington and Peking, but the door was by no means closed. The steady consolidation of Communist control in China, the step-by-step disengagement of the United States from its associations with the Nationalists, and other trends pointed toward an eventual accommodation to reality. When the Chinese Communists actively prepared in early 1950 for an invasion of Taiwan, the United States declared that it would not intervene militarily to prevent it. If this had occurred, it would have eliminated the basis for any major U.S. reintervention in the China conflict. Establishment of Peking-Washington relations might have followed in due time thereafter.

The situation fundamentally changed, however, as a result of the sudden outbreak of conflict in Korea in June 1950. In the ensuing weeks and months, both Washington and Peking made far-reaching decisions that virtually insured Sino-American hostility and conflict for many years to come. The first decisions that transformed the situation were made in Washington. It was not simply the American decision—doubtless unexpected by both Moscow and Peking—to intervene in Korea to help defend the South against the North's attack that aroused Chinese concern, although any major U.S. military action near China's borders could not but create alarm in Peking. More important were the American decisions to reintervene in the Chinese civil war, by interposing the Seventh Fleet between the China mainland and Taiwan to "neutralize" the Taiwan Strait, and—in a reversal of U.S. policy defined as recently as January—to reopen the question of Taiwan's future status, in effect challenging Peking's claim to the island.[67]

American leaders made these decisions under great pressure, probably without fully considering their possible long-run implications. Fearing that the Korean War signaled a broad military challenge by the entire Communist bloc to the entire "free world," they responded by stepping up worldwide efforts to counter any pressures or threats from Communist forces anywhere.[68] From Peking's point of view, however, the American move to reintervene in Taiwan tended to confirm its worst fears about the United States. Once again the Americans were seen to be the active protectors of their internal enemy, the Nationalists, and now they were also seen to be deliberately blocking the completion of the territorial reunification of the country.

As the Korean War progressed, and the fighting turned against the North Koreans, Chinese fear about a direct threat to northeast China increased. A crucial turning point occurred in September and October 1950. When it appeared that United Nations forces (in China's eyes, U.S. forces) might cross the 38th parallel and move north, Peking became alarmed about the possibility of a total defeat of the North Korean regime, which it considered to be a buffer essential to China's own security. It warned the Americans that if they crossed the 38th parallel, China would not stand idly by, and when the United States ignored the warning, Chinese "volunteers" moved into North Korea.[69] Within a brief period, the Korean War turned into a U.S.-China military conflict.

From late 1950 until mid-1953 the United States and China fought a major, if limited, war, which created deep feelings of mutual hostility.[70] In the fall of 1950, when China was invited to participate in UN discussion of the situation in Korea, its representative charged that the United States was "systematically building up a military encirclement...in preparation for further attack on the People's Republic of China." Washington, he said, "follows the beaten path of the Japanese imperialist aggressors."[71]

Within China, Peking's leaders stepped up their efforts to tighten political control and accelerate revolutionary change, justifying many of their harsh moves to suppress counterrevolutionaries, bourgeois businessmen, and Western-oriented intellectuals by stressing the American threat to China. The calls made by General Douglas MacArthur and others for direct military action against the mainland highlighted the potential dangers for China.[72] The Communists' "resist America, aid Korea" campaign provided an umbrella for mobilization efforts of all sorts, and under its slogans, Chinese leaders appealed strongly to Chinese nationalism and stepped up their efforts to cut China's past ties with the West.[73] In the process, they arrested several dozen American civilians, charging them with spying. Later the Chinese were to deliberately use some prisoners as bargaining chips in dealing with the United States, in ways that intensified American hostility. Peking actively fostered anti-American feeling. "Hate the United States," the Chinese people were urged in late 1950, "for she is the deadly enemy of the Chinese people. ... Despise the United States, for she is a rotten imperialist nation. ... Look with contempt upon the United States, for she is a paper tiger and can be fully defeated."[74]

The heightening of anticommunism in the United States paralleled the intensification of anti-Americanism in China, and in some respects attitudes in the two countries were mirror images. McCarthyism reached a peak of virulence in this period. Most of the American public accepted the prevalent view of China as a dangerously irresponsible and aggressive nation, dedicated to unlimited revolutionary expansionism, by military means if necessary.

Two Decades of Confrontation

The Korean War created mutual suspicions and fears that were to poison Sino-American relations for most of the 1950s and 1960s, initiating two decades of open confrontation.[75] In one sense the two countries had *no* relations during these two decades. There were no formal diplomatic ties, no trade, no legal travel back and forth, and virtually no mutual contact between ordinary citizens of the two countries (there were a few exceptions, but very few). Probably never in the modern period have two major societies been so isolated from each other for so long in peacetime—if the cold war could be considered peace. (Contacts between Washington and Moscow were considerably greater during the long period that they had no formal diplomatic ties from 1917 to the early 1930s.) China and the United States confronted each other, at a distance, as implacable adversaries.

Despite the lack of formal relations, leaders in both Peking and Washington were preoccupied by policy toward the other. In different ways and degrees, it was an obsession of both. Actually, Sino-American relations of a sort were extensive, but they were conducted to a large extent by proxy, in and through third countries. Periodically, the two countries came into direct confrontation militarily, in a series of tense crises on China's periphery. Peking and Washington constantly communicated with each other, through their official statements and actions, their propaganda, and their military deployments; such communications, however, were instruments of conflict, not accommodation.

And even though they had no conventional diplomatic relations, Chinese and American diplomatic representatives met frequently at the negotiating table, not simply in multilateral international conferences but, from 1955 on, in almost continuous bilateral talks, at the ambassadorial level, held in third countries. Ironically, diplomatic contacts with Americans during this period of "no relations" may well have been greater than those China had with any other nation except the Soviet Union. To a considerable degree, however, these contacts were sterile and simply reinforced the existing hostility between the two countries. There was almost no movement toward compromise or understanding.

United States policy toward China, in the post-Korea period, obviously posed for China its greatest and most pressing foreign-policy problems. Based on the premise that the Peking regime was an integral part of a monolithic, Soviet-led bloc, was fundamentally aggressive and expansionist, and posed great military as well as political dangers to other nations in Asia, Washington's entire Asian policy was designed to counter the "China threat" as it was then perceived. The aim, most clearly articulated by Secretary of State Dulles, was to "contain" China, isolate it, reduce its influence abroad, deter it from threatening or putting pressure on its neighbors, and exert constant external pressure on it—in the hope that it would prove to be a "passing" phenomenon.[76] The United States refused to recognize the legitimacy of the People's Republic of China and followed a diplomatic policy of nonrecognition toward it. The other side of this coin was that Washington continued to recognize the Nationalists' Republic of China on Taiwan as the only legitimate government of China, though it maintained that the status of Taiwan itself was still undetermined, and it strongly supported the Nationalists' position in the United Nations and international community generally.

To isolate Communist China, the United States continued, even after the cease-fire in Korea, to enforce an embargo on China trade, and it pressed other nations to maintain restrictive trade policies toward Peking. It forbade American travel to mainland China and tried to discourage contacts by others. In addition, it expended considerable political capital to keep the Peking regime out of the United Nations and all other international bodies and worked hard to persuade other nations not to recognize it.

Condemning all forms of neutralism or nonalignment, the United States systematically built up a network of military alliances—with Japan, South Korea, Taiwan, the SEATO powers (Thailand, the Philippines, and Pakistan were the Asian members), and the ANZUS nations (Australia and New Zealand)—to contain the Chinese.[77] Washington's large-scale military and economic assistance to its Asian allies was designed to strengthen both their defense capabilities and their ability to suppress insurrection and subversion. It also gave strong support to noncommunist leaders in the Indochina states, even though they were not formally included in the alliance system. In addition, the American government supported covert anticommunist activities against the mainland from Taiwan and a number of other areas including Thailand, Burma, and the Tibetan borderlands.[78] Washington saw all of this as a necessary response to the threat posed by Communist China.

For Peking, however, it clearly added up to a major American threat to China. Peking's leaders charged that the United States was not only infringing on China's territory but was "encircling" it militarily, threatening and pressuring it, denying it the international status and rights that were its due, and attempting to weaken its influence by all possible means. Peking was particularly outraged, and frustrated, by renewed American support of the Nationalist regime with which Washington signed a formal defense treaty in 1954.[79] More broadly, it viewed the United States as the principal nation posing a direct threat to China's security and blocking achievement of its general international goals.

Militarily Peking's response was, of necessity, defensive. China was compelled at first to rely primarily on its treaty with Russia and Soviet diplomatic and military support to deter any major military attack. But it worked hard to build up China's own strength. It also provided support to smaller Communist nations on its periphery—North Korea and North Vietnam and, for a time, Mongolia—and gave moral support and limited material aid to revolutionaries in other neighboring areas. To counter U.S. influence, it worked to expand its influence abroad, to appeal to the nonaligned nations, and to weaken the anticommunist alignment of forces confronting China. It also did all it could to undermine U.S.-

supported measures, such as trade restrictions, directed against China. In a sense, Peking's entire foreign-policy strategy, especially toward other Asian areas, was a response to its perception of an "American threat," even though its policies obviously also reflected the Communists' basic ideological outlook and other broad national goals.

From about 1952 on, China moved gradually to abandon the dichotomous world view that had shaped its policy since 1948; it returned to a united-front strategy, designed to "ally" China "with all the forces that can be allied with" in order to struggle against "American imperialism." The definition of potential allies gradually changed, and eventual, "social imperialism"—the Soviet Union—also became a prime target of the struggle, but Peking never returned to the concept of a relatively simple, clear-cut Communist-noncommunist struggle that had shaped its policy during 1948–52. The fundamental purpose of fostering such a broad united front in the 1950s and 1960s was to mobilize all possible opposition to the United States.

In dealing directly with the United States, China had very little leverage. But Peking's leaders kept trying, by varied means, to induce or compel Washington to change its policies—especially to get the United States to disengage from Taiwan.

Chinese and American Rigidity and Flexibility

Neither Chinese nor American policies were static. Ironically, Peking's leaders at the start showed considerable flexibility in their dealings with the United States and then moved toward increasing rigidity, while the United States at the start showed great rigidity and then moved toward increased flexibility.

Immediately after the Korean War, during 1954–55, Peking tried through limited military pressure to dislodge the United States from areas adjacent to China, in particular Taiwan. After this failed, it adopted more moderate and flexible policies, and during 1955–56 took a series of notably conciliatory initiatives toward the Americans, trying to achieve its goals in the Taiwan area through political means. These policies also failed to produce the desired results, at least at the pace the Chinese hoped for, and Peking's leaders shifted back to a strategy of pressure in late 1957, taking action that in 1958 produced the second major crisis in the Taiwan Strait. When the Chinese were forced to back down again, in the face of a massive mobilization of U.S. military power in the area, Peking seemed to lose hope that it could soon alter U.S. policies by either pressure or negotiation. In regard to Taiwan, leaders in Peking were compelled to think in long-range terms and to hope for an eventual erosion of American support for the Nationalists. Elsewhere they gave what support they could to China's friends and tried to induce secondary adversaries and neutral nations to oppose U.S. policies. Seemingly accepting hostile confrontation as a given, they settled into a posture of rigid inflexibility in their dealings with the Americans (although there are hints that some leaders in Peking favored greater flexibility). They continued to see many American actions in areas around China as threatening, however, and on several occasions took active measures to deter potential American threats.

In direct negotiations with the Americans, the Chinese became increasingly rigid and defensive over time, and found themselves resisting initiatives originating in Washington rather than taking new initiatives. This retreat to an essentially defensive negotiating posture was reinforced by the escalation of the Sino-Soviet dispute which resulted in the loss of Moscow's support and, eventually, created a situation in which Peking viewed itself as "encircled," pressured, and threatened by both Washington and Moscow.

The course of American policy toward China was almost the opposite. The Korean War, the effects of McCarthyism, and the succession of Dwight D. Eisenhower to the presidency and John Foster Dulles to the post of secretary of state resulted in a crusading anticommunist policy immediately after the Korean War. Seeing the Chinese as threatening everywhere on China's periphery, Dulles viewed Peking's flexibility and initiatives in the mid-1950s with deep suspicion and strongly resisted them. The U.S. government began seriously to consider alternative approaches only after the 1958 crisis in the Taiwan Strait and Dulles's death shortly thereafter. Then slow—some would say glacial—adjustments began to be made in China policy. The United States imposed new restraints on the Nationalists, to reduce the chance of conflict in the Taiwan Strait. It also began privately to propose small steps toward increased contacts, some of which were similar to those that Peking had previously urged. Changes in American public opinion and the attitudes of U.S. allies gradually exerted pressure on American leaders to consider more significant changes in China policy, and eventually Washington began to propose some changes publicly. After 1960, when the existence of a serious Sino-Soviet split became clear, the American government began to downgrade the "China threat." By the latter half of the 1960s, in striking contrast to the mid-1950s, it was the leaders in Washington who were the suitors making advances to China, and it was the leaders in Peking who were spurning them.

Crises and Negotiations

The first time that American and Chinese Communist representatives met at the negotiating table in the post-1949 period was in Korea, while the war was still under way. In mid-1951, when it became clear to both sides that any attempt to achieve victory would lead to a dangerous expansion of the war, both in effect accepted the fact of stalemate and agreed to discuss an armistice. American and South Korean military officials met with Chinese and North Korean officers in July to discuss a cease-fire. The talks which the U.S. Joint Chiefs of Staff had expected to last about three weeks finally ended with the signing of a truce at Panmunjom in June 1953.[80] In the meantime both sides had suffered huge casualties. The truce was agreed upon only after Washington had hinted that it might broaden the war, and possibly even use nuclear weapons,[81] and after the Chinese had finally accepted failure in their effort to make the Americans return all prisoners of war rather than give the prisoners a choice, which had been the prime issue in the deadlocked talks since early in the negotiating process.

These talks established a pattern of hostile negotiations, and left a residue of bitterness that was to last for years. The bitterness was compounded when, following the signing of the armistice agreement, Americans and Chinese met again at Panmunjom, in October 1953—this time represented by diplomats, not soldiers—to discuss political issues. (The armistice had included a clause recommending a political conference to negotiate the withdrawal of all foreign forces and the peaceful unification of Korea.) These talks, described by one participant as "an exercise in the diplomacy of stalemate,"[82] were interrupted by walkouts staged by both sides, and they ended in complete failure.

In the winter of 1953–54, the attention of China, the United States, and much of the world shifted to the Indochina states as the civil war there, which had been under way since soon after World War II, reached a critical point.[83] The Chinese Communists probably did not see a direct threat to themselves in Vietnam comparable to the one in Korea, but they did view North Vietnam, like North Korea, as a buffer area ruled by friendly Communist leaders and important to China's security. Since 1949 they had made clear that they would provide significant support to Ho Chi-minh and his regime, and after Chinese Communist forces reached the borders of Indochina they provided training as well as material aid to Ho's forces. In 1953–54 this aid was significantly increased.

The Americans' interest and involvement had also increased in 1948–49, when the Communist victory in China was imminent and the position of the French and noncommunist forces in the Indochinese states was deteriorating. In 1953–54 Secretary Dulles, alarmed by what he saw as another example of the worldwide dangers of expansionist "international Communism," feared direct Chinese intervention, and when the fighting reached a critical point he threatened American retaliation if Peking should send its own forces into the area.

To deal with the crisis in Indochina and with the Korean problem, the European powers convened a major international conference at Geneva in 1954. This was the first occasion since 1949 at which the principal American and Chinese Communist officials responsible for foreign policy had an opportunity to meet—as well as the first time that any top Communist leaders from the People's Republic had attended a major international conference.[84]

The conference produced a settlement that temporarily halted the fighting in Indochina and ostensibly laid the basis for a political settlement. Among other things it called for elections within two years. In accepting this compromise, the Chinese seemed to give priority to China's own security interests in the area rather than to the Vietnamese Communists' revolutionary goals. Secretary Dulles, who found the idea of compromise with the Communists basically repugnant, went along reluctantly. The United States refused to sign the agreements, but it did state unilaterally that it would not "disturb" them.

The military struggles in the Indochina states were stopped only temporarily, however. Later, when South Vietnam's leaders refused to participate in the promised elections, Washington backed them; when the North Vietnamese leaders subsequently reactivated their military struggle, Peking and Moscow supported them. Eventually, Sino-American struggle by proxy resumed in that region.

However, in 1954 Peking seemed relatively well satisfied with the immediate results of the Geneva Conference as they affected Southeast Asia. But the conference did nothing to improve Sino-American relations. In some respects, in fact, it damaged them further. Premier Chou En-lai, for example, was deeply offended when Secretary Dulles refused even to shake hands with him at the conference; he spoke bitterly of the incident many years later.[85]

Almost immediately after the Geneva Conference, the Chinese Communists turned their attention once again to Taiwan. In September 1954 they called for its "liberation" and began shelling Quemoy, a Nationalist-held island near the mainland.[86] The resulting crisis further heightened tensions in Sino-American relations and probably reinforced Peking's views about Washington's hostility and propensity to intervene in Chinese affairs. It also bolstered Washington's views on Peking's military aggressiveness.

Probably the leaders in Peking had no intention of launching a major invasion but instead were trying to exert pressure on both the Nationalists and Americans in order to achieve certain political aims. Ever since 1950, Peking had seen a steady strengthening of the Nationalist regime, with increasing U.S. support, and it feared the result would be a permanent separation of the island. The Communists' principal hopes in applying military pressures in 1954–55 could well have been to demoralize the Nationalists and convince the Americans they should disengage from the area. The results, however, were almost the opposite. Although the Communists were able to take over the Tachen Islands, which were evacuated by the Nationalists, the United States went ahead with plans to sign an open-ended mutual defense treaty with the Nationalist regime, thereby creating a formal and long-term American commitment to defend Taiwan. In addition, the U.S. Congress passed the so-called Formosa Resolution authorizing the President to use American forces to defend not only Taiwan but also the offshore islands if he so chose. At the same time, however, Washington took steps to restrain the Nationalists from embarking on military adventures against the mainland. In an exchange of notes, the Nationalists agreed that the "use of force" from Taiwan required "joint agreement."[87] Not long before, the Eisenhower administration had talked of "liberation" of Communist nations, and unleashing Chiang Kai-shek, but now Chiang was obviously leashed. It is doubtful, however, that Peking considered this any gain; its primary concern now was not any military threat from the Nationalists but rather the possibility of Taiwan's permanent separation from the mainland.[88] By 1955, the "liberation of Taiwan" seemed more remote than ever.

At this point, Peking's leaders initiated an entirely new approach toward the United States. In April 1955, while attending the Bandung Conference of Asian and African States, Premier Chou made a dramatic public offer to "sit down and enter into negotiations with the United States Government to discuss the question of relaxing tension in the Far East, and especially the question of relaxing tension in the Taiwan area." He also asserted that: "The Chinese people are friendly to the American people. The Chinese people do not want to have a war with the United States of America."[89] The conciliatory tone of Chou's statement was remarkable in light of the conflicts and tensions of the previous five years. Chou also offered soon thereafter to negotiate directly with the "responsible local authorities" on Taiwan regarding "peaceful liberation."[90] American leaders were taken aback by Chou's statements, and initially were inclined to reject his offer; but ultimately Washington agreed, and official Sino-American talks at the ambassadorial level began in Geneva in late summer of 1955.

The ambassadorial talks between the United States and the People's Republic of China, first at Geneva and later at Warsaw, provided a quasi-diplomatic link between the two countries for more than a decade and a half. They continued with only minor interruptions right up until the U.S.-China opening of 1971–72, which was followed by the direct exchange of diplomatic representatives in 1973.[91] But the talks failed to resolve any of the fundamental conflicts between the two countries. In fact, in some respects they may have exacerbated them. Yet they did provide a useful forum in which both sides could clarify their positions and intentions, and when subsequent crises erupted on China's periphery—in 1958, 1962, and 1965—they were an important communication channel that helped to reduce the dangers of miscalculation.

The first cautious contacts between American and Chinese Communist diplomats had been made at the Geneva Conference in 1954, when the question of repatriation of citizens was raised. The U.S. government was determined to obtain the release of about forty Americans still held in China; the Chinese insisted there were also Chinese citizens held in the United States who should be allowed to leave. The issue was discussed in a series of meetings between consular representatives in Geneva, but, as of 1955, without success.

When the ambassadorial talks started, Washington wanted to limit them, and felt that the release of American citizens in China should be the priority item on the agenda, to be followed by discussion of a "ceasefire" in the Taiwan area. On their part, the Chinese wished to discuss a broad range of issues, including the Taiwan problem, withdrawal of U.S. forces from the area, the end of the U.S. trade embargo, the stoppage of subversive activities directed against China, and the conclusion of an Asian-Pacific "pact of collective peace."[92] The Taiwan issue was clearly its top priority. The two sides finally agreed that the agenda should include "repatriation of civilians who desire to return to their respective countries" plus "certain other practical matters now at issue between both sides."[93]

The one and only concrete agreement reached between the two sides during the decade and a half of talks was concluded quite rapidly. In September 1955 the Americans and Chinese signed a document dealing with repatriation of citizens. But this agreement proved to be an obstacle rather than a stepping stone to further understanding, for the two sides argued about its implementation for years thereafter. The Americans felt that the agreement required the immediate unconditional release of all Americans held in China, but Peking released them in a very gradual, piecemeal fashion, and the repatriation was not completed until more than a decade later. The Chinese countered American charges of noncompliance with charges of American obstructionism in the repatriation of Chinese in the United States. Clearly, Peking viewed the repatriation issue as a lever to press the United States to move on to the larger issues that were its primary concerns, whereas Washington viewed completion of the repatriation as a prerequisite for serious discussion of other issues and regarded Peking's noncompliance as evidence of bad faith and therefore a block to agreement on other questions.

Discussion of the Taiwan problem began shortly after the repatriation agreement was signed. What Peking wanted was total disengagement of the United States from Taiwan. What the United States wanted was stabilization of the status quo and avoidance of military conflict in the area. The Americans pressed the Chinese to agree to renounce the use of force, specifically in regard to Taiwan, except for "self defense." The Chinese declared that they desired to settle Sino-American disputes by peaceful means, without the threat or use of force, and that both sides should pledge to do this, but they argued that the Taiwan issue was a purely domestic question. Although Peking was willing to say that it would settle the Taiwan problem by peaceful means *if possible*, it insisted that it could not renounce the *right* to use force to solve a domestic issue. It also asserted that there could be no question of any American right to use force for the defense of a province of China.

Altogether seven proposals and counterproposals on this issue were exchanged, but neither side was willing to compromise its basic position or to be maneuvered into weakening its stand. Peking was determined to maintain its claim to Taiwan and not to compromise its right to use force if necessary to "liberate" it. Washington was determined to defend Taiwan against any military attack and not to compromise its right to do so.

In general, however, Peking showed greater tactical flexibility in this period than Washington did. Between 1955 and late 1957 the Chinese took one initiative after another to propose higher-level negotiations— for instance, a meeting of foreign ministers—and increased contact between the two societies, including resumption of trade and an exchange of newsmen.[94] All these proposals were rebuffed by the Americans.

Conceivably, if the Americans had matched the flexibility of the Chinese at that time, the dynamics of interaction between the two countries might have begun to change. Conceivably, also, if the Chinese had rapidly implemented the repatriation agreement, Washington's responses might have been more flexible. But, even if mutual concessions had led to increased contacts, the overall relationship might not have improved very much, because of fundamental differences over the Taiwan issue. In the 1950s and 1960s neither side was prepared, as both later were, to deemphasize the issue because of more pressing concerns.

By late 1957 the Geneva talks had settled into a pattern of stalemate on the key issues. Peking, concerned at the possibility of long-term de facto separation of Taiwan, denounced the United States for pursuing a "two Chinas" policy. Proclaiming that the east wind prevails over the west wind, Mao in November 1957 called for more active worldwide opposition to the United States and urged the entire Communist bloc to stand up to the imperialists, even if this involved real risks.

In mid-1958 Peking's leaders decided again to use force to exert pressure on the Nationalists, and on the United States to alter its policy toward Taiwan.[95] Their motives were probably similar to those that had led them to precipitate the first offshore islands crisis in 1954: to demoralize the Nationalists and set in motion a process that might eventually persuade the United States to disengage from Taiwan. Peking may have calculated that a new crisis would increase divisions within the United States and between the United States and its allies, which did, in fact, occur. It clearly hoped, also, to induce the Soviet Union to give it stronger backing. Moreover, the external crisis was used to justify the new mobilizational efforts within China while the Great Leap Forward and the commune program were in full swing.

The 1958 confrontation proved to be even more dangerous than the one in 1954. When Peking's bombardment and attempt to blockade Quemoy looked as if they might succeed, the United States made it clear that it would help defend the offshore islands, and it massed tremendous naval and air forces to back up its intentions. Washington also hinted, once again, that the use of nuclear weapons was under consideration. Although the Russians backed China defensively, with statements designed to deter any American attack against the mainland, they made it clear that there were limits to what they would do and that they would not support offensive action to "liberate" Taiwan.

At the height of the crisis Peking offered to reopen negotiations with the Americans. During the previous year, the Geneva talks had bogged down and then virtually collapsed. In 1957, the U.S. government, showing the first real signs of flexibility, had offered to grant permission to American newsmen to go to China, but it had also announced that it would not assure reciprocity to Chinese newsmen. Predictably, Peking had refused to go along. Then in early 1958 the United States had proposed downgrading representation at the talks. The Chinese had immediately indicated they opposed this and wanted the talks to continue at the ambassadorial level. For more than half a year no meetings were held. They were only resumed on September 15, 1958 (now at Warsaw) following Chou En-lai's September 6 proposal to reopen negotiations, at the height of the offshore islands crisis. Although military tension did not subside until some time later, after the Communists' blockade of Quemoy had been broken, the renewal of talks underlined the desire of both sides to avoid major conflict. The talks were unsuccessful in bridging the two sides' basic differences, but they helped defuse the crisis, which petered out several weeks later.

The 1958 crisis was a watershed in many respects. It was not only a milestone in the development of the Sino-Soviet split; it had a major, if subtle, impact on both Peking and Washington that led ultimately to significant changes in Sino-American relations. Peking's hope that it could, by use of limited military pressure, weaken the Nationalists' and Americans' position or compel the United States to disengage from Taiwan was dealt a severe blow in 1958; thereafter the Chinese Communists did not renew the attempt. Before long, they became preoccupied with the deterioration of their relations with Moscow, and later with what they viewed as tacit U.S.-Soviet collaboration damaging to their interests. Apparently they concluded that both Washington and Moscow wished to prevent China from becoming a nuclear power and favored stabilization of the status quo on Taiwan. Leaders in Peking continued to see the United States as China's prime enemy, but they apparently concluded that they would have to work gradually toward trying to dislodge the United States from Taiwan and meanwhile focus their activities on other objectives.

After the 1958 crisis, the United States moved slowly toward more flexible tactics, recognizing they were needed to prevent the erosion of positions requiring international support, such as the trade embargo and opposition to the seating of Peking in the United Nations.[96] As anticommunist passions in the United States cooled, and the depth of the Sino-Soviet dispute became clear, the China threat seemed less formidable. The changes in Washington's policies began to be significant in the second half of the 1960s, but long before that a reversal of American and Chinese tactical positions had occurred.

From 1959 on it was Washington rather than Peking that pressed for agreement on secondary issues, such as the exchange of newsmen and an increase of other nonofficial contacts. On these issues, its positions became increasingly flexible.[97] For example, in 1959 Washington indicated its willingness to grant reciprocity to Chinese newsmen, and by 1965 it was prepared to have Chinese newsmen come to the United States even without any guarantee of reciprocity for American newsmen.[98] But now the Chinese were not interested.

Soon after the inauguration of John F. Kennedy's Democratic administration in 1961 there were cautious hints of possible changes in the American posture. In his debates with Richard M. Nixon, Kennedy had indicated that he believed the United States should persuade the Nationalists to withdraw from the offshore islands; later he hinted at the possibility of providing food to China and broadening nonofficial contacts and noted the need to include China in disarmament efforts.[99] (And in 1963 —just after Kennedy's death—one of his assistant secretaries of state, Roger Hilsman, called for an "open door" approach to China.) But Kennedy, fearful of the domestic political costs of dealing with the controversial China issue, deferred consideration of substantial changes in China policy.[100] Another factor arguing for caution was Peking's strong endorsement of guerrilla warfare which became a major preoccupation of the Kennedy administration. Peking, in any case, apparently did not take Kennedy's signals of possible changes in policy seriously.[101]

President Lyndon Johnson continued a cautious approach. However, following the 1966 Senate Foreign Relations Committee's hearings on China policy, which demonstrated considerable public support for a new policy, Johnson endorsed the idea of a "free flow of ideas and people and goods" between the United States and China and called for a process of "reconciliation."[102] He too, however, was unwilling to do more than alter the United States' posture toward China in very general and fairly vague terms; the Vietnam War occupied him almost totally. He took no significant concrete steps to change American policy regarding Taiwan, recognition of Peking, trade, or the China seat in the United Nations. Nevertheless, Peking probably became more aware of changing American attitudes in this period.

Trends in Peking's policies were almost the reverse of Washington's. Whereas in the 1950s the Chinese had urged agreement on secondary issues before taking up the basic—and most difficult—questions relating to Taiwan, from 1960 on they resisted American initiatives both at the Warsaw talks and publicly and maintained that the Taiwan question had to be resolved *before* agreement on any secondary issues could be reached. Chou En-lai insisted above all on agreement first on "two points of principle": that "all disputes between China and the United States, including the dispute between the two countries in the Taiwan region, should be settled through peaceful negotiations" and that "the United States must agree to withdraw its armed forces from Taiwan and the Taiwan Strait" (with the schedule subject to "subsequent discussions").[103] Since Washington showed no inclination to agree on these principles, Peking stood pat on virtually all other questions. Chinese leaders probably now feared that minor steps to improve relations with the United States might suggest Peking's tacit acceptance of the Taiwan stalemate.

There were hints in the early 1960s of debate in China on policy toward both the Soviet Union and the United States in which certain leaders may have argued for a more moderate and flexible policy toward Washington (allegedly, Liu Shao-ch'i in 1962 supported a policy of "three reconciliations," including less hostile relations with Washington).[104] And in 1964 at Warsaw the Chinese proposed a bilateral agreement on "no first use" of nuclear weapons, which the United States was not willing to consider.[105] But, overall, Peking maintained a stand-pat position on the issues that had been discussed at Geneva and Warsaw ever since 1955.

Although virtually no progress was made toward concrete agreements in the decade following 1958, both sides relaxed their view of the threat the other posed. At times when suspicions and fear mounted, the ambassadorial talks proved to be an important channel for clarifying intentions, thereby preventing inadvertent escalation of conflict. In 1961, when the Laos crisis raised new fears on both sides, the United States indicated to the Chinese at Warsaw that a failure to reach a cease-fire might result in American military intervention; the Chinese informed the Americans they were serious about their desire to negotiate an acceptable formula for neutralizing Laos. The agreement finally reached at the 1962 Geneva Conference on Laos defused this situation, at least temporarily.[106]

In 1962, when the Nationalists threatened to take military action against the mainland at a time when Peking was heavily engaged in border disputes with both India and the Soviet Union, the Communists began to build up their military forces opposite Taiwan. Washington not only imposed restraints on Taiwan but informed Peking through the Warsaw link that it did not associate itself with the Nationalists' statements and would not support any Nationalist attack on the mainland. These statements clearly helped to prevent another confrontation in the Taiwan area.[107]

Peking's doubts about U.S. intentions escalated and may have reached a new high following large-scale American military intervention in Vietnam in 1964–65, however. In response to U.S. bombing of North Vietnam, following the Tonkin Gulf incident in August 1964, Peking sent a squadron of planes (MIG-17s) plus thirty thousand to fifty thousand engineering and construction troops, including antiaircraft units, to assist North Vietnam.[108] Reports of civil as well as military defense efforts in South China reinforce other evidence that the Chinese genuinely feared escalation that might lead to American attacks on China itself, and in 1965 the leaders in Peking debated how to respond to this danger. The policy actually pursued was a relatively cautious and nonprovocative one. A contributing factor may have been the lack of complete agreement with Hanoi as well as serious differences with the Soviet Union over how to respond.[109] Peking nevertheless made clear that it would actively resist any actions against China and would strongly oppose any threat to North Vietnam's existence. The United States also exercised restraint in relation to the Chinese, to prevent a new U.S.-China conflict. Even though the escalation of U.S. involvement in South Vietnam and American air actions near the Chinese border inevitably created new Sino-American tensions, the American representatives at Warsaw assured the Chinese on several occasions that the United States did not wish to pose any threat to the security of China and had no designs on the territory of North Vietnam.[110] These assurances doubtless contributed to an abatement in Peking's fears from 1966 on. But basic Chinese and American interests and purposes continued to clash, in Vietnam and elsewhere.

Sino-American Détente

During the middle and late 1960s U.S.-China relations reached such a low point that there was little hope for any improvement. In Washington there were small signs of a more flexible attitude but no significant change in policy. Chinese leaders still viewed the United States as an extremely hostile power, pressing in on them at many points around China's periphery. Their bitterness was clearly reflected in comments made by Foreign Minister Ch'en Yi at an unusual press conference for foreign correspondents in September 1965. "For sixteen years we have been waiting for the U.S. imperialists to come in and attack us," Ch'en said. "My hair has turned gray in waiting. Perhaps I will not have the luck to see the U.S. imperialist invasion of China, but my children may see it, and they will resolutely carry on the fight."[111]

At the height of the Vietnam War, although both the United States and China took pains to avoid direct military conflict, they were engaged in a struggle by proxy. During 1966–68, moreover, when China was convulsed by the Cultural Revolution, Peking adopted an isolationist yet bellicose posture toward most of the world. Despite the fact that now "social imperialism" (the Soviet Union) became a primary target of Chinese hostility, along with "imperialism" (the United States), there was no sign of any inclination on China's part to reassess its policy toward the United States.

Then, between 1968 and 1972, both Peking and Washington reexamined their fundamental approaches and moved to redefine their basic policies toward each other.[112] The results were the dramatic steps toward détente that culminated in President Nixon's trip to Peking and the signing of the Shanghai communiqué. This remarkable turnabout started the process of "normalization" of U.S.-China relations and profoundly altered the entire pattern of big-power relations in Asia.

The process began with cautious probings in 1968–69 by both sides. Peking put out the first feeler in November 1968 when a Foreign Ministry spokesman proposed the reopening of the Warsaw talks to conclude an "agreement on the Five Principles of Peaceful Coexistence."[113] This came soon after the Soviet Union's invasion of Czechoslovakia, which had greatly alarmed the Chinese, and on the eve of the inauguration of a new Republican administration in Washington. The Cultural Revolution was drawing to a close, and relatively "moderate" pragmatic leaders began to reassert themselves. About this time Peking made some far-reaching decisions to embark on a new, far more active foreign policy designed to expand China's diplomatic relations and broaden its participation in the world community. Washington immediately agreed to reopen the Warsaw talks, but then less than forty-eight hours before the meeting scheduled for February 20, 1969, Peking canceled it. Its pretext was the defection of a Chinese Communist diplomat to the United States.[114] A more likely explanation, however, is that there was uncertainty and debate among the Chinese leaders.

When President Nixon assumed office in January 1969 he immediately initiated an examination of possible new moves in policy toward China, ordering a basic study of the subject.[115] Undeterred by the postponement of the Warsaw talks, Nixon began to put out feelers to the Chinese—first through French President Charles de Gaulle, and later through Pakistanis and Rumanians—to indicate Washington's desire to open a dialogue as well as its determination to withdraw U.S. military forces from Vietnam.[116] Then administration leaders began to speak publicly of the American desire for increased contacts with China. After the March 1969 Chinese-Russian border clashes, they stressed that Sino-Soviet military conflict should be avoided, which in a subtle way bolstered Peking against possible threats from Moscow.[117] In July, Nixon articulated, at Guam, his so-called Nixon Doctrine, calling for reduced American military involvement in all of Asia.[118] This doctrine revealed a significant downgrading of the China threat in the eyes of American leaders and implied an important reassessment of containment policies.

In July and again in December, the administration further relaxed U.S. travel and trade restrictions affecting China. Small as these steps were, they constituted important moves toward dismantling past policies. That they were taken *unilaterally*, without a request for a quid pro quo, was evidence of Washington's genuine desire to adjust its China policy. Perhaps most important, the United States on November 7 stopped active patrolling by American ships in the Taiwan Strait.[119] Throughout 1969, Peking was unresponsive, publicly, and it continued to attack both U.S. imperialism and Soviet revisionism and the alleged anti-Chinese collusion between the two. There is no doubt, however, that Chinese leaders were encouraged to reexamine their own policies.

In December 1969, when the U.S. ambassador in Warsaw contacted the Chinese to urge reopening the Warsaw talks, the Chinese were responsive, and the talks did reopen in early 1970, for the first time in about two years. Peking's tentativeness was apparent, however, when in May it canceled the next Warsaw session, just before its scheduled date, doubtless in response to the American invasion of Cambodia. China also held a "summit conference of the Indochinese peoples" and renewed its propaganda attacks on the United States.[120] Nixon had tried through intermediaries to assure Peking that the United States still desired to disengage from Vietnam and improve relations with China, but the Chinese probably remained skeptical.

During the fall and winter of 1970–71, despite developments in Vietnam, both sides continued to hint at possible policy changes and to feel out the intentions of the other. On October 1, 1970, China's National Day, Mao invited the American correspondent, Edgar Snow, to sit beside him on the public rostrum in Peking. Subsequently, in December, he told Snow that he would welcome a visit by Nixon to China.[121] Not long thereafter Nixon began secretly to explore the possibility of a high-level visit to Peking, using Pakistani and Rumanian intermediaries again.

United States support of the South Vietnamese invasion of Laos in February 1971 may have raised all the old Chinese doubts, even though Nixon again tried to reassure the Chinese about Washington's intentions; but the failure of the invasion, and Washington's acceptance of it, may have convinced Peking that the United States really intended to withdraw from Vietnam. In the spring the Chinese finally sent a definite message through the Pakistanis inviting an "American envoy" to visit China, and the United States quickly accepted.[122]

Thereafter events developed rapidly. In April the Chinese "went public" and made a major move to indicate their changed attitude, inviting an American ping pong team to China. Premier Chou met the team and hailed the visit as opening a "new page" in Sino-American relations.[123] China also began to open the door to American newsmen. On its part, Washington took further steps to liberalize travel and trade regulations. Secretary of State William Rogers declared that he hoped the "new page" in Sino-American relations would become a "new chapter."[124] And the United States redefined its position on the Chinese representation issue in the United Nations. It had begun to do this in 1970; then during 1971 Washington made its new position clear. It proposed that Peking be seated in the Security Council and General Assembly, but supported continued representation for the Nationalists in the General Assembly.

Henry Kissinger's dramatic secret trip to China then took place in July 1971. In Peking he held long discussions with Premier Chou on a broad range of issues including Taiwan and Vietnam and accepted Chou's invitation for Nixon to come to China.[125] Nixon's announcement of his planned visit took the world by complete surprise and indicated to both allies and adversaries that fundamental changes in East Asian international relations were under way. Kissinger's presence in Peking again in the fall, at the time of the UN vote on Chinese representation, virtually insured the seating of the People's Republic of China in place of the Republic of China.[126] Finally, in February 1972 Nixon, accompanied by Kissinger, arrived in Peking, met Mao, and worked out with Chou the remarkable diplomatic document, the "Shanghai communiqué," which set an entirely new framework for Sino-American relations.

The prime consideration leading Peking's leaders to alter their U.S. policy in 1971–72, as in so many major shifts in their policies toward the major powers, was their concern about national security. By the end of the 1960s, as a result of the Soviet military buildup around China, the Russian invasion of Czechoslovakia in 1968, and the Sino-Soviet border clashes of 1969, a basic qualitative change had occurred in Sino-Soviet relations. Peking now viewed Moscow as the greatest threat to China's security. In contrast, from about 1966 on, Peking seemed to cautiously downgrade the U.S. threat, especially after the Americans began to disengage from Vietnam and promised to reduce U.S. military forces elsewhere in Asia. In this new situation, the Chinese clearly decided to try to induce Washington to serve as a counterweight to restrain Moscow.

In effect, Peking decided to give higher immediate priority to this goal than to ideological considerations or to its maximum objectives regarding Taiwan and Vietnam. The Chinese doubtlessly still hoped that they could nudge the United States toward loosening its ties with Taiwan as well as accelerating its military disengagement from Vietnam. But they were now prepared to accept short-run compromise and, if necessary, delay. Some leaders in Peking (probably including Lin Piao as well as top radical leaders) apparently opposed the compromises this new approach involved, and there was clearly debate about the wisdom of it. But the strong endorsement of the new policy by both Mao and Chou made it possible. Another factor influencing Peking's decisions may have been its heightened concern about the possibility of major Japanese re-armament. It is probable the Chinese believed a reduction of U.S.-China tensions would help to prevent this.

Several mutually reinforcing motives appear to have moved Nixon and Kissinger to adopt a new policy toward China. In order to facilitate and reduce the risks of American military disengagement from Vietnam and the reduction of American military involvements throughout Asia, explicit or tacit understandings with China were obviously desirable. The downgrading of the China threat made it possible to think in new terms. Both Nixon and Kissinger also wished to obtain greater leverage in dealing with Moscow, which they viewed as Washington's primary adversary. Although some skeptics warned that Sino-American détente might harden Soviet policy toward the United States, Nixon and Kissinger chose to believe that it would impose new restraints on Moscow and push it in the direction of further compromise and détente. They proved to be right, at least in the short run.

The significant changes in American public opinion in the 1960s made it seem possible that a more flexible China policy might actually evoke favorable responses, within and outside the government. In any case, Nixon's record as a hard-line, anticommunist leader gave him a kind of protection against right-wing criticism that none of his Democratic predecessors had enjoyed.

A New Framework for Relations

The Shanghai communiqué signed by President Nixon and Premier Chou on February 28, 1972, was a skillfully drafted instrument that laid the basis for a new Sino-American relationship.[127] It expressed the desire of both sides, each for its own reasons, to end their two-decade-old confrontation and to begin a process of "normalizing relations." Both compromised on certain issues, but both also made clear that fundamental differences continued. Many of these were frankly stated. Both sides also recognized that certain crucial issues—above all the Taiwan problem—were impossible to solve immediately and that it was necessary, in effect, to lay them aside and agree to disagree. The communiqué therefore simply marked the start, not the end, of a complex process that both sides recognized would take considerable time to complete.

In the first portions of the communiqué, each side "candidly" expressed its view on many general and specific international issues. The United States stressed that a "just and secure peace" required the elimination of "the basic causes of conflict" and "the danger of foreign aggression." It emphasized support for "individual freedom and social progress . . . free of outside pressure or intervention" and proposed "improving communication between countries that have different ideologies so as to lessen the risks of confrontation through accident, miscalculation or misunderstanding." Countries should show "mutual respect" and "compete peacefully," it said, and each should "reexamine its own attitudes." It reiterated support for a "negotiated solution" in the Indochina states, and for past U.S.-South Vietnamese proposals, but it also stated that even "in the absence of a negotiated settlement the United States envisages the ultimate withdrawal of all U.S. forces from the region consistent with the aim of self-determination." It strongly emphasized its "close bonds" with Japan, placing "the highest value" on U.S.-Japan relations. It also underlined its "close ties with and support for" South Korea and the need for relaxation of tension and increased communication between North and South Korea. And it endorsed the India-Pakistan cease-fire and called for the avoidance of great-power rivalry in South Asia.

The Chinese reiterated their faith in revolution and support for "the struggles of all the oppressed people and nations for freedom and liberation." Stressing the equality of all nations, they condemned bullying by big nations, stated their opposition to "hegemony and power politics of any kind," and pledged that "China will never be a superpower." Emphasizing the importance to all of "independence, sovereignty and territorial integrity," they declared that they opposed all "foreign aggression, interference, control and subversion" and proposed that "all foreign troops" be brought home from abroad. They reiterated their "firm support" of the peoples of Vietnam, Laos, and Cambodia, and endorsed the proposals made by the Provisional Revolutionary Government in South Vietnam and the Summit Conference of the Indochinese Peoples. They also emphasized their backing for North Korean proposals for "peaceful reunification" and the abolition of UNCURK (the UN Commission for the Unification and Rehabilitation of Korea). Stressing their opposition to "the revival and outward expansion of Japanese militarism," they endorsed the "Japanese people's desire" to build "an independent, democratic, peaceful and neutral Japan." And they underlined their support for Pakistan and self-determination in Jammu and Kashmir.

After these statements highlighting the "essential differences" of their "social systems and foreign policies," the two sides declared that they would conduct their relations on the basis of the five principles of co-existence and were prepared to settle "international disputes" (a phrase that obviously did not include the Peking-Taipei conflict, at least in Peking's view) "without resorting to the use or threat of force."

Jointly they declared their desire to make "progress toward the nor-malization of relations" and "to reduce the danger of international mili-tary conflict." They also pledged that neither should "seek hegemony in the Asia-Pacific Region," which was a significant, even if vague, pledge, and declared that both opposed efforts of any other country or group of countries to do so. The latter portion of this statement, which obviously applied to the Soviet Union, was reinforced by a statement of opposition to collusion between any major powers against others, or steps by "major countries to divide up the world into spheres of interest." Both agreed they would not enter into "agreements or understandings with the other directed at other states." These statements were of great impor-tance to China since they constituted an American promise not to collude with Moscow against Peking, but they could also be interpreted as an assurance to Moscow that it should not fear U.S.-China collusion. Both sides also tried to reassure their allies, especially North and South Viet-nam, North and South Korea, and Japan, by stating they would not "negotiate on behalf of any third party."

The most difficult issue, of course, was what the Chinese referred to as the "crucial question" of Taiwan. For more than twenty years it had been the most important issue in dispute between Washington and Pe-king, and for more than ten years Peking had insisted its solution was a prerequisite to any improvement of Sino-American relations. The com-muniqué's treatment of the Taiwan issue, which was admitted to be a "long-standing serious dispute," was an exceedingly delicate exercise in deliberate ambiguity. In one sense, the issue was simply shelved. Yet both sides compromised and by doing so initiated a process of adjustment that opened the door to further change.

The Chinese reaffirmed their position that "the Government of the People's Republic of China is the sole legal government of China," that "Taiwan is a province of China which has long been returned to the motherland," and that "the liberation of Taiwan is China's internal affair in which no other country has the right to interfere." They also reiter-ated that "all U.S. forces and military installations must be withdrawn from Taiwan." But the communiqué made no direct mention of either the American defense treaty or U.S. diplomatic relations with the Nationalists.

The United States did not accept Peking's claims, but it did "acknowledge" that "all Chinese on either side of the Taiwan Strait maintain there is but one China and that Taiwan is a part of China," stating that "the United States Government does not challenge that position." These statements, while not committing the United States to any definite position, certainly moved Washington closer to Peking's view and strongly implied that the United States would not foster the separation of Taiwan from China. The United States also said it "reaffirms its interest in a peaceful settlement of the Taiwan issue by the Chinese themselves," adding that "with this prospect in mind," it "affirms the ultimate objective of the withdrawal of all U.S. forces and military installations from Taiwan." It promised that "in the meantime" it would "progressively reduce its forces and military installations on Taiwan as the tension in the area diminishes"; the "area" obviously meant Vietnam, as well as Taiwan, and possibly other Asian areas. The United States, in sum, promised military withdrawal from Taiwan, but gave no definite timetable or final target date and linked its pace to the "diminishing of tension" in "the area" and its completion to "the prospect" of "peaceful settlement of the Taiwan question by the Chinese themselves."

Clearly this compromise was far from wholly satisfactory to either side. The United States did not explicitly recognize Peking's claim to Taiwan or promise to disengage totally from the island, as Peking wished, and Peking did not renounce the use of force, as Washington wished. Deliberate ambiguity left room for differing interpretations and possibly serious misunderstanding in the future, but both sides were prepared to compromise and accept the unavoidable risks of misunderstanding, because both felt their broader interests required this.

At the end, the communiqué specified what the first steps toward normalized relations would be. The two sides agreed to "facilitate the further development of . . . contacts and exchanges" (in "such fields as science, technology, culture, sports and journalism"), "facilitate the progressive development of trade," and "stay in contact through various channels, including the sending of a senior U.S. representative to Peking from time to time."

Opening of Relations

In the period immediately following the Nixon trip, the development of new ties was far more rapid than most observers had expected. Working relations between the American and Chinese Communist embassies in Paris and Ottawa were immediately established, and businesslike discussions were begun on a variety of specific issues, including a possible agreement to settle mutual claims dating to the late 1940s and early 1950s. The most important follow-up discussions, however, took place between Kissinger and Chou. For a time, Kissinger averaged two visits a year to Peking. On these trips he regularly discussed broad international problems, including U.S.-Soviet relations.

Then, in an extremely surprising move, when Kissinger visited Peking in February 1973, the United States and the People's Republic of China agreed to establish diplomatic "liaison offices" in Washington and Peking.[128] These were opened soon thereafter; they were in fact embassies in all but name.[129] Each was headed by a prestigious senior diplomat, David Bruce in the American case and Huang Chen, a Central Committee member, in the Chinese case. Thereafter, the frequency of Kissinger's trips declined.

Peking's willingness to establish these missions while the Nationalists still maintained an embassy in Washington involved a major compromise. The Communists had consistently maintained that they would never establish diplomatic missions in the capital of any country recognizing the Taiwan regime, and Chou had stated only a short while before that Americans could not expect even visits to Washington by representatives from Peking until the Nationalist embassy in Washington was closed. By retreating on this matter, Peking gave up one possible lever for extracting concessions from the Americans. The Chinese decision to take this unprecedented step clearly demonstrated that Peking felt a strong desire to consolidate the new relationship. The desire of both sides to maintain momentum in developing the relationship was also indicated in the announcement in late 1974, at the end of still another Kissinger trip, that President Ford would visit China in 1975.

Nonofficial contacts also developed fairly rapidly. Some were exchanges, endorsed by the two governments, between private American organizations and quasi-official organizations in Peking, but most were visits by a wide variety of Americans invited by the Chinese. By late 1974 over eight thousand Americans had visited the People's Republic and about five hundred Chinese had visited the United States.[130]

Most surprising, Sino-American trade skyrocketed, rising far faster than any American estimates had projected, from about $5 million (two-way) in 1971 to almost $934 million in 1974.[131] By 1973 the United States, to everyone's surprise, was China's second largest trading partner —principally because of Peking's imports of U.S. agricultural commodities. The trade was badly imbalanced, however, since Chinese exports to the United States grew only slowly.

The United States took some further steps in this period to withdraw its military forces from Taiwan, gradually. By 1974, less than four thousand American military men remained on the island, in comparison with eight thousand to nine thousand two years earlier.[132] And in the fall of 1974, with the administration's blessing, the U.S. Senate repealed the 1955 Formosa Resolution, which was a gesture of some symbolic importance.[133]

As early as the fall of 1973, however, there began to be a "slowing down" or "cooling" in the relationship, which became increasingly apparent from 1974 on. Diplomatic negotiations on an "assets and claims" agreement, which had appeared close to conclusion, seemed to reach a stalemate. About $200 million in private claims for American property taken over by the Chinese after 1949 were to be balanced off against $75 million to $80 million of Chinese assets frozen in the United States after 1949.[134] By 1974 it appeared to the Americans that only minor technical and terminological issues blocked agreement. Since these were clearly soluble, Peking's delay seemed to be motivated by broader policy or political considerations. It was deliberately dragging its feet.

Subtle changes also occurred in nonofficial exchanges. Many sorts of Americans were invited to China, but the development of the officially endorsed "facilitated exchanges" reached a plateau. Moreover, Chinese visitors began to show increased sensitivity on the Taiwan question and sometimes raised issues about minor problems they had tended to overlook during 1973.[135] Few American newsmen other than those covering official visits were admitted to China in 1974–75, and Peking emphasized that no exchange of resident correspondents would be possible until formal diplomatic relations were established. In the United States, the Chinese showed an increasing tendency to use nonofficial exchanges politically to encourage elements strongly sympathetic to Peking. In late

1974 they enthusiastically endorsed the formation in the United States of a national U.S.-China "People's Friendship Association" and showed a definite preference in granting visas to Americans associated with its local affiliates.[136]

On the trade front, there were signs in the latter half of 1974 that Peking was beginning to cut back on imports from the United States. Although trade for the year reached a new peak, it was less than had been expected, and the 1974 trend was a prelude to a precipitous drop in 1975. Strictly economic factors helped to explain China's cancellation of important grain contracts, but political considerations were obviously also involved in the drop in overall U.S.-China trade.

Though it was evident by 1974 that the process of developing Sino-American relations had slowed down, the reasons were far from clear. Some observers argued that it simply repeated the pattern of Chinese Communist behavior in relations with other nations; almost always Western countries had at first enjoyed a honeymoon period and then relations had become more matter of fact and old and new problems had again come to the fore. But this was not a sufficient answer. The slowdown seemed to reflect deliberate decisions by Peking's leaders concerning overall strategy and tactics toward the United States, and it probably reflected internal political debate in China as well.

One very revealing discussion of the basic strategic thinking underlying Peking's new approach to dealing with the United States, and the doubts some Chinese had about it, was contained in an article entitled "Strong Weapon to Unite the People and Defeat the Enemy—Study 'On Policy,' " which was published in *Red Flag* in August 1971, immediately after Kissinger's first trip to Peking. It explained Peking's new general policy, and particularly its opening to the United States, on the basis of Mao's united-front prescriptions outlined in his 1940 directive "On Policy."[137] The article stressed the necessity for "waging struggle in a flexible way" and the need, while preserving "independence and initiative," to "unite all forces that can be united, to isolate and strike at the handful of most stubborn enemies." "Our principles must be firm," it quoted Mao saying, but "we must also have all permissible and necessary flexibility," and, employing "revolutionary dual tactics," form a united front that is "neither all alliance and no struggle nor all struggle and no alliance, but combines alliance and struggle." It pointed out that Mao clearly "distinguished between the primary enemy and the secondary enemy and between the temporary allies and the indirect allies." The message was clear: the opening to the United States was a united-front approach to dealing with the Soviet Union, which China now considered to be its primary enemy. Also clear was the fact that Peking's leaders felt they had to defend their new policy against internal criticism.

The justification, rationalization, and defense of the new policy were revealed even more clearly in a confidential document, "Outline of Education on Situation for Companies," issued by an army political department in Yunnan Province in April 1973.[138] Although this document labeled both Soviet revisionism and U.S. imperialism enemies, it bluntly stated: "Soviet revisionism is our country's most threatening enemy. . . . In terms of geographical positions, Soviet revisionism abuts on China. From this point of view, its threat to our country is much greater than that of the United States and much more direct." Moreover, it said, the Soviet Union is "stretching its arms in all directions and expanding desperately," while American strategy "has met with repeated setbacks; its aggressive power has been weakened."

Rebutting the views of cadres skeptical of the new policy, the article said: "some comrades" have a "low ability to make distinctions"; they ask whether we simply are doing what Moscow has done with the United States or whether we have the "same viewpoint" as the Americans or "have changed our policy." Mao's "revolutionary diplomatic line," it said, makes Sino-American talks "alike in form but different in essence" from Soviet-American talks. "Are we to fight these two enemies [the Soviet Union and the United States] simultaneously using the same might? No. Are we to ally ourselves with one against the other? Definitely not. We act in the light of changes in situations, tipping the scale diversely at different times. . . . This involves a high level of tactics."

The basic aims of the new policy, the article explained, were to "open the gate of contacts between us and the people of the United States," to "frustrate the strategic deployment of Soviet revisionists" (who, it was said, desire Sino-American conflict), to "aggravate the contradictions between the United States and the Soviet Union" and "between U.S. imperialism and its lackeys" (for example, Japan), and to "benefit our liberation of Taiwan" by bringing about a "gradual alienation in the relations between the United States and the Chiang gang."

There were varied indications during 1973–75 of doubt and criticism within China about the new policy and of continuing differences within the leadership. At the Tenth Party Congress in August 1973, for example, there was a noticeable difference in tone between the speeches of Premier

Chou and Wang Hung-wen, spokesman for the Shanghai "radical left."[139] Chou stressed that "necessary compromises between revolutionary countries and imperialist countries must be distinguished from collusion and compromise between Soviet revisionism and U.S. imperialism." Wang said nothing about differentiating between imperialism and revisionism. When the anti-Lin Piao, anti-Confucius campaign unfolded thereafter, the media attacked cultural contacts with the West; specific targets included film director Michelangelo Antonioni, composers Beethoven and Schubert, and the American novel *Jonathan Livingstone Seagull*. Other attacks focused on the increase in imports of Western capital goods and technology.[140] Domestic debate on these issues almost certainly contributed to the leadership's caution in developing the Sino-American relationship, at least until the United States showed a willingness to make further concessions.

Chinese officials indicated, directly and indirectly, that they were less than wholly satisfied with the pace at which the United States was changing its policies, implementing the Shanghai communiqué, and disengaging from Taiwan. In part, Peking may have been reacting to actions taken by Washington in this period that seemed to strengthen U.S. relations with the Nationalists: the appointment of a senior American diplomat, Leonard Unger, as ambassador to Taiwan, the opening of two new Nationalist consulates in the United States, the failure to withdraw all American forces from Taiwan, and new sales of American military equipment to Taiwan, on credit. Whatever the reasons, Peking seemed to have decided to exert low-pressure leverage on Washington to move ahead in implementing the Shanghai communiqué. Chou En-lai hinted at this at the January 1975 meeting of the National People's Congress, the first held in ten years. "There exist fundamental differences between China and the United States," he said, but relations "have improved to some extent" and "will continue to improve so long as the principles of the Sino-American Shanghai Communiqué are carried out in earnest."[141] The phrase "in earnest" was the revealing one.

A Plateau

In late 1974 and early 1975, both sides appeared to be cautiously feeling out the possibilities for, and limits of, further compromise on the key issues, including the Taiwan problem. The announcement in late 1974 of President Ford's planned visit in 1975 created subtle new pressure to move the relationship forward.[142] There were almost certainly men in both Peking and Washington who argued that the process of "normalization" should be completed in 1975.

Developments during the first half of 1975, however, destroyed their hopes, and Sino-American relations appeared to enter a holding pattern. The collapse of the noncommunist regimes in the Indochina states in the spring of 1975 created widespread uncertainties about the U.S. position in Asia, and U.S. leaders sought to reemphasize American commitments elsewhere in the region. Serious doubts were expressed, in Washington, about the desirability of further disengaging U.S. interests from Taiwan until greater stability emerged in East Asia. Shortly thereafter, Chiang Kai-shek's death stimulated a number of Republican party leaders to stress the importance of U.S. ties to Taiwan and to warn against further compromises that might weaken the Nationalist regime.

Within the U.S. government, some argued that an attempt should be made at the time of President Ford's visit to upgrade relations with Peking, emphasizing the advantages of doing so while Mao and Chou were still alive. But others were strongly opposed on the grounds that the immediate post-Vietnam period was not the best time. By late summer the possible political costs for President Ford, who, as the 1976 election approached, felt himself vulnerable to criticism from the Republican party's right wing, made it clear that there would be no major U.S. moves in 1975.

A variety of factors apparently led to a temporary policy freeze on the Chinese side as well. After the collapse of the noncommunist regimes in Vietnam and Cambodia, Peking seemed increasingly concerned that the U.S. position in Asia might be weakening so rapidly that Moscow could exploit the situation. This argued against pressing too hard for immediate U.S. moves regarding Taiwan, which might highlight a weakening of the U.S. position. Peking's leaders also seemed to recognize that President Ford's domestic political problems made further compromise unlikely in 1975. Perhaps fearful that Ford's trip might be canceled, Chinese leaders began to reemphasize their patience on the Taiwan problem, stressing that they wanted the President's trip to take place even if no further steps toward normalization could be taken immediately.[143]

At the same time, however, Peking's policy hardened in subtle but important ways. The Chinese became increasingly critical of U.S. efforts to promote détente with the Soviet Union, particularly after the Helsinki conference on European problems. They appeared to see a general weakening of the U.S. worldwide posture in the face of Moscow's expanding influence and may have been disturbed by the domestic confusion and irresolution in the United States in the wake of the Watergate crisis and President Nixon's resignation. Whatever the reasons, they were increasingly harsh and open in their criticism of U.S. policy toward the Soviet Union.

They also showed greater rigidity in dealing with the United States on certain issues.[144] While stating publicly that they could be patient regarding Taiwan, they indicated privately that they were not prepared to expand Sino-American ties even in relatively noncontroversial fields such as trade and exchanges until further progress could be made on the Taiwan problem. The "freeze," this seemed to suggest, was likely to continue until full normalization was achieved.

Domestic politics were almost certainly a factor affecting policy in China. Caught in the middle of the succession process, the leadership in China appeared to be uncertain about many of its policies. Chou, incapacitated by illness, faded from the scene, and Mao became less active; Vice Premier Teng Hsiao-p'ing, who was in charge of day-to-day governing of the country, could not be certain of his position as Chou had been. There was evidence, moreover, of continuing debate within China over policy toward both the United States and the Soviet Union. It is plausible to believe that radical critics of the opening to the United States argued that this policy had not paid off sufficiently. Renewed press attacks on "capitulationism" also suggested that other Chinese leaders might again be urging a more compromising approach to Sino-Soviet problems.

When Kissinger went to Peking in the fall of 1975 to arrange President Ford's trip, he was greeted with blunt public criticism of U.S.-Soviet détente. The Chinese indicated, moreover, that although they still wished Ford to come, they were not prepared to expand Sino-American relations even in minor ways. Although both sides still favored the trip, it was mainly because they believed that a cancellation might have an adverse effect on their relations. The Ford trip therefore proved to be an exercise in summitry without great substance. It was symbolically of some significance, since it demonstrated that both countries desired at least to maintain relations at their existing levels. It also enabled the top Chinese and American leaders to exchange views again on a wide range of international problems. However, it also highlighted the unwillingness or inability, temporarily at least, of the two countries to move the relationship forward. By this time it was clear that further progress would have to wait until after the U.S. presidential election in 1976.

During 1976 both countries entered periods of major domestic political change. Within China, Chou En-lai's death in January intensified the struggle between China's pragmatists and radicals, and Mao Tse-tung's death in September brought it to a climax. Within a month the outcome of the first round of post-Mao succession was clear; Hua Kuo-feng, backed by leading military leaders and civilian bureaucrats, succeeded Mao as chairman of the party and purged Mao's wife and China's other top radicals. In the United States, American leaders were preoccupied throughout the year with the presidential election campaign, and then in November the remarkable victory of Jimmy Carter over the incumbent Gerald Ford heralded a major change from a Republican to a Democratic administration.

The emergence of new leadership in both countries headed by little-known men who had not been extensively involved in foreign affairs inevitably introduced new uncertainties. Leaders in both countries indicated a desire to continue striving for normalization of Sino-American relations. But it remained to be seen how high a priority leaders in the two countries would assign to the task, and what positions they would take on the key unresolved issues. It was clear that if U.S.-China relations were to break out of the holding pattern they had been in for four years, further compromises by both sides would be required.

Problems of Normalization

In the Shanghai communiqué, the United States and China committed themselves to work toward "normalization" of relations. This term was not defined, but it was clear that in a limited sense it meant, simply, the establishment of full diplomatic relations. More broadly, however, it obviously implied that both countries should try not only to avoid overt conflict but also to resolve long-standing problems, promote détente, and achieve a degree of mutual accommodation.

The United States pledged in the communiqué to take several specific steps to remove obstacles that Peking insisted blocked the establishment of full diplomatic relations. One was the step-by-step reduction of American military forces in Taiwan leading ultimately to a complete withdrawal. The Chinese will probably not agree to full normalization of relations until this promise has been fulfilled, or its fulfillment at least appears imminent. From the U.S. point of view, this will probably not pose insuperable problems. In 1976 there were less than two thousand American servicemen on the island, and their withdrawal could be carried out without seriously damaging effects on Taiwan's defense capability or on the basic American strategic position in Asia. Peking could raise other questions about sales of military equipment to the Nationalists or American support of Taiwan's defense industries, but to date it has not done so.

Peking has been adamant, however, in insisting that the establishment of full diplomatic relations with Washington requires the severance of formal U.S. ties with Taiwan. This is obviously a more difficult step for the United States to consider. Washington would clearly prefer either not altering its relations with Taipei, or simply reducing the level of diplomatic ties with it. However, since Peking has maintained an uncompromising position on this issue for more than two decades, in dealing with all countries, not just the United States, it does not seem likely to abandon its basic position now. The Chinese have made clear, though, that they will not try to force a break in nonofficial political or economic links between the United States and Taiwan. In fact, they have indicated that the Japanese precedent is one the United States could follow, and the Japanese have demonstrated that it is possible to maintain the substance of relations with Taiwan without traditional diplomatic forms. Though the severance of formal ties with Taiwan would be more difficult for the United States than it was for Japan, and would be a greater blow to the Nationalist regime, the U.S. government seems likely to decide that consolidation of relations with Peking is sufficiently important in relation to broad American interests to justify downgrading its links with Taipei, on the understanding that the United States intends to continue important nonofficial relations with Taiwan.

The gap between Chinese and American positions regarding Taiwan's legal status poses a different kind of problem. In the Shanghai communiqué, the United States did not explicitly recognize Taiwan as Chinese territory, even though Peking would have liked it to do so. Although Peking could decide to press Washington on this issue, it does not seem likely to, at least at the time of normalization, since it did not do so even in the case of Japan. Although Tokyo went further than the United States in accommodating to Peking's desires, it still avoided unambiguous recognition of Peking's current claims regarding Taiwan. At present it

seems unlikely that Washington will be prepared to go beyond its statement in the Shanghai communiqué that it "acknowledges" that "Chinese
on either side" of the Taiwan Strait "maintain" that Taiwan is "a part of
China," and it appears that Peking will probably accept the ambiguity
in the U.S. position. However, this is a question that remains to be
clarified.

The most difficult problems that will have to be faced if U.S.-China
relations are to be normalized concern the present U.S.-Nationalist security relationship. Peking has insisted, and will almost certainly continue to insist, that the United States abrogate its defense treaty with the
Nationalists when full normalization of relations occurs. It is virtually
certain, however, that in the period immediately ahead Washington will
not be prepared to abandon totally—or risk giving the impression that
it is abandoning—any interest in, or responsibility for, the security of
Taiwan. A sense of continuing obligation to the people in Taiwan itself,
a concern about possible destabilizing effects in the region, and domestic
political considerations all will argue against total disengagement. Differences on this issue conceivably could pose an insuperable obstacle to
full normalization of relations.

However, there are ways in which the problem could be circum-
vented if both sides show the necessary will and are prepared to make
further compromises. A key question will be whether, if and when the
United States considers ending its treaty with the Nationalists, Washington and Peking can reach an understanding that from the American
viewpoint will provide a substitute for the treaty. From the U.S. point
of view, abrogation of the treaty might be acceptable if, but only if, there
were a reasonable basis for believing that Peking does not intend to impose its will on Taiwan by force. An acceptable substitute for the treaty
might consist—at a minimum—of acquiescence by Peking to American
statements and actions clearly indicating that the United States will continue to oppose any military attack on Taiwan and will continue to assist
it in maintaining a reasonable defense capability (for example, through
direct or indirect sales of military materiel), even without a formal
treaty.[145] Whether or not Peking is willing to acquiesce to the continuation of informal security links of this sort between the United States and
Taiwan could prove to be the crucial issue in the final stage of normalizing U.S.-China relations.

To conclude agreements or reach understandings that will remove
the obstacles to full normalization will require more than diplomatic

legerdemain, even though something of the skill involved in drafting the Shanghai communiqué will be essential. It will require a strong will on both sides, plus a recognition by both that no final solution of the Taiwan problem is now possible and that therefore further compromises are unavoidable. Though the compromises will not be easy to make, they are certainly within the realm of possibility if both sides are genuinely determined to consolidate their relations.

Ideology and Cultural Attitudes

Developing broader and deeper U.S.-China relations will, at best, be a long and complex process. Establishment of formal diplomatic relations will not create a close relationship; it will simply open the door to serious consideration of a wide range of other political, economic, and security issues.[146]

Among the factors that will shape Peking's approach to these issues, clearly, will be the basic cultural attitudes and ideological beliefs held by the Chinese. These factors have not predetermined China's policies toward other nations. Some of the most dramatic shifts in Chinese policy, in fact, have been dictated by realpolitik considerations that have run directly counter to some cultural and ideological predispositions. Nevertheless, such predispositions are important. They greatly affect the context in which decisions are made. They set limits on what policy options can be considered. And they are extremely important in determining the *quality* of China's relationships with other societies and governments.

The differences between China and all foreign societies in values, assumptions, and outlooks are profound. There are significant variations, however, in the degree to which cultural factors affect Chinese attitudes toward particular nations. Clearly, for example, China's historical cultural links with Japan make their relations qualitatively different from China's relations with Western nations. Some evidence supports the view that Chinese generally feel there is a larger cultural gap between China and Russia than between China and the United States. But basically the cultural barriers to Sino-American understanding are similar to those complicating China's relationships with all Western nations.[147]

Traditionally, Chinese culture has emphasized certain basic concepts and values: authority, hierarchy, collective responsibility, personal relationships, orthodoxy, conformity, and the importance of virtue and moral example. These are still important despite all the recent revolutionary changes. They contrast sharply with Western values emphasizing individualism, liberalism, pluralism, self-expression, and the rule of law. Moreover, the discipline and austerity imposed by economic imperatives in China are very different from the freedom and consumerism promoted by affluence in the West.

Traditional cultural pride, a sense of superiority and self-sufficiency, and a deep-rooted tendency toward insularity and isolationism, plus modern nationalism and xenophobia, have also strongly influenced Chinese attitudes toward all outsiders. Unquestionably, the Chinese tendency has been to regard the West not only as remote and alien but, frequently, as subversive, aggressive, and threatening as well.

United States policy is also, inevitably, influenced by cultural and ideological predispositions, and Americans have had complicated, ambivalent images of China, which have varied considerably over time. As one perceptive scholar put it: "Our concepts of China have included both a sense of almost timeless stability and almost unlimited chaos. Our notions of Chinese traits have included sage wisdom and superstitious ignorance, great strength and contemptible weakness, immovable conservatism and unpredictable extremism, philosophic calm and explosive violence. Our emotions about the Chinese have ranged between sympathy and rejection, parental benevolence and parental exasperation, affection and hostility, love and a fear close to hate."[148]

During certain periods there have been influential pro-American groups in China and pro-Chinese groups in the United States, while in other periods—including much of the 1950s and 1960s—feelings of mutual hostility have been dominant. One striking feature of public political attitudes, particularly on the American side, has been their volatility. There have been great swings of the pendulum in popular American attitudes toward China, between love and hate. The changes in Chinese attitudes may not have been as great, but significant shifts between hostility and friendliness have affected them too.

When the political climate has been favorable, interactions between Chinese and Americans have frequently been cordial, and since the reopening of Peking-Washington relations the improvement has been striking. However, as has often been the case in the past, the changes appear to have been greater in the United States than in China. On the American side, the predominant attitude rapidly swung from unreasoning hostility to uncritical euphoria, although there are already signs that the euphoria is declining.[149] In contrast, the Chinese have been politely cordial but reserved in their dealings with Americans.

The cultural differences between China and the United States, intensified by more than two decades of virtually no contact between the two societies, will obviously continue, and will work against the development of a genuinely intimate or broad relationship. A significant narrowing of the cultural gap would require more extensive contact and interaction, over an extended period, than is now possible to conceive. It is only realistic, therefore, to expect that for the foreseeable future China and the United States will continue to deal with each other across a deep cultural divide.

The profound ideological differences between the two societies will have an even greater effect, limiting the scope and breadth of the Sino-American relationship in the period ahead. In the 1950s and 1960s, ideologically based attitudes, more than traditional cultural differences, aroused passion on both sides; Chinese antiimperialism and American anticommunism seemed to guarantee intense mutual hostility for the indefinite future. In light of this background, the degree to which ideological hostilities appear to have been reduced since 1972 is remarkable in many respects. Both sides, in the effort to establish a new relationship, have stressed immediate pragmatic concerns and deemphasized ideological conflicts. This has been more true of the Americans, however, than of the Chinese. Many Americans today seem prepared to forget the fundamental ideological conflicts. In contrast, the Chinese give no indication of blurring ideological differences; they simply avoid injecting them unnecessarily into most of their dealings with Americans. This is in part because, today, their ideologically based hostility is focused on the heretical Russian revisionists rather than on their traditional ideological enemy, the imperialists. But it is mainly because they find it expedient today to give priority to pragmatic concerns over ideological issues in relations with the United States.

Ideological differences are no less basic today, however, than in the recent past. Chinese and Americans are still inhabitants of very different ideologically conceived worlds, are moved by conflicting world outlooks, philosophical assumptions, and political and economic goals, and are still in many respects adversaries on the world stage. The Chinese Communists' world is one of class struggle, mass mobilization, economic collectivism, and political totalism. The bourgeois values symbolized by the United States are still anathema, and antiimperialism continues to be a strong force motivating many of Peking's policies worldwide.

Even though the tendency of many Americans has been to assume—

or at least hope—that improved relations will make ideological conflicts unimportant, this is not going to happen in the near future. Mutual acceptance of the need for peace and coexistence can grow, and in fact already has grown, but China will continue for many years to be a revolutionary society, to view the values represented by the United States as dangerously subversive at home, and to regard imperialism as an adversary throughout the world. If the new Sino-American relationship is consolidated in the period ahead, it will be in spite of continuing ideological conflicts, not because these conflicts have disappeared.

Ideological considerations will impel the Chinese to control and limit contact and interactions with Americans in order to restrict the dangers of contamination by subversive influences. They will also lead both governments to support positions and promote policies, particularly concerning Third World areas and global economic issues, that are basically competitive.

Perhaps gradually the importance of ideology may decline in Chinese as well as American eyes. If so, the gap could become less important, and the adversary character of many of the worldwide relationships between the two nations may slowly change as parallel interests develop. But for such a trend, if it occurs, to have far-reaching effects, considerable time will be required. For the foreseeable future, ideology will continue to be a major barrier to efforts to broaden and deepen Sino-American relations.

Domestic Politics

Despite the lack of broad political contacts between China and the United States between 1949 and 1971, political factors in both countries have had an extremely important impact on their relationship. The impact of domestic politics on U.S. China policy has been particularly great, but questions concerning Sino-American relations have been controversial in China too. In the United States, the importance of politics in shaping China policy appears to have declined substantially since the reopening of Sino-American relations, but one cannot assume this will continue. And in China there is always the possibility that policy toward the United States will be a subject of serious internal debate.

Although the record of past political controversies within the Chinese leadership concerning policy toward the United States is difficult to reconstruct, there is reason to believe that as early as the 1940s Chinese Communist leaders differed on how to deal with the Americans. Debate over policy toward the United States may not have been as divisive as debate over policy toward the Soviet Union. However, in recent years, even when differences have focused mainly on Sino-Soviet relations, they have often involved issues concerning Sino-American relations too, since changes in China's relations with either of these powers usually has actual or potential implications with the other.

There was probably serious debate within the party during 1944–45, when the Chinese Communists first attempted to obtain American military assistance, over how flexible to be and what concessions to make.[150] There is evidence of differences among those at the party's Yenan headquarters, between Yenan and its representatives in Chungking who had to deal directly with the Americans, and between party leaders at the center and dispersed local leaders. Mao apparently shifted his position over time. For example, in 1944 he favored a flexible and moderate approach to the United States, but then he approved a hard antiimperialist line at the party's Seventh Congress in 1945. In many respects, Mao seems to have been ambivalent about policy toward the United States over the years, as he was on a number of other important issues, shifting position on several occasions.

Debate among the Chinese Communist leaders over U.S. policy almost certainly continued up to 1948, and possibly even until the outbreak of the Korean War.[151] When Mao defined his "lean to one side" policy in mid-1949, he went out of his way to refute the idea that help from the United States might be possible or desirable.[152] In doing so, he obviously had in mind critics of a hard line toward the United States (perhaps within the party, certainly among nonparty intellectuals friendly toward the Americans).

Existing doubts about a pro-Soviet anti-American stance were doubtless submerged, however, when the Korean War erupted, the United States reintervened in the Taiwan area, and U.S. and Chinese forces came into direct conflict in Korea. The hostility created by the war tended to unify opinion in China, as it did in the United States. When two major nations are in open military conflict, only rarely is serious criticism of policy expressed on either side. While the Communists' all-out effort to fan public hatred of the United States during the war may have reflected their fear of latent pro-American attitudes in China, there is little doubt that the war aroused deep nationalist emotions and tended to unite most of the country behind an anti-American policy.

There was little overt evidence of significant differences within the party on policy toward the United States in the years immediately following the Korean War. There was probably debate, however, whenever major shifts of broad Chinese strategy occurred—for example, when Peking adopted a more flexible policy in 1955–56, and then when it shifted back to a militantly anti-American policy in 1957–58. It is noteworthy that Chou En-lai, and professionals in the state bureaucracy, played a highly visible role in articulating a relatively moderate approach to the United States in 1955–56, whereas it was clearly Mao himself who took the lead in pushing for a militantly revolutionary policy in the late 1950s.

There is tantalizing evidence that in the early 1960s, when Mao retreated into a less prominent leadership position, some Chinese leaders may have proposed a broad shift in foreign policy, including a relatively flexible approach to the United States once again. The slogan advanced at the time was "three reconciliations and one reduction," meaning reconciliation with "reaction" and "imperialism" (the United States) as well as with "modern revisionism" (the Soviet Union), and a reduction in support for revolutionary struggles abroad. Liu Shao-ch'i, when accused during the Cultural Revolution of sponsoring this line, admitted that it might have been pushed by some but denied that he was responsible for it.[153] It is plausible to believe that it was given serious consideration but was not supported by the leadership as a whole or by Mao. For the rest of the 1960s, the only evident debates relating to policy toward Washington—for example, the 1965 controversy leading to the purge of Chief of Staff Lo Jui-ch'ing—centered on how best to cope with the perceived U.S. threat, especially in Vietnam.[154]

But there is no doubt that Peking's moves, starting in 1968, to probe the possibilities of an opening to the United States provoked major internal debate, even though Mao himself took the lead in pushing the new policy. Peking's backing and filling during 1968–71 were almost certainly due in part to internal controversy. The cancellation of the scheduled reopening of the Warsaw talks in early 1969, for example, is far more likely to have been due to unresolved differences in Peking than to a diplomat's defection.

There is ample evidence that when dramatic policy shifts were finally unveiled in 1971–72, they created doubt, shock, and strong opposition among some party members, including lower level cadres as well as top leaders, who could not understand or accept the justification given for "compromising with the enemy." The republication in 1971 of Mao's

1940 directive "On Policy" was obviously designed to counter opposition to the new policy. Its timing was important. Lin Piao was purged shortly thereafter, and there is reason to believe that he as well as some of China's leading radicals opposed the opening to the United States, arguing that China should keep up its principled opposition to both Moscow and Washington.[155] This issue may have been a factor in precipitating Lin's purge, though domestic issues were probably more important. Soviet specialists maintain that Lin strongly opposed Mao's U.S. policy and insisted on continuing the struggle against both Moscow and Washington.[156] In any case Peking thereafter mounted a major effort to indoctrinate the party's cadres and rebut "some comrades" who opposed the new policy. However, continuing leftist attacks during 1974–76 on steps to expand foreign cultural and economic contacts suggest that China's radicals never fully accepted the new policy.

It is not surprising that such a major and sudden shift of policy stirred up controversy in China. There was an obvious contradiction between the idea of improving relations with the headquarters of imperialism and continuing a basic policy of combating imperialism globally. While the logic of the new policy under existing circumstances was clear to Mao, Chou, and many other leaders who could see its practical military, political, and economic advantages, it was doubtless repugnant to many party members, especially those concerned primarily about protecting ideological purity, maintaining domestic security against subversive influences, and pushing worldwide revolution.

To date, opposition to the new policy has never been strong enough to prevent its implementation, although the slowdown of U.S.-China détente during 1974–76 probably reflected internal debate as well as external developments. The strong support both Mao and Chou gave the new policy from the start created a solid political base for it, and undoubtedly many of China's pragmatically inclined professional diplomats, economic planners, and scientists, and at least some important military leaders, have firmly supported it. Since Mao's death, Hua Kuo-feng appears to have continued backing the policy, and Teng Hsiao-p'ing—who might still make a comeback—is known to have endorsed it strongly.[157] Moreover, the purge of China's top radicals probably removed some of its most influential critics. Nevertheless, it seems very likely that many Chinese leaders still have doubts about Peking's new relationship with Washington and some may still oppose it.

It is probable that the kind of pragmatic post-Mao leadership that now appears to be emerging in China will at least wish to maintain a nonhostile relationship with the United States and probably will desire to strengthen relations. But debate on the issue could easily be revived. Whether China remains committed to a policy of improving Sino-American relations will depend in part, therefore, on domestic political trends, as well as on Peking's assessment of the value of its U.S. connection in relation to its broad international strategy. The strength of support, or opposition, to present policy will obviously be significantly affected by the judgments Chinese leaders make on the Americans' willingness to compromise on key unresolved issues in the period immediately ahead.

In the United States, internal politics has clearly had an enormous impact on policy toward China.[158] In fact from World War II until the late 1960s, China policy was one of the most politicized foreign-policy issues in the United States.

The major differences on China policy between the Republican and Democratic parties (or at least between leading individuals in the parties) have had deep roots. They arose, in part, because of differing global perspectives, priorities regarding Asia and Europe, and responses to the threat of communism. Disputes over China policy during and immediately after World War II laid the basis for acrimonious and partisan political controversy. In the late 1940s, key Republicans, especially in Congress, seized on China policy issues to launch bitter attacks on the Democratic administration.

Republican opposition to the ending of U.S. support to the Nationalists, with whom party leaders felt strong personal and emotional links, prevented decisive policy changes in 1948–49. The Nationalist government, with the help of private and congressional U.S. supporters, mounted an intensive lobbying effort to prevent U.S. accommodation to a Communist regime in China. The organized lobby was small, but many Americans who had no direct links with it supported its views.[159] The political atmosphere and the attitudes of most Americans were such that the idea of abandoning the Nationalists and dealing with the Communists was highly unpopular. By 1947, when the cooperative wartime relationship between the United States and the Soviet Union had disintegrated, anticommunism had become a major force shaping overall U.S. foreign policy. Most Americans seemed to be convinced that international communism was a monolithic as well as aggressive force and they seized upon Chinese Communist statements and actions during 1948–49 as proof that China posed a major threat.

Senator Joseph McCarthy's cynical attack in the early 1950s on those he alleged had betrayed the United States and "lost China" to the Communists helped raise anticommunist fervor to a high level.[160] The U.S. government purged a sizable proportion of its China specialists,[161] thereby severely inhibiting dispassionate analysis of China policy; any critic of unreasoning anticommunism, especially within the government but outside as well, was vulnerable to charges of being unpatriotic or worse.[162] The majority of Congress, the most powerful journalistic institutions in the country, and a large majority of the American public strongly supported a crusading anticommunist policy toward China.

These developments greatly influenced the broad direction of U.S. policy toward China and help to explain some of the crucial decisions that set the basic framework for China policy for years to come. For example, the June 1950 decision to renew support of the Nationalists and reopen the question of Taiwan's legal status was doubtless influenced significantly by the political need to obtain support for U.S. military action in Korea from key individuals in Congress and the defense establishment who had opposed U.S. disengagement from Taiwan.[163]

Following the election of Eisenhower in 1952, the new Republican administration institutionalized anticommunism and energetically pursued a policy of containment and pressure against Peking. Secretary of State John Foster Dulles epitomized the spirit of the times and the passions that the Korea War had aroused. Foreign policy tended to be viewed in black and white terms as a worldwide struggle against communism and in particular against the perceived threats posed by both Moscow and Peking.[164] Dulles's own ideological predispositions helped to shape his policies, but there is good reason to believe that domestic political considerations also influenced his actions. During the winter of 1949–50 he had written that if the Communist government of China demonstrated its ability to govern, it "should be admitted to the United Nations," but he changed his views, seemingly to accommodate to the public mood and to obtain congressional approval of his appointment as secretary of state.[165] Under Dulles, key posts in the State Department were filled by militantly anticommunist men such as Walter Robertson who were ideologically committed to a strong policy of containment and pressure against China; persons with similar views, such as Admiral Arthur Radford, were dominant in the defense establishment.

Many leading Democrats also were supporters of a hard line toward China, even after the party regained control of the White House. In a sense, the Democrats became the captives of their opposition—and of public opinion generally—on China policy issues. During the administration of John F. Kennedy, and much of the administration of Lyndon B. Johnson as well, most politicians continued to assume that the overwhelming majority of the public opposed any change of China policy in the direction of flexibility or conciliation, and that it would be prohibitively costly, politically, or too damaging to other goals, to initiate change.

At regular intervals large numbers of congressmen signed statements opposing recognition of Peking and its seating in the United Nations, and the American press was predominantly opposed to accommodation with Peking. Democratic administrations feared hostile congressional opinion, and most congressmen seemed to assume that public opinion remained rigid—long after it in fact had begun to change. In reality, opinion probably started to change in the late 1950s. By 1966, when proposals for new initiatives in China policy were articulated in congressional hearings,[166] it was evident that many Americans were receptive to the idea of establishing relations with Peking. Thereafter, proposals for a reassessment of China policy were made more frequently, in Congress and in the press as well as within the administration itself. Only then did President Johnson begin to hint publicly at the possibility of change.

No important substantive changes took place, however, until after Richard M. Nixon's Republican administration had assumed office in 1969. Even though both Kennedy and Johnson were personally prepared to consider change, both feared that major initiatives would be too costly in domestic political terms. The fact that President Nixon was a Republican with an unassailable record of anticommunism gave him a freedom of action that none of his predecessors felt they possessed. When he took dramatic steps to carry out a new policy, there was no effective opposition even from his party's extreme right wing and, in fact, he made substantial political gains from moves that a Democratic president might have expected to lead to political disaster.

The politicization of U.S. China policy and its embroilment in partisan debate from the late 1940s until the late 1960s had consequences that were obviously extremely adverse from Peking's point of view. Chinese Communist leaders tended, however, to place the blame not on American politics but on the basic nature of capitalism and imperialism and the machinations of their Nationalist adversaries. It is questionable whether they had any sophisticated understanding of the domestic political forces shaping U.S. policy. Apart from differentiating the interests of the American "people" from those of the American government, and portraying the two as being in conflict, they never made the kind of effort in the United States that they made in Japan from the early 1950s on to try to influence the political process, to attract or exert leverage on particular individuals or groups, or to appeal to general public opinion. The absence of direct contacts in the United States only partially explains this failure; more fundamentally, they appeared to assume that broad American hostility was a given, just as most Americans tended to accept Chinese hostility as a given.

The opening of contacts in 1971 and the subsequent development of diverse exchanges have created a different situation; the new patterns of interaction between the two societies, although still limited, open the door to efforts by each to influence internal political forces within the other. However, because of the nature of the exchanges, as well as the fundamental differences between the two societies, contacts between Chinese and Americans have far less direct impact within China's controlled society than in the open pluralistic setting in the United States.

Peking's policy regarding exchanges seems in one sense to be essentially practical: to gain new knowledge in important fields. However, it is clearly political, in a broad sense, fitting into well-established patterns of Chinese "people's diplomacy." Through such contacts, the Chinese hope to reinforce their official policy, build a base for "Sino-American friendship," and develop constituencies of friendly American supporters. If Peking should succumb to the temptation to be highly manipulative in these exchanges—as it has been in the case of Japan—there could be a strong reaction in the United States, and China policy questions might be politicized once again. However, if the Chinese do broaden and diversify exchanges without trying to manipulate them for short-run political gains, they should help to improve overall relations.

In the period immediately following the reopening of U.S.-China relations, China policy appeared to be successfully depoliticized. In 1974 Kissinger asserted, in fact, that "no policy of this Administration has had greater bipartisan support than the normalization of relations with the People's Republic"[167]—an extraordinary statement in light of the bitter controversy in the past, yet nevertheless probably true. But the past volatility of American attitudes and the history of partisan controversy over China policy argue for caution about projecting the euphoric attitudes of 1972–74 into the future.

The issue most likely to precipitate renewed political controversy concerns U.S. relations with Taiwan. The recent broad support for expanded Sino-American relations, even from many conservative Republicans, may have been possible in part because the United States has not yet had to make fundamental changes in its relations with the Nationalist regime. If the United States moves to sever diplomatic relations with Taiwan, or end the existing defense treaty, public criticism may well increase. Though the emotional attachments that many Americans felt to Taiwan in earlier years have clearly weakened, they have not disappeared. One cannot exclude the possibility of a public outcry against an alleged "betrayal" of Taiwan.[168] Total disengagement from all important political and economic ties with the Nationalists, or any indication of a lack of concern about Taiwan's security, would almost certainly evoke a strong reaction from a wide spectrum of political opinion.[169] Even a downgrading of U.S. ties with the Nationalist regime may reactivate some critics of relations with Peking, especially in the Republican party. In early 1975, after Chiang Kai-shek's death, Senator Barry Goldwater and former Governor Ronald Reagan spoke out against further compromise on the Taiwan issue, and later that year similar warnings were contained in a draft resolution circulated in the House of Representatives that received wide support.[170] During 1975–76 there were also signs of shifts in broad public opinion. Some leading newspapers carried editorials that reemphasized U.S. obligations to Taiwan; in mid-1976 the *New York Times*, for example, warned that "if the United States withdraws its backing" from Taiwan, this could be "the beginning of a slippery slope."[171] And a public opinion survey conducted in 1976 by the Foreign Policy Association showed greater support for "a policy looking toward the eventual independence of Taiwan" than for any other single policy option.[172]

These may be harbingers of a significant repoliticization of China policy issues that could make further moves to weaken U.S. ties with Taiwan difficult. At a minimum, political differences over policy toward Taiwan may impose limits on American flexibility in the search for formulas to reach compromises with Peking that can advance the process of normalizing relations with China.

Economic Relations

One of the most positive and unexpected developments in Sino-American relations during 1973–74 was the rapid growth of bilateral trade.

By 1975, however, it became clear that continuous growth could not be automatically assumed. Peking's economic policy toward the United States as toward other countries has been shaped with both economic and political factors in mind.[173] Although China's foreign trade has generally reflected shifts in its domestic economic policies and needs as well as changes in international market forces, in many of Peking's decisions politics has clearly overshadowed economics; this was certainly true, for example, when China's leaders decided to exert economic pressure on Japan in the late 1950s and to cut Sino-Soviet economic ties in the 1960s.

The lack of Sino-American trade between 1950 and 1971 was obviously due to American as well as Chinese policy, however. After the start of the Korean War, the United States imposed a complete embargo on trade with the People's Republic, which it continued as part of its overall policy of containment and pressure against China until the 1970s.[174] The United States also tried to induce other countries to maintain severe restrictions on China trade. In one brief period in the mid-1950s, Peking tried to induce Washington to reopen trade, but it failed. Of necessity, therefore, it focused its main effort on trying to circumvent and undermine the U.S.-sponsored system of international restrictions.

It is difficult to estimate how much Sino-American trade might have developed in the late 1950s and 1960s if the United States had removed its restrictions. There doubtless would have been some, but not necessarily very much, for political as well as economic reasons. Peking channeled the bulk of its trade to the Communist bloc in the 1950s and shifted much of it to Japan and Europe in the 1960s.

Peking's decision to develop a sizable trade with the United States after 1971 was also due to both economic and political reasons. China's leaders clearly believed that trade would help achieve normalization of political relations. In addition, its decisions reflected a broad shift in their economic policies at home and abroad. Following the Cultural Revolution, Peking decided to accelerate domestic economic growth and, to this end, to give increased priority to foreign trade in general. The nature of China's economic needs was such that the United States suddenly became a potentially important trading partner. Because it had been unable to develop agricultural output as rapidly as desired, Peking was compelled to import large amounts of agricultural products, especially grain and cotton. The United States, as the largest exporter in the world of these commodities, was a logical source of supply. It was also a potential source—though not the only one—of the capital goods and technological know-how necessary to accelerate the country's industrialization.

The rise in overall Sino-American trade immediately after 1971 was impressive.[175] It jumped from about $5 million in 1971 to $95.9 million in 1972, $805 million in 1973, and $933.8 million in 1974. The 1974 total consisted of $819.1 million of Chinese imports from the United States (13 percent of China's total imports) and only $114.7 million of Chinese exports to the United States (2 percent of China's exports), an import-export ratio of over 7 to 1. About four-fifths of the imports were agricultural commodities (wheat was 28.6 percent, corn 22.7 percent, soybeans 16.9 percent, and cotton 11.7 percent). The remaining fifth, mostly manufactured goods, included aircraft and aircraft parts (9.3 percent), telecommunications equipment, and chemical fertilizers.

Chinese exports to the United States were highly diversified; there were no very large items. Textiles and textile raw materials made up the largest category (cotton fabrics were 22.3 percent, clothing 4.9 percent, and raw silk 2.4 percent). The second largest item was tin (8.2 percent of the total). Animal products and by-products were of some importance (with pig bristles constituting 5.1 percent), as were rosin (6.9 percent) and art works and antiques (6.8 percent). Most of the rest consisted of small quantities of miscellaneous goods.

By 1974 the United States had become China's second largest trading partner. Clearly this was due in large part to China's need for grain, but it also demonstrated Peking's commitment to the new Sino-American relationship.

When in late 1974 Peking began to cancel sizable grain contracts—because of improved domestic supply, world price trends, and foreign-exchange problems—it became evident that Sino-American trade would not grow in an uninterrupted fashion. Soon, in fact, it dropped significantly. Two-way trade in 1975 was only $495 million—less than half the 1974 level.[176] China's imports, amounting to $335 million, were only double the level of its exports, which now totaled $160 million, and the volume of American manufactured goods imported rose while the volume of agricultural commodities plummeted.

There is reason to believe that Peking deliberately began to slow imports from the United States. Privately, Chinese officials hinted that bilateral trade, and especially Chinese imports of U.S. manufactured goods, might rise significantly after formal diplomatic relations were established, but would probably not change greatly before then. The level of trade in 1976 at mid-year ($119.6 million in imports by China from the United States and $90.5 million in U.S. imports from China) indicated that the year's trade was likely to be below that of 1975.[177]

It is reasonable to project a gradual increase in Sino-American trade over the next few years. However, in the period immediately ahead it may be closer to the half-billion-dollar level of recent years than to the billion-dollar peak in 1974. How much, and how rapidly, it rises above this level will depend on several factors: the overall state of U.S.-China relations, Peking's decisions on whether or not to try to accelerate China's modernization by expanding trade, the urgency of China's need for U.S. grain, capital goods, and technology, and China's ability to pay for increased imports.

In addition, it will depend on how successfully, and how soon, U.S.-China economic relationships can be institutionalized. The lack of intergovernmental agreements relating to trade is both a political and a practical impediment to more rapid trade development, and because many of the steps required will involve complicated problems, the process of institutionalizing economic relationships may take a long time to complete. Here too, progress will depend on political as well as economic factors. Domestic opposition in China as well as the desire to pressure the United States to take further steps toward normalization help to explain Peking's foot dragging on the proposed assets and claims agreement, and the Chinese may well drag their feet on all such matters until diplomatic relations can be established.

Another important reason why Sino-American trade has yet to be placed on a genuinely firm, dependable basis is that the Chinese clearly are still inclined to view the United States as a secondary or residual source of supply for most commodities. China's purchases of grain from Australia and Canada, with which Peking has formal diplomatic relations, are now based on agreements that cover several years. Peking naturally turns to them first, and to the United States only later to obtain what it cannot buy from these countries. Until Sino-American trade in grain is also based on long-term agreements, it may fluctuate unpredictably. In importing capital goods and technology Peking today seems to give priority in many fields to purchases from Japan and certain European countries, for both political and economic reasons. Consequently, the United States is in many respects still a residual supplier of manufactured goods too, except in instances where American plants or equipment are clearly unique or indisputably superior.

Achieving a reasonable balance in U.S.-China trade will probably continue to present difficulties because of the major differences in the situations and needs of the two countries. China's demand for commodities that the United States exports is potentially much greater and more important in relation to its basic needs than American demand for Chinese goods is in relation to the American economy. This helps to explain the large import-export gap in 1972–74. It was always doubtful that China would tolerate huge trade imbalances indefinitely, and now the gap is being reduced, but in part through contraction of imports as well as expansion of China's exports. For trade to be put on a more stable long-term basis, and to expand significantly, China's exports to the U.S. market will have to be increased substantially. There is a substantial potential for increase in Chinese exports of labor-intensive products such as textile goods and electronic equipment. However, Peking's sales of such commodities will encounter intense competition from areas such as Korea, Taiwan, Hong Kong, and Singapore, and considerable resistance from American producers.

Despite the many obstacles to large-scale development of U.S.-China trade, there is clearly a basis for a significant two-way exchange. China will probably continue to regard the United States as an important potential source of agricultural products and, assuming overall relations continue to improve, it is likely to show increasing interest in purchasing high-technology goods and obtaining technical know-how from the United States. Already the Chinese have bought RCA satellite stations, Boeing airplanes, Kellogg fertilizer plants, and American oil and gas equipment.[178] Purchases of such items could rise substantially.

American businessmen will doubtless continue to show an interest in China trade, despite the fact that it now accounts for only a fraction of one percent of total U.S. foreign trade, because of their hope that it will eventually become an important market. The U.S. government, like the Chinese government, will continue to regard it as symbolically important in political terms. But how much the trade grows will depend fundamentally on Chinese decisions: whether or not to mount an export drive in order to earn the foreign exchange to pay for increased imports from the United States, or to accept credits to help finance such imports, or to tolerate sizable trade imbalances in bilateral U.S.-China trade and pay for imports of U.S. goods with foreign exchange earned elsewhere. In theory, China could increase its trade with the United States fairly rapidly if it decided to do any of these things. It does not seem likely, however, to make a decision either to increase Sino-American trade suddenly and dramatically or to cut it back sharply. The likely prospect, therefore, is for fairly gradual growth.

Nevertheless, trade should continue to make a positive contribution to the process of normalizing U.S.-China relations. Gradually it should create a practical stake in the relationship for important groups in both countries and a network of personal and institutional contacts between the two societies. And, it will create new linkages of significance between the two governments. But the political importance of these economic ties should not be exaggerated. Peking will deliberately try to avoid any kind of economic dependence, and in its broad foreign policy will generally give priority to military-security and political considerations over economic ones, especially when they come into conflict. So long as China and the United States can sustain momentum toward political détente, the expansion of economic relations will both reinforce the process and in the long run help to reduce the danger of its reversal. But for the foreseeable future, trade will be less important than other factors in determining the overall state of Sino-American relations. Economic interests were not the primary ones leading to U.S.-China détente, nor will they be the crucial ones determining whether it lasts.

Strategic and Security Factors

Despite the importance of economic, ideological, and other influences, strategic and security issues have been, and will continue to be, the decisive factors shaping China's relations with the United States, as with the other major powers.[179] Security concerns, more than any others, were the crucial determinants of both the hostile confrontation between China and the United States in the 1950s and 1960s and the détente of the 1970s.

Once Peking, and especially Mao, concluded in 1968 that the Soviet Union posed the greatest immediate threat to China, the Chinese decided that some kind of link with the United States, and some sort of American presence in Asia, were desirable to create a stronger counterweight to Moscow. They apparently also concluded that Sino-American détente would reduce the dangers of future Japanese remilitarization. While U.S. aims were less clear-cut, perhaps, Nixon and Kissinger clearly wished not only to minimize the danger of direct conflict with China and facilitate the reduction of American forces in Asia but also to obtain increased leverage in dealing with Moscow. Both sides, recognizing certain common strategic interests, decided to subordinate certain other concerns in order to build a new relationship.

The opening of U.S.-China contacts significantly altered the balance among the major powers in East Asia and clearly served the security interests of both Peking and Washington by reducing their sense of mutual threat and imposing new restraints on the Soviet Union. Yet the common security interests of the United States and China are obviously still very limited, and derive in large part from factors extraneous to their bilateral relationship. To a considerable degree they depend on the state of each country's relations with the other major powers in East Asia, the Soviet Union and Japan.

The existing situation is full of contradictions. Peking and Washington are prepared to live with such contradictions at present, but they make the U.S.-China relationship extremely complex. Both recognize that, despite some common interests, the two countries remain competitors globally. However, their parallel interests mainly concern strategic and military-security problems while their competition focuses principally on broad international economic and political issues. Sometimes these different interests are intertwined, but when they conflict, both Chinese and American leaders tend to give priority to their security concerns.

The most important convergence of Chinese and American security concerns, which results in an important parallelism in some of their policies, is their common desire to prevent the expansion of Soviet influence. The degree and form of the parallelism varies considerably, however, depending on the issues and areas involved. In some instances, it is clear and explicit. In others, it is ambiguous, qualified, and tacit. At times, the Chinese publicly criticize particular American policies while privately approving them.

Peking now openly endorses a strong U.S.-supported NATO (North Atlantic Treaty Organization) and urges that no compromises with Moscow be made in Europe. At times, however, it has encouraged greater European independence from Washington. Its attitude toward the U.S.-Japanese security relationship is comparable. In South Asia, China urges greater U.S. military support of Pakistan. Publicly it condemns the activities of both superpowers in the Indian Ocean, but privately it favors a strengthening of the American naval position to match the growth of Soviet naval activity in the area. In the Middle East, Peking strongly supports the Arabs against Israel, which the United States backs, but it also makes clear that it is much more concerned about Soviet than American influence in the area. Publicly, the Chinese strongly endorse North Korea's call for a withdrawal of U.S. troops from the South, yet privately they appear to be using their influence to insure military restraint on the North's part. In Southeast Asia China now tacitly supports the continuation of a U.S. military presence in the Philippines, and even in Thailand, if Bangkok should decide its wants U.S. forces there. In sum, in most areas where American and Soviet positions are competitive, China now favors a strong U.S. stance vis-à-vis the Russians—while still publicly condemning both superpowers as oppressors of the Third World.

Yet, even in regard to the Soviet Union, Chinese and American interests are far from identical. In fact, their perspectives and policies differ in basic respects. The United States recognizes the Soviet Union to be a superpower with important and legitimate (if peaceful) roles to play in situations where its national interests are involved, and in its policy toward Moscow, Washington is committed to avoiding conflict, encouraging meaningful détente, and to the extent possible expanding ties and improving relations. Maintenance of a stable Soviet-American strategic military balance is an American goal of the highest priority—in the final analysis more important to vital U.S. interests than any aspect of Sino-American relations—and Washington considers progress in U.S.-Soviet arms control crucially important for stability.

China agrees fully with only one of these aims: avoidance of overt military conflict with the Soviet Union. Otherwise Peking's policies are very different: it strongly opposes U.S.-Soviet détente, denounces the superpowers' arms-control efforts, criticizes all signs of improvement in Soviet-American relations, and applauds any sign of increased friction between Washington and Moscow.

Moscow accuses Peking of trying, blatantly, to manipulate Soviet-American relations in order to exacerbate tension and provoke a U.S.-Soviet war.[180] Although this overstates the case, Peking does approve of continued U.S.-Soviet tension. Only if China's relations with Russia should improve is this position of the Chinese likely to change significantly.

Despite the basic differences in aims, the United States clearly backs one fundamental Chinese objective: to deter any possible Soviet military attack on China or expansion of Soviet military power elsewhere in Asia.

Although the U.S. government probably never considered the danger of a Soviet attack to be as imminent as Peking apparently did in the late 1960s, it did see war as a real enough possibility to justify deliberately throwing American political influence into the balance, not only by establishing new ties with Peking but also by openly expressing opposition to any Sino-Soviet military conflict and stressing the United States' determination to develop balanced relations with both countries. Since then, tacit American support has been a crucial element in China's deterrent against Moscow.

It is not certain, however, that the basic assumptions and expectations in Peking and Washington concerning this subtle security relationship are, or will remain, genuinely congruent. During 1975–76 the Chinese were increasingly critical of all signs of U.S.-Soviet détente and showed increasing signs of doubt about the Americans' ability or willingness to serve as an effective counterweight to the Soviet Union. During the same period there was also increasing speculation that China might wish to obtain military supplies from the United States (it did, in fact, begin purchasing military-related equipment in Europe).[181] Some Americans have publicly favored the idea, although the U.S. government clearly believes that the establishment of concrete military links with China might increase tension in the triangular U.S.-China-Soviet relationship.

For the present, the U.S.-China security relationship has an essentially political rather than military basis. The question of military contacts or cooperation remains largely hypothetical, and it seems likely to remain so in the period immediately ahead. However, one side or the other could at some point decide to explore the possibility of developing some sort of military contacts or cooperation. If Peking and Washington should decide to discuss this question, their approach to handling the problem could have far-reaching effects not only on their bilateral relations but on broader regional relationships.

The primary determinant, in fact, of future Sino-American relations will be the decisions both countries make on policies to protect their security interests, in the context of the changing overall regional balance in East Asia. The new four-power relationship involves an intricate pattern of action and reaction among the major powers. Any significant change in the triangular or quadrilateral, as well as bilateral, relations among the four will significantly affect the interests and policies of all (the implications of this are discussed in part 4). In this situation, future trends in Sino-Soviet relations could prove to be the most critical variable affecting Sino-American relations.

Korea and the Indochina States

In the years between 1949 and 1971, Korea and the Indochina states were focal points of military crises and conflicts between China and the United States.[182] In both areas local conflicts had a tremendous influence on U.S.-China relations and, conversely, the conflict between the major powers had an enormous impact on both Korea and the Indochina states. Clashes of Chinese and American interests in these areas caused one war and several tense crises between the two countries. The opening of Sino-American relations in 1972 was possible only because both sides decided to give priority to larger strategic and political interests and to downgrade or lay aside temporarily the unresolved issues in these areas.

Since the North Korean government was founded, the Chinese Communists have viewed it as a fraternal socialist regime which China should support. But Peking doubtless did not in 1949 anticipate the need to involve itself directly in Korean affairs. Its military intervention in 1950 appeared to be essentially defensive and motivated by fear that American forces, moving north, might destroy Kim Il-sung's regime and then threaten China. Peking would probably intervene again if there were a new threat to the existence of the Communist regime in North Korea, since it seems to consider the preservation of a buffer regime there to be essential to its own security. Short of that, however, China is not likely to inject its military power into the area or try to exercise direct control over it, although it is now attempting to outdo the Soviet Union in a contest for political influence in North Korea.

China has long given significant material support to North Korea,[183] and today it strongly endorses Kim Il-sung's proposals for reunification. But in recent years it has clearly emphasized the need for a peaceful rather than military reunification. And although the Chinese have publicly called for the withdrawal of U.S. forces, they seem to be concerned that any precipitate U.S. withdrawal might create a vacuum. Chinese fear of a U.S. threat in Korea appears definitely to have abated. China's overriding concern now is that Soviet influence could become dominant in this critical area next to its borders. However, the Chinese also appear uneasy about Japan's growing influence in the South.

In some respects Peking's strong political support of North Korea tends to work against stability in Korea, but China does appear to oppose actions that could lead to renewed military conflict that could involve it and the United States.

The U.S. government remains clearly committed to the goal of achieving stability on the peninsula, principally because it believes this to be of great importance to the security of Japan and therefore to peace throughout Northeast Asia. Like China, the United States will continue supporting its own ally on the peninsula. But it hopes for improved North-South relations and opposes action on either side that could create new tension and lead to conflict. Although not opposed in principle to the idea of peaceful reunification, it sees no realistic possibility of this being achieved soon, and in practice therefore it urges acceptance, de facto, of two Koreas. It continues to maintain American forces in Korea principally because it believes that their total removal might seriously destabilize the situation, and it now sees the possibility of rash action by North Korea as the main danger.

As long as the present situation and current Chinese and American perceptions of it persist, neither Peking nor Washington is likely to see the other as the primary threat in the area. However, Sino-American competition in Korea will persist, and because the hostility between North and South Korea creates one of the most volatile and dangerous situations in Asia, issues relating to the area will continue to complicate U.S.-China relations. Both Peking and Washington recognize that if a major conflict were to erupt again on the peninsula, they could be drawn in and the basis for Sino-American détente could be destroyed.

Despite some fundamental differences between the situations in Korea and in the Indochina states, there have been significant parallels in terms of conflicting Chinese and American interests. China's basic concern in the Indochina area as in Korea has been security, and its priority objective has been to protect a critical buffer area next to its southern border. Its interest in promoting revolution, though real, has been secondary.

The United States' involvement in the Indochina area in the 1950s and 1960s was also motivated by security concerns, comparable to those that impelled it to intervene in Korea. Fear of general Communist expansionism led Washington to support the existing regimes in Indochina in their struggles to prevent Communist takeovers, which it was widely assumed would lead to Chinese domination. However, American intervention heightened Chinese fears and impelled Peking to increase its material and political support to the local Communist forces, and to step up its own efforts to counter what it perceived to be a growing American threat to Chinese interests and security in Southeast Asia.

Peking probably never believed the threat in Southeast Asia, which is adjacent to relatively undeveloped areas of China, was as dangerous as American military action in Korea, which is next to China's industrial centers in Manchuria and not far from Peking itself. Nevertheless, when the United States intervened in Vietnam on a large scale in the mid-1960s and the war there escalated, Chinese fears increased. In a sense, China and the United States engaged in conflict by proxy, and in 1965–66 Peking feared the conflict might spread to China. It was difficult at this point for the Chinese even to consider the option of pursuing Sino-American détente, despite the continuing deterioration of Sino-Soviet relations and the increasing competition between Peking and Moscow for influence in Vietnam.

But the situation began to change as Chinese fears about U.S. intentions declined. Peking gave its first hint of a willingness to reassess its policy toward Washington soon after the United States had indicated, in 1968, that it intended to begin reducing its military involvement in Vietnam. China's subsequent backing and filling in its early interactions with Washington during 1969–70 were unquestionably related to the conflicting signals the United States gave about its military intentions. When U.S. forces invaded Cambodia, for example, Peking backtracked. Only when the Chinese were convinced that the United States was withdrawing its forces did they decide that the road was clear to make serious moves toward détente. Even then, they continued to stress in their first official conversations with American leaders that deescalation of the American involvement in Vietnam was a prerequisite for improvement of U.S.-China relations; at times they seemed to place even greater stress on this than on the unresolved issue of Taiwan.

When the Chinese finally decided to make dramatic overt moves toward détente, they were fully aware that the North Vietnamese would interpret this as a sign that China was placing its own interests ahead of those of local revolutionaries in Indochina. Hanoi probably did fear that Peking might pressure it to negotiate a cease-fire.[184] The Chinese attempted to soften the blow to the Vietnamese by pledging continued political and material support. But they soon demonstrated clearly that their primary concerns actually lay elsewhere. When the United States decided to mount a massive air assault on North Vietnam in late 1972, Peking was not deflected from the path of détente that it had chosen. Actually, the outcry against this new American escalatory move was louder in the United States than in China.[185] By then the Chinese had probably decided that the U.S. process of disengagement was irreversible. And they were prepared for broad geopolitical reasons to accept new strains in their relations with Hanoi in order to prepare the ground for establishing new links with the United States.

From the U.S. point of view, Chinese restraint in Vietnam was considered to be a prerequisite for steps toward détente, and one major goal in establishing a dialogue with Peking was to try to reinforce that restraint. The opening of U.S.-China relations in 1971–72 did in fact reduce the risks that would result from American military disengagement from Indochina and helped to strengthen the rationale for the new general direction in U.S. policy in East Asia symbolized by the Nixon Doctrine.

Then, in 1975, the rapid collapse of the noncommunist regimes in the Indochina states and the total U.S. military withdrawal from that area created an entirely new situation. Both Peking and Washington seemed to sense that, despite continuing differences of a basic sort, they now had some parallel interests in the Southeast Asian area as well as elsewhere. Both feared that a situation of extreme uncertainty and instability could present the Soviet Union with new opportunities to exploit. Both have ceased viewing Southeast Asia primarily in terms of U.S.-China confrontation. This by no means eliminates the possibility that conflicts of interest between the two countries in Southeast Asia could come to the fore again. But China is not now pushing for a total withdrawal of U.S. forces from Southeast Asia, and the United States no longer portrays China as a country threatening all its southern neighbors.

In the period immediately ahead, therefore, neither Peking nor Washington seems likely to view Korea and Southeast Asia, as both did in the 1950s and 1960s, primarily as arenas for Sino-American conflict. Nevertheless, serious dangers will persist. Both areas continue to be unstable, with a potential for local conflict that could involve outside powers. And both have become arenas for a new and far more complicated pattern of political competition among the four major powers in East Asia, the outcome of which will clearly have a significant impact on Sino-American relations.

The Long-run Future of Taiwan

For more than a quarter of a century, the Taiwan issue has been the most important bilateral problem in Sino-American relations, and it remains the principal obstacle to normalizing Peking-Washington ties.

There is no doubt that under the best of circumstances it will continue to complicate the U.S.-China relationship for years to come. At worst, it could again become a focus of conflict.

Difficult as it is, the short-run problem of Taiwan as an obstacle to the establishment of formal diplomatic relations between Peking and Washington should not be insoluble if both the United States and China are willing to make further compromises. However, such compromises will not alter the realities of Taiwan's present position, or determine its long-run future. Taiwan is an entity whose government and people have interests of their own and refuse to be treated simply as pawns in big-power relations.[186]

The Taiwan problem, simply stated, is that of a divided country, resulting from an uncompleted civil conflict which became internationalized in fundamental respects after the outbreak of war in Korea and at the height of the worldwide cold war between the Communist and non-communist nations. Since then, Taiwan has maintained a separate existence, which the United States has supported, while Peking has remained committed to assert its sovereignty and control over it.

Although the Nationalists still claim to be the legitimate government of all China and to be dedicated to a "return to the mainland," these myths long ago lost any credibility internationally and, for that matter, among most people on Taiwan. Under Nationalist rule, however, Taiwan has enjoyed local autonomy for more than a quarter century, and the de facto situation has become the basic reality.

Taiwan's survival as a separate entity depended, at the start, on U.S. protection and the massive aid that the Americans provided, but during the 1960s Taiwan acquired a basis for its own viability. Today it is no longer a U.S. dependency in the sense that it once was.

Peking and Taipei agree, in theory at least, that Taiwan is Chinese territory. Although the island was acquired by the Japanese in 1895 and administered by them as a colony for fifty years thereafter, the big-power agreements signed at Cairo and Potsdam during World War II promised to return it to China, and in 1945 the Nationalist government reestablished control over it. Then, as the civil war on the mainland was drawing to a close, the remnants of the Nationalist regime fled to Taiwan, and the Communists actively prepared to invade the island. It was only U.S. intervention that blocked a Communist military takeover. Statements by American leaders that reopened the question of Taiwan's legal status in a way that appeared to challenge the Chinese title to it outraged Peking's leaders who interpreted them as action aimed deliberately at insuring permanent separation of the island from China.

Ever since then Peking has pressed for the "liberation" of Taiwan and regarded reunification as a national aim of high priority.[187] It has consistently asserted that there is only one China, that Taiwan is a province of China, and that no "two Chinas" or "one China, one Taiwan" solution would be legal or tolerable. It has also insisted that no country wishing to have full diplomatic relations with Peking can maintain formal diplomatic relations with the Nationalist regime. At times the Communists have emphasized their desire to liberate Taiwan peacefully, but they have also refused to renounce the use of force, on the grounds that unification is a domestic issue and that sovereignty includes the right to use force.

The U.S. decision in June 1950 to interpose the Seventh Fleet in the Taiwan Strait to protect the island was made in an atmosphere of crisis, and in making it, Washington was not seriously constrained by legal complications. However, when it reopened the question of Taiwan's status, the U.S. government did not take an explicit position on its future status—in fact, it still has not done so.

Washington's attitudes toward Taiwan have undergone substantial changes over the years. During and immediately after the Korean War, the U.S. government supported the Nationalist regime as an active challenger to the legitimacy of the People's Republic. However, it soon imposed constraints on military action by the Nationalists, and except for one brief period, these steadily increased. Even in the original declaration on the "neutralization" of the Taiwan Strait Washington asserted that this was a two-way proposition, designed to prevent attacks by either the Communists or the Nationalists. Briefly, in the initial months of the Eisenhower-Dulles period, the new administration talked about a "liberation" policy. This proved to be meaningless rhetoric, however, and subsequently, during the offshore island crises, concrete steps were taken to "leash" the Nationalists and preclude any major military action by them against the mainland. Though U.S. support of the Nationalists steadily increased, particularly after the signature of a defense treaty in 1954, by the late 1950s it was unambiguously defensive.

Gradually, the United States appeared to move toward a de facto two-Chinas policy, and Peking increasingly feared that this would lead to Taiwan's legal independence. Washington took no explicit steps in this direction, however. Even if it had been so inclined, it would have been deterred by strong opposition from the Nationalists who were just as adamantly opposed to the idea as the Communists were. If the Nationalists in the late 1950s or early 1960s had opted to move toward independence, the United States might have approved, and possibly much of the international community would have gone along. Peking would probably have been under strong pressure to accommodate to the resulting situation eventually. By the early 1970s, however, no nation was willing to endorse such a move.

When Peking and Washington decided to explore the possibilities of détente, Peking gave up its insistence that the Taiwan problem must be solved *before* any steps toward improving U.S.-China relations could be taken, but it reiterated all of its basic claims without change. The United States in effect abandoned the two-Chinas idea as an option, yet it continued to maintain its existing relationship with the Nationalist regime.

However, there was no clear agreement in 1972 on what the long-run future of Taiwan should be, and there is not likely to be any such agreement even if Washington decides to establish full diplomatic relations with Peking and to cut its formal ties with Taiwan. Taiwan's prospects following the normalization of U.S.-China relations will then depend on the future evolution of the attitudes and policies of many actors, not only Peking and Washington, and Tokyo and Moscow as well, but above all the leaders and people on Taiwan itself.

Many factors have shaped the Chinese Communists' attitudes toward Taiwan. Strong irredentist feelings have obviously been of fundamental importance. Peking's view of the island as unliberated Chinese territory goes far toward explaining the priority it has given to the problem and the passion its leaders have frequently exhibited about it. Irredentist issues anywhere tend to be among the most explosive in international affairs because they evoke deep emotions involving national pride and self-respect. Moreover, for centuries the Chinese have insisted that all territory considered to be Chinese should be unified. Even though China has been divided for extended periods, and the territory considered to be Chinese has varied, the ideal of unity has never died.

The Chinese Communists have not, however, let irredentist passions alone determine their major policies. While they have been unyielding on some territorial claims, they have accommodated to the loss of certain areas such as Outer Mongolia. In the 1930s, Mao actually stated that he supported independence for Taiwan (a statement Peking leaders doubtless now prefer to forget).[188] In short, although Chinese irredentism has been strong in some respects, Peking has been willing to make compromises on territorial issues when broad national interests have seemed to require it.

Peking is not likely to be flexible, however, on the basic irredentist issue that the Taiwan problem poses. It can be expected for the foreseeable future, therefore, to work for the "liberation" of Taiwan simply because it views the island as Chinese territory. Conceivably this could change over the very long run, but not in the near future.

The intensity of the Chinese Communists' feelings about Taiwan has been due in part, also, to the fact that since 1949 it has been the seat of a competitive regime that has continued to challenge Peking's legitimacy. Over time, to be sure, it has become clear that the Nationalists cannot pose a major military threat to the mainland, but Taiwan could again become a base for harassment and subversion, as it was throughout most of the 1950s and 1960s. From Peking's perspective, also, Taiwan has been a symbol of continuing Western intervention in Chinese affairs. Until recently, moreover, it served as a military base for U.S. containment policies directed against the People's Republic.

Many of these factors are now less important than they once were. The Nationalists' challenge to Peking has little if any force. Especially since Chiang Kai-shek passed from the scene, the threat of the Nationalist regime has become insignificant, and efforts to harass and subvert the mainland ended some time ago. The United States is now withdrawing its forces from Taiwan and no longer views it as a major U.S. base for containment of China. Washington has made it clear that it will not itself foster Taiwanese independence, and it now stresses that the problem of Taiwan's future must be solved by the Chinese themselves. These developments have reduced the basis for Peking's resentment about Taiwan's continued separation from the rest of the country and about the United States' continued involvement. However, the irredentist issue persists, and that alone will probably impel Peking's leaders to continue striving for reunification.

Over the years, U.S. attitudes toward Taiwan have also changed. Despite an increasing American economic stake in Taiwan (which is now far larger than any U.S. economic stake in relations with the China mainland),[189] the emotional attachments that many Americans felt toward the Nationalists in earlier years have weakened. The Nationalist regime has ceased to be an ideological symbol of a worldwide struggle against communism. No leaders in the United States now view it as a potential challenger to Peking's domestic or international legitimacy. And the U.S.

government has made clear that it views the People's Republic as *the* government of China. It also acknowledges that the U.S. relationship with Taiwan in its present form poses obstacles to the kind of relations with Peking that are desirable and therefore will probably have to be adjusted.

In many respects, the United States still views the future of Taiwan in open-ended terms. Its prime stress is on the avoidance of military conflict in the Taiwan area. However, in the Shanghai Communiqué the United States implied that it might look favorably on the idea of reunification, *if* it can be accomplished peacefully. Yet few Americans would accept the idea that the United States should ignore the desires of the people on Taiwan. All of this falls considerably short of what the Chinese Communists would like to see the United States say and do, but it poses less of a challenge to Peking than the U.S. positions of earlier years.

Assuming Peking will continue to work toward reunification, one key question is whether it will try to do so rapidly or gradually; another is whether it will use peaceful or military means. Since the late 1950s Peking seems to have accepted a de facto truce in the Taiwan Strait area. When the United States fleet blocked the strait, Peking concluded that invasion was not a realistic option and probably would not be as long as the Americans remained determined to prevent it. It then tried to achieve its goals through calculated military threats and pressures in 1954–55, a policy of attraction in 1955–56, and renewed military pressure in 1958. When all these efforts failed, the Chinese Communist leaders appeared to conclude that liberation of Taiwan would have to be viewed essentially in political rather than military terms, and as a fairly long-range problem.

Since 1972, Peking's leaders have generally emphasized their desire for a peaceful reunification, and made new efforts to appeal, on the basis of Chinese nationalism, to varied groups on Taiwan.[190] They have stressed that they look at the problem in very long-range terms, and they have made some statements indicating that when reunification occurs, Peking will take Taiwan's special circumstances fully into account, will show concern for the economic welfare of the people of Taiwan, and will pursue policies of social change that do not ignore the interests of any group, including local capitalists. At times, they have hinted at a willingness to give Taiwan a special status, though they have been very vague on the degree of autonomy, if any, they might tolerate.[191]

Internationally, Peking has stopped pressing other countries to state explicitly that they recognize Taiwan as part of China. Most, in recent years, have simply "taken note" of Peking's claims.[192] And though its efforts to undermine the Nationalist regime's formal diplomatic ties everywhere and to oust it from all international bodies continue, Peking has become remarkably tolerant of the informal political ties many countries maintain with Taipei and has stopped, at least for the present, serious efforts to discourage other nations from trading with or investing in Taiwan.

All of this seems to suggest that Peking is now committed to a very long-term policy aimed at gradual and peaceful reunification, using political rather than military means. It would be unrealistic, however, to conclude that it could not revert to a policy of pressure, or even of military liberation. A shift of leadership in China could lead to a hardening of Peking's policy. Or a shift in the international balance, and Peking's perception of it, could make a policy of military action seem more practicable. Eventually, if the United States were to disengage totally from involvement in Taiwan's defense, and if the Communists' amphibious capabilities had improved, Chinese leaders might again consider a policy of threats, especially if Taiwan appeared to be moving toward independence.

Yet many factors will probably argue, in the minds of Peking's leaders, in favor of continuing a gradual political approach. There is no certainty that renewed pressure or threats alone would influence either Taiwan or the countries that continue nonofficial ties with it in ways favorable to Peking. They could be counterproductive, since they might push the government on Taiwan toward independence or impel countries such as the United States and Japan to increase rather than decrease their involvement in the area.

Actual military invasion does not seem to be a realistic possibility in the years immediately ahead even though it cannot be excluded as a possibility in the more distant future. Taiwan's present defense capability is substantial. And it could be improved, and doubtless would be, if overt threats to Taiwan's security increased. Moreover, a Chinese Communist invasion attempt, even if the United States and Japan had reduced their direct involvement in the Taiwan area, might lead both of these nations to reassess their basic policies toward the People's Republic as well as Taiwan. Peking would have to calculate what the broader international effects of the use of force against Taiwan would be. Unless the entire pattern of big-power relations in East Asia changes significantly, concern about the possible opposition of all the other major powers is likely to be a major factor inhibiting the Communists from considering an invasion.

Military moves against the small offshore islands might be a realistic possibility. Even though these islands would not be easy to take, they might well be blockaded and starved into submission if the United States stayed out of any future crisis. However, Peking itself seems to have had serious doubts, especially since 1958, about whether taking the off-shore islands alone would be in its interest, since it might simply reinforce trends toward the permanent separation of Taiwan. Moreover, here too, concern about possible American and Japanese reactions would continue to inhibit major military action.

Because of the many deterrents to military action, it seems probable that Peking will feel compelled to show continued patience and to try to achieve peaceful reunification through political attraction, or subtle pressure, or both. If a policy of attraction were to succeed, the United States and Japan would probably accommodate to peaceful reunification with relatively little difficulty. However, if one takes account of the situation on Taiwan itself, and of the desires of the island's inhabitants, there seems little possibility that this will occur soon. Today, the people on Taiwan clearly oppose the idea that their fate can be decided by Peking, or anyone else, and they show no desire to submit themselves to Communist rule.

Taiwan's political future will obviously depend fundamentally, therefore, on future trends on the island itself, the attitudes of its people, and the decisions of its leaders. Today, although its legal status continues to be uncertain, Taiwan clearly functions very successfully as an autonomous political entity. Separated from the mainland by about a hundred miles of water, its government rules a large and productive island (plus the Pescadores and offshore islands) that supports more than sixteen million people, a population larger than that of a majority of UN members. The population is almost entirely Chinese (the aboriginal groups are numerically unimportant), but more than thirteen million are local "Taiwanese." They are descendants of migrants who came from China —mainly from Fukien Province—many decades or even centuries ago. Most of the others are "mainlanders" (and their offspring) who came from various parts of China in the late 1940s; today the majority of these have been born in Taiwan.

Virtually all of both groups regard themselves as culturally Chinese, but most Taiwanese see themselves as a distinctive kind of Chinese. In many respects they clearly are. For only four years out of the last eighty has Taiwan been administered directly from the capital of China, and for long periods it had little contact with the mainland.

For fifty years the Japanese ruled the island in a classic colonial pattern. Politically their rule was repressive, and they dominated all important positions, keeping the local population in subordinate roles. Consequently, the Taiwanese showed rebelliousness repeatedly, and in 1945 they welcomed the Nationalists when China regained control of the island. However, they were soon disillusioned, as a result of the Nationalists' mismanagement at that time, which culminated in the brutal repression of the Taiwanese elite which occurred in 1947.

The Japanese, despite their political repressiveness, developed the island's economy very successfully, and as a result Taiwan was far more modernized than most of China, even in 1945. In addition, the Japanese had a significant and lasting cultural impact on the population. In the years since 1945, Taiwanese bitterness about Japanese political oppression has receded, while empathy with the Japanese based on past cultural links has tended to persist. The half century of Japanese rule set the Taiwanese apart from other Chinese, including the mainlanders who became the dominant political group.

Tension in relationships between these mainlanders and the local Taiwanese has posed serious problems ever since the late 1940s. Relations were worst in the years immediately following the 1947 repression. Dissident Taiwanese tried to organize many anti-Nationalist activities, including an independence movement. The dissidents were never able to develop substantial political power, however. And in recent years Taiwanese-mainlander relations have gradually improved. Land reform not only improved the lot of local farmers but also created an influential Taiwanese business class. Subsequent economic growth, the benefits of which have been widely distributed, has also tended to reduce political discontent.

Politically, the Taiwanese have been slowly coopted into the elite structure through participation in local elections, military conscription, administrative appointments to government posts, and recruitment into the Kuomintang party. Although mainlanders are still dominant at the top, Taiwanese now predominate at lower levels. Acute alienation has been significantly reduced, and the potential for successful rebellion, if it ever existed, seems very small. Today, many politically minded Taiwanese see a prospect for achieving predominance by gradual ascent up the political ladder. Many others remain politically apathetic.

A noncommunist Taiwanese independence movement still does exist, mostly abroad, but it is disunited, and there is little evidence that it can become a force capable of decisive political action. Moreover, as political changes have occurred, both within Taiwan and in Taiwan's international standing, even the leaders of the movement abroad have become less inclined to challenge the mainlander-led Nationalist government openly, and more predisposed to think in terms of evolutionary change. Virtually none of its leaders are pro-Communist, and while many hope for independence, they prefer the status quo to the idea of Communist rule. In the 1950s Peking sponsored a Taiwanese revolutionary movement led by activists resident in Peking. But it had little effect on Taiwan. Its leadership was purged in the late 1950s, and thereafter little was heard of it. Few overseas Taiwanese independence activists ever had any contact with it.

The Nationalist government on Taiwan, which was disorganized, corrupt, and ineffective when it arrived in 1949, has developed into a structure that, while still suffering from many shortcomings, is clearly competent to rule with considerable effectiveness. Its "succession problem" was solved without any upheaval when Chiang Kai-shek's son, Chiang Ching-kuo, stepped into his father's shoes. It remains, however, a one-party structure, authoritarian in basic respects despite democratic forms. It maintains a strong police apparatus that vigorously suppresses most Taiwanese independence activists as well as Communists or pro-Communists. But it is by no means totalistic, in the sense that the Chinese Communist regime is. Its controls over the population are in general fairly loose, and it tolerates a great deal of social pluralism and considerable freedom so long as individuals do not appear to pose subversive political threats.

The regime still retains both a national and a provincial government on Taiwan. This dual structure was justified on the basis of the leaders' intention to "return to the mainland." It was probably also considered necessary, in the mainlanders' view, to uphold the legitimacy of their political dominance on Taiwan. Increasingly, however, old slogans have become hollow, and the basis for continuing a dual structure is now questionable.

Although Kuomintang party propaganda continues to be highly ideological, the importance of ideology has steadily declined. Administrators and specialists have gradually risen in importance, though they do not control political power, and in recent years the government has focused primary attention on Taiwan's economic development, pursuing policies that are basically pragmatic and technocratic.

The development of Taiwan is in many respects a spectacular success story. Economic growth has greatly improved the life of the local population and increased the economic and social gap between Taiwan and the Communist-ruled mainland. In the 1950s it looked as if the island might remain an economic dependency of the United States for the indefinite future. But in the 1960s the process of growth "took off." For more than a decade, Taiwan's gross national product has been growing at an average rate of roughly 10 percent a year in real terms, roughly double the rate of growth in the People's Republic in the 1960s.[193] In constant dollars, Taiwan's GNP was roughly $2.2 billion in 1963 and $9.3 billion in 1973. Per-capita income has risen rapidly and is now, in constant dollars, about $533 compared to $249 in 1963; today its level is one of the highest in Asia and is at least double that in China. Moreover, the rate of net population growth has declined steadily; it was 3.8 percent in 1951 and 2.2 percent in 1970.[194] Even more important, income distribution has been far more equitable than in most developing nations. In Taiwan the difference in average income between the top 20 percent of the population and the lowest 20 percent dropped from 15 to 1 in 1950 to 5 to 1 in 1965, whereas in the Philippines, for example, it increased from 12 to 1 in 1956 to 16 to 1 in 1965.[195] Agriculture in Taiwan has been successfully modernized and impressive strides have been made toward industrialization, starting with light industry but moving toward more sophisticated industry.

One explanation for Taiwan's economic success, clearly, was the huge amount of U.S. aid it received in earlier years. In fifteen years this totaled nearly $4.5 billion, roughly a third of which was economic aid and two-thirds military assistance.[196] But the island's growth cannot be explained simply as a result of external aid—or such special factors as the relatively small size and manageability of the economy. Clearly the skills of the regime's planners and administrators, the talent and hard work of the population, and the regime's particular development strategies have been crucial factors.

The United States ended its grant aid to Taiwan in 1965.[197] Military grant aid has also ended, but the United States still makes sizable military sales to Taiwan ($293 million in fiscal 1976) under favorable credit terms.[198] In a basic economic sense, therefore, by the end of the 1960s Taiwan had become independently viable.

Foreign economic relations are of critical importance to the island. Large-scale foreign investment has provided essential capital and technology, and the entire economy has been geared to foreign trade. Taiwan has in fact become one of the most export-oriented areas in the world. In 1974, for example, its total of imports and exports, amounting to $12.62 billion, was roughly equal to the island's total GNP.[199]

The United States and Japan are the largest traders with, and investors in, Taiwan, and both play extremely important roles in Taiwan's development efforts. In 1974, Taiwan exported $2.04 billion worth of goods to the United States and imported $1.68 billion from it; for the United States this was a much larger trade turnover than with mainland China. And by 1974 U.S. investments in Taiwan were estimated to be $429 million, of a total foreign investment in Taiwan since 1952 estimated to be $1.287 billion.[200] Taiwan's economic relations with Japan are equally important, with the two-way trade in 1974 totaling over $3 billion. Taiwan has also expanded its trade elsewhere, especially with European and other industrial nations.

Although the island is now economically independent, it is so closely linked to the world economy that it is quite vulnerable to international market forces, and to the broad political as well as economic factors that affect them. This was evident in 1973–74 when international trends had seriously adverse effects on the island, and its growth rate dropped to a low level.[201] But it recovered rapidly. Clearly, Taiwan's dynamic and strong economy, based on capitalist free enterprise and tied intimately to the world economy, is profoundly different from the economy on the Chinese mainland.

In contrast to Taiwan's success economically, the international political position of the Nationalist regime has been steadily eroded in recent years, especially since Washington and Tokyo opened relations with Peking. The number of nations that officially recognize the Nationalist regime has dropped to about thirty and is still declining. In terms of traditional diplomatic relations, Taiwan can only look forward to becoming increasingly isolated.

Yet the Nationalist regime has adapted to this situation with notable pragmatism and considerable ingenuity. It has continued to trade with

well over a hundred nations and maintains "unofficial offices," many per-
forming consular and cultural as well as trade functions, in about seventy
nations that do not officially recognize it.[202] And it continues to be represented in many private international organizations. Though from Taiwan's point of view the new situation is obviously far from wholly
satisfactory, to date it has not seriously weakened the island's viability.

Taiwan has a reasonably strong defense establishment that consists of
half a million men and includes modern aircraft and naval units as well
as large ground forces.[203] The heavy economic burden of supporting this
establishment has eased as the island's economy has grown, and it can
probably be supported by the regime on its own in the future. The hundred miles of water that protect the island and the fact that most of the
men in its defense forces are local Taiwanese probably means any assault-
ing force would face stiff opposition.

But Taiwan's sense of security in recent years has depended to a considerable extent on the U.S. commitment to defend the island. If the
leaders and people on the island were to conclude that they were on their
own, militarily, the disparity in power between Taiwan and the People's Republic would create a new sense of insecurity. The ending of the
formal U.S. defense treaty would not necessarily undermine confidence
if the United States continued to demonstrate a sense of responsibility
for the security of the area. But if they concluded that the United States
had totally disengaged from the situation, leaders on Taiwan might
conceivably conclude that full accommodation to Peking's desires was
unavoidable. It is more likely, however, that if they felt desperate, they
might turn to other major powers for aid, build up their own military
forces still further—and perhaps develop an independent nuclear capability.

It is extremely difficult to predict whether military, political, and economic trends in the period ahead, both on Taiwan itself and regionally,
will impel Taiwan to explore the possibility of reassociation with the
mainland, to move toward ultimate independence, or to try simply to
preserve the status quo.

The present attitudes and aspirations of various groups on Taiwan
differ.[204] There is clearly a strong emotional tie to China among mainlanders on Taiwan. Even the Taiwanese feel they are culturally Chinese,
but most of them do not feel the same kind of emotional tie to the mainland. However, there is no sign now of any predisposition in either group
to consider rapprochement with the Peking regime in the immediate

future. Anticommunist feelings are strong, and the prevailing view seems to be that, under existing circumstances, any contact with the mainland might simply weaken Taiwan's position and make it vulnerable to Communist pressure.

Some mainlanders appear to hope that in the long run, political, social, and economic changes on the mainland will lead to a less ideological, more pragmatic, and moderate Communist regime and eventually some sort of convergence of Taiwan and China. But even those with this hope believe that Taiwan must maintain de facto separation in the short run. Some mainlanders appear tempted to try for short-term de jure independence, without foreclosing the possibility of reunification later. A great many people on Taiwan recognize, however, that in the long run Taiwan cannot be really secure without an acceptable relationship of some sort with the China mainland.

A large majority of the Taiwanese probably hope that eventually the island will become fully independent and then try to work out an acceptable relationship with Peking. Because of such hopes, they have been disturbed by the opening of Peking-Washington relations and by the pledge that the United States appeared to make in the Shanghai communiqué not to support independence for Taiwan. Some seem reluctant to accept the idea that Washington ruled out the possibility of supporting independence, and among them there are probably some who feel that if steps toward independence were actually taken, even in the face of U.S. disapproval, American leaders would have to accept a fait accompli.

On balance, however, it seems likely that no moves will be made toward de jure independence in the near future. The U.S. government will doubtless discourage overt steps in that direction, since they would pose profound policy dilemmas for the United States. Clearly Peking would react with outrage and would tend to blame the United States for such a development. It could force the U.S. government to make a clear-cut choice between two undesirable alternatives: cutting all nonofficial as well as official ties with Taiwan in order to maintain relations with Peking, or allowing its relations with Peking to deteriorate in order to maintain relations with an independent Taiwan. Many other countries that still maintain informal ties with Taiwan might feel compelled to sever them. Probably most of Taiwan's leaders today recognize that, under existing circumstances, declaring independence would clearly weaken rather than strengthen Taiwan's international position. But they cannot be expected to rule out the independence option permanently, whatever the major powers think.

The direction of long-term trends will obviously be greatly influenced by Peking's future policies. If its domestic policies become more pragmatic and moderate, attitudes on Taiwan toward the mainland might change, very slowly. And if Peking pursues a moderate and flexible policy toward Taiwan over an extended period of time, the opposition on Taiwan to all contacts may gradually decrease. However, for Peking to exert any effective attractive force on any significant number of people on Taiwan, it will have to be much more specific than it has been so far in defining the terms on which it is willing to discuss reunification. Unless it makes clear that it is prepared to offer a very substantial degree of real autonomy, its policies are more likely to reinforce trends toward ultimate Taiwanese independence than to induce the leaders on Taiwan to consider some form of reassociation with the mainland. The so-called autonomy Peking has granted to areas such as Tibet will not have any appeal.

United States policy will obviously also have a large effect on future trends. Total U.S. disengagement from Taiwan could force the island either to consider desperation moves or to capitulate to pressure from Peking, but the continuation of nonofficial relations will permit Taiwan to exercise some choice about its future. Moreover, U.S. policy will clearly have some influence on the specific policies Taiwan's leaders eventually choose. If Washington discourages steps toward de jure independence under existing circumstances, and encourages a dialogue between Taipei and Peking, this could have a significant influence on what ultimately occurs. However, if Washington were to indicate that, whatever its public posture, it would approve, or accept, steps toward de jure independence, the likelihood that leaders on Taiwan would move in that direction would be greatly increased.

Assuming that Peking pursues a moderate, long-term policy of attraction and that Washington encourages Taipei to open a dialogue with the People's Republic, it is conceivable that the two governments may eventually begin to explore, at first through intermediaries, whether any modus vivendi is possible. The process would certainly be very cautious and very gradual. It might begin with openings for trade and travel, but these might lead in time to discussions on the possibility of Taiwan's reassociation with the mainland under conditions that granted it substantial autonomy.

But trends might easily move in different directions, impelling Taiwan's leaders to move toward de jure independence or take other steps that would foreclose the possibility of reassociation with the mainland. The greatest uncertainties would arise if leaders on Taiwan were to feel a sense of desperation and had serious doubts about their survival. New pressures or threats from Peking, acute internal instability on the island, a major economic crisis resulting from a worldwide depression, or the belief that Taiwan had been totally abandoned by the United States could make them desperate. Increased political pressure from Taiwanese advocates of independence might convince Nationalist leaders that their survival domestically required steps toward de jure independence.

If Taiwan's leaders felt they were dangerously threatened by Peking, weakened at home, and abandoned by the United States, they might begin to search anywhere possible for aid. They might try to form closer links with Japan and somehow involve it in Taiwan's defense. In extremis, they might be tempted to solicit Soviet support. Despite rumors that Taipei and Moscow have already toyed with the idea of greater contacts, neither appears to have seriously considered the possibility so far.[205] Both have good reasons for not doing so. Strong nationalist and anti-Soviet feelings still make the idea repugnant to most leaders in Taipei, and the Russians appear to recognize that to deal openly with Taiwan would mean accepting Peking's enmity for the indefinite future and paying a heavy political price worldwide for a step that would widely be regarded as an exceptional example of cynical realpolitik.[206] Yet one cannot exclude this as a possibility if Taiwan's leaders were to feel desperate and Moscow-Peking relations had deteriorated further.

It is also impossible to exclude the possibility that leaders in Taipei could decide to develop an independent nuclear weapons capability.[207] Taiwan has been developing nuclear power plants for some years. It has probably already acquired the necessary knowledge of nuclear technology to produce bombs. In 1975 its premier stated publicly that Taiwan could build nuclear weapons but did not intend to.[208] It seems unlikely to do so in the near future, but its policy could change if its leaders were to feel extremely insecure.

Although the acquisition of nuclear weapons would not permit Taiwan to threaten a first strike against Peking, the ability to make a retaliatory strike would obviously enhance Taiwan's ability to deter any attack by Peking. If the Nationalists were to decide to build atomic weapons, they could decide to follow the Israelis' example and try to develop a nuclear capability without actually exploding any nuclear device.

For Taiwan to opt for such a policy might appear to be self-defeating, since it is probable that all the major powers would react strongly against it. The incentives for these powers, including the United States, to disengage completely from the Taiwan situation would clearly increase. Taiwan's international position might become even more isolated and it could find itself totally "on its own," conceivably in a dangerous situation of confrontation with Peking. It seems likely that leaders on Taiwan, considering these possibilities, will be inhibited from actually "going nuclear," yet if they were desperate, there is certainly a possibility that they would choose this route.

There is clearly no pat formula for a quick solution to the problem of Taiwan. Like many of the most difficult international problems, it is one that all parties concerned will have to live with for years to come, allowing time for gradual change to occur. At a minimum, it will remain a complicating factor and irritant in Sino-American relations. It need not, however, be an insuperable barrier to further improvement of Sino-American relations *if* both Peking and Washington view the problem in long-range terms, accept the realities and complexities of the situation, show a willingness to compromise, and continue to show flexibility and restraint. *If* Peking persists in pursuing a policy of attraction, *if* Washington gradually deemphasizes the significance of its political ties to Taiwan without abandoning it, and *if* Taipei in time sees the logic of initiating a dialogue with Peking, it may be possible eventually to work out a modus vivendi, based either on some sort of reassociation with China acceptable to Taiwan, or some sort of separate status acceptable to Peking. Until that occurs, however, Taiwan will continue to complicate Sino-American relations and will remain a potentially dangerous issue that could again become a focal point of U.S.-China conflict. It is simply not possible for Peking and Washington alone to solve the problem. Ultimately, a solution without conflict will require, as the United States asserted in the Shanghai communiqué, some kind of "peaceful settlement . . . by the Chinese themselves."

Prospects for the Relationship

The decisions made during 1971–72 by Peking and Washington to reopen contacts and start normalizing their ties profoundly altered both their bilateral relations and the entire regional balance in East Asia. Both countries decided to end the hostile confrontation that had shaped their relations for two decades, to stress certain common strategic interests, to deemphasize continuing conflicts of interest, and to try to build a new relationship.

The results have produced obvious benefits to both countries, and today the basic geopolitical and military-security reasons that led to policy changes on both sides continue to be valid. Yet in the five years since the signing of the Shanghai communiqué, progress toward establishing fully normalized relations has been very gradual, and relations between the two countries are still very limited. The new relationship rests more on common opposition to potential Soviet pressure or threats than on shared positive goals. Peking and Washington continue to view the world from very different perspectives and to pursue conflicting policies on many issues. To date, continuing differences on the Taiwan problem have prevented even the establishment of full diplomatic relations.

With new leadership in both countries, the prospects for the relationship are by no means certain. Though there are strong reasons for leaders in both countries to try to consolidate relations, and improve them further, there is no guarantee that there will be further progress. In fact, there could be retrogression. Since 1974 there has been little forward movement.

Two crucial variables are likely to shape the relationship in the period immediately ahead: the way in which the two countries handle the unresolved Taiwan problem, and trends in the triangular relationship among China, the United States, and the Soviet Union.

Bilateral relations are not likely to improve substantially until a mutually acceptable formula for dealing with the Taiwan question is agreed upon, thereby making possible the establishment of formal diplomatic ties. Further concessions will not be easy for either side to make, but compromise will be essential. Whether it occurs will depend on the importance leaders in both countries place on the relationship. Without progress in dealing with this problem, there is a real danger of deterioration in relations. Peking's leaders could consider a new strategy to exert increased pressure to alter the existing situation.

Peking could also consider a new overall strategy in dealing with the Soviet Union and the United States. There seems little possibility that China's new leaders will consider a far-reaching rapprochement with Moscow or resume a policy of openly hostile confrontation toward Washington. But it is quite possible that they may cautiously explore the possibilities for limited Sino-Soviet détente. If they do, the dynamic of interaction among China, the United States, and the Soviet Union would clearly change. The impact on the U.S.-China relationship would depend on the state of the relationship at that time. If U.S.-China relations were stalemated or deteriorating, any improvement in Sino-Soviet relations would probably weaken them further, but if U.S.-China ties were still improving, limited Sino-Soviet détente would not necessarily damage them seriously.

If Peking and Washington move to normalize diplomatic relations in the relatively near future, this should lead to increased economic and other ties. It should open the door to further efforts to narrow the differences between Chinese and American policies, and perhaps make possible limited cooperation in certain fields. However, the process of improving relations will not be easy, and for the foreseeable future the relationship will remain limited and extremely complex. There is certainly no foreseeable prospect of intimate relations. Even if the United States and China are in one sense "limited allies," they will also continue to be "limited adversaries."

Nevertheless, so long as relations continue to improve, the areas of common interest should gradually grow and the dangers of conflict decline. In time, the possibility of evolving parallel or cooperative policies to deal with regional as well as bilateral problems should increase, thereby contributing to increased regional stability.

If, however, the present limited U.S.-China relationship deteriorates, many of the unresolved problems throughout the East Asian region could again become sources of serious tension, and the potential for conflict would doubtless increase. Even assuming that neither country wished to return to the kind of hostility that existed in the 1950s and 1960s, both would see new threats to their interests and new dangers throughout East Asia.

PART FOUR

China and the New Four-Power Equilibrium

To UNDERSTAND China's relations with the other major powers in East Asia, it is necessary, but not sufficient, to analyze its bilateral relations with each of them. The overall structure of relationships in the region and China's roles in it must be examined. Treating bilateral relationships separately simplifies the problems of analysis, but it is essential also to analyze China's basic approach to dealing with *all* other powers, the domestic political, economic, and military factors that influence its capacity to deal with them, and its roles in the complex multilateral interactions that now involve them all. In recent years, as China has emerged as a "new" major power, the entire structure of big-power relations in East Asia has undergone a fundamental transformation, changing from an essentially bipolar balance into an increasingly complicated multipolar equilibrium. To understand China's position and policies—or those of any of the other powers—it is necessary to examine them in this new context.

Past Patterns of Chinese Behavior

Several conclusions emerge, from analysis of the past, about the Chinese Communists' basic approach to dealing with the other major powers in East Asia. Several are relatively simple, but they are no less important for that fact; they highlight characteristics of Chinese Communist foreign policy that have been widely ignored, or underplayed, in many discussions of China's foreign policy, which have frequently given excessive weight to Peking's rhetoric about international affairs or to its revolutionary aspirations.

One basic conclusion is that even though many factors—ideological, political, cultural, and economic—have helped to shape Chinese foreign policy, broad strategic and military-security considerations have been of overriding importance. When security interests have been at stake, Chinese Communist leaders have generally, and understandably, given them priority over other interests, including ideological and economic ones. And although relations with many foreign states, parties, and political movements have been important to a variety of China's goals, from a security point of view, Chinese Communist leaders have viewed relations with the major powers as their priority concern. For roughly four decades, since before they actually achieved national power, their security concerns have focused above all on the United States, the Soviet Union, and Japan.

Since the 1930s, they have regarded at least one of these powers as a dangerous enemy posing a major, direct military threat to China's security. And because China has been obviously inferior in military terms to the threatening powers, and Chinese leaders have clearly recognized this fact, they have attempted to devise strategies that could not only strengthen China's own defense position but also counterbalance, deter, or weaken the position of its principal foreign enemies.

Mao Tse-tung evolved a distinctive balance-of-power and "alliance" strategy based on ideas quite different from classical European concepts. Except during the brief period of Sino-Soviet alliance in the 1950s, he generally advocated a united-front strategy calling for flexible, loose, and partial alignment between China and the enemies of its enemies.

Mao's views on foreign policy as on most problems confronting the Chinese Communists had an enormous influence on the party's basic approach. In his 1940 directive "On Policy," probably the clearest statement of his strategic predispositions, he argued that, while maintaining a posture of self-reliance, the Chinese Communists should: (1) clearly identify their principal enemy at any particular time, and adopt a confrontational posture toward it; (2) try to form the broadest possible united front against it; and (3) treat "alliances" formed in the process as essentially limited and temporary. This distinctive approach represented a conscious effort to apply to foreign policy the flexible united-front strategies evolved by the Communists in their domestic struggle for power.[1] It probably also reflected, in a subtle fashion, the Chinese tradition of attempting to use "barbarians" to oppose "barbarians."[2] The Chinese Communists' preoccupation with security problems and Mao's distinctive balance-of-power approach provide the most important keys to many of the Chinese Communists' major foreign policy shifts.

These propositions, like most generalizations, are oversimplifications. They certainly do not explain everything about the Chinese Communists' overall approach to foreign policy. Although they are fundamental to an understanding of the motives that have moved Peking's leaders, and especially Mao, in their approach to dealing with the major powers, to be valid they must be qualified in various ways.

One danger of focusing attention on a single category of factors determining policy—in this case, military-security concerns—is that it tends to obscure the importance of many other interests. For instance, the Chinese Communist leaders' ideologically motivated, universalistic, messianic outlook is extremely important today to China's approach to the Third World and has influenced all its policies in varying degrees. It is essential to recognize the influence of varied political, cultural, and economic as well as ideological factors, problems, and interests on the evolution of Chinese policies. Yet, the primacy of military-security concerns in China's dealings with the major powers is highlighted by the fact that some of the most important shifts in Chinese policy have clearly run counter to ideological and economic predispositions and interests, even though they have always been rationalized in ideological terms.

Another danger of focusing attention on military-security factors is that it might seem to imply that China's policy can be fully understood in terms of rational, objective assessments by Chinese leaders of the major threats to their security and the necessary strategies to cope with them. In reality, China, like other nations, is not a "unitary rational actor" in international affairs. Chinese leaders have differed over security problems as well as other issues, especially in relation to policy toward the Soviet Union and the United States. Some of their differences have reflected varying ideological predispositions; others have resulted from divergent bureaucratic outlooks and interests. In recent years, there has probably been a consensus that China has faced serious external threats, but not on how best to respond to them. Some of Mao's critics appear to have felt that China should attempt to reduce the threats by trying to lower tension and avoid confrontation with its adversaries. Others, at the opposite pole, have argued that China should stand firm against all hostile forces, stress self-reliance, and not compromise even in the ways that Mao's united-front approach has required. As long as Mao lived, his personal predispositions regarding basic strategy generally prevailed, and China thus may have been closer to being a "unitary actor" in foreign policy than most countries are. But the underlying differences probably widened over time, and post-Mao leaders may have difficulty resolving these differences.

How "rational" Mao and other Chinese leaders have been in the past in analyzing their security problems and determining appropriate responses is debatable. Their preoccupation with external threats is understandable. The danger posed by invading Japanese armies during World War II was clear. And one can see many reasons why they feared the United States in the 1950s and 1960s and the Soviet Union from the late 1960s on. Yet, China's—and especially Mao's—approach to dealing with these powers made each of them, in turn, feel that its interests, including its security interests, were threatened by Chinese policies. In short, responding to the threats they perceived, the Chinese took actions that created reciprocal fears and stimulated hostile reactions which tended to maximize the threats that the two superpowers seemed to pose.

Chinese leaders have done their best to create an image of China as a country that holds the initiative in dealing with others. But a reactive element has been fundamental in their policies toward the other major powers. While the Chinese have taken many initiatives, some belligerent or provocative, in a broad strategic sense they have realistically recognized their weakness in the face of potential threats and have maintained an essentially defensive military posture. In practice, they have been compelled to react to others' actions more than others have had to react to China's. Often, however, they have seemed to operate on the premise that the best defense requires offensive political strategies.

Even though fear for China's security has been of crucial importance in shaping Peking's policies, Mao and his colleagues have obviously not analyzed security problems in military terms alone. They have viewed military power as one fundamental requirement for national security, and an essential ingredient of influence in a broad sense, but they have also placed tremendous stress on the ideological, political, and psychological dimensions of power. Mao in particular consistently maintained that nations, or political movements, can overcome military weaknesses and eventually defeat stronger adversaries if they adopt "correct" political and psychological strategies and tactics. In light of the military superiority of China's major adversaries, this has been a logical and reassuring position for Chinese Communist leaders to propagate; but for Mao it was not just propaganda; he appeared to have a genuine faith in the validity of this premise.

Nevertheless, the Communists have always considered military power a prerequisite for political success, and they have made a major effort to build up China's strength, devoting a sizable share of the country's gross national product to the armed forces (around 9 percent during the 1960s, and about 10 percent recently).[3] But Peking's leaders have never had illusions about China's continuing military inferiority, relative to the two superpowers, which is one reason they have generally been prudent in crises that could have escalated to major military conflict. It is reasonable to assume that avoidance of major war with any of the other big powers has been a basic aim of their policies. They have used military force on various occasions, either in response to what they perceived to be pressure or threats against China, or to achieve specific, limited objectives.[4] But they have tended to view military power primarily as a deterrent and defensive tool, and secondarily as an essential ingredient of broad political influence, rather than regarding their military forces as their principal instrument for achieving China's major foreign policy goals. They have repeatedly stated that China should "respect" its enemies "tactically" while "despising" them "strategically."[5] This has meant that while China should have faith that it can overcome its enemies eventually, primarily by political means, it should be cautious in dealing with immediate military threats posed by stronger powers, especially in situations that could lead to major conflict.

The Chinese Communists' overall approach has been based, therefore, on a more complex calculus than a simple balancing of military power. Chinese leaders have tended to think in terms of a broad "balance of forces," and in assessing the balance they have assigned great weight to political and psychological factors. They also seem to have operated on the premise that the balance of forces is shaped not only by trends in relations between *nations* but also by changes in *social forces* that cut across national boundaries. In this context, the fate of "progressive" mass movements and the actions of small and medium-sized nations are definitely relevant to the global balance and the outcome of the worldwide contest for influence, over the long run.

From the point of view of China's immediate security, however, Peking's leaders clearly regard their relations with the major powers as the crux of their problem. In determining their policies toward these powers, they have tended to think in hardheaded, realpolitik, balance-of-power terms and have recognized the ultimate, decisive importance of military power to China's security.

The Major Shifts in Chinese Alignments

From roughly the mid-1930s until the mid-1940s, the Chinese Communists were preoccupied with the basic problem of survival in the face of Japan's aggression against China. This had to take precedence for a period of time over their objective of fostering revolution within China and defeating the Nationalists, although Mao saw the struggles against foreign imperialists and domestic "reactionaries" as closely linked. Even though the Chinese Communists viewed the Soviet Union as the leader of a worldwide revolution of which the Chinese movement was a part, they could not expect significant military help from the Russians, who were preoccupied with fighting on the European front. In Asia, moreover, the Russians were pursuing a complicated policy dictated by their own security interests. They not only provided military support to the Chinese Nationalists rather than to the Communists but also signed a nonaggression pact with the Japanese. The Chinese Communists therefore looked for help elsewhere. Calling for a broad international united front against the fascists, they attempted to obtain military aid from the United States, but without success.

The end of World War II and the outbreak of renewed civil war in China fundamentally altered the strategic picture. The Soviet Union entered the war in East Asia a few days before it ended and gave various kinds of military support to the Communists in China. The Chinese Communist leadership had mixed feelings about the Russians, however, in part because of differences on such basic issues as whether or not to join a coalition with the Nationalists. Moscow continued to pursue an ambiguous China policy, giving considerably less than full support to the Communists in their struggle against the Nationalists. There were ambiguities also in U.S. policies, as Washington attempted to mediate the Chinese civil war while continuing to give various types of support to the Nationalists. In this situation, the Communists essentially went their own way, although they did what they could to influence both Soviet and American policy to serve their interests.

However, when victory was finally in sight and the Communists prepared to establish a new national regime, they decided to align closely with the Soviet Union. In broad strategic terms they were obviously concerned about the potential threat from the United States, which had filled the Asian power vacuum created by Japan's defeat, thereby becoming the predominant power in East Asia. The Americans now had a strong base for their forces in Japan, and they continued to maintain important links with the Chinese Nationalist regime. Moreover, the global cold war had begun, and Washington was clearly beginning to strengthen its position to combat communism worldwide.

Ideological, political, and economic considerations clearly were important in the Chinese Communists' decision to align with the Soviet Union. But their decision to sign a formal military treaty with Moscow— which required important Chinese concessions—was doubtless dictated above all by their sense of vulnerability and need for insurance against any U.S. threat.

The U.S. threat became a reality in Chinese eyes when, following the outbreak of the Korean War, the Americans sent troops to Korea, reintervened in the Chinese civil war, dispatched the U.S. fleet to neutralize the Taiwan Strait, and built an extensive network of alliances and bases in Asia to "contain" and exert pressure on China. Throughout the 1950s, the Chinese were preoccupied above all, therefore, by what they perceived to be a serious American threat. The central aims of their national security policy were to deter U.S. attack, dislodge the Americans from Taiwan, break out of "containment," and weaken the U.S. position throughout Asia. In the mid-1950s they briefly pursued flexible tactics, to which Washington was unresponsive, but they showed little sign of reassessing their broad strategic views. The alliance with the Soviet Union was the keystone of their foreign policy, the essential prop to China's security and protection against the principal enemy, the United States. Japan was seen as a client of the United States, weak itself but important as a base for U.S. power; Peking did what it could to weaken that connection, but with little success.

The entire strategic situation, and Chinese perceptions of it, began to change again slowly, from the late 1950s on, primarily as a result of the Sino-Soviet dispute, which became increasingly serious as differences over military-security issues grew. At three critical junctures—in 1957–59, 1962–63, and 1968–69—each of which was a basic turning point in Peking-Moscow relations, there were qualitative changes in the nature of the relationship.

Developments during 1957–59 convinced Chinese leaders that their alliance with the Russians had become of questionable value to them. Differences in strategic outlook which came to the fore at the 1957 Moscow conference, strains created by the offshore-islands crisis in 1958, disputes over naval issues, and finally Moscow's ending of nuclear weapons aid in 1959 greatly weakened Sino-Soviet ties. The intense ideological polemics of 1960 between the Chinese and Soviet parties started immediately after these developments. By 1959, the Chinese clearly doubted the value to them of the Sino-Soviet alliance, but they still hoped to convince the Russian leaders to change their views and policies. Subsequent developments, during 1962–63, destroyed that hope. In 1962, when it became apparent that the Russians—in the wake of the Cuban missile crisis—were moving toward signing an agreement with the United States that would limit nuclear testing, Peking made clear that it would regard this as a hostile act, a sign of U.S.-Soviet collusion directed against China. It demanded that the Soviet Union not sign. The Russians faced a major choice: to take steps toward arms control with the United States or to try to repair their alliance with China. They went ahead with the limited test ban, and Peking felt this was a betrayal, with consequences extremely adverse to its basic interests. Chinese leaders did not yet feel the Soviet Union posed a military threat to China, but the test ban was a "point of no return" as far as the alliance was concerned. The bitter Chinese polemical attacks of 1963–64 occurred immediately thereafter.

During much of the 1960s Peking faced two major adversaries. Although it still regarded the United States as it principal enemy, the one posing a direct military threat, it now regarded the Soviet Union as a political adversary. It still viewed Japan primarily as a base for U.S. power, but Japan's economic growth and increasing Sino-Japanese trade were gradually making it important in its own right. The Chinese stepped up their efforts to compete with Moscow for influence throughout the Communist bloc and world movement. They also tried to acquire new allies in the Third and Second Worlds. But now there was no major power aligned with China to counterbalance its principal adversaries. This was a highly unsatisfactory situation, from any Chinese perspective, and it proved to be transitional.

Finally, in the late 1960s, both Sino-Soviet relations and China's broad foreign-policy strategy underwent dramatic changes. The Soviet military buildup around China from 1965 on, the Russians' invasion of Czechoslovakia in late 1968, and the dangerous even though limited border clashes and hints of possible Soviet nuclear attack in 1969 highlighted the possibility of Sino-Soviet war. During 1968–69, when American leaders took the first steps toward withdrawal from Vietnam and proclaimed that the United States would reduce its military involvements throughout Asia, Peking concluded that American power in Asia had peaked and was beginning to decline; consequently, Chinese concern about possible U.S. military threats began to abate. In this same period Japan moved toward a more independent and influential international role. With the American decision to return Okinawa to Tokyo's control, and the Nixon-Sato communiqué issued at the time, the Chinese saw a possibility of Japan reemerging politically and feared it might remilitarize.

In response to all these trends, the Chinese revised their strategic views fundamentally during 1968–69. Thereafter, they clearly identified the Soviet Union as their principal enemy and moved to establish new relationships with the United States and Japan, hoping both would serve as counterweights to Moscow. After the opening of relations with these two powers, Peking endorsed the continuation of the U.S.-Japanese security treaty and gave its tacit approval to a U.S. military presence elsewhere in Asia.

After 1972, Mao's overall military-security strategy was designed to develop a limited alignment with both the United States and Japan, conceivably temporary, but of vital importance to China nevertheless, to deter the Soviet Union militarily and check any expansion of its influence. Globally, the Chinese leaders now seemed to see—much as Nixon and Kissinger did at the start of the 1970s—a world in which five centers of power were of crucial importance in security terms. Mao's balance-of-power strategy was based on the premise that China's security interests could best be served by encouraging opposition to the Soviet Union by all the major power centers—the United States, Japan, and Europe—as well as China itself.[6] The Chinese leaders have viewed Third World nations as increasingly important in many respects, especially in relation to China's long-run ideological, political, and economic objectives. In Peking's view, these countries could hold the key to creating a new world order in the future. But in the short run, the Third World nations are of secondary importance in relation to China's immediate security problems. Clearly, relations with the major powers—especially those directly involved in East Asia—hold the key to China's security today.

Political, Economic, and Military Trends

The deaths of both Mao Tse-tung and Chou En-lai in 1976 inevitably introduced a period of uncertainty in China. Mao had been the dominant leader of the Chinese Communist movement and regime for forty-one years, and although his policy preferences had not always prevailed, his impact on the country's leadership and policies had been enormous. Chou had been the principal government administrator, planner, and manager of both domestic development programs and foreign policy, who more than any other individual had directed day-to-day affairs.

Though their deaths were not unexpected, since both had long suffered from declining health, they nevertheless created a huge gap. For more than a decade the rest of the leadership had been deeply divided, and Mao had failed in his attempts to create a new consensus and prearrange the succession.

At the time of the succession, the differences between China's so-called pragmatists and radicals (these designations are misleading in some respects, but no better ones are available) remained unresolved. Some of the differences in Peking's leadership traced to disputes as early as the 1950s.[7] The strains these created increased throughout the 1960s and reached a climax in the extraordinarily complex, tumultuous struggle called the Cultural Revolution.

The Cultural Revolution was the culmination of a decade of debate over strategies of economic development, methods of political organization and action, policies toward culture and education, the role of the military, and foreign policy.[8] In a fundamental sense, it represented a crisis of values, caused by a polarization of views on how best to carry on the revolution and develop China. The Chinese described the differences as a "struggle between two lines" in which Maoist concepts of "uninterrupted revolution," egalitarianism, antielitism, and mass mobilization collided with more pragmatic, technocratic, institutionalized approaches to problem-solving, which the Maoists denounced as "revisionist" or "capitalist."

The Cultural Revolution precipitated an intense power struggle and resulted in a far-reaching purge. Although it shook up China's bureaucracies and checked certain revisionist trends, it did not resolve the basic underlying conflicts. China has had to live with the legacy of that upheaval, and with continuing struggles between radical and pragmatic views, ever since.

A temporary breakdown of the political system during 1966–68 resulted in a great increase in the power of the military, and by 1968, when Mao called a halt to the turmoil, the regime faced the extremely difficult tasks of cutting back the role of the military, reconstructing the party and state organizations, rebuilding the leadership, restoring social order and political stability, and increasing economic growth.

The power of the military was a critical issue in 1969–71, but in 1971 the defeat (and death) of Lin Piao, who had been designated Mao's heir during the Cultural Revolution, reestablished civilian primacy. Between then and 1973, the party gradually rebuilt the top leadership, and in 1973 it convened a party congress, the tenth, to endorse a new Politburo and Central Committee. But the struggles over power and policy continued.

During the next two years, however, there was some progress toward increased stability. Chou En-lai was able to move the regime gradually toward more pragmatic policies, and significant economic growth resumed. In January 1975, at the first meeting of China's National People's Congress in a decade, Chou outlined a forward-looking, long-term development program calling for "comprehensive modernization of agriculture, industry, national defense, and science and technology by the end of the century."[9] There is reason to believe that a majority of China's party apparatus leaders, state bureaucrats, and professional military commanders backed the kind of pragmatic policies Chou called for. Many of them had been rehabilitated with Chou's help after the purges of the Cultural Revolution. One of these, Teng Hsiao-p'ing, who had been a major target of radical attack, seemed destined to succeed him as premier.

However, China's radicals, led by Mao's wife, Chiang Ching, and three men who had risen to national prominence during the Cultural Revolution, Wang Hung-wen, Chang Ch'un-ch'iao, and Yao Wen-yuan, fought hard against these trends.[10] After Chou died in January 1976, they launched a major counterattack against all pragmatic policy trends and, probably with Mao's support, were able to bring about the purge of Teng Hsiao-p'ing.

The man who then emerged as Chou's successor to the premiership, Hua Kuo-feng, was a provincial leader who had risen rapidly after the purge of Lin Piao, becoming a Politburo leader in 1973 and minister of public security in 1975. When Hua replaced Teng as Chou's successor in early 1976, remarkably little was known about his policy views, and it was widely believed that he was a compromise choice, selected because neither the radicals nor the pragmatists were able to achieve clear predominance. Even if Hua was unaligned at the start, he did not remain so for long.

China's long succession struggle reached a climax in late 1976. By midyear, when it became evident that Mao's health was rapidly declining, jockeying for power intensified. When Mao died in September, the struggle came to a head rapidly. Hua Kuo-feng obtained the support of key military leaders and aligned himself with leading pragmatists, many of whom had been associated with Chou, and in October he succeeded Mao as party chairman and carried out a sweeping purge of the top radicals, accusing them of having plotted a coup.

A major campaign was immediately mounted to denounce the purged "gang of four" and to root out their closest followers. Local disorders and conflicts were reported in several parts of the country. Although the media were fulsome in their praise of Hua, it was clear that he faced a major task in consolidating his power. A deliberate effort was made to glorify Chou En-lai. Most of what the radicals had pushed for was criticized, directly or indirectly, and Chou's 1975 program became one of the new leadership's guiding documents. Not unexpectedly, Mao was deified, but it appeared that a subtle de-Maoization process was beginning. Hua revived a speech that Mao had made in 1956, "On the Ten Major Relationships," which had proposed policies much more moderate than those the radicals had pushed, using it to justify moves toward greater pragmatism.

In early 1977 Hua gradually consolidated his position, and seemed well in control, but there was no certainty that he would be able to hold on to power. Evidence that Teng Hsiao-p'ing might make a second comeback raised the possibility that Hua might face challenges even from other pragmatic leaders. He clearly continued to face problems from residual supporters of the radicals, though there seemed little possibility that the "gang of four" could recapture power. There was considerable evidence that the military leaders who had backed Hua had acquired increased influence, and Hua's survival required their continued support.

Despite the continuing uncertainties, it appeared by early 1977 that the immediate post-Mao succession had been relatively smooth. It had clearly involved less open conflict than pessimists had predicted, and the suppression of the top radicals seemed to have reduced, if not eliminated, the divisiveness of the "struggle between two lines."

Looking ahead, however, Hua and the Chinese leadership as a whole face a variety of major tasks. They must build a viable new collective leadership, reinstitute regularized and institutionalized processes of decision-making, and restore both organizational discipline and social order. They must also adjust or redefine policies in almost every field and try to build a consensus to make them work. The overall trend will almost certainly be in the direction of greater pragmatism. In economic policy there is likely to be increased stress on efficiency and growth which, despite many inherited problems, should enhance the prospects for China's economic development.

If no severe new power struggles break out and the trend toward more pragmatic policies continues, increased political stability and accelerated economic growth could have several important effects on the foreign-policy outlook of China's leadership. Peking's fear of manipulative intervention by outside powers, especially the Soviet Union, may gradually decrease. And, if China's rate of growth rises, its leaders' confidence in dealing with all the major powers should steadily increase. However, a new leadership that still faces many problems in consolidating its power and resolving domestic problems, and that probably will be dependent on collective decision-making for some time to come, will probably be wary of bold, dramatic, or adventurist initiatives abroad. It seems highly likely to be inclined toward cautious, centrist compromise policies. It will probably give high priority to solving concrete, immediate problems and deemphasize long-term revolutionary, ideological goals, abroad as well as at home. The new leadership seems likely to consider further steps to involve China, cautiously, in the world economy, in part to meet China's pressing needs for advanced technology. In general, current trends should strengthen the influence of those in China who favor a more outward-looking and relatively moderate foreign policy which gives priority to expanding state-to-state relationships.

In the first six months following Mao's death there was little evidence that Peking was considering any major shift in its policies toward the other major powers. Whether it does so in the months ahead will clearly depend in part on what policies these powers, particularly the United States and the Soviet Union, pursue toward China. It seems very possible, however, that in time a new leadership of the kind that now seems to be emerging may, in a very pragmatic fashion, reexamine its approach to dealing with the other major powers and consider adjusting its policies, cautiously and gradually.

The new leaders will continue to have a serious concern about China's security and will probably continue to pursue some kind of balance-of-power strategy. But they will not necessarily be wedded to Mao's concepts which called for a confrontational policy toward one principal enemy combined with flexibility toward others. Clearly, Mao's death has removed a major obstacle to considering a more flexible policy toward the Soviet Union as well as toward the United States. In time some Chinese leaders may argue in favor of exploring the possibilities of limited détente with Moscow, if—and it is a big if—the Russians are willing to alter their policies significantly. New leaders, in short, could well decide to adopt a position of greater maneuverability in dealing with all the major powers.

Although current trends point toward increasingly pragmatic and flexible Chinese policies abroad as well as at home, if a new struggle for power results in increased instability and new economic setbacks, the outlook could change. Chinese concern about foreign meddling and possible intervention would doubtless heighten. Some leaders might be tempted to manipulate international tensions, exploiting foreign threats, real or manufactured, to mobilize domestic support and justify harsh policies. A militant foreign-policy posture would be more likely.

If radical ideologues again rise to the top, which cannot be totally excluded even though it seems unlikely, they would almost certainly reemphasize both self-reliance and revolutionary militancy, as they did during the Cultural Revolution. They would probably adopt a relatively hostile posture toward all of China's potential adversaries, including the United States as well as the Soviet Union, and possibly Japan as well.

If military leaders should achieve dominance again, the prospects would be less clear. Although they would doubtless place as much stress as Mao did on the need to improve China's security, and might favor a balance-of-power strategy, their approach could differ substantially from Mao's. They would almost certainly put increased emphasis on "purely military" factors, which Mao opposed doing, and try to channel increased resources into modernization of the armed forces. They might, for very practical reasons, favor steps to reduce Sino-Soviet tensions. They would probably be realistic, and prudent, in assessing China's power position, in dealing with potential conflicts, but in crises they might favor a more "forward" defense policy and more active responses to perceived threats rather than relying heavily, as Mao did, on passive defense and popular mass resistance. However, since they have an even clearer knowledge of China's military limitations than other leaders do, they would probably not be "adventurist." In broad political terms, though, their approach to foreign policy would probably be strongly influenced by the civilian leaders with whom they aligned—who would probably be pragmatists rather than radicals.

China's leaders in the period ahead, whoever they are and whatever their predispositions may be, seem likely to recognize that China's relative weakness and the realities of the international balance of power impose major constraints on them and severely limit their foreign-policy options. Nevertheless, the ultimate outcome of the succession clearly will influence China's policies toward the other major powers. If leaders inclined toward pragmatic policies stay in power, the general thrust of Peking's policy seems likely to become increasingly outward-looking and flexible—possibly even toward the Soviet Union, eventually—and far less militant or revolutionary than it would probably have been if the radicals had triumphed in the succession struggle.

China's Economy

The state of China's economy is obviously one of the basic factors affecting its international position and role as a major power. Over the past quarter century, the Communists' economic accomplishments have been impressive in many respects, but their record has been erratic.[11] At times they have made serious policy errors and suffered major setbacks such as those during the Great Leap Forward which led to an economic depression in the early 1960s. Nevertheless, China's overall record since 1949 has been one of substantial growth, and since recovery from the post-Leap depression, the regime's economic institutions and policies appear to have been workable, though not optimal in terms of maximizing efficiency and the speed of growth.

Since the start of China's First Five-Year Plan in 1953, gross national product has grown at an average annual rate of 4–6 percent, or 2–4 percent per capita.[12] The value of industrial output has increased by roughly 10 percent a year. And the growth of agriculture, averaging 2–3 percent a year, has just kept ahead of population increases, which probably averaged about 2 percent. China's total GNP is estimated to have roughly tripled between 1953 and 1974, rising from $71 billion to about $223 billion, and the per-capita GNP has roughly doubled, rising from $122 to $243.[13] Both total and per-capita GNP are still far below the other major powers' levels, however. In 1973 the U.S. GNP was almost $1.3 trillion and close to $6,000 per capita; the Soviet Union's almost $700 billion and over $2,600 per capita; and Japan's over $400 billion and roughly $3,000 per capita.[14]

China's growth rates have been lower than those achieved by many smaller developing nations in East Asia during the 1950s and 1960s. However, in view of the country's size and the complexities of its developmental problems, they are very respectable. Moreover, in contrast to most developing nations, the Chinese have put great stress on egalitarian goals and social change as well as growth.[15] Their economic programs have involved substantial political costs, since they have been accompanied by tight political controls, enforced conformity, and compulsory mass mobilization. Nevertheless, many of their accomplishments have been impressive. They have made substantial progress in eliminating the worst poverty in China, distributing national output much more equitably than in the past so as to insure minimal living standards. China has maintained something close to full employment, although there is still widespread underemployment and inefficient use of workers. The regime has controlled inflation and maintained low and stable prices for necessities. And it has significantly expanded many basic social services, including education and health care, especially in the countryside.

But China remains, as its leaders acknowledge, a poor, developing country, the only nation almost universally regarded as a major power that still must be so categorized. Although its industrial base, the foundation for modern military power, is much stronger than it was a quarter century ago, it is still small compared to that of the other major powers. Because of the sheer size of the Chinese economy, substantial resources have been allocated for military purposes, and China has thereby made significant progress in acquiring certain elements of military strength, but economic factors continue to impose severe limits on its power.

Peking's leaders are fully aware of these limits. As Vice Premier Teng Hsiao-p'ing told a visiting group of Americans in 1974: "We are not qualified to be a superpower. Even when we have 100 million tons of steel, one cannot afford to be a superpower. . . . Some say that China is also a superpower, but we dare not accept this title. With our meagre 20 million tons of steel, we have no qualification for being a superpower, only a member of the Third World."[16] Teng's frankness in acknowledging that economic weakness now prevents China from being a super-power was striking; generally Chinese leaders simply assert that they do not wish to be a superpower.

Looking ahead, the prospect is for continuing economic growth in China. Although the likely rate cannot be accurately predicted, it is reasonable to expect that it may be comparable to that in recent years, and it could well rise if new leaders deemphasize ideology and adopt more pragmatic policies that put greater stress on efficiency and growth.

However, the problems of sustaining growth in China are formidable, and the rate of progress in the immediate future will probably not be spectacular. New policy errors could result in serious setbacks, particularly if they were to coincide with years of bad weather affecting agriculture adversely, as happened during 1959–61; Peking's leaders are not likely, however, to repeat the mistakes of the Great Leap. Political instability could also have adverse effects on economic growth, but not necessarily far-reaching or long-lasting (the Cultural Revolution's economic effects were both limited and temporary). Probably, the dynamic of growth will continue along lines foreshadowed by the program outlined by Chou En-lai in 1975.

China's leaders will have to struggle for a long time to come with policy dilemmas that have plagued them for years. A fundamental problem is how to balance efficiency and equity. Some of the most difficult specific issues concern what priorities to give to rural and urban development, what kind of incentives to use to motivate the population, whether to emphasize "expertness" (scientific and technical skills) or "redness" (ideological and political values), and how much to stress "self-reliance" both within China and in the country's foreign relations.

From the start, agriculture has posed serious problems for overall economic growth. Since the early 1960s, when Chinese leaders became fully aware of how much the level of farm output affects the economy, they have given high priority to the modernization of agriculture, especially by increasing the use of modern inputs such as chemical fertilizers. They were able in the late 1960s to raise the rate of agricultural growth significantly from about 2 percent to about 3 percent a year. They also pursued a vigorous birth-control program to slow the growth in new mouths to feed.

But the gains from such efforts may already be slowing.[17] Because traditional Chinese agriculture was highly intensive and well developed, by premodern methods, increasingly large amounts of fertilizer and more sophisticated methods will be required to raise per-acre output as much as will be needed in the years ahead. The regime's neglect of agricultural research in recent years could create a serious obstacle to solving new and more complicated agricultural problems in the future.[18] While Chinese extension services have been notably successful in disseminating currently available knowledge to peasants, China now needs new knowledge that can only be produced by highly qualified agricultural scientists, and it has been training relatively few men of this sort.

Despite these problems, it appears likely that China's agricultural output will continue to grow and perhaps keep ahead of population growth. But the race between food and population will continue to be a close one. Greatly increased investment in agricultural modernization might result in a brighter outlook. But unwise rural policies could produce new crises that could set back China's entire development process.

The outlook for China's industrial growth is brighter. There are good reasons to believe that both the capacity and output of China's industries will continue rising, probably quite rapidly. At present, the regime is stressing development of a number of important basic industries such as steel, machine building, and other metallurgical industries required for military as well as civilian purposes; petroleum, which could become an important foreign-exchange earner for China as well as providing the basis for varied petrochemical industries; synthetic fibers, which will supplement the nation's supply of cotton and reduce the need to allocate more land to cotton; and chemical fertilizers, agricultural machinery, and other products vital to improved farming.[19]

Development of some important industries is lagging, however, and transportation deficiencies create serious bottlenecks. In industry, even more than in agriculture, development problems will become increasingly complex as China's economy moves toward more sophisticated and advanced levels. But here also there has been a serious lag in the training of skilled scientists and technicians as a result of the regime's ideologically motivated policies toward education and research.[20] China today has some highly qualified experts—largely foreign-trained—in certain technologically advanced fields, including the nuclear and missile fields, but they are aging, and training of new scientists and technicians has lagged.

If this situation is not remedied, it could create very serious problems in the future. The pace of scientific and technological change is now so rapid that the Chinese will have great difficulty catching up. Since the end of the Cultural Revolution the Chinese have been trying to meet some of their most pressing technological needs by importing complete plants and advanced technology from abroad. But to accelerate industrial development across the board, particularly as they try to build sophisticated plants that will be increasingly important to their military establishment as well as their basic economy, they will have to put greater stress on the development of China's own scientific and technological skills. By early 1977 there were some signs that China's new leaders were beginning to do this.

Despite the problems they face, if Peking's leaders show flexibility in adapting their economic policies to solve new problems, China's industrial growth will continue, probably at a rate at least as high as that in recent years, which could result in roughly a doubling in overall industrial output in the next decade and a quadrupling by the end of the century.[21] Growth at this pace should permit some rise in the present low standard of living. It should also contribute positively to the prospects for internal political stability. And it should help to create a stronger base than China now possesses for modern military power.

But China is unlikely to develop into an economic superpower before the end of this century. Its huge population of close to 900 million[22] will continue to grow, even if at a declining rate, making progress in percapita terms much more difficult to achieve than in less populous nations. Technically, China will find it extremely difficult to catch up with the other major powers, and conceivably the gap between them could increase. If Peking's leaders place greater emphasis on developing science and technology, China may gradually catch up. As individuals, many Chinese have shown outstanding talent. However, at best it will take decades for China to become a developed nation in the full sense of that term.

Assuming that Peking's leaders implement a policy of "comprehensive modernization" such as Chou En-lai proposed, Chinese industry will doubtless make significant progress. And if it can achieve respectable growth rates over several decades, China will obviously become a major economic power. But since the economies of the other major powers will also continue to grow, it remains to be seen whether China will be in the "front ranks of the world" by the year 2000, which was the goal Chou set.

In the years immediately ahead, China's comparative economic weakness will continue to impose major constraints on its policies both at home and abroad. The competition for resources between the civilian and military sectors of Chinese society is intense, which clearly limits the pace of military modernization. And although China devotes a significant amount of resources to programs supporting its foreign-policy objectives, the total is still small compared to that of the other major powers.

Further development of China's economy remains one of the highest priority objectives of Peking's leaders, therefore, and avoidance of large-scale military conflict with any major power is probably considered a prerequisite for achieving this goal. A major war would almost certainly destroy most of the modern economic sector Peking's leaders have worked so hard to develop. Moreover, none of China's basic economic problems, including its food problem, are ones likely to be solved, or even significantly ameliorated, by military expansionism, and Peking's leaders appear to recognize this. Economic factors, as well as many others, argue for essentially defensive rather than expansionist policies.

One important question for the future is whether economic needs will compel China to expand its foreign trade and general involvement in the world economy. There has been limited movement in this direction, and the purge of China's top radicals may result in more.[23] If so, this should reinforce the recent tendency in China's foreign policy to stress normalized state-to-state relations and a more moderate general posture toward the outside world, rather than revolutionary goals. Eventually, expanded economic links between China and other nations could have more far-reaching effects on its overall foreign policy. But it is not likely that dramatic changes will occur suddenly. For many years to come China will be wary of increasing its foreign economic ties too extensively because of its fear of dependency on outside powers.

In sum, as China's economic development continues, its ability to play the role of a major power will be gradually enhanced. However, for the foreseeable future it will be the weakest, economically, of the four major powers in East Asia, and this will impose severe limits on its foreign policy. And although its foreign economic relationships seem likely to expand slowly, China will probably continue to be less involved in the international economy than any of the other major powers. Its economic self-reliance will in some respects limit its vulnerabilities—as it is designed to do—but it will also limit its strength, its influence, and its policy options in dealing with the outside world.

China's Military Strength

While political and economic factors will greatly influence China's ability to play the role of a major power in the future, its military position relative to the other major powers will be even more important in imposing limits on the foreign-policy choices Peking can consider. In short, the realities of military power will be a fundamental determinant of Peking's posture and policies in the future as in the past, especially in a broad strategic sense.

Since 1949, China has clearly emerged as the foremost indigenous power in Asia, with strength far overshadowing its smaller neighbors.[24] Since the 1950s it has substantially modernized its conventional forces and since 1964, when it exploded its first atomic device, it has gradually developed its nuclear capabilities. Yet it remains weak compared to the two superpowers and continues to be vulnerable to certain kinds of threats from either of them. Its primary security goal, in strictly military terms, therefore is to acquire the capability to deter attack from either the Soviet Union or the United States.

Defensively, China starts with great advantages, deriving from its enormous size and its huge, disciplined population. Both China's own leaders and leaders elsewhere recognize this. There is reason to believe, in fact, that neither the United States nor the Soviet Union has considered a massive ground invasion of China to be a feasible military option, even in the event of a major war. Japan's failure, in spite of its military superiority, to conquer China in the 1930s and 1940s provides an object lesson which no other power is likely to ignore.

Because of China's defensive advantages, some of its leaders have been inclined to rely heavily on those advantages for China's defense. Mao and those who thought like him seemed to believe that China's large ground forces and millions of militiamen could drown any invading enemy in a human sea.

But manpower alone obviously cannot protect China against all possible threats and pressures. Its major industrial and urban centers are highly vulnerable to destruction by American and Soviet naval and air forces, using either conventional or nuclear weapons. Moreover, as long as China's military establishment lacks an effective capability to defend the country at its borders, because its forces are much less sophisticated than those of the superpowers, key frontier regions will remain highly vulnerable. And as long as there is any uncertainty about the credibility of China's nuclear deterrent, both superpowers are at least theoretically capable of threatening both China's key urban centers and its conventional defense forces with destruction by selective, quick strikes. China's military inferiority has also made it vulnerable to intimidation as well as actual attack.

Because of their relative weakness, the Chinese have had to rely for deterrence in part on the political and psychological constraints inhibiting any use of nuclear weapons and in part on active political strategies aimed at neutralizing the major powers' military superiority. They have also, however, worked very hard to improve their own capability to threaten retaliation.

While defense needs have provided the most powerful motive for improving their armed forces, the Chinese have also sought to strengthen their military establishment in order to enhance China's political influence. Mao's often-quoted aphorism—"political power grows out of the barrel of a gun"[25]—did not mean that Mao advocated military expansionism, but it did underline his belief that there is an intimate link between military power and political influence. Few Chinese Communist leaders have questioned the premise that for China to play the role of a major power it must have a strong military establishment.

The Chinese have worked hard, therefore, to strengthen both their conventional and nuclear military capabilities. Since the Sino-Soviet split, they have done so almost entirely on their own, but they have nevertheless achieved notable results. The size of China's armed forces has not risen greatly, but their effectiveness has been much improved. The firepower of the ground forces, the core of the People's Liberation Army, has been substantially increased; a sizable air force has been built and a modern navy started; and China has developed a small nuclear-missile deterrent.

The primary aim of Peking's efforts has been the improvement of China's defensive rather than its offensive capabilities, and its ability to project China's power beyond its borders has remained limited. Even though the Chinese have used force in a variety of limited conflicts and crises along their borders, they have maintained an essentially defensive military posture. Moreover, despite the improvement in their defensive capabilities, they have continued to be acutely aware of their weakness compared to the superpowers, which helps to explain their continuing fear of attack and their heavy reliance on balance-of-power strategies to enhance their security.

Looking ahead, it is necessary to analyze whether this situation is likely to change in the period immediately ahead, and if so what effects the change might have on China's basic military posture and general foreign policy. A key question is how much Peking is likely to be able to improve its military capabilities, both conventional and nuclear. There is no question that the Chinese will continue to modernize their armed forces, but it is less clear how much they will be able to improve their position relative to the superpowers.

Although building and sustaining the foundations of modern military strength require large economic investments, the Chinese have demonstrated they are prepared to pay the costs. The resources they have allocated to the military are very large for a developing nation with a low per-capita national income. Because of the lack of adequate budgetary and statistical information, there is no basis for calculating these amounts with great accuracy; consequently, estimates vary and none can be regarded as more than an approximation of the truth, but they provide a general idea of rough orders of magnitude. American government specialists estimate that 7–10 percent of China's GNP (the figure has been closer to 10 percent than to 7 percent in recent years) has been allocated annually to military expenditures. Estimates by Soviet specialists on China are not very different; they calculate that about 40 percent of Peking's state *budget* goes to the military. In dollar terms, U.S. government estimates suggest that the Chinese spent between $7.5 billion and $10 billion a year on their armed forces in the late 1960s, $14–15 billion a year in the early 1970s, and $23–28 billion a year in the mid-1970s.[26]

Placing China in comparative perspective, one analyst has calculated that its military expenditures in 1972 placed China fourth in the world in total military expenditures, after the United States, the Soviet Union, and West Germany.[27] However, in absolute terms Peking's level of military expenditure was still far below that of either Washington ($78 billion) or Moscow ($65 billion). (The Soviet military budget has risen substantially since 1972, so the gap between Peking's and Moscow's expenditures has continued to increase.)[28] Yet in 1972 China's military expenditures were close to Germany's (just over $9 billion), greater than Great Britain's (over $8 billion) and France's (over $7 billion), and much greater than Japan's ($2.63 billion). However, in per-capita terms, China's military expenditures in 1972 were relatively low (just over $10), not only in comparison to those of the United States ($372) and the Soviet Union ($263) but even in comparison to countries such as Japan

($31); in fact, in per-capita military expenditures, China ranked sixty-second in the world. Nevertheless, for a poor country the economic burden of defense costs in China has been heavy.

The strains that military costs have created have clearly been serious, and there has been recurring evidence of debate over allocation of the country's limited resources, between military and civilian sectors, as well as between different branches of the military.[29] The Maoist emphasis on mobilized manpower was doubtless based not only on ideological and political considerations but also on the desire to restrict investment in expensive conventional armaments—though not necessarily in nuclear weapons or missile development. However, the pressure to expand the funds devoted to military modernization has been strong.

Military modernization has gone through several stages in China since 1949. First, the People's Liberation Army was converted organizationally from a mobile and guerrilla force to a more conventional military establishment. Rapid modernization of weapons occurred, with Soviet assistance, during the Korean War. Professionalization made significant progress soon thereafter. Then following their break with Moscow in 1960, the Chinese stepped up their efforts to develop advanced weapons, both conventional and nuclear, on their own.

Military procurement expenditures rose gradually in the early 1960s, then from 1964 to 1967 at a rate considerably faster than that of overall industrial growth. During the Cultural Revolution there was a brief cutback in 1967, but from 1968 through 1971 expenditures rose rapidly again, in a period when military leaders exercised extraordinary political power throughout China.[30] Then, in late 1971 and 1972, there was a sudden and substantial cutback in Chinese military procurement expenditures; in 1972 they dropped by as much as 25 percent,[31] falling to about the 1969 level. The sectors most affected were those involving the most sophisticated and the most expensive kinds of equipment, especially aircraft but perhaps, to a lesser extent, missiles as well. (It has been estimated, crudely, that of China's military procurement expenditures, 60–70 percent in recent years has been for aircraft, nuclear weapons, and missiles.[32]) Hence the cutbacks affected the most modern branches of China's armed forces more than the ground forces. For three years procurement remained on a plateau, before starting to rise again in 1975.[33]

Any explanation for the cutback during 1972–74 must be speculative. It is highly unlikely that Chinese military leaders felt that the PLA's modernization needs were substantially lower than before; even today the armed forces are far from achieving many of their goals. Nor was it because China no longer felt any threat from Moscow; in its worldwide policy Peking continued to urge others to adopt a strong military posture vis-à-vis the Soviet Union. It is possible, however, that by 1971–72 the intensity of Peking's fear of Soviet attack moderated to some extent, because by then China had emplaced a minimal force of operational nuclear missiles and had moved to open relations with the United States.

Probably, however, domestic considerations, both political and economic, were key factors in the cutback of military expenditures. It came immediately after the purge of Lin Piao, when a broad effort was under way to reduce the political influence of the military establishment in China. Chinese leaders in this period also began to put increased stress on the need to accelerate development of the civilian sectors of China's economy. They moved to expand foreign trade, increased imports of advanced technology, and devoted somewhat greater attention to civilian consumer needs. In general there was a shift of resources from military to civilian purposes.

Perhaps equally important, it appears that the Chinese began to encounter increasing technical problems in developing sophisticated weaponry. Such problems probably created dilemmas that argued in favor of deferring certain military programs until Chinese technical capabilities could be improved.

Basic economic and technical factors will continue to impose severe limitations on China's development as a military power for a long time to come. The Chinese, like others, have learned that continuing military modernization requires increasingly sophisticated weaponry and involves steadily escalating costs, but their resources to devote to advanced weapons are still limited.

The problems that the Chinese face in developing the industrial, scientific, and technological base necessary to create and maintain a first-rate modern military establishment are enormous. They may well feel, as they view the continuing advances in military technology elsewhere, that despite China's considerable progress, it has been progress on a treadmill.

The Chinese have built a large steel industry; its output has risen from under 2 million tons in 1952 to roughly 25 million tons.[34] And they have developed a large machine-tool industry. With a few highly skilled scientists and engineers, they have developed some facilities for producing nuclear weapons, missiles, jet engines, aircraft, electronic equipment, computers, and laser instruments. Yet the country still has a long way to go to acquire all that is required for an independent, first-rank military establishment. Shortages are still serious even in basic industries, and in various sophisticated scientific and technological fields China remains five to twenty years behind the most advanced levels of development.[35]

In recent years China has had to import 3–4 million tons of steel annually, much of it high-quality steel that is extremely important for military purposes.[36] It still relies on imports for many advanced types of equipment. China is now virtually self-sufficient in production of infantry weapons, such as rifles, mortars, rocket launchers, recoilless rifles, and light and medium artillery, and it is producing heavy artillery and tanks. But it still relies heavily, even in these fields, on knowledge gained from the Russians in the 1950s. In developing aircraft, missiles, and nuclear weapons, China has had an even greater dependence on technology acquired from the Russians. Although the Chinese have adapted and made some improvements on what they borrowed from the Soviet Union, they are clearly still in the early stages of acquiring the knowledge and the personnel required for a solid, independent, scientific, technological, and industrial base for military modernization. Their shortage of personnel in critically important military fields is illustrated by the fact that to accelerate missile development in the 1970s they apparently had to transfer specialists from their production facilities for air-breathing engines, which contributed to the slowdown of production of aircraft.[37] Moreover, their production facilities are still relatively small, concentrated, and vulnerable.

The Chinese will probably try to meet certain needs in the period ahead by importing militarily useful technology from Western Europe. They have recently, for example, obtained rights to produce Rolls-Royce aircraft engines in China[38] and have also purchased other items of possible military relevance from other West European countries. But, in the long run, their fundamental problems can only be solved by upgrading their own scientific and technological as well as industrial capabilities.

There is no prospect that the Chinese can catch up technologically with the United States or the Soviet Union in the foreseeable future, and it will be difficult for them even to narrow the existing gap. However, pressure within China, especially from top military leaders, to speed up the process of military modernization is likely to increase, and because these leaders played a key role in the power struggle following

Mao's death, they may have a large voice in deciding how resources are allocated during the next few years. The competition for resources will continue to be fierce, however, and Chinese decision makers will confront difficult dilemmas in deciding what kind of military establishment to develop, for what purposes, and how far to go in military modernization at the expense of other goals.

Today, the People's Liberation Army (which includes air and naval as well as ground forces) probably contains close to 4 million men, perhaps 80 percent of whom belong to the ground forces.[39] The regular army is now believed to consist of as many as 3.5 million men in about 210 ground force divisions.* Backing these are China's part-time militiamen, probably 5 million to 7 million of whom are well organized and partially armed, plus a large reservoir of men in the army's reserve system.

The PLA ground forces have been described by some observers as good "World War II type forces," but they are unique in many respects. Although the rank and file mostly serve short terms, under a national conscription system, the officer corps has now been professionalized. And since the 1950s the PLA's equipment has been steadily improved.† The army is an effective fighting force in many respects. Even before 1949, when the Communists' firepower was limited and they had to move mostly on foot, they showed their skill in defeating the Nationalists. In the Korean War they fought the U.S.-UN forces to a standstill. And in 1962 they performed very effectively in China's brief border conflict with India.

* Ground forces include 121 first-line infantry units backed by about 20 artillery divisions, 7 armored divisions, 4 cavalry divisions, and 6 airborne divisions, the latter under the air force. Chinese forces also include an estimated 41 railway and construction engineer divisions, perhaps 20 divisions and 40 independent regiments of special border defense and internal security forces, and a substantial number of lightly armed paramilitary "production and construction corps" in border regions.[40]

† The PLA is well supplied with artillery (including Chinese-made 152-mm and 203-mm pieces) and antitank weapons (most of which, however, are World War II types), and it has a limited number of personnel carriers and self-propelled artillery. Communications and tactical command have been improved, as China's electronics industry has developed; probably more than half of the industry's output goes to the military. The Chinese have about 9,000 tanks, including Soviet-type JS-2s, T-34s, T-54s, T-59s (reportedly a modified form of the Soviet T-54), plus Chinese-designed T-62 light tanks and T-60 amphibious tanks, some of which are excellent. However, China cannot begin to match the tank strength of the Soviet Union.

Korea also demonstrated, however, the limitations imposed by inferior firepower and lack of mobility. The Chinese suffered enormous casualties and, unable to defeat better-armed forces, had to settle for a stalemate. That experience, which was one the Chinese as well as the Americans would doubtless not like to repeat, spurred them to accelerate efforts to modernize the PLA. But much of its equipment continues to be obsolete in comparison with U.S. or Soviet weaponry. China is still deficient in logistics, transport, and communications, at least by the most advanced standards. The lag in its development of sophisticated antitank weaponry is serious. And it apparently still lacks adequate capabilities to back up and protect its ground forces with close air support and air defense. These limitations could be extremely serious in any conflict, even a limited one, with more modernized forces.

Political factors also raise questions about the potentialities of the PLA's ground forces.[41] Although a generally effective national command exists, the PLA has experienced serious internal tensions in recent years. Its top staff officers have been purged on several occasions, and the relationship between China's civil and military leadership, and between central and regional military leaders, has frequently been strained. The PLA is forced to deploy its forces over a huge territory since one of its primary functions is to garrison China itself and insure internal order, and a sizable proportion of China's total forces (the so-called regional forces, as contrasted to the main forces) are committed mainly to this task. In addition, China's defense planners must deploy their forces against outside threats from several directions.* Some Western analysts believe that Peking's ability to redeploy its forces rapidly in order to concentrate them against a threat from only one direction may be limited.[44]

Probably China's army is strong enough to deter any large-scale attempt to conquer China on the ground, but limited attacks, for example in border areas, could be extremely damaging. Peking will doubtless continue its modernization effort to try to reduce this danger. Deficiencies in advanced weaponry, transportation, and logistics greatly limit its ability to carry on protracted large-scale operations against modernized

---

* According to some estimates, in the early 1970s about 50 Chinese divisions were located in the north and northeast of China, in the Peking and Shenyang military regions; 31 in the west, southwest, and south, in the Lanchow, Sinkiang, Chengtu, and Kunming regions; 25 in the east and southeast, in the Tsinan, Nanking, and Foochow regions; and 20 in the central-south region, in the Wuhan and Canton regions.[42] A more recent estimate indicates that perhaps two-thirds of China's 121 front-line infantry divisions are now in the north and northeast.[43]

forces beyond its borders. Theoretically, the Chinese are capable of moving successfully against weak noncommunist nations in Southeast Asia, and if they were prepared to take large casualties, they might be able to do so even if a major power intervened. But this seems highly unlikely.

China's air force, which consists mainly of Soviet-type fighter planes, is also designed essentially for defensive operations.* This air force, built entirely since the 1950s, now ranks third numerically in the world, after those of the United States and Soviet Union. Its capabilities, however, are probably quite limited. Since the Sino-Soviet split, the Chinese have had to rely on their own production, and the problem of maintaining the air force as an effective arm of the PLA highlights the dilemma facing a country that is unable, economically or technically, to keep pace with the military development of its major potential adversaries. Most of China's planes are already obsolete by U.S. or Soviet standards, and their effectiveness, even defensively, in the event of large-scale attack by more modern aircraft, is very questionable. Not only do the Chinese continue to rely mainly on outdated Soviet aircraft models; they have encountered difficulties producing even them.† If their air force planes are not to become increasingly obsolete, they must produce much larger numbers

* In 1974–75 the air force was estimated to have about 4,500 aircraft and 220,000 men (if one includes strategic force and air defense personnel).[45] Roughly 3,500 planes were Soviet-type MIG fighters, a majority of them outdated models; they included some MIG-15s, about 1,700 MIG-17s, roughly 1,300 MIG-19s, and between 50 and 75 relatively advanced MIG-21s. About 400 or so were F-9s, a 1,400-mph Chinese-produced, improved version of the MIG-19, which is probably China's best fighter. (Recent models of Soviet fighters, such as the MIG-25, have performance capabilities far superior to China's aircraft. The Soviet Union has provided some other countries with MIG models more advanced than those China has.) In 1974 the Chinese bomber force consisted of roughly 500 Soviet-type aircraft. Perhaps 300 or more were IL-28s and 100 or more were TU-2 light bombers, with a fairly limited range, low speed, and small payload; 50–100 were TU-16 medium bombers, with a somewhat longer range of 1,650 nautical miles, higher payload, and faster (590-mph) speed; and a few were TU-4s. China has no long-range bombers; all are highly vulnerable to advanced antiaircraft defenses, although low-flying TU-16s, and perhaps even IL-28s, might be able to penetrate some defenses. In addition, by 1974 China had perhaps 300 helicopters, 400 military transport aircraft, and 400 or so civilian transport planes that could be directed to military use. By 1976, U.S. estimates of China's total air force had risen to 5,000, but no breakdown of types of planes is yet available.[46]

† Full production of the MIG-19 began in 1964 and continues, as does F-9 production which began in 1969.[47] Production of the MIG-21, begun in 1969, was apparently halted by 1973, probably because of production difficulties. Production of the IL-28 and TU-16 bombers, which started in the late 1960s, may also have stopped in 1973, although some reports indicate that it continues.

of improved aircraft. The production of Rolls-Royce engines in China will help substantially, but it remains to be seen how successful the Chinese are in adapting them to their needs, how rapidly they are able to initiate production, and how much they are prepared to invest in air force modernization.

Technical inferiority can have far more disastrous consequences for an air force than for ground forces. Although Peking's planes and pilots have never been fully tested in combat, they did have one limited test during the 1958 offshore islands crisis, in which they proved vulnerable to the American air-to-air missiles carried by the Chinese Nationalist planes that challenged them. Thus, the Chinese fighters, though impressive in number, may be of quite limited utility. They could doubtless inflict damage on any attacker, but it is doubtful that they could perform effectively against more advanced aircraft, which almost certainly could penetrate China's air-defense system.* China's bomber force has even more limited capabilities than its fighters. Probably its most significant mission would be to attempt a retaliatory strike—perhaps with nuclear weapons—in response to a large conventional or nuclear attack on China by a major enemy. China's IL-28s could carry one low-yield fission weapon, its TU-16s three or four. Even if most of the planes sent on such a mission were destroyed, some might get through.

There seems little doubt that China's new leaders will feel under strong pressure to improve their air force substantially, especially in quality. Further modernization is required both to make China's air defenses effective and to make its nuclear deterrent fully credible. However, the high cost of airplanes and the technological difficulty of keeping up with advances elsewhere will continue for years to impose severe constraints on what is possible.

Although the Chinese navy has been expanding in recent years, it is still the least developed of Peking's major combat service arms. Consisting largely of small coastal craft, plus a growing submarine fleet, it lacks any really large surface craft, the biggest being destroyers.† Like the air

---

* It is estimated China now has over 1,500 radars, over 4,500 antiaircraft guns, and several hundred ground-to-air missiles, mostly Chinese versions of the Soviet SA-2, in perhaps 130-plus sites. They might be relatively ineffective, however, against aircraft using sophisticated penetration aids and low-flying tactics.

† In 1974–75 the navy had about 170,000 men (including 20,000–30,000 in the naval air force and about 28,000 marines).[48] *Jane's* estimated that in 1974–75 China had about 1,450 classifiable ships (plus about 375 miscellaneous small craft), including 5 destroyers, 14 frigates (7 armed with missiles), 30 corvettes, and 51 sub-

force, it is the third largest in the world, but its capabilities are still limited and are almost entirely defensive.

It is clear, however, that Peking is committed to improving its naval capabilities. In the late 1960s it stepped up its efforts, in large part because of concern about expanding Soviet naval activity in Asia and the Pacific. China's coastal defense craft today could seriously harass any attacker, although they probably could not fend off attacks by a major navy. The Chinese navy is now able to mount small operations against weakly defended points, as it has done against the Paracel Islands.[49] But China does not yet have a "blue water navy" capable of operating far beyond its coast, and its lack of amphibious capabilities prevents it from considering offensive action against any adversary with modern air and naval forces, even in the Taiwan Strait, to say nothing of the East China, Yellow, and Japan Seas.

The most important recent development in China's navy, clearly, is the rapid growth of its submarine fleet. Although it consists of diesel submarines which are far inferior to those of the United States or the Soviet Union, and today operates almost entirely in coastal waters, it could conduct defensive operations even against a far stronger navy, and in theory, if no strong air and naval force contested it, it could attempt to blockade nearby islands such as Taiwan.

China will doubtless continue to expand its navy in order both to cope with threats from Soviet (or U.S.) forces and to increase its options in dealing with the Taiwan issue and other problems. To make its nuclear deterrent more credible, it will probably, in time, develop at least a few nuclear-powered submarines armed with sea-launched ballistic missiles (SLBMs).[50] Eventually, it could begin to develop significant amphibious capabilities.

But it will clearly take time for China to develop a major navy, and

---

marines. These numbers have continued to rise since then. Recent estimates indicate that China now has between 65 and 70 submarines, 61 principal surface combat ships, and about 1,000 coastal patrol and auxiliary craft. The increasing number of small missile-firing craft is significant. However, apart from a few old landing craft inherited from the Nationalists, the navy is almost totally lacking in ships required for amphibious operations and so far there is no evidence of any major program to build them. By 1975, the navy's air arm had 500–600 land-based aircraft, about 400 of them fighters and close to 100 of them torpedo-carrying IL-28s. The navy's principal ships are organized into the North China, East China, and South China fleets, operating out of Tsingtao and Dairen, Shanghai and Chusan, and Huanpu and Changchiang, respectively.

in the process it will probably encounter economic and technical constraints similar to those that make development of a first-class air force so difficult. For at least the next decade, the Chinese navy will probably continue to be essentially a coastal defense force, and its strength does not seem likely to expand sufficiently to broaden Peking's foreign-policy options very significantly, especially in relation to the United States or the Soviet Union. Nevertheless, as China's naval strength grows, Peking's self-confidence in dealing with the major powers will doubtless rise gradually. And neighboring areas such as Taiwan, and possibly Japan as well, will view the Chinese navy with growing unease; both will probably work to improve their own air and naval defenses. The result could be subtle but important changes in perceptions of the balance of power in East Asia.

The most important single development in recent years affecting China's military position in relation to the other major powers has been Peking's acquisition of a real, though limited, independent nuclear capability.[51] The Chinese began their nuclear program in the 1950s. Then, as the Sino-Soviet split developed, they accelerated their efforts. Mobilizing many of the country's most capable scientists, including American-trained nuclear and missile experts, they were able to build their first nuclear weapons and missile-delivery systems with remarkable speed.

Between 1964, when they exploded their first nuclear device, and 1976, the Chinese conducted twenty-one nuclear tests of devices ranging from "small" ones with 10–30 kiloton yields, which conceivably might be adapted for use in tactical nuclear weapons, to large ones with up to 4 megaton yields, usable in intercontinental ballistic missiles (ICBMs).[52]

Since the late 1960s they have steadily produced both nuclear warheads and missiles and gradually emplaced them in operational sites. They emplaced their first medium-range ballistic missiles (MRBMs), with a range of perhaps 1,000 miles, in 1966, and intermediate-range ballistic missiles (IRBMs), with a range of perhaps 2,000 miles, in 1971. More recently, they have developed missiles with a range of perhaps 3,500 miles, which some experts describe as a single-stage, limited-range ICBM. In 1970–71 they launched their first two earth satellites, demonstrating a capacity to lift sizable loads, and in 1975–76 they launched five more.

By 1974 the Chinese had manufactured 200–300 nuclear weapons and emplaced about 50 operational MRBMs and 20–30 IRBMs.[53] They are now at least theoretically capable therefore of hitting numerous targets in the Soviet Union, probably including some in European Russia, as well as targets throughout most of Asia. Some observers have speculated that the Chinese may also have been attempting to develop tactical nuclear weapons,[54] which might be usable in the Sino-Soviet borderlands or even against concentrations of invading enemy troops within Chinese territory, although there is no hard evidence that they have yet acquired such weapons.

It is noteworthy that China began to acquire the basis for an operational nuclear deterrent in the late 1960s and early 1970s when escalation of the Sino-Soviet conflict impelled Peking to reexamine its fundamental security problems and alter its basic strategic posture. Since then, it appears to have given highest priority to emplacing MRBMs and IRBMs targeted on the Soviet Union rather than the development of a full-range, 7,000-mile ICBM capable of hitting targets in the United States. There is reason to believe that the Chinese encountered serious technical problems in developing a full-range ICBM, and in solving them, they have not been able to rely on imported technology to the extent they could in earlier years. It is also possible that improvement of their relations with the United States and redefinition of their overall defense strategy led to a deliberate slowdown in the ICBM program. Cost factors may also have resulted in delay. However, work on the development of full-range intercontinental missiles continues, and the notable increase in China's nuclear tests and satellite launchings in late 1976 may have signaled an acceleration of the program. American officials now estimate that China conceivably could have some ICBMs ready for emplacement before the end of this decade.[55]

It is still possible to debate whether or not the Chinese have already acquired a credible nuclear deterrent, especially vis-à-vis the Soviet Union. Their operational nuclear capability is still extremely small, one might say embryonic, compared to that of the superpowers. The United States reportedly now has more than 30,000 nuclear weapons of varied types and the Soviet Union at least half that number.[56] And in their 1974 agreement to limit their strategic forces, both the United States and the Soviet Union are authorized to have up to 2,400 intercontinental delivery systems (ICBMs, SLBMs, and intercontinental bombers) of which 1,320 can have MIRVs (multiple independently targeted reentry vehicles) capable of hitting several targets.[57]

The huge gap in both nuclear weapons and missiles between China and the superpowers is qualitative as well as quantitative. The United States and the Soviet Union are steadily improving the efficiency and accuracy of their missiles, while China's liquid-fueled missiles are mostly slow-firing and located in "unhardened" sites (although some are "semi-mobile" and camouflaged).[58] Some specialists argue that because of qualitative disparities the gap between China and the two superpowers may actually be widening, and that therefore it will be many years before the Chinese can be confident that they have a dependable second-strike capability sufficient to make them invulnerable to the threat of a first strike by Moscow or Washington that could wipe out China's nuclear missile force.

Nevertheless, the strategic equation between China and the two superpowers has changed in important ways since Peking began emplacing its first operational nuclear missiles. Today, neither the United States nor the Soviet Union can assume that, in the event of a major conflict with China, they, or their forces abroad or their allies, might not be badly damaged by a Chinese nuclear strike. No military planner can be certain that even a massive, first-strike attack could knock out every single Chinese missile, and if any survived, China could retaliate. Already China is capable of retaliating against the Soviet Union, or against allies of the United States, and once it acquires a full-range ICBM, it will be able to retaliate against the U.S. mainland too.

China unquestionably has already acquired a deterrent that is credible in some respects, therefore.[59] Soviet and American *uncertainty* about what China might be able to do has clearly reduced the possibility that either superpower might consider threatening China with nuclear attack. It has probably also reduced the danger of even a large-scale conventional attack on China, since neither Soviet nor American leaders can ignore the danger of escalation, or exclude the possibility that in a desperate situation Chinese leaders might be tempted to retaliate, even against conventional attack, with some kind of nuclear attack, however irrational such action might appear. It is reasonable to believe, therefore, that Soviet and American military planners no longer (if they ever did) regard a first strike against China as a plausible option and that conceivably Chinese leaders now operate on the assumption that this is the case.[60] In this sense, China obviously now has at least a limited nuclear deterrent.

It does not seem likely, however, that Chinese leaders are yet fully confident of their second-strike capability, or that the basis for a genuinely stable nuclear relationship between China and the superpowers has yet been created. The disparities are still too great. If there were a serious new crisis, involving China and either of the two superpowers, there would probably be real apprehension that conflict might escalate to the nuclear level. Chinese leaders would probably still fear a preemptive first strike, and neither superpower could totally exclude the possibility of a desperation strike by China.

China's nuclear and missile development will unquestionably continue. How large a force China will build is not clear, however. It has no hope of achieving nuclear parity with the superpowers in the foreseeable future. However, it clearly can achieve a fully credible deterrent and will doubtless continue building its nuclear forces until it is confident that goal has been achieved.

China's nuclear policies will almost certainly continue to be extremely cautious. To date Peking has assiduously avoided all "bomb rattling," and it is the only nuclear power to have pledged "no first use." Eventually when China's nuclear deterrent becomes fully credible, this should, contrary to some views, improve rather than harm the prospects for developing a more stable nuclear relationship between it and the superpowers to the extent that all of them accept the concept of mutual nuclear deterrence.

In sum, although China has become a major military power in some respects during the past quarter century, it remains relatively weak in comparison with the superpowers. Security continues to be a primary preoccupation of Peking's leaders, and China's basic military posture will probably continue to be essentially defensive. Since acquiring nuclear weapons, Peking's leaders have probably acquired somewhat greater confidence in dealing with the superpowers. But they have no real basis for making offensive threats against either of them.

Because China's military forces will probably continue—in the near future at least—to be overwhelmingly defense oriented, they are essentially of regional rather than global significance, and even in the East Asian region Peking's ability to project its military power beyond its borders remains limited. Other nations cannot ignore the theoretical possibility that China's huge ground forces could overwhelm local forces in areas immediately adjacent to China on the Asian mainland, if neither superpower were to intervene. However, Chinese uncertainty about how the superpowers might react to large-scale military action by China beyond its borders will continue to reinforce many other constraints on Peking's use of force against its neighbors.

China is now able, if it so chooses, to give foreign military assistance of varying kinds that can significantly influence the outcome of some conflicts beyond its borders. However, its present leaders are doing this only on a limited scale.[61] They appear to be very sensitive to the costs, and possible dangers, of more active military involvements abroad. China's military superiority in comparison with other Asian nations does give added weight to Peking's political views, but it does not give the Chinese any decisive advantages; the competition for political influence depends on many factors other than purely military ones.

Thus, while China today is much better prepared than in 1949, militarily as well as politically and economically, to play an influential role in East Asia, its capabilities are still limited, and its realistic policy options still severely circumscribed. Clearly Chinese leaders will continue giving very high priority to security problems. They will probably continue to view the East Asian situation fundamentally in balance-of-power terms and try to enhance China's security by cultivating "allies" of some sort, while avoiding close alliances of a Western sort. Perhaps, post-Mao leaders may show greater flexibility than Mao did in dealing with both superpowers, and if their self-confidence gradually increases, they might, in time, show an increased willingness to compromise and even to cooperate with their major adversaries in efforts to prevent conflict and reduce tensions. This will depend to a considerable degree, however, on the policies of the other powers toward China, and on the way in which relationships among all four of the major powers in East Asia evolve.

A New Pattern of Major-Power Relations

The new pattern of relations among the major powers in East Asia is structurally different from any past configuration of power in the region. Today, four major states exert significant region-wide influence and interact directly. No single power is dominant, and the structure of relations is fundamentally multipolar, in striking contrast to the bipolar pattern of the recent past. A critical question for the future is whether the present four-power relationship will produce a viable equilibrium or will break down and lead to increased instability and conflict.

The new structure began to emerge in the late 1960s as a result of changes in the positions and policies of all the major powers in the region. China emerged as a stronger and more active power. Its moves, following the Sino-Soviet split, toward a self-reliant foreign policy, its acquisition of an independent nuclear capability, and its decisions after the Cultural

Revolution to reassess its strategic position, establish official relations with the United States and Japan, and broaden its diplomatic ties throughout East Asia were among the most important developments altering the overall structure of relations. Changes in the roles of all the other powers were equally important, however. Washington decided to withdraw from Vietnam and to reduce the overall American military presence in the region; Moscow decided to follow a containment policy against China and to step up its activity throughout Asia; and Japan began to exert an economically powerful and increasingly autonomous influence throughout the region. All of these developments helped to create a new regional balance.

The new pattern is unique in part because China for the first time in a century is now playing a major regional role. During the late nineteenth and early twentieth centuries, when China was weak and divided, its regional influence was minimal, and most of Asia became an arena for intense competition among the major colonial powers. Britain, France, and the Netherlands established control over Southeast Asia, except for Siam. And Britain, Russia, Japan, and others competed for spheres of influence or control over the feeble and disintegrating Chinese empire. The United States was actively involved, especially in the Philippines, but it was still a lesser actor. The competition among these powers gradually whittled away Peking's sovereignty. But because there were several competitors, and a kind of "concert of powers" limited the encroachments that any one of them could make on China, none achieved regional dominance.

This complicated, competitive balance of power broke down when Japan, under ambitious, imperialist leaders, began to expand its influence at the expense of the other colonial nations. During the first decade of this century, the Japanese worked out a brief modus vivendi with the British, and then fought and won a war with the Russians. When they kept expanding their influence, however, friction steadily increased between them and the Western powers. China remained a helpless pawn, struggled over by others. In the 1930s the Japanese embarked on an expansionist policy clearly aimed at predominant control over China. Then, during World War II they directly challenged both the United States and the European colonial powers and attempted to achieve hegemony over all of Asia. Their wartime predominance in East Asia was brief, however, and with their defeat in 1945 their forces had to return to their home islands. Prostrate and occupied, Japan was not able to play any significant regional role for almost two decades thereafter.

Throughout Asia, most of the former colonial territories achieved independence soon after the war. They were still, however, extremely weak and fragile entities. China was wracked by civil conflict. There was a vacuum left by both Japan's defeat and the European powers' retreat, and the United States immediately filled it and emerged as the predominant power in the region. However, total U.S. dominance was also brief. Soon it confronted a totally new situation created by the reunification of China under Communist rule and Peking's alignment with Moscow. China's struggle for unity and full independence had begun many years before, but the process had been delayed by war and revolution. Once the Communists achieved power, they proceeded rapidly to unify the country and build up its strength, and to put forward claims to genuine major-power status. The Soviet Union, at war's end, asserted a more important and direct role in East Asia than it had enjoyed for almost half a century. When China decided to align with the Soviet Union in 1950, they formed a seemingly monolithic bloc, openly opposed to the United States and its allies everywhere in East Asia.

The confrontations that then developed between the "Communist camp" led by Moscow, and the "free world," led by Washington, created an unprecedentedly rigid, bipolar structure of relationships. While the Chinese Communists, backed by the Soviet Union, controlled continental China, the United States, using Japan as its major base, exercised predominant influence almost everywhere else in the region and supported all nations or groups willing to oppose communism. Those nations that opted for nonalignment found it difficult to pursue independent policies; neither the Communist nor the noncommunist bloc was tolerant of neutralism at that time.

Bipolarity in its most extreme form lasted for roughly a decade. It began to break down, gradually, from the late 1950s on. Many developments contributed to this trend, but the most important was the Sino-Soviet conflict. However, both the atmospherics and the assumptions of bipolarity persisted for years thereafter. The U.S. military involvement in Vietnam in the 1960s was one of the consequences. Nevertheless, the reality of the situation steadily changed throughout the 1960s, as a new triangular relationship involving China, the Soviet Union, and the United States developed. Finally in the late 1960s, when Japan reemerged as an autonomous international actor, a quadrilateral pattern of relationships took shape. Since then all powers in the region, large and small, have had to try to adjust to the new configuration of power, which involves complex quadrilateral and triangular as well as bilateral interactions.

Four-Power Equilibrium

The present four-power relationship in East Asia is a type of "balance of power," but clearly it is one of a special kind, different from past European relationships described by that term.[62] It appears to be a kind of equilibrium in which four major nations are constantly interacting and adjusting their relationships, each trying not only to maintain and improve its position but also to prevent dangerous new imbalances from emerging. Relationships are clearly dynamic rather than static, and the situation involves, as any dynamic equilibrium does, "a state of balance between opposing forces" and "a state of adjustment between divergent influences."

There are many asymmetries within this equilibrium, and relationships among the four major powers are by no means equilateral. Militarily, the differences are tremendous. Two, the United States and the Soviet Union, are superpowers; both possess strategic capabilities of a unique sort and play major global military roles, albeit in different ways and degrees. Although China possesses an embryonic nuclear capability as well as large conventional military forces, its military power is still essentially defensive in character and regional in significance. The fourth power, Japan, has a modern but small military establishment, purely local and defensive in its functions; however, Japan's alliance with one of the superpowers and its ability to expand its military capabilities rapidly mean that it is regarded, and dealt with, as a *potential* military power of significance. Economically, three of the powers, the United States, the Soviet Union, and Japan, are highly developed, industrial nations; they possess the largest economies in the world. All three can be regarded as economic superpowers, even though significant disparities in per-capita national income continue to exist among them. In contrast, China is still a poor nation, in the early stages of economic development. Today, while two of the four, China and the Soviet Union, are locked in hostile confrontation, militarily as well as politically, the other two, the United States and Japan, are linked by a close military alliance. Maintenance of the equilibrium in its present form appears to depend, in many respects, on continuation of this asymmetry. In terms of broad political and economic relationships, all four powers now interact directly to a much greater extent than in the 1950s and the 1960s. However, unlike the basically cooperative links between the United States and Japan and the bitterly hostile contest beween China and the Soviet Union, the relationships of both the United States and Japan with both China and the Soviet Union are extremely complex mixtures of competition and cooperation.

One striking feature of the new four-power structure is the extent to which "old-fashioned" concern with the balance of power continues to be a critical factor shaping relationships. Balance-of-power concepts are often considered anachronistic in an era when many pressing global problems focus more on economic than on military issues. The problems of food, population, oil, resources, the environment, the international financial system, and, more broadly, the entire nature of the international economic order are of necessity high on the agenda of the international community. Recently, moreover, some militarily weak nations like the members of the Organization of Petroleum Exporting Countries have emerged as economic powers, and, in general, economic relations between the developed and developing nations now seem in many respects to pose more urgent problems, even in terms of national security for many nations, than old military-security questions and traditional balance-of-power issues.

These global changes have not, however, basically transformed the character of relations among the major powers in East Asia, where military-security issues and balance-of-power considerations continue to be crucial factors shaping relationships. The two countries that today appear to be most acutely sensitive to, and strongly motivated by, such considerations are China and the Soviet Union. Both are in a sense "nouveau" major powers. They are still relatively little involved in the world economy, and both are strongly moved by nationalism as well as ideology to do all they can to enhance their global status and influence. Each is motivated by strong fear of the other. Each is also apprehensive that the overall balance could shift in favor of the other and that such a shift would pose great dangers.

American policymakers remain committed to maintaining a balance of power in the area and preventing the dominance of either the Soviet Union or China; today, however, Washington appears to be prepared to adjust to the new situation of multipolarity and to strive for a new equilibrium. Japan totally eschews balance-of-power policies; and its leaders are obviously uneasy about the other powers' pursuit of such policies. The American nuclear deterrent and the oceans that separate Japan from the Asian mainland allow the Japanese a certain amount of detachment from "power politics." Yet they cannot ignore the competition that inevitably impinges on them. They are in fact extremely sensitive to any shifts, real or apparent, in the balance of power among the other three powers.

While traditional military-security considerations continue to be extremely important in East Asia, the present equilibrium clearly does not rest on military factors alone, and the constraints inhibiting major military conflict have increased. Although the possibility of large-scale war, especially between China and the Soviet Union, cannot be totally excluded, the risk of major war in East Asia appears to have been significantly reduced in recent years. Not only do the dangers posed by nuclear weapons tend to deter such conflict; the four-power pattern itself places new political constraints on all the major powers by increasing the costs that any nation tempted to initiate large-scale military action in the region must consider.

But the constraints against major war have not turned competitive relationships into cooperative ones. An intense struggle for influence continues among the four powers, especially now between China and the Soviet Union. It is primarily a political and economic competition, in which numerous variables are constantly changing, and each change affects the perception of leaders in all four nations of the current state of the equilibrium. It is, in short, a highly dynamic situation in which change is a constant.

There are important differences, however, in the ways that different leaders in the four nations try to adjust to the new multipolar structure and to maneuver within its framework. Generally speaking, those in Washington and Tokyo today seem quite prepared to accept the existing equilibrium; both stress the goal of regional stability and would like to see more cooperation and less competition. Japanese leaders, while committed to maintaining a close alliance with the United States as the keystone of their foreign policy, are attempting to maintain a posture of "equidistance" in dealing with the two Communist powers. Leaders in Washington also view the alliance with Japan as the keystone of their East Asian policy, and they, too, call for balanced relations with both the Chinese and Russians, even though the Americans try much more actively than the Japanese, whose policy remains essentially passive and reactive, to balance the two Communist powers and to use relations with each as a political lever to influence the other.

In contrast, neither Peking nor Moscow views the present situation as a satisfactory one or wishes to see it stabilized on its present basis. Wherever possible, in their policies toward the United States and Japan, and toward every other nation in the region, each does all it can not only to increase its own influence, but also to limit the influence of the other, and each would like to tilt the balance in its own favor. Neither is satisfied with the status quo, and both wish to change it. Nevertheless, both the Chinese and the Russians find it necessary to accept the new constraints imposed by the four-power relationships. Neither can ignore the danger that adventurist acts on its part could upset the situation and change relationships in ways that would be unpredictable and could be dangerous. Even though neither sees the present situation as particularly desirable, therefore, both seem to fear that any alternative might be worse. They are therefore compelled in many respects to operate within the framework of the existing balance.

Four-Power Competition

In the present competition for influence in East Asia it is no easy task for the major powers, to say nothing of others, to judge what the exact state of the balance of influence is at any particular time. Influence—the ability to affect the behavior of others—is complex and subtle; it has many ingredients and can be exercised in many ways. In the current competition, each of the powers operates from a different starting point, and each has different military, political, and economic means at its disposal to pursue its goals.

Although military strength is obviously one factor affecting China's regional influence, it is a less important one than it is for the United States or the Soviet Union. Compelled by its military inferiority to maintain an essentially defensive posture vis-à-vis the superpowers, China has had to rely heavily on political strategies to try to counterbalance them and to deter military threats from either. Nevertheless, China's large military establishment adds weight to its influence throughout the region, especially among the smaller nations, none of which can ignore China's theoretical capability to threaten them, particularly in circumstances in which no other major power exercised effective deterrence. Consequently, the inclination of many smaller nations to accommodate to

China has increased as changes in U.S. policy have altered their perceptions of Washington's ability or will to deploy and use its military power in East Asia.

China's economic influence throughout East Asia is still very limited. Both its trade and its economic assistance, other than to North Korea and North Vietnam, have been relatively small, and there is little prospect that they will soon increase dramatically. The most important basis of China's regional influence today is political and its ingredients include many intangible as well as tangible factors. It is greatly affected by the images that others have of it. These have fluctuated with changes in China's domestic and foreign policies. However, China's huge size and population, its geographical position, its history as the center of a major civilization area, and its acquisition in recent years of most of the symbols of major-power status have compelled other East Asian nations to take its views very seriously.

There is universal respect, and widespread admiration, throughout Asia for the historic achievements of Chinese culture. However, fear, or at least vague apprehension, of China is common in many of the small nations. Revolutionaries and radicals of many kinds have been attracted to or inspired by China's example, and many Asians are impressed by Chinese organizational skill and discipline. But the Chinese "model," involving disciplined mass mobilization and tight political control, has attracted relatively few dedicated adherents in neighboring countries. Leaders in Southeast Asia worry about China's ideological messianism, which conflicts with their own nationalism, its capacity to encourage and support insurrectionary revolutionary movements, even by low-keyed, low-risk means, and the possibility that Peking could try to use the large Overseas Chinese communities for subversive purposes, even though China has shown restraint in this respect.[63] In countries adjacent to China, no leader can ignore the possibilities, no matter how theoretical they may now seem, of direct Chinese military pressure or attack.

In a fundamental sense, Peking's regional political influence appears to rest on the respect that China's history, size, and location and its growing military power command, but that respect probably derives more from China's potential for doing other nations harm than from a belief in the benevolent or constructive effects of China's policies.

The foundations of the Soviet Union's regional influence in East Asia today are very different from China's. Even though Siberia and the Maritime Territory abut on China and Korea, and are close to Japan, and despite Moscow's claims that the Soviet Union is an Asian as well as a European power, few Asians regard it as such. Unlike China, the USSR deals with East Asia as an outside, and fairly remote, Western power.

Today, the critical component of Soviet influence in the region is its military power. As a nuclear superpower, it possesses a capability to threaten any nation in the region, which no country can ignore. It is not clear, however, that this power has had a positive political influence. Neither China nor Japan, whose leaders fear the pressures that Moscow could exert on them if it were not restrained by the United States, has concluded that it must accommodate politically to Soviet military power. On the contrary, Soviet threats and pressure drove Peking to adopt strategic policies directed against Moscow, and apprehension about possible Soviet threats has been the principal strategic factor that has convinced the Japanese that they must maintain an alliance with the United States. In most of the rest of Asia, strategic nuclear power is even less easily translatable into political influence—as the United States has learned—in part because few believe that it can actually be used.

The Soviet Union's conventional military power, including its growing naval forces in the region, seems likely to be more significant in the years immediately ahead as an instrument of Soviet political influence. For China, the potential Soviet threat in the north and west imposes major constraints that limit its policy options everywhere else. For Japan, the dangers of Soviet naval activity are more real and immediate than the possibility of any nuclear threat. And in Southeast Asia, the possibility that the Soviet navy may steadily increase its presence and activities in the area has introduced a significant new factor into the balance.

Except on China's borders, the Soviet Union's capacity to project even its conventional military power in a direct way in East Asia is still limited, however. It is far more limited than the United States' capability has been. The Soviet Union possesses neither clear-cut allies nor local bases within the region (apart from its own bases in the Maritime provinces) from which it can operate effectively. Nevertheless, the political impact of its military has been growing and may continue to increase. The Russians have used military aid on a large scale—notably in North Korea and North Vietnam but briefly in Indonesia as well—to promote their political influence, and they are probably prepared to offer military aid to noncommunist as well as Communist countries willing to accept it. Their naval activity in East Asian waters has been increasing, and at some point they might try to establish bases in the region—conceivably, for example, in Camranh Bay in Vietnam—if opportunities should arise. No East Asian nation has yet shown any inclination to grant the Russians base rights, or to invite them to participate directly in any local conflict, and most Asians will doubtless be wary of doing so. However, if any nation were to feel severely threatened by some other power, such as China, it might consider requesting Soviet aid. Under such circumstances Moscow might be tempted to intervene.

Diplomatically, Moscow has been expanding its bilateral ties and activities throughout the region, with some success. It has also taken region-wide initiatives, for example in proposing an Asian security pact, although so far these have evoked relatively little positive response. Its economic involvements in East Asia are still quite limited; it seems determined to expand them, however, and will probably be able to do so gradually. In some respects, it has adopted a generally conservative posture in dealing with noncommunist regimes, in part because accepting the status quo seems tactically advantageous in the competition against the Chinese, but it has obviously not abandoned all subversive activities in the region.

In a basic sense, however, the Soviet Union today exerts little positive attraction to most Asian leaders. The Russian "model" has no wide appeal. Its cultural impact has been negligible. Its diplomacy has often been heavy-handed. And its economic relations are still too limited to be of great importance to most Asians. Broadly speaking, the Soviet Union is still the least influential of the four major powers in East Asia. Perhaps the main factor working in its favor is the belief of many Asian nations today that their interests can best be served in the period ahead by expanding ties with all the major powers.

In contrast to both China and the Soviet Union, Japan today exerts no regional military influence, although its past domination is well remembered and its potential for rapid remilitarization is not ignored. At present, Japan's influence is based overwhelmingly on its economic power. The remarkable development of Japan's economic influence in recent years has clearly been an important factor changing overall relations in the area. Economically, Japan and the United States are the dominating powers in the region, and Japan's role is likely to be the more important in the long run. Extensive trade and investment relationships now link most Asian countries to Japan, and some of these countries are slipping into positions of economic dependency on Tokyo.

It is still difficult to judge the likely impact of Japan's growing economic influence. Tokyo has been cautious about translating its economic power into other kinds of influence, or trying to play a leading political role regionally. There is good reason for this caution. The resentments caused by Japan's conquests during World War II persist, and Japanese leaders recognize the great uneasiness about Tokyo's potential political as well as economic leverage, which argues for political restraint on their part. Tokyo could, however, play a more active role than it has in devising constructive solutions to major problems in the region; its failure to do so has been due in part to the limited political vision of many Japanese leaders and in part to the attitudes of other Asians. Most Asians tend to be highly ambivalent today about their economic relations with Japan. They want what Japan can provide, yet fear the dependency this could bring. Japanese technology and capital goods have stimulated economic growth in many Asian nations. However, Japanese business practices at their worst have sometimes had corrupting effects on local politics and societies. Because Japanese trade and investment policies often are oriented mainly toward the interests of Japan's own business community, their effect at times has exacerbated local problems. In Indonesia and Thailand the tremendous increase in the Japanese presence has, despite the efforts of both the Japanese government and enlightened Japanese businessmen to alleviate the resulting problems, created intense resentment and provoked strong political reactions, including anti-Japanese riots. Not surprisingly, local political groups have at times exploited anti-Japanese feelings for their own political purposes.

Thus, despite Japan's growing economic power, its regional political influence has remained limited. The unique image of the Japanese as the most successful modernizers in Asia exerts some attractive force. However, Japan's cultural uniqueness, the parochialism of many of its businessmen in dealing with other Asians, and the gap that now separates it as an advanced industrial nation from most developing nations have made the Japanese model seem of limited relevance in much of Asia. Japanese leaders are still groping for ways to define their regional political role and to assume responsibilities commensurate with their country's economic power that are acceptable to others who still remember its imperial policies.

Compared to the other major powers involved in Asia, the United States, although it is the only one whose home base is far removed from the region, has enjoyed a preeminent position. Ever since World War II it has exerted more extensive and varied kinds of influence than any other power. Militarily, its forces have been the strongest and most modern in the region. It has been the only power with naval and air forces that could be rapidly moved into almost any area. The chain of military alliances and bases that the United States created from Northeast Asia to Southeast Asia in the 1950s gave it a unique position. Economically, its aid programs and its trade and investments made it preeminent until the surge of Japanese economic growth in the 1960s. Politically, Washington has had a strong, direct influence on almost all the noncommunist governments in the countries allied to it. American popular culture has also has a great impact—few urbanites in noncommunist East Asia have been untouched by it.

Asian attitudes to the United States have been complicated, but overall, the image of U.S. society, and of the American people, has tended to be favorable in areas not under Communist control. Numerous Asian revolutionaries and radicals have obviously felt intense hostility toward the United States and all it stands for, and probably a majority of Asians have had mixed feelings about the Americans. Many have held negative views about Americans' materialism, insensitivity to Asian values, and assumptions of superiority, or have resented the power and wealth of the Americans. Some have felt that U.S. military power has frequently created rather than solved problems, often because of American clumsiness or lack of wisdom rather than malice or ill-will. Probably, however, the majority of Asians outside of the Communist-ruled areas have not feared the United States and in general have regarded it as a positive influence in the region.

Many types of Asians have looked to the United States for support, aid, and in many cases inspiration. Numerous political leaders have counted on Washington to protect their nations' security. Economic elites, planners, and businessmen have depended on American connections for development assistance or profits. Intellectuals have hoped the United States could promote progressive democratic forces in the region, even though the United States, for security reasons, has often supported authoritarian regimes. Many ordinary people seem to have regarded the Americans above all as the principal symbol of the advanced scientific and technological achievements of the so-called free world.

Today, however, the United States is no longer the predominant power in the region. It is now only one of four very influential powers in East Asia. American military and political influence has clearly declined, above all because of the failure of its policies in the Indochina states, which dramatically demonstrated the limitations of American military power in local Asian conflicts. When Washington decided to withdraw its forces from Vietnam, many Asians concluded that U.S. power in East Asia had peaked and begun to decline, and when the noncommunist regimes in Vietnam and Cambodia collapsed, the faith of some Asian leaders in the credibility of U.S. defense commitments was seriously shaken. This gave impetus to a tendency to think of local security problems less in terms of reliance on U.S. support and more in terms of self-reliance plus political strategies designed to balance all the major powers off against each other.

The economic importance of the United States to the region, though still great, has declined, relatively, as Japanese influence has grown. Its image was tarnished by its domestic political and economic crises in the late 1960s and early 1970s. Many Asian leaders concluded that, because the popular base for American foreign policy had apparently weakened, it was uncertain whether the United States would continue playing the same international roles as in the past. Some began to doubt whether Washington possessed the will to respond militarily to threats to its allies, whatever its formal commitments. As Asians' uncertainty increased about U.S. intentions, American political influence weakened. In the immediate wake of the Vietnam collapse, that uncertainty itself influenced the character of the four-power relationship in East Asia.

Yet there are good reasons to believe that virtually all nations in the region, large and small, still view the United States as the single most powerful, and influential, nation in the region. The United States still possesses the strongest military forces capable of being deployed rapidly and flexibly throughout East Asia; the questions concerning U.S. military power focus primarily on the Americans' political intentions, which it is widely recognized can change fairly rapidly and unpredictably. The United States still has important alliances and a significant, if reduced, structure of bases within the region. It still plays a key regional economic role, largely through trade and investment. Its cultural impact is still widespread and great. And although its prestige has been diminished, and its image tarnished, neither has been destroyed.

The effect of the relative decline in U.S. influence now appears to be less far-reaching, therefore, than many observers expected it to be. Although it has reinforced the inclination of Asian nations to adjust to the new multipolarity in the region, these nations still recognize the importance of American power and influence and the crucial role the

United States plays in the existing big-power equilibrium in East Asia. In adjusting to the new realities of multipolarity, some of the smaller noncommunist nations that have been most dependent on the United States will probably continue loosening their ties with Washington and make greater accommodations to the other major powers, including China. Only under extreme circumstances, however, is any likely to ask Peking, Moscow, or Tokyo to replace Washington as its protector; even after loosening their ties with Washington, most will probably continue to see their American connections as important.

As China's leaders have observed the major changes and trends in Asia, they have doubtless seen new opportunities to increase China's influence and enlarge its roles in the region. There is every reason to believe, however, that they remain acutely aware of the constraints on their capabilities and of the even greater opportunities that a fluid situation presents to the other major powers. China's leaders are most apprehensive that the Soviet Union may try to move into areas of political instability to increase its own presence and influence, and to exclude or diminish China's, as part of a broad policy designed to "contain" and "encircle" China. This has clearly replaced Peking's fear of U.S. power as its priority concern in all of East Asia. Reciprocally, Soviet leaders currently seem to be most concerned that the Chinese will attempt, wherever feasible, to limit and if possible exclude Soviet influence. Consequently, even though there is competition among all the major powers in East Asia today, the most intense contest is between Peking and Moscow, which makes the Sino-Soviet conflict a critical variable affecting relationships throughout the region, both among the four major powers themselves and between them and the smaller nations.

The Dynamics of Competition

Leaders in all four of the major powers in East Asia are sensitively attuned to any changes in existing relationships. They fear that new leadership in any of the four countries might result in sudden, major shifts of policy that could alter the existing four-power equation. They also appear apprehensive that even relatively unimportant changes in relations could have seriously adverse cumulative effects. Such fears contribute greatly to the competitiveness of the situation. Today, any move by any of the four tends to evoke countermoves by one or more of the others, which makes the situation appear more fluid and the balance more delicate than they actually are.

The intense competition between China and the Soviet Union carries over to the triangular relations in which they are involved with the United States and Japan. Because both view relations with the United States as crucial, they now compete strongly to try to influence Washington. Virtually every Chinese step toward developing its relationship with the United States has been motivated in part by Peking's desire to outcompete the Russians. China bitterly opposes any U.S.-Soviet steps toward détente, tries to highlight all conflicts of interest between Washington and Moscow, and applauds all signs that U.S.-Soviet tensions are increasing. Moscow constantly warns Washington against being taken in and manipulated by Peking and attempts in every way possible to discredit the Chinese in American eyes. The Russians have many motives in promoting U.S.-Soviet détente, but clearly the aim of further constraining and pressuring China is an important one. The conflict with China has probably been a significant factor, for example, inducing Moscow to stress its desire for greater cooperation with Washington on arms control and other problems.

Whenever the United States makes a positive move toward one of the Communist powers, the other generally attempts to take some action that reemphasizes its ties with Washington, even if only symbolically. Equally important, both Peking and Moscow appear to have been restrained from exacerbating tensions with the United States too much, especially in East Asia, for fear that the other might be able to exploit the situation. Because both have felt that a U.S. alignment with the other could have disastrous results, the United States has found itself in a relatively favorable position, with some leverage—though not as much as some observers have assumed—in dealing with both. Although Washington has tried to improve relations with both, rather than attempting to manipulate Sino-Soviet tensions to harm either side, it has nevertheless enjoyed certain advantages in dealing with them.

The triangular relationship among Peking, Moscow, and Tokyo has been similar in some respects. Although Japan is obviously not as important to China or the Soviet Union as the United States is—either as a potential ally or as a potential military adversary—Peking and Moscow have placed great importance on their relationships with Tokyo. Both have recognized its military potential as well as its present economic strength, and both have feared it might tilt toward, or even align clearly with, the other.

Each has made a major effort to expand economic relations with the Japanese, and political motives have been important in these moves. For several years, the Russians have tried to attract large-scale Japanese involvement in development projects in Siberia—for example, development of oil at Tyumen and gas at Yakutsk and construction of a pipeline to carry these products eastward—but the payoff so far has been limited. (The Japanese have invested in timber production and a few other projects, but not in the Russians' priority projects.) One reason for the Russians' limited success has been their lack of flexibility in offering the Japanese attractive terms. Another has been the reluctance of the Japanese to undertake large projects without American participation. In addition, however, Chinese political and military objections have had an important influence. Peking has made it clear, in direct warnings made through nonofficial Japanese groups, that it would view large-scale Japanese involvement in some of the proposed projects—especially the proposed pipeline, which would run close to the China border and increase the fuel available to Soviet military forces there—as a symbol of an unfriendly policy. And in trying to accelerate their own oil production and exports to Japan, the Chinese have been motivated in part by their desire to compete against the Russians and reduce the chance of large-scale Japanese involvement in energy projects in Siberia.

There has also been intense competition between Moscow and Peking to influence Japan in a broader political sense, each trying to complicate Tokyo's relations with, and prevent it from moving closer to, the other. The Chinese have strongly endorsed Tokyo's demand that the Russians return the four "northern islands" to Japan. This issue has created the main obstacle to a formal Soviet-Japanese peace treaty and, more generally, to improved overall political relations between Tokyo and Moscow. In part to differentiate their posture on territorial issues from that of the Russians, the Chinese have stopped pressing Japan, at least temporarily, to acknowledge China's claim to the Tiao-yu-t'ai/Senkaku Islands.

The strongest recent Chinese pressure on Japan has been in the negotiations for a Sino-Japanese treaty of peace and friendship. Peking has pressed hard for acceptance of a clause opposing the hegemony of any power in the region, which everyone recognizes as an anti-Soviet move, even though similar statements were included in both the Nixon-Chou communiqué and the Tanaka-Chou statement in 1972. The Japanese government has resisted this for several reasons. One is that Tokyo cannot be certain that Peking might not some day use it politically against Japan itself by claiming that Japan's economic role in Southeast Asia or elsewhere is hegemonial. The most important reason, however, has been Tokyo's desire to avoid compromising its "equidistance" posture and antagonizing Moscow. The Russians have publicly pressured Tokyo not to accept the clause, indicating that it could seriously damage Soviet-Japanese relations, and Tokyo recognizes that Peking is pressing for the clause as an overtly anti-Soviet political move.

The pressuring as well as the wooing by both Peking and Moscow have created prickly problems for Japanese politicians and diplomats. But, in reality, Japan, like the United States, obtains certain benefits that enhance its bargaining position vis-à-vis both Peking and Moscow.

In recent years, the triangular relationships involving China with the United States and Japan, and the Soviet Union with these two powers, have been less competitive or salient than they once were. They could become more complicated again, however, if U.S.-Japanese ties were to weaken, or if either Peking or Moscow were to give higher priority to the goal of dividing Washington and Tokyo.

The complexity of all of these multilateral relationships contributes to a sense of fluidity and uncertainty about the future of relations among the major powers in East Asia, but competition that simply results in minor changes in the pattern of relations is not likely to destabilize the existing balance. The present pattern seems unlikely to undergo fundamental change in the period ahead essentially because leaders in all four nations fear that actions that could destroy the existing equilibrium would involve excessive costs and dangers.

Structural Stability

A number of factors seem likely to work in favor of relative stability in relations among the major powers themselves in the period immediately ahead. None of the four appears motivated today by the kind of overtly imperialist, territorially expansionist ambitions that underlay Japanese, German, and Italian policies in the 1930s and 1940s. Not only is none of them dominant, but none seems likely to be able to establish clear predominance in the foreseeable future. The danger that any large-scale military conflict between the major powers could turn into a nuclear conflict inhibits all of their leaders even if they might otherwise be tempted to risk war. The present quadrilateral pattern is one, moreover, in which, if any one power seems to move toward an adventurist policy or threatens aggression, all the others seem likely to oppose the potential aggressor. The tendency, in short, will be for three to coalesce against one, to work in parallel if not in cooperation, to check and restrain any potential aggressor. In the event of big-power military conflict—for example, war between the Soviet Union and China—even if the other powers did not become militarily involved, on the side of the victimized nation, they would probably at least respond politically and economically in ways that could be costly to the aggressor.

Consequently, although theoretically each of the Communist powers would doubtless like to see major changes that would alter the balance in its favor, and ideally, would probably like to see the United States eventually pushed out of the region and Japan then aligned with itself, both probably feel that, in the foreseeable future, trends in such a direction would have very unpredictable consequences that could lead to a situation worse than the existing one. Neither Peking nor Moscow can exclude the possibility that Tokyo might align with its principal adversary, or that it might embark on a nationalist program of large-scale independent remilitarization and acquire its own nuclear capability. If this were to occur, and if the United States were compelled to disengage its interests from the region, the structure of relationships would be transformed from a quadrilateral to a triangular pattern, which would probably increase substantially the dangers of rising tensions, confrontations, and conflicts among China, the Soviet Union, and Japan.

On balance, the possibility now of direct large-scale military conflict between any of the major powers in the region—at least conflict resulting from deliberate military expansionism or from policies pursued without regard for the risks—seems relatively low. The greatest danger lies in the animosity between Peking and Moscow, and even there the danger seems to have been declining, and it is probable that the existing constraints will prevent war.

Nor does it seem likely that there will be major realignments among the four powers in the period immediately ahead that would fundamentally upset the existing equilibrium. Neither far-reaching Sino-Soviet rapprochement nor intimate ties between China and either Japan or the United States seem likely. Close cooperation between either the United States or Japan and the Soviet Union seems even more improbable. And although an open U.S.-Japan split that would exclude the United States from a significant regional role is not inconceivable, it is highly unlikely.

Less drastic changes in relationships are quite conceivable, however, and these could definitely affect the nature of the equilibrium, without necessarily upsetting it. A reduction of tensions between China and the

Soviet Union; a significant loosening of Japanese-American relations, especially if accompanied by expansion of Japan's military establishment; a definite tilt by the Japanese toward either Peking or Moscow (more plausibly the former)—any of these would set off tremors and create new uncertainties. The reverberations could be substantial. Some would fear that they foreshadowed major realignments that could upset the existing equilibrium. But the possibility of basic realignments actually taking place seems low, and tremors alone would not alter the equilibrium in any fundamental way. Limited Sino-Soviet détente or a partial loosening of U.S.-Japan relations might actually make the four-power pattern more nearly equilateral than at present, without weakening the mutual constraints now built into the structure of relations.

In sum, there appears to be a certain structural stability in the present equilibrium, at least in relationships among the four major powers themselves. Even though none of the four finds the situation wholly satisfactory, all of them, including China and the Soviet Union, are likely to be constrained from pushing too hard to make changes, and inhibited from taking high-risk actions that could radically change or upset the equilibrium, for fear that what would result might be worse than what now exists.

Potential Conflict Zones

While relative structural stability appears to exist today in relations among the four major powers themselves, both Northeast and Southeast Asia remain unstable. These two areas still pose dangers of conflict, which could involve the major powers.

The interests of all the major powers are involved, in varying ways and degrees, in both areas. There is reason to believe that no major power favors large-scale conflict in either, and that even Peking and Moscow will probably use their influence to try to prevent war. Nevertheless, the competitiveness of the major powers in their policies toward these areas, and the intensity of some of the competition, especially between Peking and Moscow, tends to be destabilizing.

Some of the nations in these areas, in particular North Korea and Vietnam, could themselves initiate conflicts. Both of these "middle powers" are now heavily armed and are ruled by revolutionary leaders with ambitious aims, and their neighbors are fearful of their intentions.

Although they may be restrained by internal problems as well as external pressures and constraints, there can be no certainty about their future policies.

Because of the Sino-Soviet conflict, both North Korea and Vietnam are the beneficiaries of competitive support as well as the targets of competitive pressure. Although Peking-Moscow competition subjects both to certain external restraints, it also presents each with opportunities to try to manipulate the two major Communist powers to its own advantage. The danger is that new conflicts between smaller nations in either Northeast or Southeast Asia could again draw the major powers into direct military involvement and perhaps escalate to confrontation among the major powers themselves.

Dangers in Korea

The greatest danger today exists in Northeast Asia, on the Korean peninsula.[64] Geography and history make the Korean peninsula unique. It has been a part of the traditional Chinese culture area for centuries, but it also has a distinctive history and culture of its own. Subordinate to China politically for long periods, it nevertheless has a distinguished history of independent accomplishments. For many years, it has also been a focus of international rivalries. In the modern period, it has been a cockpit for repeated clashes involving China, Russia, and Japan, and more recently the United States. Japan, after military victories over China and Russia, ruled Korea from 1910 to 1945. Then World War II brought liberation, but not the end of foreign intervention; in 1945 the Soviet Union occupied the North and the United States the South, creating the de facto division of the country. Today the strategic interests of the four major powers converge in Korea.

Both Korean regimes are strongly committed to ultimate reunification, but they have confronted each other with hostility and fear ever since the 1950–53 Korean War. Since 1953 the United States has been formally committed by treaty to help defend South Korea, and Washington now regards this as essential to maintain the credibility of its pledge to defend Japan. Since 1961 both China and the Soviet Union have been formally committed by treaty to help defend North Korea, and today they compete strongly for influence over its regime. China has demonstrated that it regards North Korea as a buffer area essential to its security. The Russians clearly regard it as important to the security of the Soviet Far East. The Japanese not only are deeply involved in

Korea economically (particularly in the South but increasingly in the North too), they also view it as critical to their security. The relationships among the six governments—two Korean and four foreign—create one of the most complex tinder boxes in the world. After the Middle East, it may well be the most dangerous trouble spot in the world, and one where local conflict could rapidly escalate into war involving the major powers.

The level of tension in Korea has fluctuated during the past decade, as local and international conditions have changed. It rose in the late 1960s when North Korea's leader, Kim Il-sung, in 1966 adopted an extremely militant posture and stepped up subversive activities aimed at the South, which reached a peak in 1968.

Then, for a brief period, it appeared that the two Korean regimes might finally be prepared to take serious steps toward reducing tension and working out a modus vivendi. In 1971 Park Chung-hee, president of South Korea, proposed North-South talks, and North Korea put forward an eight-point unification proposal. The announcement that President Nixon planned to visit Peking, which clearly shocked both Pyongyang and Seoul, impelled both North and South to further adjust their policies. In the fall of 1971, the South proposed Red Cross talks between North and South and these started soon thereafter. Secret official meetings followed, resulting in July 1972 in a dramatic announcement that the two regimes had agreed on three points: to try to achieve reunification through independent Korean efforts without external interference, to rely on peaceful means to reunify the country, and to stop slandering each other. Thereafter, a South-North Coordinating Committee and a "hot line" between Seoul and Pyongyang were established, and the much-heralded dialogue began.

The major developments that encouraged the North-South dialogue were the moves toward détente that occurred during 1971–72 between Washington and both Peking and Moscow. Whether or not China and the Soviet Union put direct pressure on their Korean allies is not known, but unquestionably the shifts in big-power relations helped to convince both Kim and Park that they should modify their policies.

At first, the prospects for progress in the North-South talks looked encouraging. North Korea's subversive efforts directed at the South dropped to a low level starting in 1972. Its general foreign-policy strategy appeared to change. It began to evolve a new policy toward Japan, and both trade and political contacts increased. For a brief period, Pyongyang also showed somewhat greater flexibility toward the United States, permitting visits by a few nonofficial Americans. It also cut back its military budget, probably for economic reasons; its economic growth rate had dropped and was lagging conspicuously behind South Korea's. On the broader international scene, Pyongyang expanded its diplomatic contacts, especially with Third World countries. It did not insist that countries recognizing it cut their ties with South Korea. By mid-1975, North Korea was recognized by over seventy nations, compared to over ninety in the case of South Korea, and there were dual relationships with a great many countries.

South Korea pressed for small steps to open up limited contacts with the North, and it too adopted a more flexible foreign policy. By 1974 it had moved quite far toward accepting a short-run, de facto two-Koreas policy. It had explicitly endorsed the idea of representation for both Korean regimes in the United Nations, which Pyongyang still adamantly opposed. Internally, although the South Korean economy was strong, due to its remarkable growth in the 1960s, political problems increased. President Park, fearful that North-South détente might expose the South to new dangers of subversion, tightened political controls and adopted increasingly repressive policies directed against virtually all opposition groups. Park's opponents continued to be strongly anticommunist, however, and there was no sign of any basis for Communist-led revolutionary action.

The initial improvement in the atmosphere surrounding North-South relations did not really narrow the gap between the two regimes' positions, however. While the South argued for a cautious, step-by-step establishment of limited Noth-South contacts, then the development of trade, leading ultimately to substantive political discussions about unification, the North called for dramatic, immediate steps toward a mutual cutback of military forces and the establishment of a North-South federation. Even though there was no objective basis for believing that two such disparate polities could be quickly reunified, this did not deter Kim from arguing for federation. The North also continued to press for a total withdrawal of U.S. military forces from Korea; the disengagement of U.S. forces was clearly one of Kim's basic objectives. Another was to isolate South Korea as much as possible internationally.

At the start, it appeared that all of the major powers involved might be prepared to use their influence in positive ways to increase stability on the peninsula. Even though Peking publicly backed all of Pyongyang's political positions, in 1973 Chinese officials privately told foreign diplomats that they were not pressing for any rapid withdrawal of U.S. military forces, and indicated that they felt a continuing U.S. military presence was desirable in Northeast Asia to check Soviet ambitions— and perhaps also to limit Japan's involvements. At the United Nations in 1973 the Chinese went along with the compromise that ended the UN Commission for Korea but left the UN Military Command intact (by 1974, however, Peking strongly backed Pyongyang's demand that the UN Command also be ended).

In 1973 the Chinese seemed to be motivated most of all by the desire to forestall conflict in Korea and to induce the United States to serve as a strong counterweight to Soviet influence throughout Northeast Asia. By 1974, however, they seemed to give priority to the aim of outcompeting the Russians in influencing Pyongyang, and to this end they increased their political support of North Korea.

The Russians, starting in 1972, also indicated that they favored stabilization of Korea on a de facto two-Koreas basis. From 1973 on, they even began to explore cautiously the possibility of developing nonofficial contacts with South Korea (privately, some Soviet specialists spoke frankly in favor of a two-Koreas policy), and they invited several Koreans from Seoul to visit the Soviet Union. They backtracked on this quickly, however, when Pyongyang showed its strong displeasure.

Japan, whose economic ties with South Korea were strong, steadily broadened its trade and nonofficial contacts with North Korea in the early 1970s. It appeared likely soon to replace China as North Korea's second most important trading partner, next to the Soviet Union. Tokyo indicated that it hoped ultimately for official relations with both regimes, making clear its desire for stabilization on the basis of two Koreas.

While emphasizing its continued commitment to South Korea's defense, Washington also stressed that it favored development of a North-South dialogue and stabilization of the existing situation on the peninsula. By 1974–75, both Washington and Tokyo had indicated, publicly, that official relations between themselves and the North might be possible, and desirable, in due time, if China and the Soviet Union showed a willingness to establish relations with the South.

Early optimism about the possibility of moderating North-South tensions largely evaporated during 1974, however. The dialogue went nowhere, and the talks settled into a stalemate. The gap between the political positions argued by representatives of the two sides, speaking for regimes ruling vastly different societies, again seemed unbridgeable. Both sides resumed hostile polemics. Moreover, the number of violent incidents increased in late 1973 and early 1974. Seoul was alarmed to discover that the North had been secretly digging tunnels under the demilitarized zone separating the two regimes—perhaps since soon after the signing of the 1972 joint communiqué. Park adopted increasingly stringent political measures to assure his control in the South, and the level of internal political tension rose. Kim returned to a militant and threatening posture. Exercising extraordinarily tight totalitarian controls, he had little concern about domestic opposition.

The regional uncertainties which the collapse of the noncommunist regimes in Indochina created in 1975 raised fears that North Korea, perhaps judging that the United States lacked the will to come to South Korea's aid, might initiate new probes, increase its subversive efforts, and actively attempt to foment revolution in the South. In April and May 1975 Kim made well-publicized visits to China and Eastern Europe, obviously to feel out what support for his policies he could count upon. When he visited Peking, although the Chinese stressed the need for a "*peaceful*" reunification of Korea, Kim was provocatively militant, stating that "if revolution takes place in South Korea, we, as one and the same nation, will not just look on it with folded arms but will strongly support the South Korean people."[65] He also induced the Chinese to state, for the first time, that they regarded the North Korean regime as the "sole legal sovereign state of the Korean nation."[66] In a sense this was Kim's payoff for his pro-Peking tilt.

In response to these developments the Park regime further tightened its internal political controls and put the South in a state of high preparedness to cope with any military, or subversive, moves from the North. The U.S. government publicly reiterated, and strongly underlined, its commitment to help defend the South. The United States still stresses the goal of stabilization, on the basis of a de facto acceptance of two Koreas, and South Korea seems willing to go along. But stabilization will not be possible without at least tacit support of new moves toward détente by China and the Soviet Union. Washington's uneasiness has been heightened by fear that political repression in the South might encourage greater risk-taking by the North and that Kim might adopt adventurist policies and induce Peking or Moscow to back him.

In actuality, in light of the military balance between North and South, probably neither Peking nor Moscow believes that major war is a realistic option for anyone to consider. Today, over a million well-armed troops confront each other in Korea, with neither side having any clear-cut military advantage. In contrast to many other unstable areas in the world, moreover, the opposing forces in Korea continue to be separated by a clear demarcation line and a demilitarized zone. The North's air force is stronger than the South's, and its backup militia forces are reputedly superior, but the South's 650,000 regular troops outnumber the North's 425,000. (The South's total population, over thirty million, is twice the size of the North's.)

What the South continues to fear, however, is a quick strike by the North, aimed at capturing Seoul, slightly over thirty miles from the border. Some evidence suggests that Pyongyang has been trying to develop modern mobile forces capable of launching such a strike. But an American division, armed with tactical nuclear weapons, still blocks the route to Seoul, and even if that division is withdrawn, neither North Korea nor its allies in Peking and Moscow can contemplate the possibility of a major attack without calculating the response that the United States might make.

It is plausible to believe, therefore, that both China and the Soviet Union still oppose any large-scale conflict in Korea and probably will be able to constrain Kim from taking actions that might lead to war. Yet North Korea's militancy, and the temptation to exploit political instability in the South, plus the intense competition between Peking and Moscow in their relations with the North, create major uncertainties about the situation. It is impossible to answer with any certainty a number of disturbing questions. Might Kim, even if Peking and Moscow disapprove, step up his probes and subversive acts against the South, especially if political instability under Park's regime leads to outbreaks of disorder and if Kim concludes the U.S. defense commitment is not credible? Might Kim then be able to exploit the Sino-Soviet dispute to his advantage and induce China and the Soviet Union to back actions they really did not approve? If tensions were to escalate, would China and the Soviet Union be able to restrain North Korea effectively? If not, might either be drawn into involvement in ways that would compel the United States to respond?

Certain trends since 1974 suggest that the competition between Peking and Moscow might make both of them susceptible to some degree of manipulation by Kim, and that Kim is trying to exploit the situation to his own advantage. Since late 1973, Peking has given few signals, as it did earlier, that it privately approves the continuing U.S. military presence in South Korea; since 1975, in fact, Chinese diplomats have argued strongly, privately as well as publicly, for the withdrawal of U.S. troops from Korea. They also have become more dogmatic and inflexible in their support for North Korea's international positions. During 1974 Moscow, on its part, stopped most of its cautious efforts to establish nonofficial contacts with South Korea, and although since then it has made a few small gestures in this direction, it has not got very far. In both cases the probable explanation is that Kim has had at least partial success in pressuring his allies to increase their support of his policies (North Korea's growing economic problems, however, could make it susceptible to increased pressure in the future from its allies—particularly the Soviet Union).

Even though the Sino-Soviet conflict, and moves by both Peking and Moscow to improve relations with the United States and Japan, appear to have virtually precluded united action by the Chinese and Russians to support adventurist North Korean policies, Sino-Soviet competition clearly still gives Kim opportunities to exert leverage on both. Today, certainly, there seems to be little basis for openly cooperative efforts by Peking and Moscow together with Washington and Tokyo to impose reliable constraints on both Korean regimes, or to develop four-power understandings on how to increase stability on the peninsula and encourage North-South détente. Without such cooperation or understandings, the danger remains that local conflict might break out, escalate, and reach a point where the major powers, despite their opposition to war in Korea, would feel compelled to become involved.

Dangers in Southeast Asia

In comparison to Korea, Southeast Asia today is less threatening to regional stability and poses fewer dangers of big-power conflict. But conditions are even more fluid, unstable, and complex, and here too, although the new pattern of four-power relations imposes restraints on all nations involved in the region, the competition among the major powers, and especially between China and the Soviet Union, has certain destabilizing effects.[67]

Southeast Asia, for centuries a crossroads, is a huge area, measuring roughly three thousand miles from east to west and two thousand north to south. Never unified, it has always been characterized by striking cultural and political diversity. Historically, both China and India have had a significant cultural impact on the region—hence the term *Indochina*—and their emigrants, especially the Overseas Chinese, have acquired substantial economic power throughout the region. However, Chinese and Indian influence was limited, and over the centuries many distinctive local cultures developed and thrived in the region; some of them, such as the Java-based Majapahit Kingdom, in what is now Indonesia, and the Khmer Kingdom, in what is now Cambodia, for a time developed strong local political regimes.

In the early sixteenth century, the major European trading and colonial nations, the Portuguese, Spaniards, Dutch, English, and French, and by the end of the nineteenth century the Americans as well, began to exert their influence in the region, and eventually all Southeast Asia except Siam (Thailand) was under their domination. The British, Dutch, and French achieved predominant positions. Their colonial rule brought enforced order and stimulated considerable economic development, but the metropolitan powers pursued policies designed primarily to serve their own interests, and colonial rule prevented the emergence of modern nation-states.

World War II changed all of this. The Japanese conquest of Southeast Asia destroyed the European colonial regimes there. It also accelerated the growth of modern nationalism within territorial entities that colonial rulers had established. When, at war's end, Japanese colonialism was, in its turn, destroyed, nationalist movements flourished and led rapidly, despite abortive attempts by the Dutch and French to reestablish their rule, to the establishment of new nations.

Most of the states in Southeast Asia—Indonesia, Burma, Malaysia, Singapore, Thailand, Philippines, Laos, Cambodia, and Vietnam—started with fragile political entities. In many places, statehood was achieved before genuine nationhood, and nation-building was a difficult task. Nationalists assumed leadership in most places, but in every nation in the region, Communist movements mounted violent, revolutionary struggles and difficult minority problems led to numerous local rebellions. In addition, emotion-laden border disputes created many serious tensions. The political institutions in the new nations were subjected to tremendous strains, and the newly created democratic institutions soon broke down in many places.

In spite of the complexity and diversity of Southeast Asia, certain broad trends within the region, and in the big powers' involvement there, are apparent. The strength of nationalism has proved to be greater than the force of communism everywhere except in the Indochina states—in Vietnam especially, Ho Chi-minh's marriage of nationalism and communism gave the Communist movement a legitimacy and strength unique in the area. Elsewhere, noncommunist leaders have contained the insurrections they faced and made gradual progress in their efforts at nation-building. In many nations, however, the breakdown of democratic forms has led to new kinds of authoritarian regimes, usually dominated by military men.

Most of the noncommunist nations have achieved substantial economic growth, even though it has generally been less than what they hoped for. The variations have been great, however. Between 1963 and 1973, while the average rate of growth in gross national product was only 2.7 percent in Burma, it was 5–6 percent in Indonesia, Malaysia, and the Philippines, 7.6 percent in Thailand, and 12.4 percent in Singapore.[68] Many Southeast Asian states have faced great problems caused by unstable international prices and markets, rapid urbanization, and internal economic and social inequities. As in many other developing nations, modernization has strained the social fabric in most Southeast Asian nations. And all of them have had also to cope with a very uncertain international environment. Although modest steps have been taken toward regional cooperation, mainly through the Association of Southeast Asian Nations (ASEAN), which includes Malaysia, Singapore, Indonesia, Thailand, and the Philippines, progress toward regionalism has been slow.

Because of the power vacuum created by the defeat of Japan and the subsequent instability in the region, it was probably inevitable that Southeast Asia—an area rich in resources and strategically located—would again become an arena for big-power competition. This did not happen immediately, however. For several years after World War II none of the four major powers that now play key roles in Southeast Asia was deeply involved in the region, although the United States reestablished close ties with the Filipinos after granting them independence in 1946 and for a brief period the former European colonial nations made abortive efforts to inject their power back into the region.

The situation changed fundamentally, however, in the late 1940s and early 1950s. The rise to power of a dynamic Communist regime in China, the extension of the cold war to East Asia, and the American decision to pursue an active "containment" policy designed to check the spread of Communist influence made Southeast Asia a cockpit for East-West competition.

The new Chinese Communist regime adopted a highly revolutionary posture toward Southeast Asia in 1949. Peking encouraged insurrections throughout most of the region, specifically endorsing several Communist uprisings that had broken out in 1948. As soon as Chinese Communist forces reached the borders of Indochina, they began giving Ho Chi-minh tangible support, in the form of training and materiel, in his struggle against the French. The United States, committed to combat the spread of communism everywhere, first gave aid to the French in Vietnam, then initiated varied programs to support noncommunist governments elsewhere in the area. Subsequently it moved to build an anticommunist military alliance system in the region.

Despite their fears both of China and of local Communist movements, a number of Southeast Asian nations tried to avoid involvement in the developing U.S.-China confrontation. Only Thailand and the Philippines lined up clearly with the United States, by joining the Southeast Asia Treaty Organization formed in 1954. The SEATO powers extended their protection, however, to the noncommunist regimes in South Vietnam, Cambodia, and Laos. Most Southeast Asian nations, including Indonesia and Burma, to a lesser degree Malaya and Singapore, and at times (though not consistently) Laos and Cambodia, adopted some kind of nonalignment posture.

In the late 1950s and early 1960s, Moscow became more active in the region, but China and the United States were the major powers most involved, and they engaged in conflict by proxy, especially in Vietnam. China increased its support of North Vietnam, even though it did not sign any formal military treaty with it or send Chinese combat troops to the area. The Americans, after replacing the French as the main supporters of South Vietnam in 1954, steadily increased their involvement, first with economic and military aid, then advisers, and finally U.S. forces.

The Chinese always made clear their hope that a Communist-led revolution would ultimately triumph in all of Vietnam. But their immediate goal seemed to be to exclude Western power and insure that North Vietnam would remain as a friendly buffer area. Their policies over the years suggest that they tended to view their revolutionary interests throughout Southeast Asia in fairly long-range terms and were not inclined to take large risks to achieve short-run objectives.

The Chinese first demonstrated their willingness to compromise to a degree that the North Vietnamese found disturbing at the Geneva Conference in 1954. In signing the Geneva agreements that divided the country, the Chinese doubtless hoped that the separation of North and South would be temporary, and that the Communists would soon win their struggle by political means, in the elections that the agreements called for. Nevertheless, Peking was prepared to endorse agreements that called for a halt to the fighting and at least a temporary stabilization of the situation, which the Vietnamese Communists must have disapproved. Peking's principal motive, it seems clear, was to minimize the dangers of new major-power confrontations in the region which could pose threats to China itself.

When the Vietnamese Communists stepped up their revolutionary activities in the 1960s, China provided increased support, but some evidence suggests that it questioned the wisdom of the North Vietnamese leaders' inclination to press for rapid victory and advised them to think in longer range terms and pursue a strategy of "protracted warfare." Peking probably feared that any attempt to achieve rapid victory could provoke increased American intervention, as in fact it did. In Laos, the Chinese were clearly prepared to compromise, and did so in 1972, to prevent escalation of conflict. And while strongly backing the revolutionaries in Cambodia in the late 1960s, they avoided military intervention themselves.

Although Peking obviously viewed Vietnam as the most important area in Southeast Asia, in terms of its own security interests, it also attempted to expand Chinese influence throughout the region. It gave moral support, and limited material aid, to several Communist parties and movements in the region, and the majority of these looked to China rather than to the Soviet Union as their prime source of inspiration. Peking also applied limited pressure on certain areas immediately adjacent to China, especially Burma, to insure that they would not join any U.S.-led anticommunist grouping.

Briefly, during the 1955–57 Bandung period, China adopted an activist but conciliatory posture toward the noncommunist regimes throughout Southeast Asia, endorsing neutralism and emphasizing its desire to develop diplomatic ties with them. It also adopted a policy of restraint in dealing with Overseas Chinese problems in the area. However, it still obviously hoped to weaken U.S. influence throughout Southeast Asia. Because this approach paid only limited immediate dividends, however, by the late 1950s Peking had returned to a more militant posture, which increased fears of Chinese intentions throughout the region.

China did make major progress in the late 1950s and early 1960s in developing closer relations with Indonesia and Cambodia. In the early 1960s it appeared, in fact, that a Peking-oriented Vietnam-Cambodia-Indonesia axis was developing, which might provide a basis for substantially increased Chinese influence in the region as a whole. Then, the failure of the Communist coup in Indonesia in 1965, which Peking had openly endorsed, followed by a strong anticommunist repression campaign carried out by the Indonesian military leaders who succeeded Sukarno, destroyed any immediate hopes for such an axis that China might have had.

American policy throughout this period aimed primarily at combating both Chinese and local Communist influence. In addition to adopting the role of protector of South Vietnam, the United States gradually increased its role in Laos and gave major assistance to Thailand and the Philippines. It also supported anticommunist forces elsewhere and exerted pressure on the nonaligned states in the area to abandon neutralism and join the United States in helping to "contain China."

Although the Soviet Union provided sizable aid to North Vietnam, exercised considerable influence in Indonesia for a brief period, and developed important ties with Burma, in general its role in Southeast Asia remained much less important than that of either China or the United States. Tokyo's involvement in the region was beginning to be felt economically, but it was not yet important; the rapid expansion of Japanese trade and investment still lay in the future. In the 1950s and much of the 1960s, therefore, the clash of big-power interests in Southeast Asia was essentially a confrontation, in part through proxies, between the United States and China, focusing above all on Vietnam.

In the mid-1960s, however, changes began to occur that by the mid-1970s had fundamentally altered the situation. Most important, the escalation of the conflict in Vietnam brought large-scale but unsuccessful U.S. military intervention, involving enormous costs in both lives and dollars. The ultimate U.S. failure and decision to withdraw its forces from the entire Indochina area had a far-reaching impact not only in Southeast Asia but also on the basic pattern of big-power relations throughout East Asia. Then, the development of Sino-Soviet competition and the rapid growth of Japan's economic role in the region accelerated the transition from a bipolar to a multipolar situation.

In 1965 the Vietnam war took on a new character when North Vietnam, with large-scale Chinese and Soviet material aid, and the United States, in support of the South Vietnamese, both greatly increased their military efforts. The situation that resulted was similar in some respects to that in Korea in the early 1950s. The United States was now fighting directly alongside a small Asian ally against a small but strong Asian Communist nation supported by Peking and Moscow.

However, there were also profound differences between Vietnam in the late 1960s and Korea in the early 1950s. For one thing, the war itself was very different; the political and mobile nature of the struggle made it much more difficult to apply U.S. power effectively. Also, although both the Chinese and the Russians gave large amounts of aid to North Vietnam, neither sent its own military forces to engage in active combat, as China had done in Korea. Moreover, Peking and Moscow were now political antagonists, competing bitterly against each other for influence in Hanoi. Most important, the South Vietnamese regime, unlike the government in South Korea, proved unable to create an independently viable base of political strength.

The basic failures of the South Vietnamese and Americans—fighting a "limited war" because of Washington's determination to avoid provoking intervention by Chinese forces—to defeat the Communist forces ultimately led to: the alienation of the American public which compelled Washington to change its policies; the steps taken from late 1968 on to disengage U.S. forces; the tortuous road to a negotiated truce, with some military escalations along the way which greatly raised the level of conflict in Cambodia; the ultimate breakdown of the Paris agreements due to violations by both North and South Vietnam; and then the final collapse in 1975 of the noncommunist governments in both Cambodia and Vietnam, and the less violent but no less effective takeover of power by the Communists in Laos.

All of these developments have helped to create a new pattern of relations and configuration of power in Southeast Asia. American influence has clearly declined, although the United States continues to be a very important political and economic factor in the situation and still is the only external power that maintains mobile naval and air forces in the area. Washington's primary goals in the region are now much more limited than they used to be, but it is still committed to use its influence to work toward greater stability and to maintain access to the region. China's political influence has grown substantially, as Peking has broadened its diplomatic ties with the noncommunist states, and it still gives verbal encouragement to several revolutionary movements in the area. It appears to be pursuing very limited aims, however. Vietnam, under a disciplined, ambitious, and well-armed Communist regime, has emerged as the strongest Southeast Asian nation in purely military terms. But it faces major problems of internal consolidation. The Soviet Union has stepped up its diplomatic and economic activities, especially in the Indochina states, but elsewhere in the region as well. Yet outside of Vietnam and Laos it remains the least influential of the major powers. Japan has emerged as the strongest economic power in the region, and its political influence, though still limited, is gradually growing. Although Japan's goals are primarily economic, its need for oil from the Middle East creates a vital security interest in transit rights.

Sino-American confrontation no longer dominates the scene, and the newest element is increasing Soviet and Japanese influence. The Russians are competing everywhere against Chinese influence, as the Chinese are competing against theirs. Politically and economically, the Russians now tend deliberately to be conservative rather than revolutionary, but they could be tempted to try to increase their military presence in the area, through expanded naval activity and perhaps increased military aid, which would have disruptive and destabilizing effects.

The balance among the major powers in Southeast Asia today makes it very unlikely that any single power will be able to establish clear dominance in the foreseeable future. All four will play important roles, but none can ignore the numerous constraints limiting their influence and freedom of action.

There is widespread uncertainty, however, about the future policies of the Communist regimes in the Indochina area, their relationships with Peking and Moscow, and the consequences of Sino-Soviet competition for the region as a whole.[69] Hanoi, having rapidly unified North and South Vietnam, probably believes that it should strive for a hegemonial position in the entire Indochina area. However, Moscow and especially Peking seem unlikely to endorse such a policy. Their competition for influence over Vietnam has escalated substantially since Hanoi achieved final victory. The Vietnamese clearly do not wish to be subordinate to either and are trying to maintain good relations with both, while pursuing their own goals. Recently, they have tilted in a pro-Soviet direction. Historically, the Vietnamese have feared China, and they may feel that closer ties with the Soviet Union will help to counterbalance China's influence. The result has been to increase strains in Peking-Hanoi relations. The Chinese seizure in 1974 of the Paracel Islands, which the Vietnamese consider theirs, and the occupation by Vietnamese in 1975 of some islands in the Spratleys, which the Chinese claim, have created new tensions. In the period ahead, Hanoi will probably be inhibited from leaning too far in a pro-Soviet direction, however, for fear of provoking stronger Chinese opposition to its aims elsewhere in the region. It has shown a desire to expand economic and other ties with Japan and has also indicated that it is probably prepared to establish diplomatic relations with the United States.

In 1975 the new Cambodian regime carried out drastic revolutionary policies at home and cut off most foreign ties. It showed strong hostility against Moscow, as well as Washington, in part because the Russians had continued to deal with its noncommunist enemies right to the end. Its most important external link now is with China, which has long cultivated and supported not only Prince Sihanouk (who has disappeared from view) but also Khieu Samphan and the other leaders of the Khmer Rouge who have exercised real power. China's energetic efforts to cultivate close ties with Cambodia have clearly been motivated in part by its desire to minimize Moscow's influence, but it seems inclined to try to limit Hanoi's influence as well. There is evidence that, despite Hanoi's aid to the Khmer Rouge, the new rulers in Phnom Penh wish to restrict North Vietnamese influence. Traditionally, many Cambodians have feared the Vietnamese, and there is no reason to believe that fear has disappeared. Conceivably, important Sino-Vietnamese differences could develop over Cambodia.

In Laos, the situation, as always, has been the fuzziest. More than a decade ago, in 1962, a framework for a coalition government was established, with the endorsement of the leaders of China, the Soviet Union, and the United States, all of whom seemed to prefer compromise to open conflict that might provoke increased big-power military intervention. Thereafter, all these powers continued to be involved in Laos, politically and economically, but the Laotian Communists relied above all on support from Hanoi and Peking. While Hanoi was the main conduit for military assistance, Peking made clear its strong interest in the area by building important roads linking the Pathet Lao areas in northern Laos to China. The noncommunist groups in Laos had relied for years on backing from the United States, but when, in 1975, the coalition finally broke down, the Pathet Lao assumed control, and the U.S. role rapidly diminished; by 1976 it had, for all practical purposes, been eliminated, despite the continuation of diplomatic representation in the country. The greatest gains since 1975 have been made by the Soviet Union, which today appears to have more influence in Laos than any other foreign power. But both Peking and Hanoi also continue to be heavily involved, and it now appears that a complex Chinese-Vietnamese-Russian competition for influence is under way.

Since the 1975 Communist takeovers in the Indochina states, apprehensions have grown in the rest of Southeast Asia, especially in Thailand, which borders on Cambodia and Laos and is very close to both China and Vietnam. There is doubt about the future U.S. role in the region, and it is now widely assumed, probably correctly, that in the foreseeable future the United States will avoid committing any of its ground forces in local conflicts in Southeast Asia. Most countries in the region hope for continuation of a significant U.S. political and economic role, and many still desire some sort of American military presence in the area, even if only a naval and air presence, but do not know what can be expected.

Noncommunist Southeast Asians' fears, differing in different nations, have focused most of all on North Vietnam, secondarily on China, and thirdly on the Soviet Union. They worry that one or more of these nations may try to exploit the new instabilities in order to expand their areas of control or influence, conceivably by direct military expansionism but more likely by exerting new pressure or increasing support of insurrectionary groups. Although these fears did not begin in 1975, they increased when the United States moved to withdraw militarily from Vietnam, opened relations with China, and scaled down its regional military role. The rapid Communist takeovers in 1975 heightened apprehensions and stimulated virtually every nation in Southeast Asia to reassess its policies.

Since the U.S.-China opening in 1972, and especially since 1975, all of the noncommunist Southeast Asian nations have adjusted their policies in important ways. Most have moved toward broadening relations with all four major powers. Several have also probed the possibility of establishing relations with the Communist regimes in the Indochina area. Generally, it seems clear their hope is that the major powers will balance and check each other and also restrain Vietnam. Even nations such as Thailand and the Philippines that have been most closely aligned with and dependent on the United States have deliberately loosened their ties with the Americans and moved to establish or broaden diplomatic links with Peking as well as Moscow. Among Southeast Asian nations, the slowest to move toward new relationships with China have been Singapore and Indonesia, but in 1976 Singapore's prime minister, Lee Kuan-yew, visited Peking. All of this movement reflects the trend toward multipolarity and reinforces it.

International trends are not the only causes of instability in Southeast Asia. Internal political conditions are at least as important. Few regimes in the area are genuinely stable, and the trend regionally has been toward military rule and increased authoritarianism. Virtually all of the non-communist nations continue to face armed dissidents, more often than not Communist guerrillas, to whom the Communist nations, and especially China and Vietnam, give moral support and in some cases limited material aid.

Yet, despite all their problems, the majority of Southeast Asian nations have strong assets that make their prospects for survival, and development, better than some observers seem to believe. Nationalism is a powerful force in most of them; it reinforces a natural determination to oppose both internal and external threats. Most are relatively well endowed with natural resources, which eases their economic problems. In none, at present, is the Communist movement strong enough to threaten the survival of the existing regime; outside of Indochina the Communists have still not captured control of the main force of local nationalism. Guerrilla movements could pose greater problems if China or Vietnam increased material support to them, but this could provoke a strong nationalist counterreaction, regionally as well as locally.

Therefore, even though the prospects for genuine stability within most Southeast Asian nations, or in their regional relationships, are clouded, there is no imminent danger that these countries will rapidly succumb, in domino fashion, to internal Communist takeovers such as those that occurred in the Indochina states. Moreover, even though most noncommunist nations in the area will almost certainly accommodate to some degree to the Communist powers, they are unlikely to align closely with any one of them or to abandon their important links with the United States and Japan. The main effect on most Southeast Asian nations of the new multipolarity of power relationships is likely to be to encourage self-reliance in dealing with internal problems and flexibility in dealing with all external powers.

China in the period ahead will undoubtedly continue to view Southeast Asia as a region of special interest. Because of geographical propinquity and the long history of China's involvement in the region, the Chinese have many intangible as well as tangible interests in Southeast Asia. Vietnam, traditionally regarded, like Korea, as part of the Sinic civilization area, borrowed Confucian philosophy, ideographic writing, and a great deal more from China. And in earlier centuries the Chinese ruled Annam, in what is now northern Vietnam, for long periods. Elsewhere, Peking's historic role was less important. However, the Chinese have invaded Burma on several occasions; in the fifteenth century, Ming rulers sent large naval expeditions throughout the area; and Chinese ties with Siam (Thailand) were extensive. Apart from invasions and incursions in Annam and Burma, China's imperial rulers never embarked on broad territorial expansion in Southeast Asia, but Chinese cultural and political influence was widely felt, and the large Overseas Chinese minorities that settled in the region—they now total somewhere between ten million and twenty million people—still maintain many links to China. Peking has not crudely manipulated them as a fifth column, but it does foster ties of varied sorts with them, and it regards protection of their interests as an important responsibility. Peking also has an economic interest in the region; even though its trade is still limited, the potential for the future is important.

In recent years, however, China's main interests in Southeast Asia have related to its political and security goals. One political goal has been to encourage revolutionary change. Since 1949 China has supported various Communist groups and movements in the area. Although it has not in general considered direct military intervention with Chinese forces to be either a feasible or a desirable option, it has provided significant material support to the Communists in Vietnam, Cambodia, and Laos. Elsewhere, while giving important moral support, it has usually restricted its concrete assistance to advice and training, although in a few instances it has provided very limited material assistance. Chinese involvement in Burma over the years (and in Indonesia in the 1960s) has been somewhat larger than in most other countries, though still very limited in terms of what Peking could do.

Although China has never renounced support of Communists in Thailand, Malaysia, and the Philippines, as well as in Burma and Indonesia, in practice the emphasis China has given to revolutionary objectives has varied greatly. When Peking has given high priority to state-to-state relations—as it did in the mid-1950s and is now doing—it has tended to deemphasize revolutionary goals. Almost always, immediate national interests have taken precedence over revolutionary interests, except when they have been mutually reinforcing.

China will doubtless continue to take an active interest in revolutionary movements in Southeast Asia but view revolutionary goals in long-range terms and limit Chinese intervention to support them. And as its relations with existing noncommunist regimes expand, there will be increased pressure to deemphasize revolutionary activity. Competition with Moscow and Hanoi may impel Peking to reemphasize revolutionary aims in certain situations. But in its overall policy toward Southeast Asia, revolutionary goals will probably continue to be secondary rather than primary factors shaping Chinese policy toward the region.

Peking can be expected to place highest priority on the protection of China's concrete interests and the expansion of China's general influence in the region through conventional means. This has been true in the past and is likely to be even more true in the future. China can be expected to compete actively against the other major powers, but largely by using traditional diplomatic, political, and economic instruments. In such competition, even though Peking's economic capabilities are limited, especially in comparison to those of Japan and the United States, it has important assets that it will try to use, and probably will be able to use quite effectively, in diplomatic and political competition.

China's single most important aim in Southeast Asia will almost certainly continue to be the protection of its national security. Throughout the 1950s and 1960s, the main concern of Chinese leaders was the potential threat they saw in U.S. military involvements in Southeast Asia. China's relative military weakness deterred it from responding to U.S. military action with Chinese military intervention, but if Chinese leaders had feared for the survival of North Vietnam, they probably would have dispatched combat forces as they did in Korea in the 1950s. In the event, their policy toward the region was essentially cautious and reactive, but they left no doubt that they would do all they could, without excessive risks, to counter the American threat that they perceived at that time.

Today, Peking still sees a potential threat to China in the region, but it now sees the Soviet Union as posing the danger. It views the growing Russian activity and influence in the region as part of a deliberate Soviet policy of containing and encircling China, and even though the problems posed by Soviet policy have been more political than military, Peking fears that a strengthened Soviet political position will lead to an increased Soviet military presence in the region and pose a serious military threat in the future. Today, the Chinese place the highest priority, therefore, on the need to compete against, and check, the growth of Soviet influence, in every possible way, in Southeast Asia as elsewhere.

In a basic sense, China's approach to Southeast Asia is still essentially reactive, and militarily it remains cautious because most of the constraints that have limited its options in the past continue to be operative. But politically it now competes very actively against Soviet influence in every way that it can. Because this is now its primary preoccupation, it has adopted a tolerant, and in some respects even favorable, attitude toward the continuation of an American military presence in Southeast Asia, as in Northeast Asia, hoping this will help keep Soviet influence in check.

The situation in Southeast Asia at present is significantly different from that in Northeast Asia, however. None of the major powers—including China—sees the region today as being as potentially dangerous to its immediate security interests as Korea could be. But the major powers do continue to see relationships in Southeast Asia, as in Northeast Asia, as highly competitive, and there is no basis yet for genuine four-power cooperation.

The Soviet Union is now pursuing an overtly anti-Chinese policy in Southeast Asia, not because its own interests are yet very heavily involved in the region, or because the Chinese pose any threat from that area to the Russians themselves, but rather as part of its broad global strategy of exerting pressure on China. Currently, Moscow relies primarily on diplomatic and economic means to pursue its goals in the region, but it could become more involved militarily at some point in the future.

Although the present structure of four-power relations clearly imposes important constraints on all the major powers, in Southeast Asia, as throughout East Asia, relationships among the powers continue to be highly competitive, and fundamentally the situation remains unstable. Apprehensive about the dangers of new foreign intervention, the majority of Southeast Asian states now believe that their long-term interests require them to develop closer cooperation within the region, establish ties with all the major powers, and work to limit and perhaps eventually eliminate all external powers' bases and forces.

Efforts to organize regional cooperation have been under way for many years, with only limited results. However, the Association for Southeast Asian Nations is now making some progress and its leaders have called for neutralization of Southeast Asia, through the creation of a "zone of peace and neutrality." Even though this concept is still vague, it symbolizes a growing desire to promote regional self-reliance and check big-power intervention.

The goals of increased regional cooperation and neutralization clearly have widespread support among Southeast Asian nations, but neither will be easily achieved. Even among the noncommunist nations, numerous conflicts of interest persist. And there are still deep divisions between them and the Communist states in the Indochina area. If these divisions cannot be bridged, the region could polarize into two loose blocs, one consisting of noncommunist nations with ASEAN as its core and Indonesia its strongest member, and the other consisting of the Communist states in the Indochina area with Vietnam playing the leading role. Such a polarization would heighten tensions, increase the dangers of conflict, and set back any prospect of creating a "zone of peace."

China has gone further than the other major powers, so far, in endorsing the concept of neutralization. There is little prospect, however, that neutralization will be realized until there is much greater regional cooperation among the ASEAN nations, a closing of the gap between them and the Indochina states, and agreement among all the major powers to respect the new restraints that neutralization would impose on them.

In time all the major powers, as well as the nations in Southeast Asia themselves, may recognize that neutralization would serve their interests. But in the years immediately ahead, the only realistic prognosis is for the continuation of considerable instability within the region and continuing competition among the four major powers. The prospects for maintaining the peace and gradually increasing regional cooperation will depend fundamentally on whether the new big-power equilibrium can be maintained and gradually stabilized, or whether it will break down and lead to renewed conflict. Conversely, trends in Southeast Asia will inevitably affect the prospects for a stable equilibrium among the major powers throughout East Asia.

Retrospect and Prospect

Looking back over the past quarter century, Chinese leaders may well regard their strategies in dealing with the other major powers in East Asia as successful in certain fundamental respects. In an international

environment that they have viewed as generally hostile, they have deterred major attacks by the powers that they have regarded as most
threatening. They have successfully demonstrated that, despite China's
relative military weakness, it will not capitulate in the face of pressure
or intimidation. They have steadily built up their defense capabilities
and maintained a position of basic self-reliance. They have also been able
to take advantage of "contradictions" between other powers, gaining
useful support first from the Soviet Union to counterbalance U.S. power
and then from the United States to check Soviet threats. They have supported Communist regimes in Korea and Vietnam and helped preserve
friendly buffer areas in both places. They have greatly expanded their
international diplomatic ties, especially since the start of the 1970s, obtained general recognition as a major power, and asserted their views on
most global as well as regional problems. They have increased their foreign economic ties and obtained needed grain, capital goods, and technology from diverse foreign sources. And as leaders of the largest developing nation, they have become vocal spokesmen for the Third World
in dealing with the industrial powers.

Yet the balance sheet is far from wholly favorable. Chinese policies
have helped to create the hostile environment that Peking has had to face.
At no time have Chinese leaders felt free from threats from the other
major powers, and their strategies have merely checked perceived
threats, not eliminated them. They have experienced one crisis after
another on China's periphery and have had to devote a great deal of
their energy and resources to dealing with them. They have had to invest
huge resources in building their military establishment, which has inevitably reduced what they could devote to developing the civilian
economy and raising living standards. Although they have reduced
China's military inferiority compared to its major adversaries, China remains relatively weak and vulnerable and has no close allies among the
major powers. They have been unable to sustain friendly relations with
most of the large nations in Asia—including India and Indonesia as well
as the major powers—over any prolonged period. They still face very
hostile and potentially threatening forces, which are far stronger than
China's, along virtually their entire northern and western borders. They
remain uncertain about areas such as Korea and Vietnam because of
Sino-Soviet competition. They have failed to achieve their basic goal of
"liberating" Taiwan and therefore consider China's reunification to be
incomplete. None of the Communist movements to which they have

given moral support—outside of the Indochina states—have succeeded in their struggles for power. More broadly, despite China's increased voice in international affairs, its capacity to make its influence felt effectively is still very limited on most issues. And although its foreign economic relations have increased, China is still not extensively involved in the world economy and still therefore must forgo many benefits that greater involvement could bring.

Looking ahead, it is difficult to judge exactly how China's post-Mao leaders will assess the balance sheet of the past, or how they will perceive their interests and define their goals and strategies in the future. There will doubtless be both continuity and change. There is no question that certain basic Marxist-Leninist and Maoist concepts will continue to influence Chinese thinking. China's leaders will probably still view the world in terms of constant change, shifting "contradictions," and struggle. Although their schematic definitions of the "balance of forces" in the world may change, their concept of three worlds will probably continue to influence their outlook. China will doubtless continue to identify itself on many issues with the Third World and to lend its weight to promoting change—both revolutionary change in the Communist sense and systemic international change in relations between the developing and developed nations.

At the same time, China's new leaders will doubtless continue to give the highest priority to national security and thus to devote primary attention to relations with the other major powers. They will certainly continue their efforts to strengthen China militarily. And they seem likely to continue stressing self-reliance and pursuing some kind of balance-of-power strategy designed to enhance China's security.

Yet future leaders will not necessarily view the world, assess their interests, and define their policies in exactly the same way as past Chinese leaders. Mao's personal, idiosyncratic conceptions of the conflict of forces in the world, and of the best strategies to cope with them, greatly influenced the particular balance-of-power policies China pursued while he lived. Post-Mao leaders with different perspectives may question the validity of old policies. Certain long-term trends affecting China's position may argue for modifying inherited policies, especially if the leadership moves generally toward more pragmatic approaches to problems, which seems likely judging by the immediate results of China's succession struggle.

Although China remains relatively weak compared to its potential adversaries, its acquisition of a nuclear deterrent may persuade post-Mao leaders that they can deal with the other powers with somewhat greater self-confidence—and less preoccupation with China's vulnerability— than in the past. If they are less obsessed than Mao with the Soviet Union's political and ideological as well as military threat, they could be more willing to consider alternative strategies for dealing with Russia. If they reassess their basic security problems, they could opt for greater flexibility in dealing with all the powers, instead of concentrating on counterbalancing one principal enemy, as Mao was inclined to do. If they give increasing priority to the need to accelerate China's economic development, they may put increased stress on policies designed to expand "normalized" political and economic relations with other countries, and somewhat less emphasis on ideological and political conflicts. And if, over time, China's interests become more deeply involved in the international community, and especially in the global economy, the willingness of China's leaders to participate in some cooperative international ventures could gradually increase.

It is highly unlikely that China's new leaders will totally abandon self-reliance, or try to ally closely with any other power, unless they see no other alternative in order to survive. They are not likely therefore either to try to achieve a broad rapprochement with Moscow that would restore a close alliance or to try to work toward a close alliance with either the United States or Japan. It is possible, however, that Peking could decide to adopt a more balanced approach, try to defuse existing threats by greater compromise, and attempt to achieve increased maneuverability and leverage in dealing with both superpowers through a carefully calculated approach of "equidistance."

The direction in which China moves, if its leaders do consider important policy changes, will be significantly influenced by the nature of Peking's new leadership, once it is consolidated, and by the imperatives, dictated by basic internal problems and needs, that the new leaders perceive. It will also be greatly influenced, however, by the policies toward China pursued by the other major powers, especially the two superpowers. Specifically, it will depend on whether the Soviet Union is prepared to reduce its military pressure on China, compromise on border problems and other issues, and modify its containment efforts on all of China's periphery; whether the United States is willing to compromise further on the Taiwan issue and move toward fully normalized relations with Peking, and maintains a credible overall regional and global position; and whether Japan continues to abjure major remilitarization, remains an important source of capital goods and technology for China, and avoids any significant pro-Soviet tilt. Future Chinese policy will also be greatly influenced by the general character of four-power relations in East Asia, the quality of relations between the other powers, and the balance of influence among the powers in areas of potential conflict such as Korea and Southeast Asia.

In the immediate future, China's new leaders will probably continue to view the Soviet Union as the main potential threat to China's security, but the likelihood of open military conflict will remain low. While a far-reaching rapprochement is unlikely, China may try, cautiously, to probe the prospects for reducing Sino-Soviet tensions and moving toward limited détente; if so, it will have to be prepared to modify its own policy in order to reduce the Soviet threat. Whether compromise is possible will also depend on Moscow's policies, and on whether it demonstrates a willingness to modify many of its past policies. The possibilities may increase after new men replace the aging leadership in Moscow. If, however, Peking's leaders remain convinced that Moscow is implacably hostile, continues to pursue threatening policies, and is unwilling to make any significant compromises, they will doubtless continue to pursue strongly anti-Soviet policies not very different from those of recent years.

If pragmatists predominate in China's post-Mao leadership, Peking is likely to continue to view relations with Washington as important. No return to openly hostile confrontation seems likely under foreseeable circumstances. However, whether the relationship continues to be very limited, as at present, or is gradually strengthened, or deteriorates, will depend on Peking's perception of the U.S. willingness to compromise further on the Taiwan issue and on the state of triangular Chinese-American-Soviet relations. If Washington moves toward full normalization of relations and makes the adjustments in relations with Taiwan that this will doubtless require, and if Peking continues to view the United States an an effective counterweight that constrains the Soviet Union, Chinese leaders will probably work gradually to expand and improve relations—even if they also explore the possibilities of Sino-Soviet détente. If, however, relations with the United States are not fully normalized, and especially if it proves possible to reduce Sino-Soviet tensions, Peking may try to exert increased pressure on Washington to compromise on the Taiwan problem, and Sino-American relations could retrogress.

Chinese leaders are very likely to continue efforts to expand relations —especially economic relations—with Japan in the period ahead. And they will doubtless persist in their efforts to deter Japan from developing closer relations with the Soviet Union. China is likely to approve of the U.S.-Japan security treaty so long as U.S.-China relations continue to improve. However, they would probably attack it again if Sino-American relations were to deteriorate. Even assuming Sino-Japanese ties improve, however, the relationship will probably continue to be restricted; and it will clearly still contain elements of both cooperation and competition. Over time, the competitive elements, based on divergent interests regarding Taiwan, Korea, Southeast Asia, and the oceans in East Asia, may grow. And if Japan were to decide to embark on major remilitarization, Sino-Japanese relations could become increasingly antagonistic.

In their policies toward Korea and Southeast Asia, the Chinese will persistently try to increase their roles, but their influence will probably continue to be limited and counterbalanced by that of the other powers. China will attempt to use its influence to try to reduce the influence of any other power that might pose a direct threat to China's security from either area; and in the immediate future the Soviet Union will doubtless continue to be viewed as more dangerous than the United States in this respect. The Chinese will probably avoid adventurist policies toward either area, however, and they seem likely to use their influence to prevent major conflicts that could lead to new military interventions by other powers. They can be expected to give some support to revolutionaries elsewhere, if they are oriented toward China rather than the Soviet Union, but in the period immediately ahead they will probably stress the development of conventional state-to-state relations much more than the promotion of revolutionary change.

Broadly speaking, no sudden drastic changes seem likely in the pattern of four-power relations in East Asia, or in China's roles in that pattern, in the years immediately ahead. Limited détente between Peking and Moscow, or other changes that seem possible, could alter the existing pattern marginally, but they would not necessarily upset the existing equilibrium. Conceivably, if one takes an optimistic view, a gradual improvement in Sino-Soviet relations, if not accompanied by a deterioration in Sino-American relations, could remove one major obstacle to four-power cooperation in the region and improve the possibility of achieving cooperation or understandings among the powers designed to reduce the danger of conflict and enhance the prospects for regional stability. If one takes a less optimistic view, what is likely is the continuation of competition rather than cooperation among the major powers throughout most of the region. Yet in either case, the balance is not likely to change fundamentally in the period ahead. All four of the major powers, including China, can be expected to continue playing major roles, but none of the four will have a realistic basis for trying to achieve regional hegemony.

Sources

BECAUSE this study is a broad interpretive analysis rather than a limited, detailed monograph, the documentation is designed primarily to give supporting data and bibliographic guidance on major points. Although primary sources are generally cited for quotations and statistics, many of the notes cite secondary sources containing useful background information.

No study of recent international developments can be based on archival materials. Apart from a few important U.S. documents that have been declassified or leaked, the full official record is not available and will not be for many years for any of the four powers dealt with; in the cases of China and the Soviet Union, it probably never will be. Therefore, I have had to rely primarily on the public record, especially as it has been revealed in newspapers and journals in the four countries.

I have followed the Chinese Communist press since Feb. 2, 1949, when I purchased my first issue of the *People's Daily*, the Chinese Communist party's official paper, on the streets of Peking immediately after the Communist takeover of that city. In recent years I have relied heavily on the English-language translations of published Chinese materials and transcripts of Chinese broadcasts contained in *Survey of People's Republic of China Press* [SPRCP] (formerly *Survey of China Mainland Press* [SCMP]), *Selections from People's Republic of China Magazines* (formerly *Selections from China Mainland Magazines*), and *Current Background*, all put out by the American Consulate in Hong Kong; and *Foreign Broadcast Information Service* [FBIS] *Daily Report: People's Republic of China* [PRC] (formerly *Communist China*), distributed by the National Technical Information Service of the U.S. Department of Commerce. *Peking Review*, a weekly publication of the Chinese Communist party, contains most important official statements on Chinese foreign policy. Translations in the U.S. government-produced *Joint Publications Research Service*, as well as the Hong Kong-published *Union Research Service* are also useful, though they concentrate more on domestic than on foreign affairs.

I have used the U.S. press—especially the *New York Times* and *Washington Post*—extensively, but for texts of U.S. government documents and speeches I have relied primarily on official publications such as the *Department of State Bulletin*. I have followed the Soviet and Japanese press, in translation, in the *Foreign Broadcast Information Service [FBIS] Daily Report: Soviet Union* and in the *Daily Summary of Japanese Press* issued by the American Embassy in Tokyo. I have also used selectively the *Current Digest of the Soviet Press*, put out by the American Association for the Advancement of Slavic Studies. These press and radio sources have informed all my judgments, even though I cite them only for certain facts and texts of major statements.

The majority of the sources I cite are monographic studies in English that are readily available in major American libraries. Many of them have extensive citations of primary sources. In addition to the published writings of many students of Chinese foreign policy, I cite some unpublished studies that have been especially useful to me. Two scholarly periodicals have been particularly useful: the *China Quarterly* (Contemporary China Institute, London) and *Asian Survey* (University of California Press).

While my interpretations derive from my formal research over the years, they are also based on the less tangible benefits of my contacts with Chinese of varied political persuasions over the past three decades, plus considerable contact during the past decade with Japanese specialists on Chinese affairs and, to a lesser extent, Soviet specialists on Asia. In 1972–73 I was fortunate to spend a month in the People's Republic of China at the invitation of the Chinese People's Institute for Foreign Affairs, and a month in Japan spent largely in meetings with scholars and officials specializing on foreign affairs, including Sino-Japanese relations, and in 1974 to spend two weeks in the Soviet Union at the invitation of the Soviet Academy of Sciences, meeting and talking with China specialists in and out of government. Visits to Southeast Asia in 1976 and Taiwan and Korea in early 1977 were also helpful. In recent years, I have also had frequent conversations with Chinese, Soviet, Japanese, and other Asian diplomats in Washington and New York. My interviews with M. S. Kapitsa (of the Soviet Foreign Ministry) in Moscow and Ch'iao Kuan-hua (then vice minister, and subsequently minister, of foreign affairs) in Peking produced especially useful insights.

For many years I have had close, continuous contact with American officials dealing with China policy, and my understanding of the U.S. side of the U.S.-China equation has also been enhanced by my own involvement as a foreign service officer in the American consulate-general in Hong Kong during 1951–52, a member of the Department of State in 1956–57, a member of the Department of State's Panel of Advisors on China during 1966–69, and a consultant to the National Security Council during 1968–70.

Introduction: China—A New Major Power

1. For broad surveys of China's foreign policy since 1949, see Harold C. Hinton, *China's Turbulent Quest: An Analysis of China's Foreign Policy*

Since 1949, enlarged ed. (Macmillan, 1972), and *Communist China in World Politics* (Houghton Mifflin, 1966); J. D. Simmonds, *China's World: The Foreign Policy of a Developing State* (Columbia University Press, 1970); Vidya Prakash Dutt, *China's Foreign Policy, 1958–62* (Bombay: Asia Publishing House, 1964); R. G. Boyd, *Communist China's Foreign Policy* (Praeger, 1962); and A. Doak Barnett, *Communist China and Asia: Challenge to American Policy* (Harper and Brothers for Council on Foreign Relations, 1960).

John Gittings, *The World and China, 1922–1972* (London: Methuen, 1974), interprets the concepts that have helped to shape Chinese foreign policy; see also, Ishwer C. Ojha, *Chinese Foreign Policy in an Age of Transition: The Diplomacy of Cultural Despair* (Beacon, 1969); and Michael Lindsay, *China and the Cold War: A Study in International Politics* (Melbourne, Australia: Melbourne University Press, 1955).

Two legal studies that throw important light on Chinese foreign policy are Jerome Alan Cohen and Hungdah Chiu, eds., *People's China and International Law: A Documentary Study*, 2 vols. (Princeton University Press, 1974); and James Chieh Hsiung, *Law and Policy in China's Foreign Relations: A Study of Attitudes and Practice* (Columbia University Press, 1972). A. M. Halpern, ed., *Policies Toward China: Views from Six Continents* (McGraw-Hill for Council on Foreign Relations, 1965), concentrates on the policies of other nations but is also illuminating on Chinese policy. Useful textbook treatments are Allen S. Whiting, "Foreign Policy of Communist China," in Roy C. Macridis, ed., *Foreign Policy in World Politics*, 2nd ed. (Prentice-Hall, 1962); and Robert C. North, *The Foreign Relations of China*, 2nd ed. (Dickenson, 1974). Collections of short analyses include Tang Tsou, ed., *China in Crisis*, vol. 2, *China's Policies in Asia and America's Alternatives* (University of Chicago Press, 1968); King C. Chen, *The Foreign Policy of China* (Seton Hall University Press, 1972); Jerome Alan Cohen, ed., *The Dynamics of China's Foreign Relations*, East Asian Monograph 39 (Harvard University Press, 1970); and Devere E. Pentony, *China, the Emerging Red Giant: Communist Foreign Policies* (Chandler, 1962).

Valuable analytical articles include Allen S. Whiting, "The Logic of Communist China's Foreign Policy: The First Decade," *Yale Review*, vol. 50 (Autumn 1960), pp. 1–17, and "The Use of Force in Foreign Policy by the People's Republic of China," *Annals of the American Academy of Political and Social Science*, vol. 402 (July 1972), pp. 55–66; A. M. Halpern, "Communist China and Peaceful Coexistence," *China Quarterly*, no. 3 (July–September 1960), pp. 16–31, "The Chinese Communist Line on Neutralism," ibid., no. 5 (January–March 1961), pp. 90–115, "The Foreign Policy Uses of the Chinese Revolutionary Model," ibid., no. 7 (July–September 1961), pp. 1–16, and "China in the Postwar World," ibid., no. 21 (January–March 1965), pp. 20–45; Tang Tsou and Morton H. Halperin, "Mao Tse-tung's Revolutionary Strategy and Peking's International Behavior," *American Political Science Review*, vol. 59 (March 1965), pp. 80–99; Robert A. Scalapino, "China and the Balance of Power," *Foreign Affairs*, vol. 52 (January 1974), pp. 349–85; Michael B. Yahuda, "China's New Era of International Relations," *Political*

Quarterly, vol. 43 (July–September 1972), pp. 295–307, and "Chinese Foreign Policy: A Year of Confirmation," in Peter Jones, ed., *The International Yearbook of Foreign Policy Analysis*, vol. 1 (London: Croom Helm, 1975); Ross Terrill, "How China Makes Its Foreign Policy" and "How Do the Chinese See the World," *800,000,000: The Real China* (Little, Brown, 1972), chaps. 17 and 19; and Donald W. Klein, "Peking's Evolving Ministry of Foreign Affairs," *China Quarterly*, no. 4 (October–December 1960), pp. 28–39, and "The Management of Foreign Affairs in Communist China," in John M. H. Lindbeck, ed., *China's Management of a Revolutionary Society* (University of Washington Press, 1971), pp. 305–42.

For a useful topically organized bibliography of English-language works on Chinese foreign policy, see Roger Dial, *Studies on Chinese External Affairs: An Instructional Bibliography of Commonwealth and American Literature* (Halifax, Nova Scotia: Centre for Foreign Policy Studies, Dalhousie University, 1973).

2. The text is in *Long Live the Victory of People's War* (Peking: Foreign Languages Press, 1965), reprinted in A. Doak Barnett, *China after Mao* (Princeton University Press, 1967). D. P. Mozingo and T. W. Robinson analyze the statement's meaning and significance in *Lin Piao on 'People's War': China Takes a Second Look at Vietnam*, RM-4814-PR (Santa Monica, Calif.: Rand Corp., 1965).

3. *Peking Review*, Apr. 30, 1969, pp. 16–35.

4. Ibid., Sept. 7, 1973, pp. 17–25.

5. Ibid., Jan. 24, 1975, pp. 21–23.

6. Ibid., Apr. 12, 1974, supplement, pp. 1–5.

7. Gittings, *The World and China*, discusses the evolution of these concepts; see especially pp. 144 ff. The Russians have denounced the concepts; see M. Kudrin, "A False Concept of the Maoists," *Foreign Broadcast Information Service Daily Report: Soviet Union*, Apr. 26, 1974, pp. C1–C8.

8. For analyses of China's relations with Southeast Asian Third World countries, see Melvin Gurtov, *China and Southeast Asia—The Politics of Survival: A Study of Foreign Policy Interaction* (Johns Hopkins Press, 1971); Jay Taylor, *China and Southeast Asia: Peking's Relations with Revolutionary Movements* (Praeger, 1974); David Mozingo, *Chinese Policy Toward Indonesia, 1949–1967* (Cornell University Press, 1976); Sheldon W. Simon, *The Broken Triangle: Peking, Djakarta, and the PKI* (Johns Hopkins Press, 1969); Daniel D. Lovelace, *China and 'People's War' in Thailand 1964–1969* (Center for Chinese Studies, University of California, 1961); and Chae-Jin Lee, *Communist China's Policy Toward Laos: A Case Study 1954–67* (Center for East Asian Studies, University of Kansas, 1970).

On China and South Asia, see Neville Maxwell, *India's China War* (Doubleday Anchor Books, 1972); Wayne Wilcox, *India, Pakistan, and the Rise of China* (Walker, 1964); Bhabani Sen Gupta, *The Fulcrum of Asia: Relations Among China, India, Pakistan and the USSR* (Pegasus, 1970); Alistair Buchan, ed., *China and the Peace of Asia* (Praeger, 1965); and D. E. Kennedy, *The Security of Southern Asia* (Praeger, 1965).

On China's relations with other Third World areas, see Bruce D. Larkin, *China and Africa, 1949–1970: The Foreign Policy of the People's Republic of China* (University of California Press, 1971); Zbigniew Brzezinski, ed., *Africa and the Communist World* (Stanford University Press, 1963); George Yu, *China and Tanzania: A Study in Cooperative Interaction* (Center for Chinese Studies, University of California, 1960); and Cecil Johnson, *Communist China and Latin America, 1959–1967* (Columbia University Press, 1970).

On revolutionary aspects of Chinese policy toward the Third World, see Peter Van Ness, *Revolution and Chinese Foreign Policy: Peking's Support for Wars of National Liberation* (University of California Press, 1971); Chalmers Johnson, *Autopsy on People's War* (University of California Press, 1973); Samuel B. Griffith, *Peking and the People's War* (Praeger, 1966); Robert A. Scalapino, ed., *The Communist Revolution in Asia: Tactics, Goals, and Achievements* (Prentice-Hall, 1965); and A. Doak Barnett, ed., *Communist Strategies in Asia: A Comparative Analysis of Governments and Parties* (Praeger, 1963).

The "Chinese model" is discussed in Michel Oksenberg, ed., *China's Development Experience* (Columbia University Press, 1973); and Werner Klatt, ed., *The Chinese Model: A Political, Economic, and Social Survey* (University of Hong Kong Press, 1965).

On the problem of the Overseas Chinese, see Stephen Fitzgerald, *China and the Overseas Chinese: A Study of Peking's Changing Policy 1949–1970* (Cambridge University Press, 1972); and Lea E. Williams, *The Future of the Overseas Chinese in Southeast Asia* (McGraw-Hill for Council on Foreign Relations, 1966).

9. In 1975 Peking established formal relations with the Common Market; see *New York Times*, Sept. 16, 1975. No major studies of China's relations with Western Europe have yet been published. Useful articles include Dick Wilson, "China and the European Community," *China Quarterly*, no. 56 (October–December 1973), pp. 647–66; Vladimir Reisky de Dubnic, "Europe and the New U.S. Policy Toward China," *Orbis*, vol. 16 (Spring 1972), pp. 85–104; and Giovanni Bressi, "China and Western Europe," *Asian Survey*, vol. 12, no. 10 (October 1972), pp. 819–45. On Chinese-East European relations, see pt. 1, n. 1.

10. President Nixon stated that "there are five great power centers in the world today," including China, which will "inevitably [be] an enormous economic power" (*Department of State Bulletin*, July 26, 1971, p. 95). When Kissinger arrived in Peking in July 1971, Chou En-lai expressed great interest in the speech and loaned his copy, with personal marginal notes, to Kissinger, who had left Washington before seeing the final text (Marvin Kalb and Bernard Kalb, *Kissinger* [Little, Brown, 1974], pp. 247–48). Some months later, Nixon elaborated on his concept: "I think it will be a safer world and a better world if we have a strong, healthy United States, Europe, Soviet Union, China, Japan, each balancing the other, not playing one against each other, an even balance" (*Time*, Jan. 3, 1972, p. 11).

Part One: China and the Soviet Union

1. For scholarly analyses and collections of documents giving both Chinese and Soviet views on Sino-Soviet relations since 1949, see Donald S. Zagoria, *The Sino-Soviet Conflict, 1956–61* (Princeton University Press, 1962); John Gittings, *Survey of the Sino-Soviet Dispute: A Commentary and Extracts from the Recent Polemics, 1963–1967* (Oxford University Press, 1968); Harold C. Hinton, *The Bear at the Gate: Chinese Policymaking Under Soviet Pressure* (Washington: American Enterprise Institute for Public Policy Research; and Stanford, Calif.: Hoover Institution on War, Revolution and Peace, 1971); William E. Griffith, *Peking, Moscow, and Beyond: The Sino-Soviet-American Triangle* (Center for Strategic and International Studies, Georgetown University, 1973); Zbigniew K. Brzezinski, *The Soviet Bloc: Unity and Conflict* (Harvard University Press, 1960); G. F. Hudson, Richard Lowenthal, and Roderick MacFarquhar, eds., *The Sino-Soviet Dispute* (Praeger, 1961); Kurt London, ed., *Unity and Contradiction: Major Aspects of Sino-Soviet Relations* (Praeger, 1962); Klaus Mehnert, *Peking and Moscow* (London: Weidenfeld and Nicolson, 1963); Donald S. Zagoria, ed., *Communist China and the Soviet Bloc, Annals of the American Academy of Political and Social Science*, vol. 349 (September 1963); Alexander Dallin, ed., *Diversity in International Communism: A Documentary Record, 1961–1963* (Columbia University Press, 1963); William E. Griffith, *The Sino-Soviet Rift* (M.I.T. Press, 1967); Richard Lowenthal, *World Communism: The Disintegration of a Secular Faith* (Oxford University Press, 1964); *Sino-Soviet Conflict*, H. Doc. 237, 89:1 (Government Printing Office, 1965); John G. Stoessinger, *Nations in Darkness: China, Russia, and America* (Random House, 1971); and Donald Treadgold, ed., *Soviet and Chinese Communism: Similarities and Differences* (University of Washington Press, 1967).

For useful books by journalists, see David Floyd, *Mao Against Khrushchev: A Short History of the Sino-Soviet Conflict* (Praeger, 1963); Edward Crankshaw, *The New Cold War: Moscow v. Pekin* (Penguin, 1963); and Harrison Salisbury, *War Between Russia and China* (Norton, 1969).

Among valuable studies by Rand Corp. of Santa Monica, Calif., are Thomas W. Robinson, *A National Interest Analysis of Sino-Soviet Relations*, P-3319 (1966); and Allen S. Whiting, *Contradictions in the Moscow-Peking Axis*, P-1183 (1957), *The Sino-Soviet Alliance: How Durable?* P-1714 (1959), and *Conflict Resolution in the Sino-Soviet Alliance*, P-2029 (1960).

In addition, see listings in standard bibliographic guides under William Ballis, O. Edmund Clubb, Shen-yu Dai, Franz Michael, Harry Gelman, James C. Hsiung, Shao-chuan Leng, Charles McLane, George Modelski, Robert North, Uri Ra'anan, Robert A. Scalapino, Benjamin I. Schwartz, Harry Schwartz, Michael Tatu, and Richard Thornton.

Soviet views are contained in M. S. Kapitsa, *The CPR: Two Decades—Two Policies* (Moscow: Political Literature Publishing House, 1969), trans. JPRS 51425 (Arlington, Va.: Joint Publications Research Service, Sept. 22,

1970); O. B. Borisov and B. T. Koloskov, *Soviet-Chinese Relations, 1945–1970* (Moscow: MYSL Publishing House, 1971), ed. Vladimir Petrov (University of Indiana Press, 1975); and S. Sergeichuk, *Through Russian Eyes: American-Chinese Relations*, trans. Elizabeth Cody-Rutter (Arlington, Va.: International Library, 1975). No comparable book-length Chinese analyses are available in English, but Chinese views are well documented in the studies cited earlier.

2. For a comprehensive treatment of the history of Sino-Russian relations, see O. Edmund Clubb, *China and Russia: The Great Game* (Columbia University Press, 1971). For historical background on relations in the decades immediately before the Communist takeover in China, see Max Beloff, *Soviet Policy in the Far East, 1944–1951* (Oxford University Press, 1953); Harriet Moore, *Soviet Far Eastern Policy, 1931–1945* (Princeton University Press, 1945); Aitchen K. Wu, *China and the Soviet Union: A Study of Sino-Soviet Relations* (London: Methuen, 1950); Henry Wei, *China and the Soviet Union* (Van Nostrand, 1956); and Victor A. Yakhontoff, *Russia and the Soviet Union in the Far East* (London: George Allen and Unwin, 1932).

3. On relations between the Chinese and Soviet Communist parties before 1949, see Conrad Brandt, *Stalin's Failure in China, 1924–1927* (Harvard University Press, 1958); Conrad Brandt, Benjamin Schwartz, and John K. Fairbank, *Documentary History of Chinese Communism* (Harvard University Press, 1952); Xenia Joukoff Eudin and Robert C. North, *Soviet Russia and the East, 1920–1927: A Documentary Survey* (Stanford University Press, 1957); Charles B. McLane, *Soviet Policy and the Chinese Communists, 1931–1946* (Columbia University Press, 1958); Richard C. Thornton, *The Comintern and the Chinese Communists, 1928–1931* (University of Washington Press, 1969); Allen S. Whiting, *Soviet Policies in China, 1917–1924* (Columbia University Press, 1954); and C. Martin Wilbur and Julie Lien-ying How, eds., *Documents on Communism, Nationalism, and Soviet Advisers in China, 1918–1927* (Columbia University Press, 1956).

4. Chang Kuo-t'ao, one of the founders of the Chinese Communist party, described Maring (Hendricus Sneevliet), the Comintern representative at the founding meeting of the Chinese party, as "endowed with the social superiority complex of the white man" (*The Rise of the Chinese Communist Party, 1921–1927* [University Press of Kansas, 1971], p. 139). "Maring apparently saw himself sitting on top of the world with the main strings of the Chinese revolution held in his hands" (ibid., p. 265). Chang blames the Russians for imposing a wrong revolutionary strategy on the Chinese party.

5. See Brandt, *Stalin's Failure in China*.

6. For differing views on the degree to which Mao evolved his united-front positions independently, see Lyman Van Slyke, *Enemies and Friends: The United Front in Chinese Communist History* (Stanford University Press, 1967), p. 57; and Gregor Benton, "The 'Second Wang Ming Line' (1935–38)," *China Quarterly*, no. 61 (March 1975), pp. 61 ff.

7. See Stuart R. Schram, *The Political Thought of Mao Tse-tung* (Praeger, 1963, 1969 rev. ed.); and Stuart R. Schram with Hélène Carrère d'Encausse,

Marxism and Asia: An Introduction with Readings (London: Allen Lane, Penguin, 1969).

8. See Clubb, *China and Russia*, pp. 306–18.

9. See, for example, *Foreign Relations of the United States, Diplomatic Papers, 1944,* vol. 6, *China* (GPO, 1967). Stalin told U.S. Ambassador W. Averell Harriman: "The Chinese Communists are not real Communists, they are 'margarine' Communists" (p. 799). Foreign Minister V. M. Molotov remarked to Donald Nelson: "Some of these people called themselves 'Communists' but they had no relation to communism. . . . The Soviet Government could not be blamed in any way for this situation nor should it be associated with these 'Communist elements' " (p. 255).

10. See Boris Koloskov, *The Soviet Union and China: Friendship or Alienation?* (Moscow: Novosti Press Agency Publishing House, 1971), pp. 11–13. His statement that "all of the arms of the Kwangtung Army were handed to the Chinese Communists" (p. 12) is an exaggeration. The Soviets did, however, time many of their force withdrawals to permit Chinese Communist forces to take over Japanese arms, and they deliberately blocked the entry of Chinese Nationalist forces into certain key areas.

11. See Clubb, *China and Russia*, pp. 337 ff.; and Edwin W. Pauley, *Report on Japanese Assets in Manchuria to the President of the United States July 1946* (U.S. Department of State, 1946), pp. 21–35.

12. See A. Doak Barnett, *China on the Eve of Communist Takeover* (Praeger, 1963), pp. 247 ff.

13. See Vladimir Dedijer, *Tito* (Simon and Schuster, 1953), p. 322; Milovan Djilas, *Conversations with Stalin* (Harcourt, Brace and World, 1962), pp. 182–83; and Mao Tse-tung, "Speech at the Tenth Plenum of the Eighth Central Committee," in Stuart Schram, ed., *Chairman Mao Talks to the People* (Pantheon, 1974), p. 191.

14. Liu Shao-ch'i, *Internationalism and Nationalism* (Peking: Foreign Languages Press, 1949). This article originally appeared in November 1948.

15. Mao Tse-tung, *On People's Democratic Dictatorship* (Peiping: English Language Service, New China News Agency, 1949). In this article, dated July 1, 1949, Mao declared: "Travel the road of the Russians—this was the conclusion" (p. 4). He asserted that, "internationally, we belong to the anti-imperialist front, headed by the U.S.S.R." (p. 9).

16. The Chinese and Russians agreed that if either were "attacked by Japan or any state allied with it" (that is, the United States), the other would "immediately render military and other assistance by all means at its disposal." *Sino-Soviet Treaty and Agreements* (Peking: Foreign Languages Press, 1951), pp. 5–8.

17. Alexander Eckstein, in Howard L. Boorman and others, *Moscow-Peking Axis, Strengths and Strains* (Harper for Council on Foreign Relations, 1957), p. 92. See also Alexander Eckstein, *Communist China's Economic Growth and Foreign Trade: Implications for U.S. Policy* (McGraw-Hill for Council on Foreign Relations, 1966), pp. 135 ff.

18. Mao argued that "we can only look for genuine friendly aid" from the

antiimperialist front headed by the USSR and that it was "childish" to expect aid from the British and American governments (*On People's Democratic Dictatorship*, p. 9). Mao did call for trade with the Western nations, however.

19. Nikita Khrushchev, *Khrushchev Remembers* (Little, Brown, 1970), pp. 367 ff.

20. See Allen S. Whiting, *China Crosses the Yalu: The Decision to Enter the Korean War* (Macmillan, 1960). Robert R. Simmons, *The Strained Alliance: Peking, P'yongyang, Moscow and the Politics of the Korean Civil War* (Free Press, 1975), supports the consensus regarding China's entry into the war, but argues strongly that serious Sino-Soviet tensions existed in 1949-50 and throughout the war. I believe he exaggerates the seriousness of tensions and frictions in this early period.

21. For overall trade figures, see Eckstein, *Communist China's Economic Growth*, p. 98. Russian claims regarding aid to China are in Koloskov, *The Soviet Union and China*.

22. Hans Heymann, Jr., asserts this; see *China's Approach to Technology Acquisition: Part I—The Aircraft Industry*, R-1573-ARPA (Santa Monica, Calif.: Rand Corp., 1975), p. 9.

23. *New York Times*, June 4, 1956, citing a speech made in Warsaw in March 1956. Khrushchev charged Stalin with creating serious strains that jeopardized the Sino-Soviet alliance, by "demanding too much in return for aid" and insisting on the establishment of several joint-stock companies.

24. Mao described the negotiation of this treaty as a "struggle" and said that at one point Stalin was reluctant to sign because he lacked confidence in the Chinese Communists (Schram, *Chairman Mao Talks to the People*, p. 191).

25. *Khrushchev Remembers: The Last Testament* (Little, Brown, 1974), p. 247. Mikhail A. Suslov stated on Feb. 14, 1964, that after 1953 "elements of inequality in the relations between our countries [Soviet Union and China] imposed during the Stalin personality cult were removed"; Russian officials subsequently acknowledged publicly that the joint-stock companies had been a mistake (Gittings, *Survey of the Sino-Soviet Dispute*, p. 57).

26. M. S. Kapitsa, chief of the First Far East Department, Ministry of Foreign Affairs, Moscow, mentioned in an interview with me on Apr. 26, 1974, that Stalin maintained direct correspondence with Kao without going through the Chinese Central Committee and Politburo. *Khrushchev Remembers: The Last Testament* confirms this (pp. 243-44).

27. Several Soviet scholars and officials frankly acknowledged this in conversations with me in Moscow, April 1974.

28. See Eckstein, *Communist China's Economic Growth*, pp. 154 ff.

29. Ibid., pp. 153-60 and 167; by Eckstein's calculations, $825 million to $1.145 billion of the total was extended from 1953 on, after China's First Five-Year Plan was under way. Kapitsa, *The CPR: Two Decades—Two Policies*, p. 177, states the total of Soviet credits to China was 1.86 billion rubles.

30. Koloskov, *The Soviet Union and China*, pp. 66 and 74.

31. Roderick MacFarquhar, *The Hundred Flowers Campaign and the Chinese Intellectuals* (Praeger, 1960), p. 50.

32. Simmons, *The Strained Alliance,* discusses these, but he probably overstates the strains.

33. A. Doak Barnett, *Communist China and Asia* (Harper, 1960), p. 348; and Gittings, *Survey of the Sino-Soviet Dispute,* p. 57.

34. Harold C. Hinton, *Communist China in World Politics* (Houghton Mifflin, 1966), p. 87, n. 119.

35. "On the Historical Experience of the Dictatorship of the Proletariat" and "More on the Historical Experience of the Dictatorship of the Proletariat," *People's Daily,* Apr. 5 and Dec. 29, 1956, in *Communist China, 1955–1959, Policy Documents With Analysis* (Harvard University Press, 1962), pp. 144–51 and 257–72.

36. Quoted in "Mao Tse-tung on Imperialists and All Reactionaries are Paper Tigers," *People's Daily,* Oct. 31, in *Current Background,* no. 534 (Nov. 12, 1958), pp. 1–14.

37. In "Statement by the Spokesman of the Chinese Government," Sept. 1, in *Peking Review,* Sept. 6, 1963, pp. 7–16, the Chinese accused Khrushchev of "asking China to agree to the U.S. scheme of creating 'two Chinas'" at the time of his visit to China in the fall of 1959.

38. Officially, the Chinese stated: "In August and September of 1958, the situation in the Taiwan Straits was indeed very tense as a result of the aggression and provocations by the U.S. imperialists. The Soviet leaders expressed their support for China on September 7 and 19 respectively. Although at that time the situation in the Taiwan Straits was tense, there was no possibility that a nuclear war would break out and no need for the Soviet Union to support China with its nuclear weapons. It was only when they were clear that this was the situation that the Soviet leaders expressed their support for China" (ibid.).

39. In a "Statement by the Spokesman of the Chinese Government," Aug. 15, in *Peking Review,* Aug. 16, 1963, pp. 7–15, the Chinese declared that on June 20, 1959, the Soviet government "unilaterally tore up the agreement on new technology for national defense concluded between China and the Soviet Union on October 15, 1957, and refused to provide China with a sample of an atomic bomb and technical data concerning its manufacture." *Khrushchev Remembers: The Last Testament,* p. 269, states that "a prototype atomic bomb" was packed and ready to send to China but that at the last minute a decision was made not to send it. See also Raymond L. Garthoff, ed., *Sino-Soviet Military Relations* (Praeger, 1966), p. 90.

40. My judgments about the effects of the 1958 offshore islands crisis on Sino-Soviet relations are influenced by my Apr. 26, 1974, interview with M. S. Kapitsa as well as by all the factual data publicly available. There are varying interpretations by other analysts. Donald S. Zagoria's analysis, in *The Sino-Soviet Conflict,* p. 206, supports the Chinese charge that the Russians gave support only "when the crisis had passed its peak" (his book was published *before* the Chinese published their charge in September 1963). See also John

R. Thomas, "The Limits of Alliance: The Quemoy Crisis of 1958," in Garthoff, *Sino-Soviet Military Relations*, pp. 114–49. Some U.S. government analysts argue that the Russians probably knew of Peking's plans and agreed to support them (within limits). They stress that the crisis did not end until the U.S. navy had broken the Chinese blockade of Quemoy in late September, or until the Chinese ended major shelling in early October. They argue that Khrushchev's Sept. 7 and 19 statements, conveying strong warnings to the United States, significantly helped the Chinese (they were clearly designed to deter any U.S. attack on the mainland). Morton H. Halperin, in *China and the Bomb* (Praeger, 1965), p. 55, n. 46, argues that "in fact the Soviet Union did provide to the Chinese the kind of nuclear cooperation and protection that they desired." Nikita Khrushchev, in *Khrushchev Remembers: The Last Testament*, pp. 262–63, implies that the Russian leaders supported the idea of taking the offshore islands and were baffled by Chinese statements suggesting they had not really wanted to take the islands.

However, Kapitsa, in his interview with me, emphasized that the crisis seriously disturbed Moscow, and he indicated that the Russians' decision to reassess their policy of nuclear weapons aid to the Chinese soon thereafter was precipitated in part by the crisis. He strongly maintained that the Chinese did not fully inform Khrushchev about their intentions in regard to the offshore islands when Khrushchev visited China just before the crisis (Kapitsa has also stated this publicly in his account in *The CPR: Two Decades—Two Policies*, p. 194). The credibility of this claim is increased by the recent revelation that, in an unpublished speech on Nov. 30, 1958, Mao declared that his July–August talks with Khrushchev "did not contain a word about the question of the Taiwan situation." (This is one of many revelations in recently published collections of Mao's unpublished statements; the originals were issued in China in 1967 and 1969; copies were obtained by Nationalist sources later and released in 1973. These volumes, titled *Mao Tse-tung Ssu-hsiang Wan-sui—Long Live Mao Tse-tung's Thought*—are analyzed by Stuart R. Schram in *China Quarterly*, no. 57 [January–March 1974], pp. 156 ff. Mao's statement is in the 1969 volume, p. 254, cited by Allen S. Whiting, "New Light on Mao, 3. Quemoy 1958; Mao's Miscalculations," *China Quarterly*, no. 62 [June 1975], p. 269.) Kapitsa and Gromyko flew to Peking and met with Mao and the Chinese Politburo, where, Kapitsa asserts, they were further disturbed (as they had been in November 1957) by statements Mao made regarding possible nuclear war. The plausibility of Kapitsa's allegation that Mao made deprecating statements about the danger of nuclear war at the Chinese Politburo meeting Gromyko is said to have attended is bolstered by a speech made on Sept. 5, 1958, the day before the Politburo meeting, in which Mao discussed at some length the nuclear problem and indicated his willingness to risk nuclear attack (extracts in Whiting, "New Light on Mao," p. 268).

The timing of events is suggestive. On Sept. 6, the date of Gromyko's reported meeting with the Chinese Politburo, Chou En-lai offered to reopen the Warsaw talks with the United States. Khrushchev's first letter to President Eisenhower was sent on the following day, Sept. 7. It is plausible to believe that Gromyko made clear the limits of Soviet support, that the Chinese then decided to reopen Sino-American talks, and that only thereafter was Khrushchev willing to make a strong public pledge of support of the Chinese.

The most significant point emerging from my interview with Kapitsa was that the crisis probably helped to precipitate a reassessment of the Soviet policy of nuclear aid to China, apparently because it heightened the USSR's awareness of risks its alliance with China could involve.

41. This point was stressed in an interview I had with a leading Soviet scholar in Moscow in April 1974.

42. M. S. Kapitsa, in my April 26 interview, stated that the Chinese requested Soviet help in constructing a large number of submarines, but Khrushchev said no, offering instead to help build only a few and proposing that the Soviet navy have access to facilities on the China coast in the event of war, to which Mao reportedly said no. One Chinese official stated in 1964 that in 1958 the Russians had proposed forming a joint Sino-Soviet fleet and constructing a long-range navigational aid station in China (*China Quarterly*, no. 18 [April–June 1964], p. 238). Malcolm Mackintosh, a British specialist on Soviet affairs and Sino-Soviet relations, believes the Russians wanted a joint Sino-Soviet fleet, naval bases in China, and a joint early-warning system (*Sino-Soviet Relations and Arms Control* [East Asian Research Center, Harvard University, 1966], vol. 2, pp. 13–14).

43. In *The Origin and Development of Differences Between the Leadership of the CPSU and Ourselves* (Peking: Foreign Languages Press, 1963), p. 26, the Chinese assert that in 1958 the Soviet Communist party "put forward unreasonable demands designed to bring China under Soviet military control." In a 1973 classified document "Outline of Education for Companies" (see *Issues and Studies*, June 1974, pp. 90–108, and July 1974, pp. 94–105), the Chinese Communists alleged that the Soviets proposed "building long-wave radio stations" in China and "forming a joint fleet" (ibid., p. 99).

44. On the Chinese reaction, see Zagoria, *The Sino-Soviet Conflict*, pp. 280–83; and Gittings, *Survey of the Sino-Soviet Dispute*, pp. 112–15.

45. Soviet scholars stressed this to me in interviews in Moscow in April 1974. The Russians have charged that Chinese actions "which undermine the policy of neutralism, in effect help the imperialist powers to increase their influence in the emancipated countries and especially in India" (Gittings, *Survey of the Sino-Soviet Dispute*, p. 112).

46. See, for example, Khrushchev's statements quoted in Senator Hubert H. Humphrey's article, "My Marathon Talk with Russia's Boss," *Life*, Jan. 12, 1959.

47. In April 1974, one Soviet scholar said to me: "In the early phases of the Great Leap Forward many people even in Russia believed that perhaps Mao had discovered the secret of rapid development. . . . Many people were terribly impressed by the Great Leap at first. Even I was . . . until I discovered what the true facts were."

48. For a general account, from the Soviet perspective, of these frictions, see Koloskov, *The Soviet Union and China*, pp. 77–79. Michael A. Klochko, *Soviet Scientist in Red China* (Praeger, 1964), gives a first-person account.

49. *People's Republic of China: An Economic Assessment*, Compendium of Papers Submitted to the Joint Economic Committee of Congress, 92:2 (GPO, 1972), p. 345.

50. See David A. Charles, "The Dismissal of Marshal P'eng Teh-huai," *China Quarterly*, no. 8 (October–December 1961), pp. 63–76; and Garthoff, *Sino-Soviet Military Relations*, pp. 93 and 168. The charge against P'eng was that he had had illicit relations with Soviet leaders; he probably favored a more compromising approach to Sino-Soviet relations.

51. "Long Live Leninism," *Red Flag*, no. 8 (Apr. 16, 1960); it was later published in book form by Foreign Languages Press, Peking, in 1960.

52. Koloskov, *The Soviet Union and China*, p. 79.

53. Ibid., p. 80.

54. The Chinese stated to the Russians that their "peremptory orders to the Soviet experts to discontinue their work and return to the Soviet Union . . . inflicted enormous losses upon China's socialist construction . . . going completely against communist ethics. . . . Now you have again suggested sending experts to China. To be frank, the Chinese people cannot trust you" ("Letter of the Central Committee of the CPC of February 29, 1964, to the Central Committee of the CPSU," in *Seven Letters Exchanged Between the Central Committees of the Communist Party of China and the Communist Party of the Soviet Union* [Peking: Foreign Languages Press, 1964], p. 27).

55. Eckstein, *Communist China's Economic Growth*, p. 160.

56. Koloskov, *The Soviet Union and China*, p. 80.

57. See *An Economic Assessment*, pp. 347 and 350–51. The decline proceeded relentlessly: $1.65 billion in 1960, $915 million in 1961, $750 million in 1962, $600 million in 1963, $450 million in 1964, $415 million in 1965, $320 million in 1966, $105 million in 1967, $95 million in 1968, $55 million in 1969, and finally $45 million in 1970.

58. For general background, see Boorman and others, *Moscow-Peking Axis*, especially chap. 4; Clubb, *China and Russia*, especially chaps. 1–7; and the sources cited in n. 131, below.

59. See Dennis J. Doolin, *Territorial Claims in the Sino-Soviet Conflict: Documents and Analysis* (Stanford, Calif.: Hoover Institution, 1965), p. 43; and Tai Sung An, *The Sino-Soviet Territorial Dispute* (Westminster, 1973), p. 68.

60. See *The Origin and Development of Differences; Peking Review*, Sept. 13, 1963, p. 18; and Tai, *The Sino-Soviet Territorial Dispute*, p. 77. Some reports indicate that, after the Chinese loosened exit requirements, large numbers of minority people in Sinkiang applied to the Soviet consulate in Kulja to enter the Soviet Union; the Chinese tried to stop the flow, accusing the Russians of subversion.

61. Ibid.

62. Doolin, *Territorial Claims*, p. 28.

63. Ibid., pp. 29–31; and *A Comment on the Statement of the Communist Party of the USA* (Peking: Foreign Languages Press, 1963), pp. 13–14.

64. *Tass International Service* (Moscow), Jan. 3, 1964; and Doolin, *Territorial Claims*, pp. 33–36.

65. Hinton, *The Bear at the Gate*, p. 17.

66. *Sekai Shuho* (Tokyo), Aug. 11, 1964; and Doolin, *Territorial Claims*, pp. 42–44.

67. Gittings, *Survey of the Sino-Soviet Dispute*, p. 160.

68. See Dallin, *Diversity in International Communism;* and Griffith, *The Sino-Soviet Rift.*

69. See ibid.; and Hudson, Lowenthal, and MacFarquhar, *The Sino-Soviet Dispute*, pp. 157 ff. For a succinct analysis of the Sino-Soviet dispute's effect on other Communist parties in the 1960s and early 1970s, see Joseph C. Kun, "Peking and World Communism," *Problems of Communism*, vol. 23, no. 6 (November–December 1974), pp. 34–43.

70. See William E. Griffith, *Albania and the Sino-Soviet Rift* (M.I.T. Press, 1963).

71. *The Origin and Development of Differences*, p. 42.

72. See Charles Neuhauser, *Third World Politics: China and the Afro-Asian People's Solidarity Organization, 1957–1967*, Monograph 27 (East Asian Research Center, Harvard University, 1968).

73. "Statement by the Spokesman of the Chinese Government," *Peking Review*, Sept. 6, 1963, p. 14.

74. Gittings, *Survey of the Sino-Soviet Dispute*, pp. 176–78.

75. *Peking Review*, Nov. 8, 1963, p. 20.

76. In memorandums sent to the Soviet government on Sept. 3 and Oct. 20, 1962, and June 6, 1963, China stated that it hoped the Russians "would not infringe on China's sovereign rights and act for China in assuming an obligation to refrain from manufacturing nuclear weapons" ("Statement by the Spokesman of the Chinese Government," Aug. 15, in *Peking Review*, Aug. 16, 1963, p. 15).

77. See the Chinese government statement of July 21, *Peking Review*, Aug. 2, 1963, p. 7.

78. A leading Soviet scholar analyzed the choice in these terms in an interview with me in April 1974.

79. See *Seven Letters Exchanged Between the Central Committees* and the articles cited in n. 81, below.

80. *Peking Review*, July 26, 1963, pp. 28–46.

81. A comprehensive statement of the Chinese position is contained in "A Proposal Concerning the General Line of the International Communist Movement," June 14, in *Peking Review*, July 26, 1963, pp. 10–26. The nine joint articles by the editorial department of *People's Daily* and *Red Flag* commenting on the Soviet "Open Letter" began with "The Origin and Development of the Differences between the Leadership of the C.P.S.U. and Ourselves" on Sept. 6, 1963, and ended with "On Khrushchev's Phoney Communism and Its Historical Lessons for the World," on July 14, 1964; for texts of the articles, see *Peking Review*, Sept. 13, 20, and 27, Oct. 25, Nov. 22, and Dec. 20, 1963, and Feb. 7, Apr. 3, and July 17, 1964.

82. See A. Doak Barnett, *China after Mao* (Princeton University Press, 1967).

83. Harold C. Hinton, *China's Turbulent Quest: An Analysis of China's Foreign Relations Since 1945* (Macmillan, 1970), pp. 128 ff.

84. See Donald S. Zagoria, *Vietnam Triangle: Moscow, Peking, Hanoi* (Pegasus, 1967); and Gittings, *Survey of the Sino-Soviet Dispute*, pp. 260–70.

85. See Robert A. Scalapino, "The Cultural Revolution and Chinese Foreign Policy," *Current Scene*, vol. 6, no. 13 (Aug. 1, 1968), pp. 1–15; Melvin Gurtov, "The Foreign Ministry and Foreign Affairs in the Chinese Cultural Revolution," in Thomas W. Robinson, ed., *The Cultural Revolution in China* (University of California Press, 1971); and Hinton, *China's Turbulent Quest*, pp. 127–62.

86. Interviews in September 1974 with U.S. government specialists on Sino-Soviet relations.

87. Although Soviet writers attempt to analyze Peking's "errors" in political and social terms, they generally fall back on pejorative accusations of "adventurism," "chauvinism," "hegemonism," and "recklessness." See, for example, Kapitsa, *The CPR: Two Decades—Two Policies*, chaps. 3 and 5; and I. Alexandrov, *Where is Peking Heading?* (Moscow: Novosti Press Agency Publishing House, 1973).

88. Peking charged that Moscow had stepped up its "military provocations over China's air space," asserting these were "in support of its atrocities of aggression against Czechoslovakia" (*Peking Review*, Sept. 20, 1968, p. 41). For the immediate Chinese reactions, see Hinton, *The Bear at the Gate*, pp. 21–24.

89. See Thomas W. Robinson, *The Sino-Soviet Border Dispute: Background, Development, and the March 1969 Clashes*, RM-6171-PR (Santa Monica, Calif.: Rand Corp., 1970). For Peking's version, see Neville Maxwell, "The Chinese Account of the 1969 Fighting at Chenpao," *China Quarterly*, no. 56 (October–December 1973), pp. 730–39.

90. Lin Piao, "Report to the Ninth National Congress of the Communist Party of China," *Peking Review*, Apr. 30, 1969, p. 33.

91. *Peking Review*, Aug. 22, 1969, pp. 4–5.

92. Victor Louis, a Soviet journalist with close links to the authorities in Moscow, conveyed the most highly publicized implied threats (*New York Times*, Sept. 18, 1969). For other threats, see Hinton, *The Bear at the Gate*, pp. 29–30.

93. See *Issues and Studies*, July 1969, pp. 5–8.

94. *Peking Review*, Oct. 10, 1969, pp. 3–4.

95. The figures were $45 million in 1970, $154 million in 1971, $255 million in 1972, $272 million in 1973, $285 million in 1974, and $310 million in 1975. For 1970–73 figures, see Central Intelligence Agency, *People's Republic of China: International Trade Handbook*, A 73-29 (CIA, 1973), p. 10, and A (ER) 74-63 (CIA, 1974), p. 10; for 1974–75 figures, see CIA, "China: Trade, by Area and Country, 1974–75" (CIA, 1976; processed).

96. *Peking Review*, Jan. 25 and Mar. 29, 1974, p. 3 and p. 5; the Chinese claimed that the helicopter was captured during one of several landings on Chinese territory for espionage activities.

97. See *New York Times* and *Washington Post*, Nov. 8, 1974, and *Foreign Broadcast Information Service* [*FBIS*] *Daily Report: People's Republic of China* [*PRC*], Nov. 7, 1974, p. A1.

98. See *New York Times*, Dec. 28, 1975.

99. Hinton, *The Bear at the Gate*, analyzes this approach perceptively; see especially pp. 27 ff.

100. *China Quarterly*, no. 76 (September 1976), p. 687

101. *Washington Star*, Oct. 19, 1976.

102. Alexander O. Ghebhardt, "The Soviet System of Collective Security in Asia," *Asian Survey*, vol. 13, no. 12 (December 1973), pp. 1075-91, argues that the Soviets had both the United States and China in mind.

103. The Soviet-Indian treaty, signed Aug. 29, 1971, was particularly important; the text is in *Survival*, vol. 13, no. 10 (October 1971), pp. 351-53.

104. For background, see Michael Pillsbury, *SALT on the Dragon: Chinese Views of the Soviet American Strategic Balance*, P-5457 (Santa Monica, Calif.: Rand Corp., 1975). John Newhouse argues that the Sino-Soviet conflict provided the impetus, or pretext, for Soviet deployment of an ABM system around Moscow, for the timing of the opening of the SALT negotiations in 1969, for the Russians' July 1970 feeler to the Americans about possible agreement on "joint action" to deter or punish any other nuclear power taking "provocative actions"; he argues that the results "hastened the sluggish pace" of Moscow's détente policy (*Cold Dawn: The Story of SALT* [Holt, Rinehart and Winston, 1973], pp. 164-65, 189, 220, 222-23, and 237).

105. The ideological factor is stressed in most studies written in the 1960s; see Brzezinski, *The Soviet Bloc*; Dallin, *Diversity in International Communism*; Griffith, *The Sino-Soviet Rift*; Schram, *The Political Thought of Mao Tse-tung*; and Benjamin I. Schwartz, *Communism and China: Ideology in Flux* (Harvard University Press, 1968).

106. Lowenthal used this as the subtitle of his study, *World Communism*.

107. For a succinct analysis of the issues involved, see Dallin, *Diversity in International Communism*, introduction.

108. By 1966, Chinese media were describing the thought of Mao Tse-Tung as "the apex of contemporary Marxism" (Barnett, *China after Mao*, pp. 41-43). The party constitution adopted on Apr. 4, 1969, asserts: "Mao Tse-tung thought is Marxism-Leninism of the era in which imperialism is heading for total collapse and socialism is advancing to worldwide victory" (*Peking Review*, Apr. 30, 1969, p. 36). On the question of authority, see Schwartz, *Communism and China*, pp. 130 ff.

109. See Liparit Kyuzajhyan, *The Chinese Crisis: Causes and Character* (Moscow: Novosti Press Agency Publishing House, 1967); A. Malukhin, *Militarism—Backbone of Maoism* (Moscow: Novosti Press Agency Publishing House, 1970); O. Leonidov, *Peking Divisionists* (Moscow: Novosti Press Agency Publishing House, 1971); and N. Simoniya, *Peking and National Liberation Struggle* (Moscow: Novosti Press Agency Publishing House, 1970). The Soviet press and radio express similar views, as do Soviet officials and scholars, though they are less polemical in conversation than in print.

110. For years, Soviet as well as Chinese leaders, while arguing for im-

proved state relations, have asserted that their ideological differences are "irreconcilable"; see Brezhnev's report to the Soviet Twenty-fourth Party Congress, cited in Hinton, *The Bear at the Gate*, p. 73.

111. See, for example, Brezhnev's June 7, 1969, speech to the Moscow international Communist conference, in *Current Digest of the Soviet Press*, vol. 21, no. 23, especially pp. 10–12. In a speech in Tashkent, Brezhnev called for state relations on the basis of the "principles of coexistence" (*FBIS Daily Report: Soviet Union*, Sept. 25, 1973, pp. R1–R13). Edgar Snow, "A Conversation with Mao Tse-tung," *Life*, Apr. 30, 1971, p. 48, quotes Mao as saying that the existing Sino-Soviet ideological differences are "irreconcilable," but that state problems can be settled "eventually." Chou En-lai, in "Report to the Tenth Congress of the Communist Party of China" (*Peking Review*, Sept. 7, 1973, p. 23), reiterated China's ideological opposition to Moscow and accused it of hegemonial aims, but stated that "controversy on matters of principle should not hinder the normalization of relations between the two states on the basis of the Five Principles of Peaceful Coexistence." For a summary of worldwide divisions among Communist parties, see David E. Albright, "The Soviet Model: A Development Alternative for the Third World?" in Henry W. Morton and Rudolf L. Tökés, eds., *Soviet Politics and Society in the 1970s* (Free Press, 1974), pp. 299–339.

112. From 1952 on, during the early years of the First Five-Year Plan, a primary slogan of China's development program was "Learn from the Soviet Union."

113. This was a recurring theme in interviews I had with Russians in the Soviet Union in April 1974 as well as in conversations with visiting Soviet scholars and diplomats in the United States.

114. See, for example, the Alexander Solzhenitsyn letter to Soviet leaders in 1973 in which he speaks of the "dynamic pressure of a billion Chinese against our thus far undeveloped Siberian lands" and warns of the danger of war with China which he said could be "the largest and bloodiest in the history of mankind" (*New York Times*, Mar. 3, 1974). Andrei Almarik in "Will the Soviet Union Survive Until 1984?" predicted Russia's defeat in any conflict with China; Sino-Soviet war "will start sometime between 1975 and 1980," he said (C. L. Sulzberger, ibid., Dec. 17, 1969). Yevgeny Yevtushenko in a March 1969 poem asserted that "the new Mongol Khans [the Chinese] have bombs in their quivers" and declared that "if we are dragged into war ... we shall have enough warriors for the new battle of Kulikova" (ibid., Mar. 23, 1969).

115. "On Khrushchev's Phoney Communism and Its Historical Lessons for the World" (*Peking Review*, July 17, 1964) is one of the most important as well as comprehensive Maoist indictments of the Soviet Union. Even more revealing of Mao's personal views are his unpublished speeches collected in *Long Live Mao Tse-tung's Thought*. (See "Miscellany of Mao Tse-tung Thought, 1949–1968, pts. 1 and 2," *Joint Publications Research Service*, JPRS 61269-1 and -2, Feb. 20, 1964. See also Schram, *Chairman Mao Talks to the People*, pp. 82–83, 99, 103, 128–30, 181, 191, and 287; and Jerome Ch'en, *Mao* [Prentice-Hall, 1969].)

116. Khrushchev's dictated memoirs are extremely revealing, even though

lapses of memory and selective, self-serving rationalizations clearly affect his account. Khrushchev declared that Mao "has played politics with Asian cunning ... [and] has always been a master at concealing his true thoughts and intentions. ... I was always on my guard with him" (*Khrushchev Remembers*, pp. 461–62). For his views on Mao, see ibid., especially pp. 367–73 and 461–79; and *Khrushchev Remembers: The Last Testament*, especially pp. 235–89, 307–11, and 329.

117. See *Khrushchev Remembers: The Last Testament*, pp. 291–92.

118. See Schram, *The Political Thought of Mao;* and Schram and Carrère d'Encausse, *Marxism and Asia.*

119. Michael Pillsbury, *Patterns of Chinese Power Struggles: Three Models* (paper prepared for the University Seminar on Modern China, Columbia University, Mar. 27, 1974; processed), p. 24, argues that in the "ten big struggles"—the major leadership conflicts within the Chinese Communist party since 1927—"the Soviets have consistently identified contending factions or opinion groups ... and have attempted to influence the outcome in favor of Soviet interests, not always successfully." Several analyses of Chinese purges note evidence of Chinese differences regarding relations with Russia. On the 1959 purge, see Charles, "The Dismissal of Marshal P'eng Teh-huai," especially pp. 65–67 and 75. On the Lo Jui-ch'ing case, see Zagoria, *Vietnam Triangle;* Maury Lisann, "Moscow and the Chinese Power Struggle," *Problems of Communism*, vol. 17, no. 6 (November–December 1969), pp. 32–41; and Uri Ra'anan, "Peking's Foreign Policy 'Debate,' 1965–1966," and Donald Zagoria, "The Strategic Debate in Peking," in Tang Tsou, ed., *China in Crisis*, vol. 2, *China's Policies in Asia and America's Alternatives* (University of Chicago Press, 1968). For interpretations different from those in the latter two studies, see Harry Harding and Melvin Gurtov, *The Purge of Lo Jui-ch'ing: The Politics of Chinese Strategic Planning*, R-548-PR (Santa Monica, Calif.: Rand Corp., 1971), in which it is argued that although Lo did differ with Mao on strategic policy, he did not advocate amelioration of relations with Moscow. Michael Yahuda, "Kremlinology and the Chinese Strategic Debate, 1965–66," *China Quarterly*, no 49 (January–March 1972), pp. 32–75, questions Ra'anan's and Zagoria's basic methodology as well as their conclusions. However, I find their analyses plausible.

Lin Piao, like Liu Shao-ch'i, was charged implicitly with having had "illicit relations" with the Soviet Union (*Survey of China Mainland Press*, Jan. 10–14, 1972, p. 78). What seems likely is that Lin opposed normalization of relations with the United States but did not favor rapprochement with Moscow; see Philip Bridgham, "The Fall of Lin Piao," *China Quarterly*, no. 55 (July–September 1973), p. 446.

In 1974–75, several Chinese articles, written in allegorical, historical terms, indicate that debate continued on whether to make compromises with the Soviet Union or to stand firm; those favoring compromise appeared still to include some Chinese military leaders. See especially "Lo Ssu-ting Discusses Patriotism, National Betrayal," *Red Flag*, in *FBIS Daily Report: PRC*, Nov. 20, 1974, pp. E1–E10, which strongly warns against compromise. In the same issue of *Red Flag,* another article gave counter arguments, asserting that it is a mistake to "overlook the limitations imposed by objective conditions"; this article opposed both "adventurism" and "capitulationism"; see Wu Chen-hsuan, "Correctly Assess the Objective Situation—Some Experiences in Studying Chairman Mao's Military Writings," in ibid., Nov. 21, 1974, pp. E1–E6.

120. Russian officials and scholars whom I interviewed in Moscow in 1974 made significant distinctions in their judgments of the attitudes of key Chinese leaders toward the Soviet Union. Generally, they viewed Kao Kang as strongly pro-Soviet, P'eng Teh-huai as more friendly to Moscow than Mao, Liu Shao-ch'i as generally reasonable and less hostile to Moscow than Mao, and Lin Piao as anti-Soviet but equally anti-American.

121. On Aug. 12, 1975, a major blast appeared in *People's Daily* against persons favoring compromise with Moscow; see An Miao, "Confucianist Capitulationism and Traitor Lin Piao," in *Survey of People's Republic of China Press,* Aug. 22, 1975, pp. 171–80. The return of the Soviet helicopter crew in December (see *New York Times,* Dec. 28, 1975) was interpreted by some as a move by leaders favoring a more compromising approach.

122. As noted in Bridgham, "The Fall of Lin Piao," however, some radicals opposed Mao's U.S. policy in the late 1960s and early 1970s.

123. These judgments are based on interviews in 1974 with U.S. government specialists on Soviet and Sino-Soviet affairs and with scholars specializing on the politics of Moscow's foreign policy, as well as published analyses. I am grateful to Jiri Valenta for information and useful insights on Soviet bureaucratic politics, including many relevant to Moscow's China policy ("Soviet Foreign Policy Decision-Making and Bureaucratic Politics: Czechoslovak Crisis 1968" [Ph.D. dissertation, School of Advanced International Studies, Johns Hopkins University, 1975]). Richard C. Thornton discusses the subject in "The Soviet Union's 'China Policy,' 1949–1972," *Intercollegiate Review,* Winter 1972–73, pp. 99–107, "Soviet Strategy in Asia Since World War II" (paper prepared for the fourth annual Sino-American Conference on Mainland China, Dec. 12–15, 1974; processed), and "Soviet Strategy and the Vietnam War," *Asian Affairs,* no. 4 (March–April 1974), pp. 205–28. Useful analyses of the relationship of internal politics and foreign policy in the Soviet Union include Vernon V. Aspaturian, *Process and Power in Soviet Foreign Policy* (Little, Brown, 1971), especially pts. 4 and 6; Alexander Dallin, "Soviet Foreign Policy and Domestic Politics: A Framework for Analysis," *Journal of International Affairs,* vol. 23, no. 2 (1969), pp. 250–65; and Morton Schwartz, *The Foreign Policy of the USSR: Domestic Factors* (Dickinson, 1975).

124. I obtained useful insights on this aspect of Sino-Soviet interactions from Harry Gelman, who is engaged in a long study of the subject.

125. See Wang Ming, *Lenin, Leninism and the Chinese Revolution* (Moscow: Novosti Press Agency Publishing House, 1970). Wang died in 1974.

126. Gelman argues that the available evidence suggests that Mao strongly supported Khrushchev versus Malenkov. Richard C. Thornton argues that Mao initially supported Malenkov but shifted during 1953–54 to support

Khrushchev ("The Soviet Union's 'China Policy,'" p. 100; and "The Structure of Communist Politics," *World Politics*, vol. 24, no. 4 [July 1972], p. 509). It is possible that Mao supported Malenkov briefly, then Khrushchev during 1954-55 and immediately thereafter, and then anti-Khrushchev Soviet leaders after 1957.

127. Lin Piao in his "Report to the Ninth National Congress," p. 32, stated: "We firmly believe that the proletariat and the broad masses of the people in the Soviet Union... will surely rise and overthrow this clique consisting of a handful of renegades.... I will advise comrades to remain firm in the conviction that the masses of Soviet people and of Party members and cadres are good, that they desire revolution and that revisionist rule will not last long." Wang Ming, in *Lenin, Leninism, and the Chinese Revolution*, published in Moscow with the obvious endorsement of the Soviet party leaders, asserts that "the tragedy and misfortune caused by the 'thought' of Mao Tse-tung, by his activity are a temporary, transient phenomenon.... the defeat of Mao Tse-tung is inevitable.... the time is not far off when Leninism and the cause of socialism will again triumph on Chinese soil" (pp. 26-27). Such statements give each side a basis for accusing the other of trying to subvert and overthrow its leaders.

128. The best general treatment of Sino-Soviet economic relations through the mid-1960s is Eckstein, *Communist China's Economic Growth*. Other useful studies include Cheng Chu-yuan, *Economic Relations Between Peking and Moscow* (Praeger, 1964); and Sidney Klein, *The Road Divides: Economic Aspects of the Sino-Soviet Dispute* (Hong Kong: International Studies Group, 1966). As Sino-Soviet trade declined, so too did U.S. study of Sino-Soviet economic relations; very few studies have tried to estimate future possibilities.

129. M. I. Sladkovskii, a leading specialist on the Chinese economy and director of the Institute of Far Eastern Studies, Academy of Sciences, Moscow, argued this strongly in an interview with me in Moscow on Apr. 16, 1974.

130. Trade figures are from CIA, *People's Republic of China: International Trade Handbook*, A 73-29 (1973) and A(ER) 74-63 (1974), and "China, Trade, By Area and Country."

131. For a comprehensive study of the issues, see Tai Sung An, *The Sino-Soviet Territorial Dispute* (Westminster, 1973). Other useful studies include Doolin, *Territorial Claims in the Sino-Soviet Conflict*; Francis Watson, *The Frontiers of China* (Praeger, 1966); and George N. Patterson, *The Unquiet Frontier: Border Tensions in the Sino-Soviet Conflict* (Hong Kong: International Studies Group, 1966). Chinese views are summarized in official statements; additional details are in Neville Maxwell, "The Chinese Account of the 1969 Fighting at Chen Pao," *China Quarterly*, no. 56 (October–December 1973), pp. 730-39. Soviet views, in addition to official statements, are presented in A. Kruchinin and V. Olgin, *Territorial Claims of Mao Tse-tung: History and Modern Times* (Moscow: Novosti Press Publishing House, [1970]). See also Department of State, Bureau of Intelligence and Research, *China–U.S.S.R. Boundary*, International Boundary Study 64 (1974).

132. For texts of the Chinese statements, see *Peking Review*, May 30 and

Oct. 10, 1969, pp. 3–9 and pp. 3–4. For texts of the Soviet statements, see *Current Digest of the Soviet Press*, Mar. 26–Apr. 1 and July 9, 1969, pp. 3–5 and pp. 9–13; and *Reprints from the Soviet Press* (New York: Compass Publications), vol. 9, no. 2 (July 1969), pp. 50–64. See also C. L. Sulzberger's interview with Chou En-lai, *New York Times*, Oct. 29, 1973.

133. Soviet Foreign Ministry officials used a figure of 20,000 square kilometers in interviews with me in April 1974. An, *The Sino-Soviet Territorial Dispute*, p. 114, uses the figure 12,000 square miles. In 1976, a generally conciliatory Soviet article on Sino-Soviet relations cited 13,000 square miles as the area in dispute (*China Quarterly*, no. 67 [September 1976], p. 687).

134. M. S. Kapitsa, in my April 26, 1974, interview, stated that the Soviet government had officially informed the Chinese government in 1973 that it was prepared to accept the thalweg principle in settling the river borders and that if accepted by both sides this would involve recognizing as Chinese over 400 islands that hitherto had been regarded as Soviet. He also stated categorically that the Soviet government would not give up Hei-hsia-tzu.

135. My interviews with Chinese and Soviet officials suggest that (1) the Chinese regard military withdrawal as a crucial issue (while generally relating this issue to the problem of "disputed areas," they gave the impression that the huge deployment of Soviet troops near China is their basic cause of concern); and (2) the Russians give no indication they are yet prepared to consider any significant withdrawals, even from areas the Chinese label "disputed." The Chinese and Russians also differ on what Kosygin and Chou agreed to in this respect in 1969.

136. The Chinese have used the one million figure for several years. The two million figure used by the Russians is more recent and may simply be their propaganda response to the Chinese propaganda charge; see, for example, *La Stampa* (Turin, Italy), Dec. 13, 1973, in *FBIS Daily Report: Soviet Union*, Jan. 9, 1974, pp. C1 ff. The two million figure was consistently used in my April 1974 interviews in the Soviet Union.

137. Estimates of forces on the border vary depending on the area on both sides of the border considered. The figures I use are based on interviews with Western intelligence specialists on Sino-Soviet affairs in September 1974. No major change has occurred since then. For background, see Thomas W. Wolfe Statement, in *United States–China Relations: A Strategy for the Future*, Hearings before the Subcommittee on Asian and Pacific Affairs of the House Committee on Foreign Affairs, 91:2 (GPO, 1970), pp. 56 ff. For general discussion of Sino-Soviet military affairs, see Garthoff, *Sino-Soviet Military Relations;* and An, *The Sino-Soviet Territorial Dispute*, chap. 4.

138. Chou En-lai warned against "surprise attack" in an Aug. 24, 1973, speech (*Peking Review*, Sept. 7, 1973, p. 24). The Chinese have given publicity to their underground shelter program and from the start of the opening of China to American correspondents have shown outsiders the results; see Seymour Topping, "Air Raid Shelters in City and Valley," in New York Times, *Report from Red China* (New York Times Co., 1971), pp. 32–35.

139. In September 1969, the Soviet press discussed the 1939 Soviet defeat

of Japanese forces at Khalkin-gol, seemingly to warn the Chinese of a possible repeat performance against them (An, *The Sino-Soviet Territorial Dispute*, pp. 136–37). For an account of what happened in the 1930s, see Clubb, *China and Russia*, especially pp. 313–17.

140. See Allen S. Whiting and Sheng Shih-ts'ai, *Sinkiang: Pawn or Pivot?* (Michigan State University Press, 1958).

141. Phillips Talbot, "The President's Letter: Views From Peking," *Asia* (Asia Society newsletter), vol. 3, no. 1 (January–February 1976), p. 2.

Part Two: China and Japan

1. The paucity of Western studies dealing with Sino-Japanese relations since 1949 is striking. It may be due to a tendency to view recent Sino-Japanese relations simply as a corollary of U.S.-China relations. Among the few books focused on Sino-Japanese relations that have been useful in my research for this volume are Leng Shao-chuan, *Japan and Communist China* (Kyoto: Doshisha University Press, 1958), which covers the early years after 1949; and Yoshifusa Beppu, *Development of Japan's Relations with China* (Tokyo: Sano-Shobo, 1973), which covers the period through 1970. One very useful unpublished dissertation is Nathan N. White, "An Analysis of Japan's China Policy under the Liberal Democratic Party, 1955–1970" (Ph.D. dissertation, University of California, Berkeley, 1971; Ann Arbor, Mich.: University Microfilms, 1971).

For broad studies of Chinese foreign policy that discuss Sino-Japanese relations in some detail, see Harold C. Hinton, *Communist China in World Politics* (Houghton Mifflin, 1966); and A. Doak Barnett, *Communist China and Asia: Challenge to American Policy* (Harper for Council on Foreign Relations, 1960), chap. 10.

For general studies of Japan's foreign relations that deal with Sino-Japanese interactions, see Donald C. Hellmann, *Japan and East Asia: The New International Order* (Praeger, 1972); James W. Morley, ed., *Forecast for Japan: Security in the 1970s* (Princeton University Press, 1972); Lawrence Olsen, *Japan in Postwar Asia* (Praeger, 1970); John K. Emmerson, *Arms, Yen and Power: The Japanese Dilemma* (Dunellen, 1971); Frank C. Langdon, *Japan's Foreign Policy* (Vancouver: University of British Columbia Press, 1973); Martin E. Weinstein, *Japan's Postwar Defense Policy, 1947–1968* (Columbia University Press, 1971); and Robert A. Scalapino, *Asia and the Major Powers* (Stanford, Calif.: Hoover Institution on War, Revolution and Peace, and Washington: American Enterprise Institute for Public Policy Research, 1972).

Among the best brief analyses of Sino-Japanese relations that I have found are A. M. Halpern, "The Chinese Communist Approach to Japan, 1957–1963" (1963; processed), and *Peking and the Problem of Japan, 1968–72*, Professional paper 99 (Arlington, Va.: Center for Naval Analyses, 1972); Alice L. Hsieh, "The Strategy and Tactics of Communist China's Policy Toward Japan (1949–1956)" (n.d.; processed); Tang Tsou and T. Najita, "Sino-Japanese Relations in the 1970s" (paper prepared for a conference on Japan's Emerging Role in the International System and Japanese-American Relations in the 1970s–1980s, Sophia University, Tokyo, n.d.; processed); and Paul F. Langer, "Japan's Relations with China—A Look Into the Future," P-3071 (Santa Monica, Calif.: Rand Corp., February 1965; processed).

2. See Edwin O. Reischauer and John K. Fairbank, *East Asia: The Great Tradition* (Houghton Mifflin, 1958 and 1960).

3. See ibid.; and G. B. Sansom, *Japan, A Short Cultural History* (Appleton-Century, 1943).

4. Mary C. Wright, *The Last Stand of Chinese Conservatism: The T'ung-Chih Restoration, 1862–1874* (Atheneum, 1966), analyzes the Chinese response. A good discussion of the contrast is in William W. Lockwood, "Japan's Response to the West, The Contrast with China," *World Politics*, vol. 9, no. 1 (October 1956), pp. 37–54.

5. John King Fairbank, *The United States and China* (Harvard University Press, 1955), p. 167. The political links between Japan and Chinese revolutionaries in this period are discussed in Marius B. Jansen, *The Japanese and Sun Yat-sen* (Harvard University Press, 1954).

6. Japanese expansionism in China is traced in Harold M. Vinacke, *A History of the Far East in Modern Times*, 4th ed. (Crafts, 1941); and Franz H. Michael and George E. Taylor, *The Far East in the Modern World* (Holt, Rinehart and Winston, 1956).

7. See Chow Tse-tung, *The May Fourth Movement: Intellectual Revolution in China* (Stanford University Press, 1960). A revealing personal account by one of the founders of the party is Chang Kuo-t'ao, *The Rise of the Chinese Communist Party* (University Press of Kansas, 1971), especially chap. 1.

8. Lyman P. Van Slyke, *Enemies and Friends: The United Front in Chinese Communist History* (Stanford University Press, 1967), p. 43; and James Pinckney Harrison, *The Long March to Power: A History of the Chinese Communist Party, 1921–72* (Praeger, 1972), p. 232.

9. Chalmers A. Johnson, *Peasant Nationalism and Communist Power: The Emergence of Revolutionary China, 1937–1945* (Stanford University Press, 1962), elaborates this thesis. However, the Communists' reformist policies were also important; they are stressed in Mark Selden, "The Yenan Legacy: The Mass Line," in A. Doak Barnett, ed., *Chinese Communist Politics in Action* (University of Washington Press, 1969), pp. 99–151.

10. This discussion of Sino-Japanese relations in the 1950s relies heavily on Hsieh, "The Strategy and Tactics of Communist China's Policy"; and Barnett, *Communist China and Asia*, chap. 10.

11. If one side were attacked by "Japan or any state allied with it," the other would immediately give assistance (*Sino-Soviet Treaty and Agreements* [Peking: Foreign Languages Press, 1951], pp. 5–8).

12. See Robert A. Scalapino, *The Japanese Communist Movement, 1920–1966* (University of California Press, 1966), pp. 61–64 and 78 ff.; and Rodger Swearingen and Paul Langer, *Red Flag in Japan: International Communism in Action, 1919–1951* (Harvard University Press, 1952), pp. 199 ff.

13. Nikita Khrushchev, *Khrushchev Remembers* (Little, Brown, 1970), pp. 367 ff.

14. "In the Spring of 1951 John Foster Dulles, as a special envoy of President Truman, suggested to Premier Yoshida a U.S.-Japan security treaty and strongly demanded the immediate rearming of Japan" (Shigeharu Matsumoto, "Japan and China: Domestic and Foreign Influences on Japan's Policy," in A. M. Halpern, ed., *Policies Toward China: Views from Six Continents* [McGraw-Hill for Council on Foreign Relations, 1965], p. 127).

15. Barnett, *Communist China and Asia*, pp. 259–60.

16. The complications that the existence of two Chinese governments created in the drafting of the treaty are analyzed in Richard P. Stebbins, *The United States in World Affairs, 1951* (Harper for Council on Foreign Relations, 1952), pp. 207 ff.

17. The texts of the Yoshida and Dulles letters are in *Department of State Bulletin*, Jan. 28, 1952, p. 120.

18. Notes accompanying the treaty specified that it applied only to the "territories which are now or which may hereafter be under the control of" the government in Taipei (see Matsumoto, "Japan and China," p. 130; and Richard P. Stebbins, *The United States in World Affairs, 1952* [Harper for Council on Foreign Relations, 1953], p. 213).

19. For useful discussions of Japanese attitudes toward China, see C. Martin Wilbur, "Japan and the Rise of Communist China," in Hugh Borton and others, *Japan Between East and West* (Harper for Council on Foreign Relations, 1957), pp. 189–239; and Marius B. Jansen, *Japan and Communist China in the Next Decade*, RM62TMP-81 (Santa Barbara, Calif.: General Electric Co., 1962), especially pp. 5–17. For historical background on earlier Japanese attitudes toward China, differentiating varied opinions, see K. H. Kim, *Japanese Perspectives on China's Early Modernization: The Self-Strengthening Movement, 1860–1895* (Center for Chinese Studies, University of Michigan, 1974).

20. The analysis of the period from 1952 on draws on Beppu, *Development of Japan's Relations with China*, pp. 82 ff; and on my study, *Communist China and Asia*, especially pp. 261 ff.

21. The conference resolutions strongly opposed Japanese "remilitarization" and U.S. bases in Japan (New China News Agency [NCNA] releases, Oct. 12, in *Survey of China Mainland Press* [SCMP], Oct. 14–15, 1952, pp. 11–13).

22. See White, "An Analysis of Japan's China Policy," p. 151; and Yang Ching-An (Alexander), "The Japanese Business Interests and Foreign Policy: Sino-Japanese Trade, May 1958–April 1962, A Case Study" (Columbia University, n.d.,; processed), p. 13.

23. See NCNA releases, Jan. 7 and 8 in *SCMP*, Jan. 8 and 9, 1953, p. 1 and pp. 3–4; and Beppu, *Development of Japan's Relations with China*, p. 114.

24. Barnett, *Communist China and Asia*, p. 263.

25. Ibid. See also Beppu, *Development of Japan's Relations with China*, pp. 90 ff., regarding increasing public pressure for promoting trade with China.

26. For the text of the declaration, see NCNA release, Oct. 12, *SCMP*, Oct. 12, 1954, pp. 3–4.

27. See Chou En-lai to Ikuo Oyama, NCNA release, Oct. 9, in *SCMP*, Oct. 10–13, 1953, pp. 19–20; and Kuo Mo-jo's statement to visiting Japanese, NCNA release, Oct. 30, in *SCMP*, Oct. 31–Nov. 1, 1953, pp. 5–6.

28. For data on the 1953–54 developments, see Barnett, *Communist China and Asia*, pp. 264–66.

29. Hatoyama eased the restrictions on Japan-China travel, allowed a trade delegation from Peking to visit Tokyo, and endorsed a private Japanese fishery delegation's trip to China. Nevertheless, the Chinese were very critical of his policy; for negative comments, see NCNA release, Dec. 20, and *People's Daily* editorial, Dec. 30, in *SCMP*, Dec. 21 and 31, 1954, p. 10 and p. 18.

30. George McT. Kahin, *The Asian-African Conference, Bandung, Indonesia, April 1955* (Cornell University Press, 1956), p. 28.

31. For a summary of the agreement, see NCNA release, Apr. 15, in *SCMP*, Apr. 16–18, 1955, pp. 36–42.

32. For the Chinese objectives, see NCNA release, Apr. 2, and for the text of the agreement and its appendix, NCNA release, May 4, in *SCMP*, Apr. 2–4 and May 5, 1955, pp. 7–10 and pp. 4–7.

33. Chou stated that even though Peking rejected the two-Chinas idea and objected to Tokyo's relations with the Nationalists, it was willing to take steps toward normalizing relations (NCNA release, Aug. 17, in *SCMP*, Aug. 18, 1955, pp. 4–5).

34. Barnett, *Communist China and Asia*, pp. 268–69.

35. Halpern, "Chinese Communist Approach to Japan," p. 4.

36. NCNA release, May 8, in *SCMP*, May 11, 1956, p. 27.

37. Beppu, *Development of Japan's Relations with China*, p. 96.

38. For data on Japanese visitors to China, see Chou's June 28 speech, in *Current Background*, no. 395 (July 5, 1956), pp. 1–15; Leng, *Japan and Communist China*, pp. 21–23; Halpern, "Chinese Communist Approach to Japan," p. 4; and Barnett, *Communist China and Asia*, p. 274.

39. Barnett, *Communist China and Asia*, p. 257.

40. For one example of the communiqués, see joint statement of Inejiro Asanuma and Chang Hsi-jo (president of the Chinese People's Institute of Foreign Affairs), NCNA release, Apr. 22, in *SCMP*, Apr. 25, 1957, pp. 48–51. Halpern, "Chinese Communist Approach to Japan," pp. 4–5, talks of China's dealing with the Japanese Socialist party "in the capacity of a shadow government."

41. Kenzo Uchida, "A Brief History of Postwar Japan-China Relations," *Developing Economies*, vol. 9, no. 4 (December 1971), pp. 541–42 and 551. For a general discussion of Sino-Japanese trade relations in the 1950s, see Leng, *Japan and Communist China*.

42. White, "Analysis of Japan's China Policy," pp. 143–44; and Wilbur, "Japan and the Rise of Communist China," pp. 215–17.

43. For discussion of the developments in the Kishi period, see Halpern, "Chinese Communist Approach to Japan," pp. 7–14; Beppu, *Development of Japan's Relations with China*, pp. 102–12; Gene T. Hsiao, "Nonrecognition

and Trade: A Case Study of the Fourth Sino-Japanese Trade Agreement," in Jerome A. Cohen, ed., *China's Practice of International Law: Some Case Studies* (Harvard University Press, 1972); and Barnett, *Communist China and Asia*, pp. 237–38 and 272–80.

44. See Gene T. Hsiao, "The Role of Trade in China's Diplomacy with Japan," in Jerome Alan Cohen, ed., *The Dynamics of China's Foreign Relations*, East Asian Monograph 39 (Harvard University Press, 1970), pp. 41–56; and Hsiao, "Nonrecognition and Trade."

45. See Halpern, "Chinese Communist Approach to Japan," pp. 9–11; and Hsiao, "Nonrecognition and Trade," pp. 16–19.

46. See White, "Analysis of Japan's China Policy," p. 150; Halpern, "Chinese Communist Approach to Japan," pp. 11–14; and Barnett, *Communist China and Asia*, pp. 237–38 and 272–80.

47. It is debatable whether Peking genuinely thought it could help the Japanese Socialists, but there is little question that it wished to pressure Kishi by causing new economic problems (Halpern, "Chinese Communist Approach to Japan," p. 12).

48. The Japanese Socialist and Communist parties increasingly competed for control of labor and other organizations (ibid., p. 18).

49. For discussion of the Chinese campaign against the treaty, see Beppu, *Development of Japan's Relations with China*, pp. 156–64.

50. Uchida, "Brief History of Postwar Japan-China Relations," p. 547.

51. Ibid., pp. 154–55; and Halpern, "Chinese Communist Approach to Japan," pp. 20–21.

52. White, "Analysis of Japan's China Policy," p. 448.

53. See Beppu, *Development of Japan's Relations with China*, pp. 153–55; and Olin L. Wethington, "The Politics of Sino-Japanese Trade: Chou's Four Principles, April 1970" (Columbia University, July 1973; processed), pp. 5–6.

54. For the text of Chou's statement, see *Peking Review*, Sept. 14, 1960, pp. 25–26.

55. Halpern, "Chinese Communist Approach to Japan," p. 26. See also Leng Shao-chuan, "Sino-Japanese Trade," *Law and Policy in International Business*, vol. 5, no. 3 (1973), especially pp. 782–84.

56. Uchida, "Brief History of Postwar Japan-China Relations," p. 547.

57. Halpern, "Chinese Communist Approach to Japan," p. 27; and Leng, "Sino-Japanese Trade," p. 785.

58. See Leng, "Sino-Japanese Trade," p. 803; White, "Analysis of Japan's China Policy," pp. 154–55; and Beppu, *Development of Japan's Relations with China*, p. 218.

59. See George P. Jan, "Japan's Trade with Communist China," *Asian Survey*, vol. 9, no. 12 (December 1969), especially pp. 913–14; and Leng, "Sino-Japanese Trade," pp. 791–92.

60. Leng, "Sino-Japanese Trade," p. 803.

61. Halpern, "Chinese Communist Approach to Japan," pp. 31–32.

62. See Scalapino, *Japanese Communist Movement*, pp. 136 ff.

63. Peking charged that "Hayato Ikeda is in no way second to Nobusuke

Kishi in subservience to the United States and hostility to China" (*Peking Review*, Oct. 18, 1960, pp. 9–11).

64. Lawrence W. Beer, "Some Dimensions of Japan's Present and Potential Relations with Communist China," *Asian Survey*, vol. 9, no. 3 (March 1969), p. 170. See also Beppu, *Development of Japan's Relations with China*, pp. 180–83.

65. Premier Sato stated in August 1965 that although Yoshida's letter was "private" and not legally binding on it, the Japanese government would continue Yoshida's policy (Leng, "Sino-Japanese Trade," p. 792).

66. Scalapino, *Japanese Communist Movement*, pp. 266–76.

67. Uchida, "Brief History of Postwar Japan-China Relations," p. 551.

68. *People's Daily*, Sept. 10, in *Peking Review*, Sept. 15, 1967, p. 32.

69. See text of the communiqué in *Department of State Bulletin*, Dec. 15, 1969, pp. 555–58. In an interview on Dec. 23, 1972, in Peking, Ch'iao Kuan-hua (then vice minister of foreign affairs) stressed that the communiqué had seriously disturbed him and others in Peking, which helps to explain Peking's 1970 campaign against Japanese remilitarization.

70. See text of the communiqué in *Peking Review*, Apr. 10, 1970, pp. 3–5; it charges that "the Japanese reactionaries are now stepping up the fascistization [sic] and militarization of Japan."

71. See Uchida, "Brief History of Postwar Japan-China Relations," p. 551; and Leng, "Sino-Japanese Trade," p. 803.

72. Halpern, *Peking and the Problem of Japan*, pp. 8–9, 17–21, and 27–31.

73. Ibid., pp. 10–11; see also Wethington, "Politics of Sino-Japanese Trade."

74. Leng, "Sino-Japanese Trade," pp. 803 and 794.

75. Such concerns seemed to underlie Ch'iao's comments in his Dec. 23, 1972, interview. See also Ralph Clough, "Sino-Japanese Relations: A New Era?" *Current History*, vol. 65, no. 385 (September 1973); and Halpern, *Peking and the Problem of Japan*, especially pp. 26–27.

76. A Komeito–China–Japan Friendship Association communiqué signed in Peking in 1971 specified these principles and two others: withdrawal of all U.S. troops from the Taiwan area and "restoration" of the rights of the People's Republic of China in the United Nations (text in *Peking Review*, July 9, 1971, pp. 20–21).

77. Gene T. Hsiao, "The Sino-Japanese Rapprochement: A Relationship of Ambivalence," in Gene T. Hsiao, ed., *Sino-American Detente and Its Policy Implications* (Praeger, 1974), p. 165.

78. Ibid., p. 167.

79. For the text, see *New York Times*, Sept. 30, 1972.

80. For the relevant parts of the Potsdam and Cairo agreements, see *A Decade of American Foreign Policy: Basic Documents, 1941–49*, S. Doc. 123, 81:1 (Government Printing Office, 1950), pp. 49 and 22. The Cairo agreement states that "Manchuria, Formosa, and the Pescadores shall be restored to the Republic of China."

81. *Bungei Shunju*, December 1972, cited in Tsou and Najita, "Sino-

Japanese Relations in the 1970s," p. 49. In an interview with Michio Royama, Ohira stated: "Japan is in no position to determine the territorial title legally" (*Tokyo Shimbun*, Oct. 1, in *Daily Summary of Japanese Press*, Oct. 5, 1972, pp. 13–14). For a clear exposition of Japanese official views, see Takakazu Kuriyama, "Some Legal Aspects of the Japan-China Joint Communiqué," *Japanese Annual of International Law*, no. 17 (1973), pp. 42–51.

82. Hisahiko Okazaki, "Japan's Taiwan Relations After Normalization with Peking," in Yung-Hwan Jo, ed., *Taiwan's Future* (Hong Kong: Union Research Institute for Arizona State University, 1974), p. 112. Public opinion supports this; see Douglas H. Mendel, Jr., "Japanese Public Views on Taiwan's Future," *Asian Survey*, vol. 15, no. 3 (March 1975), pp. 215–33.

83. See Kuriyama, "Some Legal Aspects," p. 48. Ohira also stated: "As for the question of the ending of the Japan-ROC Treaty, it is not that a treaty will live or die by one word spoken by me. It is that, as a result of the normalization of Japan-China diplomatic relations, there now remains no room any more for the Japan-ROC Treaty to operate" (*Nihon Keizai*, Oct. 1, in *Daily Summary*, Oct. 4, 1972, p. 18).

84. See David Nelson Rowe, *Informal 'Diplomatic Relations': The Case of Japan and the Republic of China, 1972–1974* (Hamden, Conn.: Shoe String Press for Foreign Area Studies Publications, 1975).

85. *Asahi*, Jan. 27, 1973; see also *Asahi*, Jan. 18, in *Daily Summary*, Jan. 20–23, 1973, pp. 6–7. Takeo Kimura also reported that Chou asserted Ohira had assured the Chinese that the U.S.-Japan security treaty will not apply to Taiwan (*Nihon Keizai*, Jan. 26, in *Daily Summary*, Jan. 26, 1973, pp. 19–20). However, a Japanese diplomat informed me that this was not true, but that Chou stated to the Japanese that in his view the security treaty would not now apply to Taiwan. It was also reported that "Premier Chou En-lai stated that it probably cannot be helped that Japan stays under the umbrella of American nuclear weapons" (ibid.).

86. *Yomiuri*, Mar. 12, 1973, cited in Tsou and Najita, "Sino-Japanese Relations in the 1970s," p. 23. *Yomiuri*, Mar. 25, in *Daily Summary*, Mar. 27, 1973, p. 27, has a slightly different version of Liao's comment.

87. *Kyodo*, Dec. 17, 1973, in *Foreign Broadcast Information Service [FBIS] Daily Report: People's Republic of China [PRC]*, Dec. 18, 1973, p. A1.

88. *Nihon Keizai*, Jan. 12, in *Daily Summary*, Jan. 17, 1974, p. 24.

89. *Asahi*, Aug. 21, in *Daily Summary*, Aug. 24–26, 1974, p. 20.

90. *China Quarterly*, no. 62 (June 1975), pp. 373–74. Chou made this statement to Shigeru Hori, a right-wing Japanese politician.

91. *JETRO China Newsletter*, no. 3 (March 1974), p. 1. Japan External Trade Organization (JETRO) is a government agency.

92. Ibid., no. 10 (April 1976), p. 1. Worldwide inflation and revaluations of the yen made the rise seem greater than it was in real terms.

93. In the fall of 1974, Ryutaro Hasegawa, chairman of the Japan-China Oil Importing Association, stated, on his return from a trip to China, that under favorable conditions China might be able by 1980 to produce 400 million

tons of oil and export 100 million to Japan (*Sankei*, Aug. 16, in *Daily Summary*, Aug. 20, 1974, p. 10). This is an extremely high estimate. A more frequently used estimate of Chinese exports to Japan by 1980 is 50 million tons (see, for example, *Journal of Commerce* [New York], July 16, 1975, p. 1). JETRO's figures vary up to 50 million, but some are considerably lower (*JETRO China Newsletter*, no. 7 [April 1975], pp. 12–17). See also Tatsu Kanbara, "The Petroleum Industry in China," *China Quarterly*, no. 60 (December 1974), pp. 699–719 (his estimate for 1980 exports is 20 million tons); Nicholas Ludlow, "China's Oil," *U.S.-China Business Review*, vol. 1, no. 1 (January–February 1974), pp. 21 ff.: Joseph A. Yager and Eleanor B. Steinberg, *Energy and U.S. Foreign Policy* (Ballinger, 1975), chap. 12; and Ralph N. Clough, "Chinese Oil, Japanese Markets, and U.S. Technology" (Jan. 20, 1975; processed). A conservative figure for possible exports in 1980 would appear to be 20 million tons; however, figures between 35 million and 50 million tons are plausible.

94. *Nikkan Kogyo*, July 11, in *Daily Summary*, July 25, 1974, p. 14. See also *Mainichi*, Feb. 22, in *Daily Summary*, Feb. 28, 1975, p. 6.

95. Sheldon W. Simon, "The Japan-China-USSR Triangle," *Pacific Affairs*, vol. 47, no. 2 (Summer 1974), p. 129.

96. During the first nine months of 1973, in fact, at least 53 Chinese technical teams visited Japan; see *China Trade Reports*, no. 322 (September 1973), cited in Hans Heymann, Jr., *China's Approach to Technology Acquisition: Part III, Summary Observations*, R-1575-ARPA (Santa Monica, Calif.: Rand Corp., 1975), p. 28.

97. See Clough, "Sino-Japanese Relations," p. 110; and Simon, "The Japan-China-USSR Triangle," p. 129.

98. Leng, "Sino-Japanese Trade," p. 796.

99. For the text and an analysis of the agreement, see *JETRO China Newsletter*, no. 3 (March 1974), pp. 9–17.

100. See Gene T. Hsiao, "Prospects for a New Sino-Japanese Relationship," *China Quarterly*, no. 60 (December 1974), pp. 721–27.

101. Ohira's positions, which were leaked to the press, became a cause célèbre; see *Tokyo Shimbun*, Apr. 11, in *Daily Summary*, Apr. 12–15, 1974, pp. 23–24. See also *Tokyo Shimbun*, Apr. 16, in *Daily Summary*, Apr. 20–22, 1974, pp. 21–36.

102. Hsiao, "Prospects for a New Sino-Japanese Relationship," p. 724.

103. The agreement is summarized in *New York Times*, Apr. 21, 1974.

104. For the text of the statement, see NCNA release, Apr. 20, in *Survey of People's Republic of China Press* [SPRCP], Apr. 29–May 3, 1974, pp. 173–74.

105. Simon, "Japan-China-USSR Triangle," p. 138.

106. Fox Butterfield, *New York Times*, Apr. 21, 1974.

107. *Washington Post*, July 9, 1975.

108. For the text, see *Yomiuri*, Nov. 13, in *Daily Summary*, Nov. 20, 1974, pp. 32–34; for comment, see *Tokyo Shimbun*, Nov. 14, in *Daily Summary*, Nov. 16–18, 1974, pp. 3–4.

109. *Mainichi*, Feb. 26, and *Yomiuri*, Mar. 11, in *Daily Summary*, Feb. 28 and March 18, 1975, p. 16 and p. 7. See also *Kyodo*, June 20, in *FBIS Daily Report: Asia and Pacific*, June 20, 1974, p. C1. For extensive background, see Choon-ho Park, "Fishing Under Troubled Waters: The Northeast Asia Fisheries Controversy," *Ocean Development and International Law Journal*, vol. 2, no. 2 (Summer 1974), pp. 93–135.

110. See *China Quarterly*, no. 62 (June 1975), pp. 374–75.

111. *Washington Post*, Aug. 16, 1975.

112. See *Peking Review*, Feb. 8, 1974, p. 3. For other Chinese statements on shelf issues, see ibid., Nov. 27 and Dec. 11, 1970, and Jan. 1, 1971, pp. 8–10, pp. 15–16, and p. 22. For the resulting inhibitions in Japan, see *Yomiuri*, Mar. 15, and *Mainichi*, Mar. 16, in *Daily Summary*, Mar. 25, 1975, p. 1 and p. 3.

113. The issue is discussed in Peter N. Upton, "International Law and the Sino-Japanese Controversy over Territorial Sovereignty of the Senkaku Islands," *Boston University Law Review*, vol. 52, no. 4 (Fall 1972), pp. 763–90; and Choon-ho Park, "Oil Under Troubled Waters: The Northeast Asia Sea-Bed Controversy," *Harvard International Law Journal*, vol. 14, no. 2 (Spring 1973), pp. 212–60, and *Continental Shelf Issues in the Yellow Sea and the East China Sea*, Occasional Paper 15 (Law of the Sea Institute, University of Rhode Island, 1972).

114. *Kyodo*, Oct. 4, in *FBIS Daily Report: PRC*, Oct. 8, 1974, p. A8.

115. See Liao Ch'eng-chih remarks to Japanese visitors, in *Yomiuri*, Mar. 12, 1973 (cited in Clough, "Sino-Japanese Relations," p. 110). See also *Yomiuri*, Mar. 12, in *Daily Summary*, Mar. 23, 1973, p. 20.

116. See Teng Hsiao-p'ing's statement reported in *Nihon Keizai*, Jan. 12, in *Daily Summary*, Jan. 17, 1974, p. 24.

117. Ibid., for the Chinese view.

118. For succinct summaries of the problems, see *China Quarterly*, nos. 63 and 64 (September and December 1975), pp. 593–94 and pp. 799–800.

119. The Russians warned the Japanese on several occasions, and kept doing so in 1976. For example, Foreign Minister Andrei Gromyko, on a visit to Japan in January 1976, reportedly "warned...that Moscow would be forced to 'reconsider' its relations with Tokyo if Japan took political sides with China against Russia" (*New York Times*, Jan. 13, 1976).

120. Wilbur, "Japan and the Rise of Communist China," in Borton and others, *Japan Between East and West*; Jansen, *Japan and Communist China*; and Kim, *Japanese Perspectives*, discuss Japanese attitudes. See also the books on Japan's foreign relations listed in n. 1, and Sadako Ogata, "Japanese Attitude Toward China," *Asian Survey*, vol. 5, no. 8 (August 1965), pp. 389–98; Kan Ori, *Japanese Public Opinion of Sino-Japanese Relations, 1969–72*, Sophia University Research Papers series A-11 (Tokyo, 1972); Chalmers Johnson, "How China and Japan See Each Other," *Foreign Affairs*, vol. 50, no. 4 (July 1972), pp. 711–21; and A. Doak Barnett, "Japanese Views on China," *American Universities Field Staff Report*, ADB-5-54, Apr. 20, 1954. For poll data, see Douglas H. Mendel, Jr., *Japanese People and Foreign Policy: A Study of Public Opinion in Post Treaty Japan* (University of California Press, 1961),

and "Japanese Opinion on Key Foreign Policy Issues," *Asian Survey*, vol. 9, no. 8 (August 1969), pp. 625–39; and *Sankei*, Mar. 25, in *Daily Summary*, Apr. 23, 1975, pp. 11–13.

121. Chou En-lai, commenting about Japan to James Reston, said: "Economic expansionism is bound to bring about military expansionism" (*New York Times*, Aug. 10, 1971). Such views may well still exist.

122. At times, polls have indicated considerable Japanese dislike of China; see Donald C. Hellmann, "Japan's Relations with Communist China," *Asian Survey*, vol. 4, no. 10 (October 1964), pp. 1085–92; and Douglas H. Mendel, Jr., "Japan's Taiwan Tangle," ibid., pp. 1079–84. A 1974 poll (*Sankei*, Nov. 16, in *Daily Summary*, Nov. 28–29, 1974, p. 27) showed that a large majority of the public believed Japan and China will coexist, but it indicated differences on whether it will be on "friendly terms" or "in confrontation." In an October 1974 poll, China rated seventh as the nation most-liked, with 9 percent of the vote, and third as the nation most-disliked, with 13 percent of the vote; the United States ranked second, after Switzerland, as the nation most-liked, with 24 percent of the vote, and fourth, just below China, as the nation most-disliked, with 12 percent of the vote. The Soviet Union was near the bottom of most-liked nations, at eleventh with only 2 percent of the vote, and at the top of most-disliked nations with 32 percent of the vote. In a 1975 poll (*Sankei*, Mar. 25, in *Daily Summary*, Apr. 23, 1975, pp. 11–13) the United States was still the second most-liked nation but now was the third most-disliked; China ranked as the seventh most-liked and fourth most-disliked; the Soviet Union and the Republic of Korea continued to rank as the first and second most-disliked nations. Since 1970 there has been no greater than a 6 percent difference in China's rating as the most-liked and the most-disliked (*Sankei*, Nov. 6, in *Daily Summary*, Nov. 9–11, 1974, p. 24).

123. Marius B. Jansen, "Comments," in Tang Tsou, ed., *China in Crisis*, vol. 2, *China's Policies in Asia and America's Alternatives* (University of Chicago Press, 1968), p. 458.

124. Emmerson, *Arms, Yen and Power*, p. 222.

125. Ibid. See also Hellmann, *Japan and East Asia*, pp. 222–23; and Martin E. Weinstein, "Strategic Thought and the U.S.-Japan Alliance," in Morley, *Forecast for Japan*, pp. 39 and 43.

126. Polls on interest in books, movies, and so on indicate a strong interest in American culture, however.

127. On the roles of Liao and Kuo in Sino-Japanese relations, see Donald W. Klein and Anne B. Clark, *Biographical Dictionary of Chinese Communism, 1921–1965* (Harvard University Press, 1971), pp. 544–50 and 458–65.

128. On the politics of Sino-Japanese relations, see the sources in n. 1 and Frank C. Langdon, "Japanese Liberal Democratic Factional Discord on China Policy," *Pacific Affairs*, vol. 41, no. 3 (Fall 1968), pp. 403–15; Chae-Jin Lee, "Factional Politics in the Japan Socialist Party: The Chinese Cultural Revolution Case," *Asian Survey*, vol. 10, no. 3 (March 1970), pp. 230–43; Sheldon Simon, "Maoism and Inter-Party Relations: Peking's Alienation of the Japan Communist Party," *China Quarterly*, no. 35 (July–September 1968), pp. 40–

57; Hellmann, "Japan's Relations with Communist China"; and Mendel, "Japan's Taiwan Tangle," pp. 1073–84. My judgments are based also on numerous conversations with Japanese and U.S. Japan specialists.

129. The *JETRO China Newsletter*, initiated in June 1973, is an indispensable source of trade information. See also White, "Analysis of Japan's China Policy"; Beppu, *Development of Japan's Relations with China;* Uchida, "Brief History of Postwar Japan-China Relations"; Hsiao, "Role of Trade" and "Nonrecognition and Trade"; Wethington, "Politics of Sino-Japanese Trade"; Leng, "Sino-Japanese Trade"; Yang Ching-An, "The Policy-Making Process in Japan's Policy Toward the People's Republic of China: The Making of the Liao-Takasaki Trade Agreement of November 1962" (Ph.D. dissertation, Columbia University, 1969); Jan, "Japan's Trade with Communist China," pp. 900–18; David G. Brown, "Chinese Economic Leverage in Sino-Japanese Relations," *Asian Survey*, vol. 12, no. 9 (September 1972), pp. 753–71; and Hsiao, "Prospects for a New Sino-Japanese Relationship," pp. 720–49.

130. *JETRO China Newsletter*, no. 10 (April 1976), p. 1. See also Central Intelligence Agency, *People's Republic of China: International Trade Handbook* (CIA, 1975), pp. 1 and 6; and "China: Trade, by Area and Country, 1974–75" (CIA, 1976; processed).

131. For overall Chinese trade figures, see CIA, *People's Republic of China: International Trade Handbook*, A(ER) 74-63 (CIA, 1974), especially p. 9. For overall Japanese trade figures, see Japan Tariff Association, for the Ministry of Finance, *Summary Report, Trade of Japan*, vol. 238 (November 1975), pp. 1–2. Figures for both China and Japan are f.o.b. for exports and c.i.f. for imports.

132. See CIA, *People's Republic of China: International Trade Handbook*, A(ER) 74-63 (1974), pp. 5 and 16.

133. *Economic Information File: Japan 1973*, pp. 53 and 148. In some years, China has bought over 80 percent of Japan's fertilizer exports (*JETRO China Newsletter*, no. 4 [July 1974], p. 4).

134. *JETRO China Newsletter*, no. 4 (July 1974), p. 1, and no. 7 (April 1975), pp. 1 and 24.

135. Ibid., no. 7 (April 1975), p. 27.

136. See n. 93.

137. The drop in Chinese petroleum exports in early 1976 was due to declining Japanese interest as well as to production problems in China. Chinese oil has a high wax content, and the Japanese are reluctant to make the investments required to refine large quantities imported from China unless the Chinese assure them of uninterrupted supplies. Long-term agreements at attractive prices may, therefore, be a prerequisite for large increases in exports of Chinese oil to Japan.

138. Observers disagree on how their competition in Asia will affect relations between China and Japan. See n. 151 below.

139. *Asahi*, Jan. 18, 1973, cited in Tsou and Najita, "Sino-Japanese Relations in the 1970s," p. 39.

140. *Yomiuri*, Jan. 19, in *Daily Summary*, Jan. 23, 1973, pp. 16–17.

141. Selig S. Harrison, *Washington Post*, Mar. 4, 1973. This was one article in a series by Harrison.

142. Ibid., Feb. 25, 1973.

143. *The Summary Trade Report of Japan* (Tokyo: Japan Tariff Association for Ministry of Finance, 1973), pp. 33–36; figures on Japan's trade with Brunei, Burma, Indonesia, Khmer (Cambodia), Laos, Malaysia, the Philippines, Singapore, Thailand, Timor, and the Republic of Vietnam were compiled by Thomas Rohback (Japanese statistics on trade with Southeast Asia often include South Korea, Taiwan, Hong Kong, India, Pakistan, Sri Lanka, and other countries not included in Western calculations). All calculations are based on f.o.b. export prices and c.i.f. import prices.

144. Harrison, *Washington Post*, Feb. 25, 1973. See also *New York Times*, Jan. 4, 1974.

145. For 1972 and 1973 figures, see news release RECN-75, Department of State, Bureau of Public Affairs, Office of Media Service, Oct. 23, 1973. For 1974 figure, see *Nihon Keizai*, Apr. 1, in *Daily Summary*, Apr. 4, 1974, p. 24.

146. Harrison, *Washington Post*, Feb. 25, 1973.

147. *Nihon Keizai*, May 12, in *Daily Summary*, May 21, 1974, p. 15. See also Franz Michael and Gaston J. Sigur, *The Asian Alliance: Japan and United States Policy* (New York: National Strategy Information Center, 1972), pp. 44–47.

148. A leading Japanese economist, Saburo Okita, estimates that Japan's trade with "Southeast Asia" (as defined by the Japanese) was roughly a third of its total trade a decade ago, is about a quarter now, and may drop to about a fifth in 1980 (Harrison, *Washington Post*, Feb. 25, 1973). The trend in the narrowly defined Southeast Asia area is about the same as in the broader area.

149. Statistics are from CIA, *People's Republic of China: International Trade Handbook*, A(ER) 74-63 (1974), p. 10, and A 73-29 (1973), p. 10; and Thomas R. Kershner, *China and Southeast Asia: The Anomalies of Trade, Aid, and Politics*, Asian Studies Occasional Paper 4 (Southern Illinois University, 1972); the 1970 figures are from the 1973 handbook, all others from the 1974 edition.

150. Based on discussions with Franklin B. Weinstein, who has been conducting a study of Japan's recent impact on Southeast Asia.

151. Views on future Sino-Japanese relations differ widely. Hellmann, *Japan and East Asia*, foresees intense rivalry; Ross Terrill, in Ian Wilson, ed., *China and the World Community* (Sydney and London: Angus and Robertson, 1973), sees a potential for rivalry. Harrison, in the 1973 *Washington Post* series, foresees increasingly close cooperation; Derek Davies, editor of *Far Eastern Economic Review*, expressed a similar view to me in 1974. Discussing the "Japanese love-hate syndrome regarding China," Shinkichi Eto, "Japan and China—A New Stage?" *Problems of Communism*, vol. 21, no. 6 (November–December 1972), p. 17, states that if economic competition "should become unexpectedly severe," or other conflicts of interest develop, "Japanese attitudes toward China could grow exceedingly negative." Harrison cites

examples of very optimistic Japanese views and conciliatory Chinese views. However, the Chinese have also attacked Japan's economic expansion (see "Japanese Monopoly Capital Steps up Economic Expansion in Southeast Asia," *Peking Review*, Oct. 8, 1971, pp. 18–20). The Russians fear Sino-Japanese cooperation. For example, a broadcast, revealing Russia's concern, alleged that many Southeast Asians believe "that if a Japanese-Chinese rapprochement occurs, the two countries may jointly try to seek hegemony in Asia." The broadcast emphasized that "Japan possesses great economic potential and is carrying out financial and trade infiltration into Southeast Asian countries. China has abundant natural resources and large manpower and is continuously strengthening its military might while stepping up subversive activities against Southeast Asian countries. Therefore, one can imagine what would happen if these two countries are united. Japanese industry's high technical level may be used by Peking to improve its rocketry and nuclear arsenal to attack Southeast Asian countries anytime" (Radio Peace and Progress, Moscow, June 21, in *FBIS Daily Report: Soviet Union*, June 23, 1975, p. C2).

152. See Upton, "International Law"; and Park, "Oil Under Troubled Waters" and *Continental Shelf Issues*.

153. The basic Chinese position is outlined in Foreign Ministry statement of Dec. 30, 1971, in *Peking Review*, Jan. 7, 1972, pp. 12–14; for additional statements, see *Peking Review*, Jan. 1 and May 7, 1971, p. 22 and pp. 14–15.

154. See, especially, Park, "Oil Under Troubled Waters," p. 250; and Upton, "International Law," p. 768.

155. Upton, "International Law," p. 781.

156. On a few issues, China has defined its own positions; see Chinese working papers, submitted to the UN Committee on the Peaceful Uses of the Sea-Bed and the Ocean Floor Beyond the Limits of National Jurisdiction: "Working Paper on Sea Area Within the Limits of National Jurisdiction," A/AC.138/SC.II/L.34, July 16, 1973; "Working Paper on General Principles for the International Sea Area," A/AC.138/SC.I/L.25, Aug. 2, 1973; and "Working Paper on Marine Scientific Research," A/AC.138/SC.III/L.42, July 19, 1973.

157. See Park, *Continental Shelf Issues;* and Donald R. Allen and Patrick H. Mitchell, "The Legal Status of the Continental Shelf of the East China Sea." *Oregon Law Review*, vol. 51 (Summer 1972), pp. 789–812.

158. See NCNA, Dec. 28, 1970, and Apr. 3, 1974, in *FBIS Daily Report: PRC*, Dec. 29, 1970, and Apr. 4, 1974, p. A6 and p. A5. See also n. 112 above.

159. See discussion on Taiwan and Korea in pt. 3, p. 231 ff., and sources cited in pt. 3, n. 186, and pt. 4, n. 64.

160. See Tsou and Najita, "Sino-Japanese Relations in the 1970s," p. 50.

161. The text is in *Collective Defense Treaties*, prepared for the House Committee on Foreign Affairs, 91:1, rev. ed. (GPO, 1969), pp. 82–84.

162. *Asahi*, Oct. 1, in *Daily Summary*, Oct. 3, 1972, p. 24.

163. *Asahi*, Nov. 8, in *Daily Summary*, Nov. 10, 1972, p. 20, reports the "unified view" of the Tanaka government: "The Taiwan Clause set forth the

recognition of the top leaders of Japan and the U.S. at the time in 1969. Since then, the situation surrounding Taiwan has changed, and the possibility of armed conflict arising has disappeared. In the light of this background, the recognition has also changed."

164. *Nikkan Kogyo*, July 11, in *Daily Summary*, July 25, 1974, p. 14. The *New York Times*, Apr. 25, 1974, cites the figure $2.5 billion (see *China Quarterly*, no. 59 [July–September 1974], p. 650).

165. *Sankei*, Feb. 1, in *Daily Summary*, Feb. 7, 1975, p. 6, gives the figures for the first 11 months of 1974 as follows: Japanese exports to Taiwan, over $2 billion; Japanese imports from Taiwan, $770 million.

166. Harrison, *Washington Post*, Feb. 25 and 26, 1973. *Nihon Keizai*, Feb. 14, in *Daily Summary*, Feb. 15, 1974, p. 25, reported that Japanese investment (presumably direct investment) in Taiwan was $45 million in 1973. In 1974 the rate of investment decreased. *Sankei*, Feb. 1, in *Daily Summary*, Feb. 7, 1975, p. 6, reported that in January–October 1974, "there were 45 cases of investment in Taiwan from our country . . . amounting to a total of $3,430,000, way below the actual results in the same period of the preceding year—67 cases amounting to $33,570,000."

167. Harrison, *Washington Post*, Feb. 26, 1973.

168. Based on my interviews with other countries' diplomats and U.S. government officials during 1974 and 1975, and with People's Republic of China diplomats during 1975. During late 1974 and early 1975, such Chinese hints ended. In the wake of the changes that occurred in Vietnam in early 1975, there were more, although the Chinese then made it clear that they intended to back up the North Korean political positions strongly, in the United Nations and elsewhere. In 1976, they ended again.

169. Prime Minister Takeo Miki stressed this in his August 1975 meeting with President Gerald Ford; Korea was the major item on the agenda of that meeting. See *New York Times*, Aug. 7, 1975, and *Washington Post*, Aug. 13, 1975.

170. Harrison, *Washington Post*, Feb. 27, 1973.

171. For general background on security issues in the region, see Ralph N. Clough, *East Asia and U.S. Security* (Brookings Institution, 1975); Fred Greene, *Stresses in U.S.-Japanese Security Relations* (Brookings Institution, 1975), and *U.S. Policy and the Security of Asia* (McGraw-Hill for Council on Foreign Relations, 1968).

172. For background on Japan's security, see Weinstein, *Japan's Postwar Defense Policy*; Morley, *Forecast for Japan*; Emmerson, *Arms, Yen and Power*; Hellmann, *Japan and East Asia*; and Paul F. Langer, *Japanese National Security Policy—Domestic Determinants*, R-1030-15A (Santa Monica, Calif.: Rand Corp., 1972).

173. Weinstein, *Japan's Postwar Defense Policy*, p. 123.

174. Japan Defense Agency, *Defense of Japan*, Japan Defense Agency, 1973, p. 5.

175. Ibid., p. 2. The *New York Times*, Jan. 12, 1975, reported that the

government had adopted a $4.4 billion budget for 1975 (this amounted to 6.3 percent of the operating budget and was an increase of 21 percent over the previous year).

176. Japan Defense Agency, *Defense of Japan*, p. 6.

177. Figures are from Japan Defense Agency, "Japan's Fourth Five-Year Defense Plan" ([1973]; processed), p. 10.

178. Hisao Iwashima, "Trends in Peace Research and Military Studies in Japan" (paper prepared for the 1972 convention of the International Studies Association, Dallas, Texas; processed), p. 5.

179. See text of the interview in *New York Times*, Aug. 10, 1971.

Part Three: China and the United States

1. For a survey of American writings on the history of U.S. relations with East Asia, including Sino-American relations, see Ernest R. May and James C. Thomson, Jr., eds., *American-East Asian Relations: A Survey* (Harvard University Press, 1972). For background on interactions between China and the outside world, and on American policy toward East Asia, in the pre-Communist period, see: John K. Fairbank, ed., *The Chinese World Order: Traditional China's Foreign Relations* (Harvard University Press, 1968); John K. Fairbank, *Trade and Diplomacy on the China Coast* (Harvard University Press, 1953), and *China's Response to the West* (Atheneum, 1963); Earl Swisher, *China's Management of the American Barbarians: A Study of Sino-American Relations, 1841–1861, With Documents* (New Haven: Far Eastern Association, 1953); Immanuel C. Y. Hsu, *China's Entrance Into the Family of Nations: The Diplomatic Phase, 1858–1880* (Harvard University Press, 1960); Hosea Ballou Morse, *The International Relations of the Chinese Empire*, 3 vols. (London: Longmans, Green, 1910); Werner Levi, *Modern China's Foreign Policy* (University of Minnesota Press, 1953); Tyler Dennett, *Americans in Eastern Asia* (Macmillan, 1922); A. Whitney Griswold, *The Far Eastern Policy of the United States* (Harcourt, Brace, 1938); Foster Rhea Dulles, *China and America: The Story of Their Relations since 1789* (Princeton University Press, 1941); Paul Clyde, *The Far East* (Prentice-Hall, 1958); Akira Iriye, *Across the Pacific: An Inner History of American-East Asian Relations* (Harcourt, Brace and World, 1967); Dorothy Borg, *American Policy and the Chinese Revolution, 1925–28* (Macmillan, 1947); Herbert Feis, *The Road to Pearl Harbor* (Princeton University Press, 1950); and Warren I. Cohen, *America's Response to China: An Interpretive History of Sino-American Relations* (Wiley, 1971).

On Sino-American relations during World War II, see Tang Tsou, *America's Failure in China, 1941–50* (University of Chicago Press, 1963); Herbert Feis, *The China Tangle: The American Effort in China from Pearl Harbor to the Marshall Mission* (Princeton University Press, 1953); C. F. Romanus and R. Sutherland, *U.S. Army in World War II: The China-Burma-India Theater*, 3 vols. (U.S. Department of the Army, 1953, 1956, 1959); Barbara Tuchman, *Stillwell and the American Experience in China, 1911–45* (Macmillan, 1971); John S. Service, *The Amerasia Papers: Some Problems in the History of U.S.-China Relations*, Research Monograph (Center for Chinese Studies, University of California, 1971); and John Paton Davies, Jr., *Dragon by the Tail* (Norton, 1972).

Documentary material on U.S.-China relations during and immediately after World War II is available in the "white paper" of the Department of State, *United States Relations with China, With Special Reference to the Period 1944-49*, Publication 3573, Far Eastern Series 30 (Government Printing Office, 1949); in Joseph W. Esherick, ed., *Lost Chance in China: The World War II Despatches of John S. Service* (Random House, 1974); in *The Amerasia Papers: A Clue to the Catastrophe of China*, prepared for the Senate Committee on the Judiciary, 91:1, 2 vols. (GPO, 1970); and, most important, in the volumes covering U.S.-China relations, through the year 1949, of Department of State, *The Foreign Relations of the United States* (GPO, annual).

2. Department of State, *U.S. Relations with China*, p. xv.

3. Ibid., p. xi.

4. Y. C. Wang, *Chinese Intellectuals and the West, 1872-1949* (University of North Carolina Press, 1966), appendix, cited in John K. Fairbank, *China Perceived: Images and Policies in Chinese-American Relations* (Knopf, 1974), p. 99.

5. See Griswold, *Far Eastern Policy of the United States*, chap. 2; and Department of State, *U.S. Relations with China*, pp. 1-5.

6. Department of State, *U.S. Relations with China*, chap. 1.

7. Ibid., p. 19.

8. Ibid., pp. 28-33; and Feis, *China Tangle*, especially chaps. 2-7.

9. This involvement is the major theme of Tsou, *America's Failure in China*; Feis, *China Tangle*; and Tuchman, *Stillwell*.

10. John K. Fairbank places special emphasis on the differences between the Chinese and the American perspectives; see *Trade and Diplomacy; China's Response to the West; China Perceived; China: The People's Middle Kingdom and the U.S.A.* (Belknap Press of Harvard University Press, 1967); and *Chinese-American Interactions* (Rutgers University Press, 1975). For examples of Chinese views from opposing ideological positions, see Chiang Kai-shek, *China's Destiny* (Roy Publishers, 1947); and Hu Sheng (a leading Chinese Communist propagandist), *Imperialism and Chinese Politics* (Peking: Foreign Languages Press, 1955).

11. See Dennett, *Americans in Eastern Asia*, pp. 128 ff. American naval intimidation helped to overcome Chinese reluctance.

12. Department of State, *U.S. Relations with China*, pp. 7-8.

13. Although the origins of this nationalism can be traced back at least to the 1890s, it increased during World War I and was focused on Japan as a result of the Twenty-One Demands, but was also directed against the Western powers because of their acquiescence to Japanese demands at Versailles. See Chow Tse-tsung, *The May Fourth Movement: Intellectual Revolution in Modern China* (Harvard University Press, 1960).

14. See George Kennan, *American Diplomacy, 1900–1950* (University of Chicago Press, 1951), who argues that a basic cause of U.S. problems was a tendency, on one hand, to accept involvements with few "inhibitions" (attributable, he argues, to "emotional complexes") and an unwillingness, on the other, to operate on the basis of "power realities" (pp. 53–54); he asserts that "sentimentality toward the Chinese" shaped U.S. policy. Tsou, *America's Failure in China*, charges that the United States did not back its words or pursue its interests and goals with appropriate power.

15. Tsou, *America's Failure in China*, p. 9.

16. Some two hundred Soviet "volunteer" airmen flew Soviet planes in aid of the Nationalist defense effort in the late 1930s, and more than a hundred Soviet airmen were lost; see O. Edmund Clubb, *China and Russia: The Great Game* (Columbia University Press, 1971), p. 310.

17. See works on World War II cited in n. 1 above, and Theodore H. White and Annalee Jacoby, *Thunder Out of China* (Sloane, 1946).

18. See, for example, the statement by a liberal Chinese editorialist in A. Doak Barnett, *China on the Eve of Communist Takeover* (Praeger, 1963), pp. 22–24.

19. In April 1946, Mao Tse-tung stated to the American correspondent Anna Louise Strong: "As you know, both Hitler and his partners, the Japanese warlords, used anti-Soviet slogans for a long time as a pretext for enslavement of the people at home and aggression against other countries. Now the U.S. reactionaries are acting in exactly the same way" (*Selected Works of Mao Tse-tung* [Peking: Foreign Languages Press, 1961], vol. 4, p. 98). On Aug. 18, 1949, he stated: "The war to turn China into a U.S. colony, a war in which the United States of America supplies the money and guns and Chiang Kai-shek the men to fight for the United States and slaughter the Chinese people, has been an important component of the U.S. imperialist policy of world-wide aggression since World War II" (ibid., p. 433).

20. This judgment is based in part on my observation, as a reporter and scholar during 1947–48, of rural and urban areas in every major region of the country under Nationalist control. American visitors to Communist-held areas encountered relatively little anti-American feeling among ordinary people. During the half year I spent under Communist rule in Peking in 1949, the new government made a deliberate effort to foster anti-Americanism.

21. John K. Fairbank notes, "All in all, the white peril in the 1850s in China became a good deal more sinister than the yellow peril of the 1900s in America" (*The United States and China* [Harvard University Press, 1955], pp. 134–35). Frederick Wakeman, Jr., discusses xenophobia in south China in the mid-nineteenth century in *Strangers at the Gate: Social Disorder in South China, 1839–1861* (University of California Press, 1966), pp. 54 ff. Xenophobia was a powerful force in the Boxer uprising of 1900, in the Nationalists' rise to power in 1927, and in many other populist movements. Latent or manifest, it continues in varying forms and degrees.

22. Steven Goldstein, "The View from Yenan: Chinese Communist Per-

spectives on International Relations, 1937–1941" (preliminary draft of Ph.D. dissertation, Columbia University, 1975; processed), concludes (p. 241) that a "dichotomous Leninist view ... was the central factor which informed the CCP's strategic image" of world affairs in the 1930s, and that this "image would posit that more often than not there would be a confrontation of *all* the revolutionary forces of the world and *some* members of the imperialist camp," in "an interaction of forces whose ultimate loyalty was to one or another of the two camps," even though there would not always necessarily be a confrontation between *all* revolutionary forces and *all* reactionary forces. The Chinese later had more flexible, united-front views. James Reardon-Anderson, "Yenan: The Foreign Policy of Self-Reliance" (preliminary draft of Ph.D. dissertation, Columbia University, 1975; processed), argues that in the mid-1940s the Chinese Communists' flexibility was such that it suggested the possibility of long-term Sino-American cooperation rather than the inevitability of two-camp confrontation. This, however, is debatable. As early as 1948, Liu Shao-ch'i, then second-ranking party leader, stated bluntly: "The world today has been divided into two mutually antagonistic camps ... the world imperialist camp ... [and] the world anti-imperialist camp. ... To remain neutral or sitting on the fence is impossible" (Union Research Institute, *Collected Works of Liu Shao-ch'i, 1945–1957* [Hong Kong: Union Research Institute, 1969], p. 140).

23. On the origins and evolution of Chinese united-front policies, see Lyman P. Van Slyke, *Enemies and Friends: The United Front in Chinese Communist History* (Stanford University Press, 1967). Goldstein, "The View from Yenan," illuminates the development of Chinese Communist united-front approaches toward the Western powers in the late 1930s.

24. See Van Slyke, *Enemies and Friends*, pp. 48 ff.; and Gregor Benton, "The 'Second Wang Ming Line' (1935–38)," *China Quarterly*, no. 61 (March 1975), pp. 61–94.

25. Mao's concepts are discussed in detail in Goldstein, "The View from Yenan," pp. 240 ff.

26. The term *basic national policy* was applied to fundamental principles, and *flexibility* to foreign policy (ibid., p. 254).

27. Edgar Snow, *Red Star Over China*, rev. ed. (Grove, 1968), p. 103.

28. *Selected Works of Mao Tse-tung*, vol. 2 (1965), pp. 443–44.

29. See Kenneth E. Shewmaker, *Americans and Chinese Communists, 1927–1945: A Persuading Encounter* (Cornell University Press, 1971).

30. For an account of this mission by its head, see David D. Barrett, *Dixie Mission: The United States Army Observer Group in Yenan, 1944*, Research Monograph (Center for Chinese Studies, University of California, 1970). For diplomatic reports from the mission, see Service's dispatches in Department of State, *U.S. Relations with China; Esherick, Lost Chance in China; The Amerasia Papers: A Clue;* and Department of State, *Foreign Relations of the United States, 1944*, vol. 6, *China* (1967).

31. Department of State, *Foreign Relations of the United States, 1944*, vol. 6, *China* (1967), p. 730.

32. *The Amerasia Papers*, vol. 1, p. 796.

33. Department of State, *Foreign Relations of the United States, 1945*, vol. 7, *The Far East, China* (1969), pp. 273–74.

34. Ibid., p. 209. See also, Barbara Tuchman, "If Mao Had Come to Washington: An Essay in Alternatives," *Foreign Affairs*, vol. 51, no. 1 (October 1972), pp. 44–64.

35. Tung Pi-wu, a second-level leader.

36. See, for example, Department of State, *Foreign Relations of the United States, 1944*, vol. 6, *China* (1967), pp. 618–22.

37. This is a major theme in Reardon-Anderson, "Yenan."

38. Ibid., pt. 5, p. 58.

39. Ibid., pp. 1–26.

40. A succinct summary of Marshall's mission is in Department of State, *U.S. Relations with China*, chap. 5, pp. 127–229; the detailed record is in the relevant volumes of Department of State, *Foreign Relations of the United States*. Reardon-Anderson analyzes Chinese reactions in "Yenan," pt. 7.

41. See Marshall's Jan. 7, 1947, statement to the President, in Department of State, *U.S. Relations with China*, pp. 686–89.

42. John F. Melby, adviser to Marshall, reported this to Allen S. Whiting; see Whiting's testimony in *United States–China Relations: A Strategy for the Future*, Hearings before the Subcommittee on Asian and Pacific Affairs of the House Committee on Foreign Affairs, 91:2 (GPO, 1970), p. 179.

43. See Boris Koloskov, *The Soviet Union and China: Friendship or Alienation?* (Moscow: Novosti Press Agency Publishing House, 1971), pp. 11–13.

44. See Vladimir Dedijer, *Tito* (Simon and Schuster, 1953), p. 322; Milovan Djilas, *Conversations with Stalin* (Harcourt, Brace and World, 1962), pp. 182–83; and Stuart Schram, ed., *Chairman Mao Talks to the People* (Pantheon, 1974), p. 191.

45. Some months before the formal end of the Marshall mission, when the Communists were again engaged in military conflict with the Nationalists, Mao called for a "war of self-defense" to "smash Chiang Kai-shek's offensive" (*Selected Works of Mao Tse-tung*, vol. 4, p. 89). On Sept. 29, 1946, in an interview with the American correspondent A. T. Steele, he said, "I doubt very much that the policy of the U.S. government is one of 'mediation'." He added that "the policy . . . is to use the so-called mediation as a smoke-screen for strengthening Chiang Kai-shek in every way" (ibid., p. 109).

46. Department of State, *U.S. Relations with China*, p. 712.

47. See Tsou, *America's Failure in China*, chaps. 11 and 12.

48. Tsou, ibid., p. 441, labels it a process combining "partial withdrawal" and "limited assistance."

49. These conversations are described in Seymour Topping, *Journey Between Two Worlds* (Harper and Row, 1972), pp. 83–86; and Robert M. Blum, *The United States and Communist China in 1949 and 1950: The Question of*

Rapprochement and Recognition, prepared for the Senate Committee on Foreign Relations, 93:1 (GPO, 1973).

50. Stuart's May 11, 1949, dispatch to the secretary of state, cited in Blum, *The United States and Communist China,* p. 8; see also John Leighton Stuart, *Fifty Years in China: The Memoirs of John Leighton Stuart, Missionary and Ambassador* (Random House, 1954), p. 247.

51. Department of State, *U.S. Relations with China,* p. xvi.

52. See the text of President Truman's Jan. 5 statement, in *Department of State Bulletin,* Jan. 16, 1950. See the text of Acheson's Jan. 12 statement, in ibid., Jan. 23, 1950, p. 113.

53. See Richard P. Stebbins, *The United States in World Affairs, 1950* (Harper for Council on Foreign Relations, 1951), p. 195. A useful general account of this period is in Frederick B. Williams, "The Origins of the Sino-American Conflict, 1949–1952" (1973; processed).

54. Union Research Institute, *Collected Works of Liu Shao-ch'i, 1945–1957,* p. 140.

55. *Selected Works of Mao Tse-tung,* vol. 4, pp. 370–71.

56. See the text in ibid., pp. 411–24.

57. Ibid., p. 442.

58. Union Research Institute, *Collected Works of Liu Shao-ch'i, 1945–1957,* pp. 178–79.

59. For text, see *Sino-Soviet Treaty and Agreements* (Peking: Foreign Languages Press, 1951), pp. 5–8.

60. *Department of State Bulletin,* Jan. 23, 1950, p. 119.

61. See Blum, *The United States and Communist China;* Topping, *Journey Between Two Worlds;* and Donald S. Zagoria, "Mao's Role in the Sino-Soviet Conflict," *Pacific Affairs,* vol. 47, no. 2 (Summer 1974), pp. 139–53, and "Choices in the Postwar World (2): Containment of China," in Charles Gati, ed., *Caging the Bear: Containment and the Cold War* (Bobbs-Merrill, 1974), pp. 109–27. Barbara Tuchman, in "If Mao Had Come to Washington," pp. 44–64, argues, similarly, about an opportunity lost in January 1945 when the idea of a trip to Washington by Mao and Chou was raised.

62. Topping, *Journey Between Two Worlds,* was the first to bring this fact to light; see also Blum, *The United States and Communist China.*

63. Topping, *Journey Between Two Worlds,* indicates there may have been feelers about a trip as early as April, but there is no evidence of a definite invitation until June 28.

64. A Soviet China specialist stated this in a conversation with me in Moscow in April 1974.

65. *People's China,* May 16, 1950, p. 4.

66. In his letter transmitting the white paper to President Truman, Acheson said future U.S. policy would be influenced by "the degree to which the Chinese people come to recognize that the Communist regime serves not their interests but those of Soviet Russia" (Department of State, *U.S. Relations with China,* pp. xvi–xvii). In his Jan. 12, 1950, speech, he declared, "The Soviet

Union is detaching the northern provinces" from China; "we must not undertake to deflect from the Russians to ourselves the righteous anger, and the wrath, and the hatred of the Chinese people which must develop" (*Department of State Bulletin*, Jan. 23, 1950, p. 115). This line became more extreme after Chinese intervention in the Korean War. Dean Rusk, then assistant secretary of state, declared on May 18, 1951: "The independence of China is gravely threatened" by the Russians; "we do not recognize the authorities in Peiping for what they pretend to be. The Peiping regime may be a colonial Russian government—a Slavic Manchukuo on a larger scale. It is not the Government of China. It does not pass the first test. It is not Chinese" (ibid., May 28, 1951, p. 847).

67. Truman declared that "in these circumstances the occupation of Formosa by Communist forces would be a direct threat to the security of the Pacific area.... The determination of the future status of Formosa must await the restoration of security in the Pacific, a peace settlement with Japan, or consideration by the United Nations"; see his June 27, 1950, statement in ibid., July 3, 1950, pp. 5–6.

68. The minutes on the June 1950 meetings (Department of State memorandums of June 25, 26, and 27, 1950), at which the President discussed these issues with his top advisers, have recently been declassified and released; I am grateful to Morton H. Halperin for providing me copies. Significantly, a memorandum dated June 14 from General Douglas MacArthur was read at the start of the first meeting; it argued that it was essential for the United States to keep Taiwan out of Communist hands. There was fairly quick agreement with Acheson's proposal that the U.S. fleet should be sent to prevent attacks either way across the Taiwan Strait. Acheson stated that the United States "should not tie up" with Chiang Kai-shek, but that he thought "the future status of Taiwan might be determined by the UN"; the President said "he wished consideration given to taking Formosa back as part of Japan and putting it under MacArthur's Command," but no decision was made to do this, and Acheson emphasized that it would be "undesirable that we should get mixed up in the question of the Chinese administration of the Island." The President later stated that "we needed to lay a base for our action in Formosa." The primary considerations were military. Dean Rusk has stated, in interviews with me and others, that the decisions regarding Taiwan were motivated by a genuine fear of broad Communist expansion. It is plausible to believe, however, that domestic political considerations were also very important; President Truman needed to get support for U.S. action in Korea from American military commanders, the Pentagon, and Republican congressmen who had been urging that the United States defend Taiwan. Doubtless the decision to reopen the question of Taiwan's legal status was also motivated by the need, as the President put it, to "lay a basis for our action in Formosa." Nowhere, however, is there evidence of sober, thorough consideration of the potential long-run political consequences for U.S. relations with China.

69. This is thoroughly discussed in Allen S. Whiting, *China Crosses the*

Yalu: The Decision to Enter the Korean War (Macmillan, 1960). The Chinese made clear that they were prepared, if necessary, to risk a U.S. nuclear attack, but they probably counted on the Soviet alliance to deter such action.

70. The war is analyzed in detail in David Rees, *Korea: The Limited War* (Penguin, Pelican, 1970).

71. *Current Background*, no. 36 (Dec. 5, 1950).

72. See Dean Acheson, *Present at the Creation: My Years in the State Department* (Norton, 1969), pp. 422–25, 471–77, and 514–20. The Chinese could not know, however, how much MacArthur's views were out of line with U.S. policy.

73. On this campaign, see Richard L. Walker, *China Under Communism: The First Five Years* (Yale University Press, 1955), pp. 91 ff. The Communists also mounted a major campaign accusing the United States of engaging in "germ warfare."

74. From *Shih-shih Shou-ts'e* [Current affairs handbook], quoted in *Current Background*, no. 32 (Nov. 29, 1950).

75. Among the most useful studies of Sino-American relations since 1949 are Foster Rhea Dulles, *American Policy Toward Communist China: The Historical Record: 1949–1969* (Crowell, 1972); Kenneth T. Young, *Negotiating with the Chinese Communists: The United States Experience, 1953–1963* (McGraw-Hill for Council on Foreign Relations, 1968); J. H. Kalicki, *The Pattern of Sino-American Crises* (Cambridge, England: Cambridge University Press, 1975); Sheldon Appleton, *The Eternal Triangle? Communist China, the United States and the United Nations* (Michigan State University Press, 1961); Willard L. Thorp, ed., *The United States and the Far East*, 2nd ed. (Prentice-Hall, 1962); Roderick MacFarquhar and others, *Sino-American Relations, 1949–1971* (Praeger, 1972); Williams, "Origins of the Sino-American Conflict"; Robert Blum, *The United States and China in World Affairs* (McGraw-Hill for Council on Foreign Relations, 1966); Robert P. Newman, *Recognition of Communist China?* (Macmillan, 1961); A. T. Steele, *The American People and China* (McGraw-Hill for Council on Foreign Relations, 1966); Richard Moorsteen and Morton Abramowitz, *Remaking China Policy: U.S.-China Relations and Governmental Decisionmaking* (Harvard University Press, 1971); A. Doak Barnett, *A New U.S. Policy Toward China* (Brookings Institution, 1971); Fred Greene, *U.S. Policy and the Security of Asia* (McGraw-Hill for Council on Foreign Relations, 1968); Alexander Eckstein, ed., *China Trade Prospects and U.S. Policy* (Praeger for National Committee on United States–China Relations, 1971); and Gene T. Hsiao, ed., *Sino-American Detente and Its Policy Implications* (Praeger, 1974).

Useful chronologies and documentation are in Congressional Quarterly, *China and U.S. Far Eastern Policy, 1945–1966* (Congressional Quarterly Service, 1967), and *China and U.S. Foreign Policy*, 2nd ed. (Congressional Quarterly, Inc., 1973).

Congressional hearings that contain valuable material are *United States Policy Toward Asia*, Hearings before the Subcommittee on the Far East and the Pacific of the House Committee on Foreign Affairs, 89:2 (GPO, 1966); *U.S. Policy with Respect to Mainland China*, Hearings before the Senate Committee on Foreign Relations, 89:2 (GPO, 1966); *United States–China Relations: A Strategy for the Future*, Hearings before the Subcommittee on Asian and Pacific Affairs of the House Committee on Foreign Affairs, 91:2 (GPO, 1970); *United States–China Relations*, Hearings before the Senate Committee on Foreign Relations, 92:1 (GPO, 1971); *United States Relations with the People's Republic of China*, Hearings before the Senate Committee on Foreign Relations, 92:1 (GPO, 1972); *The New China Policy: Its Impact on the United States and Asia*, Hearings before the House Committee on Foreign Affairs, 92:2 (GPO, 1972); *United States–China Relations: The Process of Normalization of Relations*, Hearings before the Subcommittee on Investigations of the House Committee on International Relations, 94:1 and 2 (GPO, 1976); and *United States–Soviet Union–China: The Great Power Triangle*, Hearings before the Subcommittee on Future Foreign Policy Research and Development of the House Committee on International Relations, 94:1 and 2 (GPO, 1976).

76. For comprehensive statements of U.S. policy toward China in this period, see Dulles's June 28 speech on "Our Policies Toward China" (press release, Department of State, Public Service Division, series S, no. 58, June 28, 1957), in which he labeled Communist rule in China "a passing and not a perpetual phase"; and the State Department memorandum, "United States Policy Regarding Non-Recognition of Communist China," to all diplomatic missions (press release, Department of State, no. 459, Aug. 11, 1958).

77. See Greene, *U.S. Policy and the Security of Asia*, pt. 2.

78. Allen S. Whiting, "Statement," in *The Economics of National Priorities*, Hearings before the Subcommittee on Priorities and Economy in Government of the Joint Economic Committee of Congress, 92:1 (GPO, 1971), pp. 448–52.

79. See "Foreign Minister Chou En-lai's Statement on U.S.–Chiang Kai-shek 'Mutual Security Treaty,'" in *Oppose U.S. Occupation of Taiwan and 'Two China's' Plot* (Peking: Foreign Languages Press, 1958), pp. 18–27.

80. See Rees, *Korea*, pt. 3, pp. 289 ff.

81. Ibid., p. 417.

82. Young, *Negotiating with the Chinese Communists*, p. 24.

83. For background, see Melvin Gurtov, *The First Vietnam Crisis: Chinese Communist Strategy and United States Involvement, 1953–54* (Columbia University Press, 1967); and King C. Chen, *Vietnam and China, 1938–1954* (Princeton University Press, 1969).

84. The conference, and China's role in it, are discussed in ibid., and in Robert F. Randle, *Geneva 1954: The Settlement of the Indochina War* (Princeton University Press, 1969).

85. Edgar Snow, *The Other Side of the River: Red China Today* (Random House, 1961), pp. 94–95.

86. On the 1954 offshore islands crisis, see Tang Tsou, "The Quemoy Imbroglio: Chiang Kai-shek and the United States," *Western Political Quar-*

terly, vol. 12, no. 4 (December 1959), pp. 1075–91; and Harold Hinton, *Communist China in World Politics* (Houghton Mifflin, 1966), pp. 258 ff.

87. See A. Doak Barnett, *Communist China and Asia: Challenge to American Policy* (Harper for Council on Foreign Relations, 1960), p. 411.

88. For Chinese statements reflecting this concern, see *Important Documents Concerning the Question of Taiwan* (Peking: Foreign Languages Press, 1955).

89. George McT. Kahin, *The Asian-African Conference* (Cornell University Press, 1956), pp. 28–29; see also A. Doak Barnett, "Chou En-lai at Bandung, Chinese Communist Diplomacy at the Asian-African Conference," and "Asia and Africa in Session, Random Notes on the Asian-African Conference," *American University Field Staff Reports,* ADB-4-55 and ADB-5-55, May 4 and 18, 1955.

90. July 30, 1955, speech, in *Current Background,* no. 342 (Aug. 3, 1955).

91. This discussion relies on Young, *Negotiating with the Chinese Communists,* the best source on the talks.

92. Ibid., pp. 55–56.

93. Ibid., p. 52.

94. Ibid., pp. 76–77 and 116 ff.

95. For analyses of the offshore island crisis in 1958, see Tsou, "The Quemoy Imbroglio"; Morton H. Halperin and Tang Tsou, "United States Policy Toward the Offshore Islands," *Public Policy,* vol. 15 (1966); Morton H. Halperin and Tang Tsou, "The 1958 Quemoy Crisis," in Morton H. Halperin, ed., *Sino-Soviet Relations and Arms Control* (M.I.T. Press, 1967), pp. 265–303; Tang Tsou, "Mao's Limited War in the Taiwan Strait," *Orbis,* vol. 3, no. 3 (Fall 1959), pp. 332–50; Allen S. Whiting, "New Light on Mao: Quemoy 1958, Mao's Miscalculations," *China Quarterly,* no. 62 (June 1975), pp. 263–70; John R. Thomas, "The Limits of Alliance: The Quemoy Crisis of 1958," in Raymond L. Garthoff, ed., *Sino-Soviet Military Relations* (Praeger, 1966), pp. 114–49; Melvin Gurtov, "The Taiwan Strait Crisis Revisited, Politics and Foreign Policy in Chinese Motives," *Modern China,* vol. 2, no. 1 (January 1976), pp. 49–103; and Young, *Negotiating with the Chinese Communists,* pp. 137 ff. There are still differing interpretations of this crisis.

96. By 1957 the American-sponsored system of trade restrictions directed against China had begun gradually to erode as other major trading nations started to reduce their restrictions. The U.S. position on the China seating issue in the United Nations did not weaken seriously, however, until the 1960s.

97. See Young, *Negotiating with the Chinese Communists,* pp. 221 ff.

98. Ibid., pp. 278–79.

99. Ibid., pp. 238–46 and 252–68. For analysis of President Kennedy's approach to China policy, see Roger Hilsman, *To Move a Nation: The Politics of Foreign Policy in the Administration of John F. Kennedy* (Dell, Delta, 1968), pp. 302–57; and James C. Thomson, Jr., "On the Making of U.S. China Policy, 1961–69: A Study of Bureaucratic Politics," *China Quarterly,* no. 50 (April–June 1972), pp. 221–43.

100. See Theodore C. Sorensen, *Kennedy* (Harper and Row, Bantam, 1966), pp. 750–51; and Arthur M. Schlesinger, Jr., *A Thousand Days: John F. Kennedy in the White House* (Houghton Mifflin, 1965), pp. 479–84. Chinese Nationalist opposition to U.S. moves favoring admission of Outer Mongolia to the United Nations, and Peking's conflict with India in 1962, also helped to deter U.S. initiatives. Kennedy continued to view the Chinese as "tough," in "the Stalinist phase," and threatening (Sorensen, *Kennedy*, p. 750).

101. The Chinese Communist press adopted a hostile attitude toward Kennedy from the start. Confidential Chinese Communist publications did too; the People's Liberation Army's classified "Bulletin of Activities" stated on Apr. 25, 1961: "The smell of gunpowder is more evident in Kennedy's administration than in Eisenhower's, for it is more reactionary, treacherous, elusive and deceitful" (J. Chester Cheng, ed., *The Politics of the Chinese Red Army: A Translation of the Bulletin of Activities of the People's Liberation Army* [Stanford, Calif.: Hoover Institution, 1966], p. 486). In a conversation I and others had with Vice Foreign Minister Ch'iao Kuan-hua on Dec. 23, 1972, he still expressed very hostile attitudes toward Kennedy and asserted that Peking never took seriously the Kennedy administration's hints about the possibility of a more flexible U.S. China policy.

102. Thomson, "On the Making of U.S. China Policy," discusses the Johnson period; see especially p. 241.

103. Young, *Negotiating with the Chinese Communists*, p. 231.

104. See n. 153 below.

105. Young, *Negotiating with the Chinese Communists*, pp. 261–63.

106. The background is discussed in A. M. Halpern and H. B. Fredman, *Communist Strategy in Laos*, RM-2561 (Santa Monica, Calif.: Rand Corp., 1960). The U.S. approach to Laos is discussed in Hilsman, *To Move a Nation;* Schlesinger, *A Thousand Days;* Sorensen, *Kennedy;* and Young, *Negotiating with the Chinese Communists.* The Chinese approach is analyzed in Arthur Lall, *How Communist China Negotiates* (Columbia University Press, 1968).

107. I have benefited from Allen S. Whiting's analysis of the 1962 period, in "U.S.-Chinese Political Relations" (paper prepared for a conference on the foreign policy of Communist China, Puerto Rico, Jan. 4–8, 1970; processed).

108. Allen S. Whiting, "How We Almost Went to War with China," *Look*, Apr. 29, 1969, pp. 76–79.

109. See Donald S. Zagoria, *Vietnam Triangle: Moscow, Peking, Hanoi* (Pegasus, 1967).

110. Young, *Negotiating with the Chinese Communists*, pp. 268–69.

111. Franz Schurmann and Orville Schell, eds., *The China Reader: Communist China, Revolutionary Reconstruction and International Confrontation, 1949 to the Present* (Random House, 1967), p. 553.

112. For valuable background, see Marvin Kalb and Bernard Kalb, *Kissinger* (Little, Brown, 1974), pp. 216–83 (based partly on interviews with Kissinger); Allen S. Whiting, "U.S.-Chinese Political Relations," and statements in *United States–China Relations: A Strategy for the Future*, Hearings, pp. 178–82, and in *United States Relations with the People's Republic of*

China, Hearings, pp. 194–204; Barnett, *A New U.S. Policy Toward China;* Congressional Quarterly, *China and U.S. Foreign Policy;* Jerome Alan Cohen, "China and the United States: When Will the 'Normalization' of Relations Be Completed?" in Francis O. Wilcox, ed., *China and the Great Powers* (Praeger, 1974), pp. 65–84; *The New China Policy*, Hearings; and Hsiao, ed., *Sino-American Detente and Its Policy Implications.*

113. See the text in *Peking Review*, Nov. 29, 1968, p. 31.

114. Whiting, "U.S.-Chinese Political Relations," p. 30.

115. Nixon's article, "Asia After Viet Nam" (*Foreign Affairs*, vol. 46, no. 1 [October 1967], pp. 111–25), revealed the views he held on China policy in the period just before his election. His order for a reexamination of U.S. policies was in National Security Study Memorandum no. 14, Feb. 1, 1969 (John P. Leacacos, "Kissinger's Apparat," *Foreign Policy*, no. 5 [Winter 1971–72], p. 14). (One source indicates the date of the memorandum was Feb. 5; perhaps it was distributed on that date.) Many officials had long favored a broad policy review and many options had already been carefully examined.

In early 1969 Nixon and Kissinger also consulted with specialists outside the government, and I participated in the first of their meetings on April 24, 1969, when five academic specialists on Asia met first with Kissinger and then with the President. (I had suggested such a meeting to Kissinger in December 1968, and, at his request, Edwin O. Reischauer and I sent him memorandums in early January outlining views on U.S. policy toward China and Asia.) The discussion focused on possible new directions in China policy. The President did not reveal his views but hinted that he favored change.

116. Kalb and Kalb, *Kissinger*, especially pp. 222–25 and 233–38.

117. See, for example, Secretary of State Rogers's news conference, Apr. 7, *Department of State Bulletin*, Apr. 28, 1969, p. 361; and Under Secretary of State Elliott L. Richardson's speech in ibid., Sept. 22, 1969, p. 26.

118. See *United States Foreign Policy, 1969–1970: A Report of the Secretary of State*, Department of State publication 8575 (GPO, 1971), pp. 36–37. For a transcript of Nixon's Guam press conference, see Richard Nixon, *Public Papers of the Presidents of the United States, 1969*, no. 279, "Informal Remarks in Guam with Newsmen," July 25, 1969 (GPO, 1971).

119. Kalb and Kalb, *Kissinger*, p. 225.

120. See *Peking Review*, special issue, May 8, 1970, on this conference.

121. Edgar Snow, *The Long Revolution* (Random House, Vintage, 1973), p. 172; this was first published in *Life*, Apr. 30, 1971.

122. Kalb and Kalb, *Kissinger*, p. 237.

123. On Apr. 14, 1971, Chou En-lai stated to the American table tennis team: "You have opened a new page in the relations of the Chinese and American people. I am confident that this beginning again of our friendship will certainly meet with the majority support of our two peoples" (*New York Times*, Apr. 15, 1971).

124. Secretary Rogers at his April 23 news conference declared: "We would hope that this opening is not the last. We would hope it was the begin-

ning of new relations between our two countries. I think it was the Prime Minister of the People's Republic of China who said that it was a new page in our relations. We would hope that it becomes a new chapter, that there will be several pages to follow" (*Department of State Bulletin*, May 10, 1971, p. 595).

125. See Kalb and Kalb, *Kissinger*, pp. 237 ff. The text of Nixon's acceptance of the invitation is in *Department of State Bulletin*, Aug. 2, 1971, p. 121; he said the purpose of the visit was "to seek the normalization of relations and also to exchange views on questions of concern to the two sides."

126. The United States had argued for "dual representation" which amounted to a two-Chinas policy in the United Nations in August 1971 (a position toward which it had been leaning for some time). However, it was too late for this to be successful, and the United Nations voted to seat Peking and expel Taipei on Oct. 25. This was not unexpected by American officials.

127. Text in ibid., Mar. 20, 1972, pp. 435–38. I also found useful a typescript of Kissinger's important and revealing "backgrounder" to American newsmen in China on Mar. 1, 1972, concerning the trip and the communiqué.

128. The joint communiqué announcing this on Feb. 22, 1973, stated they agreed "the time was appropriate for accelerating the normalizaton of relations" (*Department of State Bulletin*, Mar. 19, 1973, p. 313).

129. Huang Chen and his deputy, Han Hsu, soon let it be known that they would both use the title *ambassador*.

130. National Committee on United States–China Relations, *Prospects for United States–China Relations* (Wingspread, Wisc.: Johnson Foundation, 1975), p. 18.

131. See ns. 173 and 175 below.

132. Joseph Lelyveld, "A 1½-China Policy," *New York Times Magazine*, Apr. 6, 1975, p. 69.

133. *Prospects for United States–China Relations*, p. 23.

134. See *U.S.-China Business Review*, vol. 1, no. 1 (January–February 1974), p. 42, which discusses the likely basis for an agreement.

135. As late as November 1973 when Kissinger visited Peking, the Chinese seemed to be softening rather than hardening on the Taiwan issue. The joint communiqué issued on Nov. 14 made no specific mention of the withdrawal of U.S. forces from Taiwan and stated that normalization of relations "can be realized only on the basis of *confirming the principle* [emphasis added] of one China" (*Department of State Bulletin*, Dec. 10, 1973, p. 716), which seemed to imply greater Chinese flexibility. However, the line on Taiwan hardened in 1974. This was evident in U.S.-China exchange relations. The Chinese began to show great sensitivity regarding the Taiwan issue again (as I observed first hand as a member of the Committee on Scholarly Communication with the People's Republic of China and member of the board of the National Committee on United States–China Relations). Then in 1975 there was a brief softening and in 1976 a hardening once more of the public line. Although changes in the level of domestic tension doubtless contributed to these changes, I believe they also reflected deliberate policy shifts.

136. *Foreign Broadcast Information Service* [FBIS] *Daily Report: People's Republic of China* [PRC], Sept. 10, 1974, p. A25.

137. Text in ibid., Aug. 18, 1971, pp. B-1–B-7. The Communist leaders also revived Mao's Oct. 17, 1945, statement "On the Chungking Negotiations" which analyzed the rationale for negotiating with and making some concessions to a political adversary. In 1945, addressing "some comrades [who] can't understand why we should be willing to negotiate with Chiang Kai-shek," Mao made a pessimistic assessment of the possibility of reaching any lasting agreement but justified negotiations on "realistic," pragmatic, tactical grounds. Chiang "was realistic in inviting us, and we are realistic in going to negotiate with him." He asserted that "the capitalist and the socialist countries will yet reach compromises on a number of international matters, because compromise will be advantageous," but "there will be twists and turns in our road." Original text in *Selected Works of Mao Tse-tung*, vol. 4, pp. 53–61; extracts in *Red Flag*, reprinted in *Peking Review*, July 28, 1972, pp. 5–8.

138. The document is probably authentic. Translated in *Issues and Studies*, vol. 10 (June and July 1974), pp. 90–108 and pp. 94–105.

139. Texts in *Peking Review*, Sept. 7, 1973, pp. 17–25 and 29–33.

140. On the cultural issues, see an article in ibid., Feb. 1, 1974, pp. 7–10, which charged that Antonioni "looked specifically for material that could be used to slander and attack China" and deliberately produced an "anti-China" film; and another article in ibid., Mar. 1, 1974, pp. 15–17, which attacked a "slavish mentality" regarding all things foreign, including music. On the issues concerning trade and the import of technology, see Chin Feng, "Down with Underestimation of Oneself," *Study and Criticism*, Aug. 20, in *Selections from People's Republic of China Magazines*, Sept. 20, 1974, pp. 1–3, criticizing excessive foreign imports, which attacked "servile lackeys of imperialism" who "view foreigners as hundred percent perfect and ourselves as totally incompetent," and "China Develops Science and Technology Independently and Self-Reliantly," *Peking Review*, Nov. 15, 1974, pp. 13–15, which stressed the importance of "maintaining independence and keeping the initiative in our own hands." In contrast, the minister of foreign trade, Li Chiang, in an article summarized in *FBIS Daily Report: PRC*, July 9, 1974, pp. 1–3, stressed that "under no circumstances" should self-reliance mean pursuing a "closed-door" policy.

141. *Peking Review*, Jan. 24, 1975, p. 24.

142. Secretary Kissinger clearly indicated that at that time he believed President Ford's visit would "be one further step along [the] route" toward "normalization of relations" (*Department of State Bulletin*, Dec. 30, 1974, p. 913). However, in the wake of the Indochina disasters, President Ford, in reassuring U.S. allies, stated that it was his "aim" to "reaffirm our commitments to Taiwan" (ibid., May 26, 1975, p. 678).

143. An American editor who participated in an interview with Vice Premier Teng Hsiao-p'ing in mid-1975 paraphrased Teng: "China will be happy to have Ford come whether or not the visit accomplishes anything. . . . Relations between the U.S. and Communist China can never be normal

until the U.S. has severed diplomatic relations with the Chinese Nationalists on Taiwan, withdrawn its troops and broken its treaties. But there is no hurry. China has told the U.S. government that it will wait until the time is right for the U.S. to act." (Richard H. Leonard, *Milwaukee Journal*, July 8, 1975.)

144. In October 1975 the Chinese Foreign Ministry publicly denounced the U.S. government for conniving with Tibetan "traitors" in the United States (*China Quarterly*, no. 65 [March 1976], p. 206).

145. A Chinese Communist newspaper in Hong Kong stated in October 1976: "Some commentators see these sales of arms to Taiwan as perhaps a way for the United States to free itself of the Taiwan-U.S. joint defense treaty" (*Wen Wei Pao*, Oct. 4, in *FBIS Daily Report: PRC*, Oct. 6, 1976, p. N-1).

146. The entire range of U.S.-China issues is analyzed in detail in A. Doak Barnett, *China Policy: Old Problems and New Challenges* (Brookings Institution, 1977).

147. Problems created by cultural and attitudinal differences are discussed in Iriye, *Across the Pacific;* Cohen, *America's Response to China;* Ishwer C. Ojha, *Chinese Foreign Policy in an Age of Transition: The Diplomacy of Cultural Despair* (Beacon, 1969); John Gittings, *The World and China, 1922–1972* (London: Methuen, 1974); and Fairbank, *China's Response to the West; Trade and Diplomacy; China: The People's Middle Kingdom and the U.S.A.; China Perceived;* and *Chinese-American Interactions.* Useful articles include Mark Mancall, "The Persistence of Tradition in Chinese Foreign Policy," *Annals of the American Academy of Political and Social Science,* vol. 349 (September 1963), pp. 14–26; and Albert Feuerwerker, "Chinese History and the Foreign Relations of Contemporary China," ibid., vol. 402 (July 1972), pp. 1–14. American attitudes toward China are perceptively analyzed in Harold R. Isaacs, *Images of Asia: American Views of China and India* (Harper and Row, Torchbooks, 1972; published in 1958 as *Scratches on Our Minds*). For other analyses, see Tang Tsou, *America's Failure in China,* and "Western Concepts and China's Historical Experience," *World Politics,* vol. 21, no. 4 (July 1969), pp. 655–91; Richard H. Solomon, "Parochialism and Paradox in Sino-American Relations," *Asian Survey,* vol. 3, no. 12 (December 1967), pp. 831–50; John G. Stoessinger, *Nations in Darkness: China, Russia, America* (Random House, 1971); Edward Friedman and Mark Selden, eds., *America's Asia: Dissenting Essays on Asian-American Relations* (Random House, 1971); and Bruce Douglass and Ross Terrill, eds., *China and Ourselves: Explorations and Revisions by a New Generation* (Beacon, 1969).

148. Isaacs, *Images of Asia,* p. 64.

149. See Sheila K. Johnson, "To China, With Love," *Commentary,* June 1973, pp. 37–45; and Lucian W. Pye, "Bringing Our China Policy Down to Earth," *Foreign Policy,* no. 18 (Spring 1975), pp. 123–32.

150. See Reardon-Anderson, "Yenan," chaps. 4 and 5.

151. Zagoria, "Mao's Role in the Sino-Soviet Conflict," believes Mao may have been open-minded until at least mid-1949. I believe that the basic decision to align with Moscow was probably made in 1948.

152. Mao asserted that it was "a naive idea in these times" to believe that

"we need help from the British and U.S. governments" (*Selected Works of Mao Tse-tung,* vol. 4, p. 417). On Aug. 18, 1949, commenting on the departure of U.S. Ambassador Leighton Stuart, he said: "There are still some intellectuals and other people in China who have muddled ideas and illusions about the United States. Therefore we should explain things to them, win them over, educate them and unite with them, so they will come over to the side of the people and not fall into the snares set by imperialism" (ibid., p. 438).

153. In one of Liu's "confessions" in the summer of 1967, he said it "was put forward by an individual comrade in rough draft and was not brought up at a Central Committee meeting. At the time I still did not know this point of view had appeared. Afterwards, it was removed from that comrade's safe." (See Union Research Institute, *Collected Works of Liu Shao-ch'i, 1958–1967,* p. 367.) In an earlier "self-criticism" in October 1966, however, Liu had implied that "Teng [Hsiao-p'ing] . . . proposed the so-called 'three reconciliations and one reduction' " at the Central Committee's Ninth Plenum (ibid., p. 361). See also Lowell Dittmer, *Liu Shao-ch'i and the Chinese Cultural Revolution: The Politics of Mass Criticism* (University of California Press, 1974), pp. 98, 107, and 225.

154. See Zagoria, *Vietnam Triangle;* and John Gittings, *Survey of the Sino-Soviet Dispute: A Commentary and Extracts from the Recent Polemics, 1963–1967* (Oxford University Press, 1968).

155. Officially, Peking accused Lin Piao (identified simply as a "swindler") as well as Liu Shao-ch'i of having had "illicit relations with foreign countries" and having "attempted to change the line and policies" of Mao (Ying-mao Kao, ed., *Chinese Law and Government,* vol. 5, nos. 3–4 [Fall–Winter 1972–73], pp. 5 and 97–98).

156. This was a consistent Soviet line in my conversations with China specialists in Moscow in April 1974.

157. When still a vice-premier, Teng Hsiao-p'ing stated in an interview with leading U.S. senators, in 1974, that China would "feel more comfortable" with the United States than with the Soviet Union for the "foreseeable future" (as a participant in that meeting told me). In June 1975, moreover, in an interview with U.S. editors, he clearly indicated a willingness to defer any attempt to solve the Taiwan problem (but not to compromise on the key issues) (*Christian Science Monitor* and *Washington Post,* June 3, 1975).

158. A brief summary of lobbying on China policy, the role of Congress, and the China issue in U.S. elections is in Congressional Quarterly, *China and U.S. Foreign Policy,* pp. 38–58. Ross Y. Koen, *The China Lobby in American Politics* (Macmillan, 1960), describes the lobbying structure. Public opinion and pressure groups are analyzed in A. T. Steele, *The American People and China* (McGraw-Hill for Council on Foreign Relations, 1966). Discussion of competing views in public debate on China policy issues is contained in Robert P. Newman, *Recognition of Communist China?* (Macmillan, 1961).

159. "One of the astonishing things about the China Lobby," according to Max Ascoli, *Reporter,* Apr. 29, 1952, "is that, as far as one can find out, it has no leaders, only mouthpieces."

160. Steele, *The American People and China,* pp. 38–42.

161. E. J. Kahn, Jr., *The China Hands: America's Foreign Service Officers and What Befell Them* (Viking, 1975). For a revealing personal account by one of those "purged," see O. Edmund Clubb, *The Witness and I* (Columbia University Press, 1975).

162. Such attacks continued until the opening of Washington-Peking relations; see, as examples, Robert Hunter and Forrest Davis, *The 'New' Red China Lobby* (Whittier, Calif.: Constructive Action, Fleet Publishing, 1963); and American Council on World Freedom, *Red China and Its American Friends* (Washington: American Council on World Freedom, 1971).

163. The State Department memos of June 25, 26, and 27, 1950, cited in n. 68 do not definitely prove this, but I believe it is highly likely. So, too, do some other analysts; see Morton H. Halperin, *Bureaucratic Politics and Foreign Policy* (Brookings Institution, 1974), pp. 61 and 77.

164. See Townsend Hoopes, *The Devil and John Foster Dulles* (Little, Brown, 1973), especially pp. 77 ff., 115 ff., 262 ff., 415 ff., and 442 ff.

165. John Foster Dulles, *War or Peace* (Macmillan, 1950), p. 190; and Hoopes, *The Devil and John Foster Dulles*, pp. 131 and 262.

166. As the initial witness at the Senate Committee on Foreign Relations hearings on China policy in 1966, I called for major changes in China policy. Instead of criticism, the reaction in the press and in letters to me was overwhelming approval. Peking's *People's Daily's* reaction was negative and skeptical, but mildly so; one of its articles argued that the policy of "containment without isolation" which I had urged was merely a cover-up of U.S. policy failure, but it ended with the statement that "we are convinced that some day the Chinese and American people will smash the schemes of the U.S. reactionaries, sweep away all obstacles and establish close contact, to bring about a tremendous growth of the friendship between our two peoples" (*Atlas*, June 1966, pp. 459–60). Not surprisingly, the reaction on Taiwan was hostile; see *Issues and Studies*, vol. 2 (May 1966), pp. 1–10.

167. Press release, National Committee on United States–China Relations, June 3, 1974.

168. While attending Chiang Kai-shek's funeral in April 1975, Senator Barry Goldwater warned against further U.S. concessions regarding Taiwan. He denounced Washington's "shabby treatment of a former ally" and warned that if the administration was considering withdrawal of recognition from Nationalist China, "I can assure the Secretary of State and the President that this will not be accomplished without strong opposition from myself and other Americans" (press release from the office of Senator Goldwater, Apr. 11, 1975). Shortly thereafter, House minority leader John J. Rhodes stated that no steps are likely now to further loosen U.S. ties with Taiwan, "if President Ford wants to be renominated by the Republican party" (Leslie H. Gelb, *New York Times*, May 10, 1975). President Ford on May 6, in the wake of U.S. defeats in Southeast Asia, had stated that his "aim" was "to reaffirm our commitments to Taiwan" (*Department of State Bulletin*, May 26, 1975, p. 678). Within his administration, however, varied options continued to be actively considered in anticipation of Ford's trip to Peking. Warnings by Republican

leaders continued during 1976: Ronald Reagan stated that the United States "should not abandon Taiwan to improve relations with China," and he warned against letting the Chinese succeed in "talking us into abandoning an ally and violating a treaty" (*New York Times*, Feb. 14, 1976). Both Goldwater and Reagan seemed ambivalent, however. Goldwater, while opposing compromise on Taiwan, argued that the United States needs to further develop relations with the People's Republic to maintain a "counterbalancing force to the U.S.S.R." (*Congressional Record*, vol. 121, no. 85 [1975], p. 2). Similarly, Reagan implied that in strategic terms the United States should develop a better relationship with China, accusing President Ford of causing "cracks in our relationship with mainland China," and saying the United States "has failed miserably to uphold its end of the bargain as the senior power and superpower in the relationship with China" (*Honolulu Star-Bulletin*, Mar. 6, 1976). Neither seemed to see any contradiction in such statements and their uncompromising positions regarding Taiwan. Reagan put his position in a nutshell when he said he supported more normal relations with China but would require a pledge from China to recognize the right of Taiwan to "independence" (*New York Times*, Jan. 31, 1976). Despite such statements, however, none of the presidential candidates chose to make China policy a major issue in the 1976 campaign.

169. In a 1974 Gallup poll, 45 percent of the respondents favored the seating of the Peking regime in the United Nations, 37 percent disapproved; 58 percent felt it was not "fair" that the Nationalist regime was excluded from the United Nations, 15 percent that it was fair; 45 percent thought it was "fair" for the United States to try to normalize relations with Peking (36 percent that it was not), but 72 percent indicated they would be opposed to establishing diplomatic relations with Peking if it required breaking ties with Taipei (11 percent said they would favor it); and 48 percent said they believed the United States should honor its treaty to defend Nationalist China (35 percent said it should not) (*A Gallup Study of Public Attitudes Toward Nations of the World* [Princeton, N.J.: Gallup Organization, Inc., August 1974], pp. 23-32). A 1975 poll indicated that while 61 percent favored "establishing diplomatic relations with mainland China" (23 percent opposed), 70 percent favored "continuing relations with Nationalist China" (14 percent opposed) (ibid. [Oct. 1975]).

170. H. Con. Res. 360, 94:1 (1975), the so-called Mathis Resolution, stated: "That it is the sense of the Congress that the United States Government, while engaged in a lessening of tensions with the People's Republic of China, do nothing to compromise the freedom of our friend and ally, the Republic of China and its people." A majority of House members indicated approval of the resolution but it was not put to a formal vote.

171. June 17, 1976.

172. News release, "Great Decisions '76 Opinion Ballots," Foreign Policy Association, June 30, 1976.

173. For background on China's overall trade, see Alexander Eckstein, *Communist China's Economic Growth and Foreign Trade* (McGraw-Hill

for Council on Foreign Relations, 1966); Feng-hua Ma, *The Foreign Trade of Mainland China* (Aldine, 1971); A. H. Usack and R. E. Batsavage, "The International Trade of the People's Republic of China," in *People's Republic of China: An Economic Assessment*, Joint Economic Committee of Congress, 92:2 (GPO, 1972), pp. 334–82; and Nai-Ruenn Chen, "China's Trade, 1950–74," in *China: A Reassessment of the Economy*, Joint Economic Committee of Congress, 94:1 (GPO, 1975), pp. 617–52.

For analyses of U.S.-China trade, see Eckstein, *China Trade Prospects*; Patrick M. Boarman, ed., *Trade with China: Assessments by Leading Businessmen and Scholars* (Praeger, 1974); William W. Whitson, ed., *Doing Business with China: American Trade Opportunities in the 1970s* (Praeger, 1974); Jerome Alan Cohen, "Implications of the Detente for Sino-American Trade," in Hsiao, ed., *Sino-American Detente and Its Policy Implications*, pp. 46–75. The best periodical source on Sino-American trade is *U.S.-China Business Review*, which has been published bimonthly since January 1974 by the National Council for U.S.-China Trade.

174. See John R. Garson, "The American Trade Embargo Against China," in Eckstein, *China Trade Prospects*, pp. 3–124.

175. For statistics on recent U.S.-China trade I have used William Clarke and Martha Avery, "The Sino-American Commercial Relationship," in *China: A Reassessment of the Economy*, especially pp. 512–14; Central Intelligence Agency, "China: Trade, by Area and Country, 1974–75" (CIA, 1976; processed); and *U.S.-China Business Review*, especially vols. 2 and 3, no. 2 (March–April 1975 and 1976), p. 19 and p. 30. There are some discrepancies between their figures, mainly on Chinese imports. The Department of Commerce figures on Chinese imports used in Clarke and Avery are based on U.S. f.a.s. (free alongside ship in the United States) values and CIA's figures on c.i.f. (cost, insurance, and freight) values.

176. CIA, "China: Trade, by Area and Country." Commerce Department figures in Clarke and Avery are slightly different: $462 million total, consisting of $304 million in U.S. exports to China and $158 million in Chinese exports to the United States.

177. *U.S.-China Business Review*, vol. 3, no. 5 (September–October 1976), p. 11.

178. Ibid., vol. 1, no. 2 (March–April 1974), p. 10, also lists other sales of U.S. plants, equipment, and technology.

179. The discussion here concerns broad strategic considerations; China's military forces are discussed in pt. 4.

180. A *Pravda* editorial of Feb. 22, 1975, assailed "the present Chinese rulers' perfidious and far-reaching calculations aimed at pushing the peoples of the Soviet Union and the United States into a thermonuclear war" (*FBIS Daily Report: Soviet Union*, Feb. 25, 1975, p. C3). For a general analysis of U.S.-China relations by a leading Soviet specialist, see B. N. Zanegin, "Certain Aspects of U.S.-Chinese Relations," *USA: Economics, Politics, Ideology*, no. 2 (1975), in *FBIS Daily Report: Soviet Union*, Feb. 14, 1975, pp. C1–C12.

181. Russian speculation that China seeks military assistance from the

United States began even earlier, in late 1973; see Michael Pillsbury, *Soviet Apprehensions About Sino-American Relations*, P-5459 (Santa Monica, Calif.: Rand Corp., 1975).

182. For general sources on Korea and Vietnam, and big-power involvements in these two countries, see pt. 4, ns. 64 and 67.

183. China's economic aid to North Korea through 1971 totaled $330 million, not including some significant military aid that could not be calculated (Leo Tansky, "Chinese Foreign Aid," in *People's Republic of China: An Economic Assessment*, pp. 378–79).

184. Hanoi's press treatment of the U.S.-China opening revealed its disapproval and apprehensions. How much Peking used its influence to encourage a cease-fire in Vietnam is debatable, however. Reportedly Chou En-lai told Kissinger in 1971 that China would not press Hanoi one way or the other. However, Mao told French Foreign Minister Maurice Schumann that he had advised the North Vietnamese to be more compromising. (Tad Szulc, "How Kissinger Did It: Behind the Vietnam Cease-Fire Agreement," *Foreign Policy*, no. 15 [Summer 1974], pp. 44–45.) In any case, Chinese as well as Soviet aid continued during 1973–74 and was important to Hanoi's ultimate victory.

185. As a member of a visiting delegation in China when this bombing occurred, I observed the extraordinary degree to which the Chinese underplayed the issue, at least in dealings with American visitors.

186. For background on Taiwan, see Mark Mancall, ed., *Formosa Toa* (Praeger, 1964); Yung-Hwan Jo, *Taiwan's Future* (Hong Kong: Union Re search Institute for Arizona State University, 1974); Fred W. Riggs, *Formosa under Chinese Nationalist Rule* (Macmillan, 1952); Joseph W. Ballantine, *Formosa: A Problem for United States Foreign Policy* (Brookings Institution, 1952); H. Maclear Bate, *Report from Taiwan* (Dutton, 1952); George H. Kerr, *Formosa Betrayed* (Houghton Mifflin, 1965); Douglas Mendel, *The Politics of Formosan Nationalism* (University of California Press, 1970); and Paul K. T. Sih, ed., *Taiwan in Modern Times* (St. John's University Press, 1973).

For discussion of the policy problems for the United States, see Jerome Alan Cohen and others, *Taiwan and American Policy: The Dilemma in U.S.-China Relations* (Praeger, 1971); William M. Bueler, *U.S. China Policy and the Problem of Taiwan* (Colorado Associated University Press, 1971); Hung-dah Chiu, ed., *China and the Question of Taiwan: Documents and Analysis* (Praeger, 1973); Lung-chu Chen and Harold D. Lasswell, *Formosa, China, and the United Nations* (St. Martin's, 1967); Lelyveld, "A 1½-China Policy"; James Laurie and Stefan Leader, "Coming to Terms with Two Chinas," *Far Eastern Economic Review*, Jan. 24, 1975, pp. 22–24; J. Bruce Jacobs, "Taiwan 1972: Political Season" and "Taiwan 1973: Consolidation of the Succession," *Asian Survey*, vols. 13 and 14, no. 1 (January 1973 and 1974), pp. 102–12 and pp. 22–29; Bruce R. Simmons, "Taiwan and China: The Delicate Courtship," *Current History*, vol. 65, no. 385 (September 1973), pp. 111 ff.; Sheldon L. Appleton, "Taiwan: The Year It Finally Happened," *Asian Survey*, vol. 12, no. 1 (January 1972), pp. 32–37; Robert A. Scalapino, "The Question of 'Two

Chinas,'" in Tang Tsou, ed., *China in Crisis*, vol. 2, *China's Policies in Asia and America's Alternatives* (University of Chicago Press, 1968), pp. 109–27; and Robert W. Barnett, "China and Taiwan: The Economic Issues," *Foreign Affairs*, vol. 50, no. 3 (April 1972), pp. 444–58.

187. Peking's positions are discussed in detail in Young, *Negotiating with the Chinese Communists*. For official Chinese statements revealing Peking's growing fear of a two-Chinas outcome in the 1950s, see *Oppose U.S. Occupation of Taiwan*.

188. Mao said to Edgar Snow: "Manchuria must be regained. We do not, however, include Korea, formerly a Chinese colony, but when we have re-established the independence of the lost territories of China, and if the Koreans wish to break away from the chains of Japanese imperialism, we will extend them our enthusiastic help in their struggle for independence. The same thing applies for Taiwan." (Snow, *Red Star Over China*, p. 110.)

189. In 1974, U.S. trade with Taiwan totaled $3.7 billion (about four times that with the mainland), U.S. investments in Taiwan totaled about $375 million, and the Export-Import Bank had made loans to Taiwan of $1.2 billion and its guarantees totaled about $700 million (Ralph N. Clough, "The Taiwan Issue in Sino-American Relations" [1976; processed], p. 7).

190. See Teng Hsiao-p'ing's statement to a group of visiting American editors (*New York Times*, June 3, 1975). Chou En-lai reportedly told a group of American students "that liberation [of Taiwan] is not something that will occur in one or two years. Instead, he said that it would take many years. He probably would not live to see it although we probably would.... The Chinese people are prepared for liberation by military means but strongly hope that that would not be necessary" (from notes made by a participant). In early 1977, *People's Daily* asserted that "China has always favored solving the problem through negotiation and not by force" (*Washington Post*, Jan. 14, 1977).

191. Chinese leaders have stated, in interviews, their willingness to negotiate with Nationalist leaders, their intention of absorbing Taiwan gradually, and their willingness to permit Taiwan to retain a higher average living standard than other parts of China, their intention of going slow in nationalizing enterprises, and their willingness to give subsidies to replace foreign investment. Chou emphasized to some Overseas Chinese from North America "that one should not be too impatient" (Joseph J. Lee, "Peking's View of Taiwan: An Interview with Premier Chou En-lai," in Jo, *Taiwan's Future*, pp. 65–70). Former Nationalist leaders in the Peking government have periodically urged negotiation; see, for example, Fu Tso-yi's interview with a visitor of Chinese origin from the United States, reported in *Asahi*, July 10, 1973. In 1975 Peking gave great publicity to the release of high-ranking Nationalist officials who had been imprisoned ever since the Communist takeover of China. Repeatedly in recent years Peking's press and radio have appealed to Taiwanese to help work toward a peaceful reunification.

192. The terms used include "take note," "respect," and "acknowledge" (Takakazu Kuriyama, "Some Legal Aspects of the Japan-China Joint Communiqué," *Japanese Annual of International Law*, no. 17 [1973], p. 46).

193. Statistics are from U.S. Arms Control and Disarmament Agency, *World Military Expenditures and Arms Trade, 1963–1973*, Publication 74 (GPO, 1975), p. 27.

194. Overseas Development Council, "Comparative Table" (Washington: the Council, 1974; processed), p. 1.

195. Ibid.

196. Lelyveld, "A 1½-China Policy," p. 76; and Leo Moser, "Taiwan, China and the World," in Jo, *Taiwan's Future*, p. 98.

197. As of July 1, 1971, Taiwan was regarded as a "developed nation" by the U.S. government (see Robert C. North, "The Population, Technology and Resources of Taiwan: Implications for Political Power," in Jo, *Taiwan's Future*, p. 134).

198. See *New York Times*, Aug. 4, 1976; the figure represents arms actually transferred. In 1974 and 1975 the figures were $198 million and $215 million. For other data on U.S. military aid, see *Far Eastern Economic Review*, Jan. 24, 1975, pp. 22 ff. The U.S. government authorized a military credit agreement in 1973 worth about $250 million under which Northrop Corp. started production of F-5E fighter planes on Taiwan (Lelyveld, "A 1½-China Policy," p. 69).

199. Trade figures are from *Business and Industry* (Taiwan), Jan. 24, 1975. For additional data, see Chen Fu Chang, "The Balance of Payments of Taiwan, 1966–72," *Asian Survey*, vol. 14, no. 6 (June 1974), pp. 546–57; and Arthur Dornheim, "Taiwan's Trade Perspectives," in Jo, *Taiwan's Future*, pp. 117–25; and numerous articles in *Free China Weekly* (Taiwan).

200. Estimates, obtained in February 1975, of the head of the Republic of China desk, Department of State.

201. In 1975 the rate of GNP growth turned up again; it was 4.3 percent for the year (*Free China Weekly*, Mar. 21, 1976, p. 1).

202. See Don Oberdorfer on Nationalist representation abroad, in *Washington Post*, Oct. 5, 1974.

203. Taiwan's defense expenditures in 1974–75 totaled an estimated $774 million, and its military forces included: (1) Army, 340,000 men, 2 armored divisions, 12 infantry divisions, 6 light divisions, 2 armored cavalry divisions, 2 airborne brigades, 4 special forces groups, 2 surface-to-air missile (SAM) battalions (one with HAWK missiles, and one with NIKE-HERCULES); (2) Air force, 80,000 men, with about 206 combat aircraft (6 fighter-bomber squadrons with 90 F-100s, 2 fighter squadrons with 36 F-5s, 3 interceptor units with 63 F-104s); (3) Navy, 36,000 men, 2 submarines, 18 destroyers, 16 escorts, 6 torpedo boats, 21 tank landing ships, 4 medium landing ships, and 22 other landing craft; (4) Marines, 35,000 men, 2 divisions (Laurie and Leader, "Coming to Terms with Two Chinas," p. 23). See also Angus M. Fraser, "Military Posture and Strategic Policy in the Republic of China," *Asian Affairs*, no. 5 (May–June 1974), pp. 308–18.

204. For statements indicating official Chinese Nationalist positions, policies, and attitudes, see *Free China Review*. My judgments on the attitudes of various groups on Taiwan are also based on interviews with Taiwanese politicians and students as well as Republic of China diplomats and officials on

several visits to Taiwan, and on the analyses made by leading American specialists on the Republic of China.

205. The rumors increased substantially in 1974 following a visit to Taiwan by a Soviet correspondent, Victor Louis, but there have been no recent contacts reported.

206. These judgments are in part based on my conversations and interviews with both Chinese Nationalist officials and Russian officials and scholars.

207. See George H. Quester, "Taiwan and Nuclear Proliferation," *Orbis,* vol. 17, no. 1 (Spring 1974), pp. 140–50.

208. *Washington Post,* Sept. 18, 1975.

Part Four: China and the New Four-Power Equilibrium

1. The idea of concentrating on one principal enemy also reflected Mao's personal relations; "his practice has been to engage one person, a single 'main foe,' with whom he would lock himself in the embrace of conflict" (Lucian W. Pye, *Mao Tse-tung, The Man in the Leader* [Basic Books, 1976], p. 309).

2. On traditional Chinese approaches to dealing with the outside world, see John K. Fairbank, ed., *The Chinese World Order: Traditional China's Foreign Relations* (Harvard University Press, 1968); Earl Swisher, ed., *China's Management of the American Barbarians: A Study of Sino-American Relations, 1841–1861, with Documents* (Yale University for Far Eastern Association, 1953); Lin Kuo-chung, *Classical Chinese Concepts of International Politics and Their Influence on Contemporary Chinese Foreign Policy* (Ph.D. dissertation, University of Oklahoma, 1974), which discusses early Chinese balance-of-power concepts; and Richard L. Walker, *The Multi-State System of Ancient China* (Hamden, Conn.: Shoe String Press, 1953), which analyzes the "international relations" among Chinese states before unification of the country by Ch'in-shih Huang-ti.

3. See n. 26 below.

4. See Allen S. Whiting, "The Use of Force in Foreign Policy by the People's Republic of China," *Annals of the American Academy of Political and Social Science,* vol. 402 (July 1972), pp. 55–56, and *The Chinese Calculus of Deterrence: India and Indochina* (University of Michigan Press, 1975).

5. See Mao Tse-tung, "Imperialists and All Reactionaries Are Paper Tigers" (*Foreign Broadcast Information Service* [FBIS] *Daily Report: Far East,* Nov. 3, 1958, pp. 1–21).

6. The Chinese have strongly emphasized, privately as well as publicly, the need for all the major powers to maintain their strength to counterbalance the Soviet Union. See, for example, report on the conversations with Chinese leaders in January 1975 of Franz Joseph Strauss, head of the German opposition Christian Democratic Union, in *China Quarterly,* no. 62 (June 1975), pp. 384–85. Privately the Chinese argue that Europe and the United States must cooperate, and that Europe should have its own nuclear force; see Phillips Talbot's report on an interview with Teng Hsiao-p'ing, *Asia,* vol. 3, no. 1

(January–February 1976), p. 1. Chinese concern about a possible decline in U.S. strength relative to that of the Soviet Union is revealed in Foreign Minister Ch'iao Kuan-hua's May 20, 1975, speech to party cadres (*Issues and Studies*, December 1975, pp. 93–108). The Chinese now appear to believe that the danger of Soviet attack on China has lessened, but that it will increase if the Soviet Union's power position improves in any other areas of the world; see John Burns's report, based on discussions with high officials in Peking, in *Washington Post*, Oct. 5, 1974.

7. On policy disputes and debates, see Parris H. Chang, *Power and Policy in China* (Pennsylvania State University Press, 1975); Roderick MacFarquhar, *The Origins of the Cultural Revolution*, vol. 1, *Contradictions Among the People, 1956–1957* (Columbia University Press, 1974); Lowell Dittmer, *Liu Shao-ch'i and the Chinese Cultural Revolution: The Politics of Mass Criticism* (University of California Press, 1974); Richard Baum, *Prelude to Revolution: Mao, the Party, and the Peasant Question, 1962–66* (Columbia University Press, 1975); and A. Doak Barnett, *Uncertain Passage: China's Transition to the Post-Mao Era* (Brookings Institution, 1974).

8. On the Cultural Revolution, see Thomas W. Robinson, ed., *The Cultural Revolution in China* (University of California Press, 1971); Stanley Karnow, *Mao and China: From Revolution to Revolution* (Viking, 1972); Edward E. Rice, *Mao's Way* (University of California Press, 1972); and Richard H. Solomon, *Mao's Revolution and the Chinese Political Culture* (University of California Press, 1971).

9. *Peking Review*, Jan. 24, 1975, p. 23.

10. See criticism of the pragmatic trends encouraged by Chou En-lai in Yao Wen-yuan, "On the Social Basis of the Lin Piao Anti-Party Clique," *Peking Review*, Mar. 7, 1975, pp. 5–10; and Chang Ch'un-ch'iao, "On Exercising All-Round Dictatorship Over the Bourgeoisie," *Peking Review*, Apr. 4, 1975, pp. 5–11.

11. For comprehensive, up-to-date data on the economy, see *China: A Reassessment of the Economy*, Joint Economic Committee of Congress, 94:1 (Government Printing Office, 1975). An excellent general analysis is Alexander Eckstein, *China's Economic Development: The Interplay of Scarcity and Ideology* (University of Michigan Press, 1975). Other important studies (which contain useful bibliographies) include Dwight H. Perkins, *Market Control and Planning in Communist China* (Harvard University Press, 1966); Nai-Ruenn Chen and Walter Galenson, *The Chinese Economy Under Communism* (Aldine, 1969); and Audrey Donnithorne, *China's Economic System* (London: George Allen and Unwin, 1967).

12. In *China: A Reassessment of the Economy*, p. 23, Arthur G. Ashbrook, Jr., estimates China's average annual GNP growth during 1953–74 at 5.6 percent, per-capita growth at 3.4 percent (three years earlier, his estimate of GNP growth was 4 percent a year from 1952 through 1971; see *People's Republic of China: An Economic Assessment*, Joint Economic Committee of Congress, 92:2 [GPO, 1972], pp. 8 and 39–40).

13. *China: A Reassessment of the Economy*, p. 23.

14. U.S. Arms Control and Disarmament Agency (ACDA), *World Military Expenditures and Arms Trade, 1963–73* (GPO, 1975).

15. The transferability of China's policies to other societies is probably limited. For discussion of the "Chinese model," see Michel Oksenberg, ed., *China's Development Experience* (Academy of Political Science, Columbia University, 1973); Donald S. Zagoria, "China by Daylight," *Dissent* (Spring 1975), pp. 135–47; Donald S. Keesing, "Economic Lessons from China," *Journal of Development Economics*, no. 2 (1975), pp. 1–32; and A. Doak Barnett, "Development in China—The Political and Social Context" (paper prepared for a conference sponsored by Directorate for Science, Technology and Industry, Organisation for Economic Co-operation and Development, Paris, December 1975; processed).

16. From notes of Professor Merle Goldman.

17. There is evidence of a "declining rate of increase" in grain output in recent years; the annual average rate was 2.2 percent during 1957–67, 1.7 percent during 1968–71, and 1.3 percent during 1971–74 (Alva Lewis Erisman, "China: Agriculture in the 1970's," in *China: A Reassessment of the Economy*, p. 342). In 1975 China started a major program, initiated at Tachai, to achieve farm mechanization by 1980; it appeared to mix pragmatic and ideological goals (*New York Times*, Sept. 17, 1975).

18. American agricultural specialists visiting China in 1974 were impressed by China's agricultural progress and by the effectiveness with which agricultural knowledge is disseminated, but were disturbed by the decline in agricultural research and training (*New York Times*, Oct. 7, 1974).

19. See Robert Michael Field, "Civilian Industrial Production in the People's Republic of China, 1949–74," in *China: A Reassessment of the Economy*, pp. 146–74. Small-scale industry has played a significant, but secondary, role in recent years ("Rural Small-scale Industry in the People's Republic of China" [draft of a report by the American Rural Small-scale Industry Delegation to the National Academy of Sciences, American Council of Learned Societies, and Social Science Research Council, 1975; processed]).

20. There was a gradual restoration of standards in education and research during 1974–75, but a radical counterattack in late 1975 set back the process. See the article on educational policy in *Red Flag*, no. 12 (Dec. 1, 1975), in *Selections from People's Republic of China Magazines*, Dec. 24–31, 1975.

21. This is a rough estimate, made by U.S. government analysts in 1975.

22. Because of the lack of reliable statistics, all estimates are tentative; see Leo A. Orleans, "China's Population Statistics: An Illusion?" *China Quarterly*, no. 21 (January–March 1965), pp. 168–78. (The statistical problem has changed little since 1965.) In 1974 the Chinese stated that their population was "nearly 800 million" (Leo A. Orleans, "China's Population: Can the Contradictions Be Resolved?" in *China: A Reassessment of the Economy*, p. 69). John S. Aird estimates the population is well over 900 million ("Population Policy and Demographic Prospects in the People's Republic of China," in *People's Republic of China: An Economic Assessment*, p. 328).

23. There was continuing debate on this issue in the period just before

Mao's death. For opposing views, see articles by Li Chiang, minister of foreign trade, favoring increased involvement (*FBIS Daily Report: People's Republic of China,* July 9, 1974, pp. 1–3); and Chin Feng, "Down with Underestimation of Oneself," stressing the necessity for self-reliance (*Selections from People's Republic of China Magazines,* Sept. 20, 1974, pp. 1–3). Chou's death in early 1976 obviously precipitated an even more intense debate on this issue; see *New York Times,* Feb. 19, 1976, citing Chinese press attacks on men who put economic development ahead of politics.

24. For data on China's military capabilities, see Morton I. Abramowitz, deputy assistant secretary of defense, East Asia and Pacific affairs, statement to Subcommittee on Future Foreign Policy Research and Development of the House International Relations Committee (Apr. 6, 1976; processed); International Institute for Strategic Studies, *The Military Balance, 1974–75* (London: IISS, 1974); John E. Moore, ed., *Jane's Fighting Ships, 1974–75* (Huddersfield, England: Netherwood, Dalton, 1974); James R. Schlesinger, *Report of Secretary of Defense on FY 1976 and Transition Budgets, FY 1977 Authorization Request and FY 1976–80 Defense Programs* (GPO, 1975); *Allocation of Resources in the Soviet Union and China,* Joint Economic Committee of Congress, 93:2, 94:1 and 2 (GPO, 1974, 1975, and 1976); Angus M. Fraser, *The People's Liberation Army: Communist China's Armed Forces* (Crane Russak, 1973); Hans Heymann, Jr., *China's Approach to Technology Acquisition: Part I, The Aircraft Industry,* R-1573-ARPA (Santa Monica, Calif.: Rand Corp., 1975); and John R. Dewenter, "China Afloat," *Foreign Affairs,* vol. 50, no. 4 (July 1972), pp. 738–51. In *China: A Reassessment of the Economy,* see Sidney H. Jammes, "The Chinese Defense Burden, 1965–74," pp. 459–66; Robert F. Dernberger, "The Economic Consequences of Defense Expenditure Choices in China," pp. 467–99; and Angus M. Fraser, "The Utility of Alternative Strategic Postures to the People's Republic of China," pp. 438–58.

25. Mao Tse-tung, *Selected Works of Mao Tse-tung,* vol. 2 (Peking: Foreign Languages Press, 1965), p. 224.

26. Only crude estimates can be made because of the inadequacy of budgetary and statistical information from China. Figures for the late 1960s and early 1970s are from ACDA, *World Military Expenditures and Arms Trade, 1963–1973,* p. 27; for the mid-1970s, from *Aviation Week,* Dec. 6, 1976, p. 19. ACDA estimates have varied between 7.35 percent and 9.21 percent, but they are above 8 percent for the years from 1968 on. Ruth Leger Sivard estimated military expenditures at $9 billion in 1972 (*World Military and Social Expenditures, 1974* [New York: Institute for World Order, 1974]), and at $12 billion in 1973 (*World Military and Social Expenditures, 1976* [New York: Arms Control Association, Institute for World Order, and Members of Congress for Peace Through Law Education Fund, 1976], p. 22). Even ACDA figures have not been entirely consistent; in *World Military Expenditures, 1971* (GPO, 1972), p. 12, ACDA estimated 1970 military expenditures at $10 billion, but in its 1963–1973 volume at $12 billion in current dollars and $13 billion in constant dollars. Jammes, "The Chinese Defense Burden," p. 466,

states that Chinese military expenditures in 1974 were "less than" 10 percent of GNP; Dernberger, "The Economic Consequences," p. 468, estimates they were "about" 10 percent. The U.S. government estimate, reported in the *Aviation Week* article cited above, was roughly 10 percent.

27. Sivard, *World Military and Social Expenditures, 1974,* pp. 4 and 24–25.

28. *Allocation of Resources in the Soviet Union and China—1976,* pp. 16–20 and 32.

29. See, for example, Jammes, "The Chinese Defense Burden," pp. 463–64.

30. Testimony of CIA Director William E. Colby in *Allocation of Resources in the Soviet Union and China—1974,* pp. 76–78; Colby's estimates are of military procurement, not overall military expenditures. Estimates of overall military expenditures show a steady upward trend, without significant cutbacks, although the rates of increase have varied (ACDA, *World Military Expenditures and Arms Trade, 1963–1973,* p. 27).

31. Jammes, "The Chinese Defense Burden," p. 463.

32. This is a rough estimate by a U.S. official.

33. *Allocation of Resources in the Soviet Union and China—1976,* p. 80.

34. Field, "Civilian Industrial Production in the People's Republic of China, 1949–74," p. 166. Central Intelligence Agency, *Handbook of Economic Statistics,* Research Aid A(ER) 75-65 (CIA, 1975), p. 91, gives a figure of 23.8 million for 1974.

35. Colby's estimate, in *Allocation of Resources in the Soviet Union and China—1974,* p. 71.

36. Central Intelligence Agency, *China's Minerals and Metals Position in the World Market,* Research Aid ER 76-10150 (CIA, 1976), p. 15.

37. For background on China's aircraft industry, see Heymann, *China's Approach to Technology Acquisition.* China was believed in 1975 to have three plants to produce fissile material, five to produce air frames, and five to produce jet engines; some of them may not have been in operation (information from an unattributable source).

38. On the negotiations to obtain the right to produce the Rolls-Royce Spey engine, see ibid., pp. 57–60. Agreement was reached in late 1975 (*New York Times,* Dec. 15, 1975).

39. See Abramowitz statement to House subcommittee, p. 4; and Colby testimony in *Allocation of Resources in the Soviet Union and China—1974,* pp. 27 and 36. Colby stated, "We believe they have nearly as many men under arms as the U.S.S.R.," which he estimated to be "nearly four million." Until recently most estimates of China's forces were between 3 million and 3.5 million.

40. For data on divisions and equipment, see Abramowitz statement to House subcommittee, p. 4; and Fraser, *The People's Liberation Army,* pp. 4–5. Where these sources differ, Abramowitz's figures, which are more recent, are used.

41. Most China specialists focus on the political rather than the strategic aspects of Peking's military establishment. See William W. Whitson, with

Chen-hsia Huang, *The Chinese High Command: A History of Communist Military Politics, 1927–71* (Praeger, 1973); John Gittings, *The Role of the Chinese Army* (London: Oxford University Press, 1967); Ellis Joffe, *Party and Army: Professionalism and Political Control in the Chinese Officer Corps, 1949–1964*, East Asian Monograph (Harvard University Press, 1965); Samuel B. Griffith II, *The Chinese People's Liberation Army* (McGraw-Hill, 1967); Alexander L. George, *The Chinese Communist Army in Action* (Columbia University Press, 1967); and Harvey W. Nelson, *An Organizational History of the Chinese People's Liberation Army, 1966–1969* (Ph.D. dissertation, George Washington University, 1972). Whitson especially stresses the political constraints limiting flexibility of deployment of Chinese forces.

42. IISS, *The Military Balance, 1974–1975*, p. 49; and Fraser, *The People's Liberation Army*, p. 18. In recent years, 25 percent more forces have reportedly been assigned to north and northeast China than in the early 1970s.

43. Abramowitz statement to House subcommittee, p. 4.

44. Whitson, *The Chinese High Command*, pp. 542–43.

45. See IISS, *The Military Balance, 1974–1975*, p. 50.

46. Abramowitz statement to House subcommittee, pp. 4–5.

47. Heymann, *China's Approach to Technology Acquisition*, pp. 26–27.

48. For data on naval personnel and units, see Moore, *Jane's Fighting Ships, 1974–75*; Fraser, *The People's Liberation Army*; and Abramowitz statement to House subcommittee. Abramowitz, the most up-to-date, authoritative source, states that by 1976 China had about 65 diesel submarines and one prototype nuclear attack submarine (the latter still lacks missiles).

49. See *New York Times*, Jan. 25, 1976.

50. Press release, Joint Economic Committee of Congress, July 16, 1975, p. 10, stated that the one nuclear submarine the Chinese were then building was to be nuclear powered but was probably designed for conventional rather than nuclear missiles.

51. On China's nuclear development policy and strategy, see Morton H. Halperin, *China and the Bomb* (Praeger, 1965), and "Chinese Attitudes Toward the Use and Control of Nuclear Weapons," in Tang Tsou, ed., *China's Policy in Asia and America's Alternatives* (University of Chicago Press, 1968), pp. 135–57; Alice Langley Hsieh, *Communist China's Strategy in the Nuclear Era* (Prentice-Hall, 1962), and *Communist China's Military Policies, Doctrine, and Strategy* (Santa Monica, Calif.: Rand Corp., 1968); Harry Gelber, *Nuclear Weapons and Chinese Policy*, Adelphi Paper 99 (London: International Institute for Strategic Studies, 1973), and "Nuclear Weapons in Chinese Strategy," *Problems of Communism*, vol. 20, no. 6 (November–December 1971), pp. 33–34; Jonathan D. Pollack, "Chinese Attitudes Toward Nuclear Weapons, 1964–9," *China Quarterly*, no. 50 (April–June 1972), pp. 244–71; H. C. Hinton, *Communist China's External Policy and Behavior As a Nuclear Power*, Research Paper P-75 (Washington, D.C.: Institute for Defense Analyses, 1963); and Arthur Huck, *The Security of China: Chinese Approaches to Problems of War and Strategy* (Columbia University Press, 1970).

52. The latest test was in November 1976 (*Peking Review*, Nov. 26, 1976, p. 10).

53. IISS, *The Military Balance, 1974–1975*, p. 49.

54. See Alice Langley Hsieh's testimony in *ABM, MIRV, SALT and the Nuclear Arms Race*, Hearings before the Subcommittee on Arms Control, International Law, and Organization, of the Senate Foreign Relations Committee, 91:2 (GPO, 1970).

55. Whereas in February 1975 Secretary of Defense Schlesinger stated that some might be "ready for deployment in silos by mid-1980" (*Annual Defense Department Report FY 1976 and FY 197T*, p. II-17), CIA Director Colby indicated in June 1975 that this might occur by "1978 or 1979 at the very earliest" (*Allocation of Resources in the Soviet Union and China—1975*, pp. 44–45).

56. In 1975 James Reston reported that the United States then had about 8,500 strategic nuclear weapons and about 22,000 tactical nuclear weapons (*New York Times*, June 6, 1975).

57. *SALT and MBFR: The Next Phase*, Report of a Trilateral Conference, *Survival*, January/February 1975, p. 32.

58. Semimobile missiles, while not invulnerable, increase the uncertainty for an attacker.

59. In *Statement by General George S. Brown, United States Air Force, Chairman, Joint Chiefs of Staff, to the Congress on the Defense Posture of the United States for Fiscal Year 1977* (Jan. 20, 1976), p. 46, General Brown declared that China has "a modest, but credible, nuclear capability against the U.S.S.R."

60. In the May 26, 1973, *Washington Post*, Marquis Childs summarized an interview with Chou En-lai: "As for China's policy, the Premier is confident that a Soviet strike across the northern border, so long a major threat, has been deterred. The deterrence has been achieved by successful diplomacy on the one hand and by extensive and costly measures of preparedness—a strong army, rapid nuclear missile development, tunnel digging—on the other hand." A Soviet diplomat who called this interview to my attention saw it as an indication that the Chinese leadership believes that by 1973 China had acquired at least a minimal nuclear deterrent. In my April 1974 conversations with China specialists in Moscow, they consistently stated that the Soviet Union accepts the reality of China having already acquired a minimal deterrent.

61. See Leo Tansky, "Chinese Foreign Aid," in *People's Republic of China: An Economic Assessment*, pp. 379–80.

62. My views on the likely emergence of a new kind of four-power relationship took shape during 1969–70 before any U.S.-China opening had actually occurred (see *Annals of the American Academy of Political and Social Science*, vol. 390 [July 1970], pp. 73–86). The articulation by President Nixon, during 1971–72, of his concept of "five great power centers" (see introduction, n. 10) stimulated numerous critiques of balance-of-power concepts; see Zbigniew Brzezinski, "The Balance of Power Delusion," and Stanley Hoffman, "Will the Balance Balance at Home?" *Foreign Policy*, no. 7 (Summer

1972), pp. 54–59 and 60–86. Hedley Bull, "The New Balance of Power in Asia and the Pacific," *Foreign Affairs*, vol. 49, no. 4 (July 1971), p. 669, stated "the new balance will rest primarily upon an equilibrium among the three great powers—the United States, the Soviet Union, and China—and the principal uncertainty is whether they will be joined by a fourth, Japan." Harold C. Hinton sees Japan as less "important in the balance than the other three major powers" (*Three and a Half Powers: The New Balance in Asia* [Indiana University Press, 1975]). Robert A. Scalapino, *Asia and the Road Ahead: Issues for the Major Powers* (University of California Press, 1975), analyzes relationships among the four East Asian powers plus India and Indonesia. Ralph N. Clough, *East Asia and U.S. Security* (Brookings Institution, 1975), discusses four-power relationships and stresses the key role of U.S.-Japan relations. Franz Schurmann, *The Logic of World Power: An Inquiry into the Origins, Currents, and Contradictions of World Politics* (Random House, 1974), focuses on the U.S.-China-Soviet triangle. See also Alistair Buchan, *The End of the Post-war Era* (Saturday Review Press, 1974); and Steven I. Levine, "China and the Superpowers," *Political Science Quarterly*, vol. 90, no. 4 (Winter 1975).

63. Peking has made a deliberate effort to allay Southeast Asian fears; see texts of its joint communiqués with the Philippines and Thailand, in *China Quarterly*, nos. 63 and 64 (September and December 1975), pp. 598–99 and pp. 809–10. However, despite Chinese pledges supporting the principles of noninterference, opposition to subversion, and renunciation of claims of dual citizenship by Overseas Chinese, Southeast Asian nations remain uneasy because of continued Chinese propaganda supporting Communist insurrections in the area. Peking has been unwilling to stop clandestine radio broadcasts from stations in China directed at Communist parties in Southeast Asia.

64. For background on Korea, see Shannon McCune, *Korea's Heritage: A Regional and Social Geography* (Tuttle, 1956); Andrew J. Grajdanzev, *Modern Korea* (John Day, 1944); Young C. Kim, ed., *Major Powers and Korea* (Silver Spring, Md.: Research Institute on Korean Affairs, 1973); Gregory Henderson, *Korea, The Politics of the Vortex* (Harvard University Press, 1968); Gregory Henderson, Richard Nedlebow, and John G. Stoessinger, eds., *Divided Nations in a Divided World* (Makay, 1974); Robert A. Scalapino and Chong-sik Lee, *Communism in Korea*, 2 vols. (University of California Press, 1973); and Dae-Sook Suh, *The Korean Communist Movement, 1918–1948* (Princeton University Press, 1970). Recent trends in North-South relations and big-power involvements are discussed in Donald S. Zagoria and Young C. Kim, "North Korea and the Major Powers," *Asian Survey*, vol. 15, no. 12 (December 1975), pp. 1017–35; Ralph N. Clough, *Deterrence and Defense in Korea: The Role of U.S. Forces* (Brookings Institution, 1976); Edwin O. Reischauer, "The Korean Connection," *New York Times Magazine*, Sept. 22, 1974, pp. 15 ff.; Joungwon A. Kim, "The Unification of Korea," *Pacific Community*, vol. 2, no. 3 (April 1971), pp. 564–76, and "North Korea's New Offensive," *Foreign Affairs*, vol. 48, no. 1 (October 1969), pp.

166–79; Nathan White, "Japan's Security Interests in Korea," *Asian Survey*, vol. 16, no. 4 (April 1976), pp. 299–318; Kyung-won Kim, "The Torment of Detente," Harold C. Hinton, "China and Korea," and Chong-sik Lee, "The North Korean Policy and Its Strategy Toward South Korea" (papers prepared for a George Washington University conference on Korea and the major powers, May 1–3, 1975; processed); Robert A. Scalapino, "The Two Koreas—Dialogue or Conflict," Donald S. Zagoria, "The Impact of Detente on Korea," and William J. Barnds, "The Two Koreas in East Asian Affairs" (papers prepared for a Council on Foreign Relations discussion group, January–March 1975; processed); and Young Whan Kihl, "The Nixon Doctrine and South-North Relations" (paper prepared for the Sixth International Conference of the Korean Institute of International Studies, July 1973; processed).

65. Kim Il-sung speech, in *Peking Review*, Apr. 25, 1975, p. 17.

66. Joint communiqué signed by China and North Korea, *Peking Review*, May 2, 1975, p. 9.

67. For background on Southeast Asia and U.S. policy toward the region, see George McTurnan Kahin, *Governments and Politics of Southeast Asia* (Cornell University Press, 1964); William Henderson, ed., *Southeast Asia: Problems of United States Policy* (M.I.T. Press, 1963); Robert Tilman, ed., *Man, State, and Society in Contemporary Southeast Asia* (Praeger, 1969); Lucian W. Pye, *Southeast Asia's Political Systems* (Prentice-Hall, 1967); Cora Du Bois, *Social Forces in Southeast Asia* (University of Minnesota Press, 1949); Harry J. Benda and others, *World of Southeast Asia* (Harper and Row, 1967); Richard Butwell, *Southeast Asia Today—and Tomorrow: Problems of Political Development* (Praeger, 1969); Bernard K. Gordon, *Toward Disengagement in Asia: A Strategy for American Policy* (Prentice-Hall, 1969), and *Dimensions of Conflict in Southeast Asia* (Prentice-Hall, 1966); Kenneth P. Landon, *Southeast Asia: Crossroads of Religion* (University of Chicago Press, 1974); Melvin Gurtov, *South-East Asia Tomorrow: Problems and Prospects for U.S. Policy* (Johns Hopkins Press, 1970); and Russell H. Fifield, *Americans in Southeast Asia: The Roots of Commitment* (Crowell, 1973), and *Southeast Asia in United States Policy* (Praeger, 1963).

On Sino-Soviet relations and Vietnam, see Donald S. Zagoria, *Vietnam Triangle: Moscow, Peking, Hanoi* (Pegasus, 1967); P. J. Honey, *Communism in North Vietnam: Its Role in the Sino-Soviet Dispute* (Greenwood Press, 1973); Oliver E. Clubb, Jr., *The United States and the Sino-Soviet Bloc in Southeast Asia* (Brookings Institution, 1962); and chapter by Jacques Guillermaz and Basile H. Kerbley in Kurt London, ed., *Unity and Contradictions: Major Aspects of Sino-Soviet Relations* (Praeger, 1962), pp. 233–47.

On China's relations with Southeast Asia as a whole, see sources cited in introduction, n. 8. On China's relations with Vietnam, see Melvin Gurtov, *The First Vietnam Crisis: Chinese Communist Strategy and United States Involvement, 1953–1954* (Columbia University Press, 1967); King C. Chen, *Vietnam and China, 1938–1954* (Princeton University Press, 1969), and "The Chinese Role in the Indochina Crisis," in Gene T. Hsiao, ed., *The Role of the External Powers in the Indochina Crisis* (Southern Illinois University

Press, 1973); D. P. Mozingo and T. W. Robinson, *Lin Piao on "People's War": China Takes a Second Look at Vietnam*, Rand Study 4814-PR (Santa Monica, Calif.: Rand Corp., 1965); Harold C. Hinton, *China's Relations with Burma and Vietnam: A Brief Survey* (New York: Institute of Pacific Relations, 1958), and "China and Vietnam," in Tang Tsou, ed., *China in Crisis*, vol. 2, *China's Policies in Asia and America's Alternatives* (University of Chicago Press, 1968), pp. 201–24; Robert Simmons, "China's Cautious Relations with North Korea and Indochina," *Asian Survey*, vol. 9, no. 7 (July 1971), pp. 629–44; and Ishwer C. Ojha, *The Changing Pattern of China's Attitude Toward a Negotiated Settlement in Vietnam, 1964–71*, Asian Studies Occasional Paper no. 2 (University of Southern Illinois, 1972).

On Vietnam itself, see writings of Bernard B. Fall, in particular *Two Viet Nams: A Political and Military Analysis* (Praeger, 1967). Most writings on the United States and Vietnam focus on the Vietnam War. Official statements and reports can be found in *Department of State Bulletin;* the President's annual reports to Congress, *U.S. Foreign Policy in the 1970's;* and the secretary of state's reports, *United States Foreign Policy*. Revealing classified U.S. documents are to be found in *The Pentagon Papers: The Secret History of the Vietnam War* (Bantam, 1971). On U.S. involvement in the war, see George McTurnan Kahin and John W. Lewis, *The United States in Vietnam: An Analysis in Depth of the History of America's Involvement in Vietnam* (Delta, 1967); David Halberstam, *The Best and the Brightest* (Fawcett, 1973); Committee of Concerned Asian Scholars, *The Indochina Story* (Bantam, 1970); Frances Fitzgerald, *Fire in the Lake: The Vietnamese and the Americans in Vietnam* (Atlantic Monthly, Little, Brown, 1972); Robert Shaplen, *The Lost Revolution* (Harper and Row, 1965); Leslie H. Gelb, "Vietnam: The System Worked," *Foreign Policy*, no. 3 (Summer 1971), pp. 140–67; James C. Thomson, Jr., "How Could Vietnam Happen? An Autopsy," *Atlantic*, April 1968, pp. 47–53; and Tad Szulc, "How Kissinger Did It, Behind the Vietnam Cease-Fire Agreement," *Foreign Policy*, no. 15 (Summer 1974), pp. 21–69.

68. ACDA, *World Military Expenditures and Arms Trade, 1963–1973*, pp. 24, 37, 45, 51, 54, and 59.

69. On the complexity of the new situation, see Joseph C. Kun, *Communist Indochina: Problems, Policies, and Superpower Involvement* (Center for Strategic and International Studies, Georgetown University, 1976); and Brewster Grace, "Postwar Thailand: Indochinese Domino or Chinese Checker?" *Fieldstaff Reports*, Southeast Asia Series, vol. 23, no. 5 (Hanover, N.H.: American Universities Field Staff, 1975). Some of the complexities have been reported by the U.S. press; see *New York Times*, May 2 and 12, June 4, 11, and 22, Aug. 15 and 18, and Oct. 9, 1975; and *Washington Post*, June 21, 24, and 25, and Aug. 17, 1975, and Apr. 25, 1976.

Index of Authors Cited

The spelling of Asian surnames follows usage in works cited rather than any standard romanization system.

General Index